SOCIAL SCIENCE

RESEARCH

ON LATIN AMERICA

SOCIAL SCIENCE
RESEARCH
ON LATIN AMERICA

REPORT AND PAPERS OF A SEMINAR

ON LATIN AMERICAN STUDIES IN THE UNITED STATES

HELD AT STANFORD, CALIFORNIA,

JULY 8–AUGUST 23, 1963

Edited by CHARLES WAGLEY

COLUMBIA UNIVERSITY PRESS

NEW YORK AND LONDON 1964

COPYRIGHT © 1964 COLUMBIA UNIVERSITY PRESS

LIBRARY OF CONGRESS CATALOG CARD NUMBER 65-11971

MANUFACTURED IN THE UNITED STATES OF AMERICA

Foreword

The present volume represents a major step in advancing the program of the Joint Committee on Latin American Studies, appointed by the American Council of Learned Societies and the Social Science Research Council in 1959. The Committee's primary objectives are to improve communications among those interested in research relating to Latin America, to consider ways in which the development of such research might be furthered, and to administer a program of grants for field research.

With financial support from the Carnegie Corporation of New York, the Ford Foundation, and the Council on Higher Education in the American Republics, the Joint Committee has already taken a number of steps toward achievement of its aims. Individual research grants have been provided for seventy-five scholars working in many different branches of the humanities and social sciences and associated with fifty-eight different institutions throughout the United States. Moreover, the Committee has cooperated with other agencies whose objectives harmonize with its own. It helped plan the Conference on the Status of Latin American Studies in the United States, co-sponsored in 1961 by the University of California at Los Angeles and the Council on Higher Education in the American Republics. It gave partial financial assistance to the First Inter-American Conference on Musicology (Library of Congress, 1963) and made possible a meeting on Portuguese language development in relation to Brazilian area studies (University of Texas, 1964). And the Joint Committee co-sponsored, with the Hispanic Foundation of the Library of Congress, a conference of historians to discuss plans for a "Guide to Historical Literature on Latin America."

In an effort to improve communication between social scientists in the United States and those in Latin America, the Joint Committee, with funds provided by the Council on Higher Education in the American Republics, took the major responsibility in organizing two conferences. The Inter-American Conference on Research and Training in Sociology, planned in cooperation with the American Sociological Association, was held in Palo Alto in 1961. Latin American participants at the meeting shortly afterwards formed an active "Latin American Group for the Development of Sociology." The second meeting—the Inter-American Conference on Research and Training in Economics—was held in Santiago, Chile, in 1962 with the co-sponsorship of the Instituto de Economía of the University of Chile. Its proceedings were distributed to interested scholars and institutions in Latin America and the United States.

John J. Johnson, Stanford University, accepted major responsibility for arranging an entirely different kind of conference, which was held by the Joint Committee at Scottsdale, Arizona, from January 30 through February 2, 1963. Its purpose was to focus the attention of scholars from many different disciplines upon one major general subject—"Continuity and Change in Latin America." The papers presented at that meeting, with an introduction by Mr. Johnson, have been published by the Stanford University Press under the title *Continuity and Change in Latin America.*

The present volume is the product of another Joint Committee meeting—a seminar held at the Center for Advanced Study in the Behavioral Sciences from July 8 through August 23, 1963. During those seven weeks a continuing nucleus of the seminar, in discussions with various visiting disciplinary groups, sought answers to two major questions: What is the status of our present knowledge of Latin America? How can we improve our understanding of that area? The fruitfulness of the seminar can best be determined from the pages which follow. It remains only for me, on behalf of the Joint Committee, to thank all of those participants who helped make this report possible and in particular those members of the seminar's continuing panel who were not members of the Joint Committee. They included Raymond Carr of Oxford University, H. Field Haviland, Jr., of the Brookings Institution, Robert Heussler of the Ford Foundation, Frederick Olaf-

son of John Hopkins University, and Carl B. Spaeth of Stanford
University. A special word of appreciation is due to Ralph W.
Tyler, Director of the Center for Advanced Study in the Behavioral Sciences, who served as the chairman of our seminar and
was our host, to Bryce Wood, who carried the major responsibility for the organization of the meeting, and to Charles Wagley, who has fulfilled the task of making the seminar's results
available to a wider audience. Finally, the Committee acknowledges the generosity of the Ford Foundation in making the seminar financially possible.

ROBERT N. BURR
*Chairman, Joint Committee
on Latin American Studies*

Preface

The Seminar on Latin American Studies consisted of a core group of participants who attended all or several of the various meetings during the seven weeks from July 8 to August 23, 1963, at the Center for Advanced Study in the Behavioral Sciences in Stanford, California. These were Robert N. Burr, Raymond Carr, Joseph Grunwald, H. Field Haviland, Jr., Robert Heussler, Frederick A. Olafson, Carl B. Spaeth, Charles Wagley, and Bryce Wood. The chairman was Ralph W. Tyler, and Richard J. Walter served as rapporteur and as a colleague in our discussions.

Each week this core group was joined by a panel of specialists from a social science discipline. Each panel remained with us from three to five days. During this period, there was discussion of a paper prepared beforehand as well as general discussions of Latin American studies in the United States. From July 11 to 13, a panel of political scientists joined the core seminar group. Anthropologists held forth from July 22 to 24. Between July 31 to August 2, we discussed, not a discipline of the social sciences, but an almost universal Latin American problem, namely, land tenure and legal institutions relating to land tenure and agrarian reform. For these particular sessions, the participants were drawn from several disciplines of the social sciences and from the professions. From August 5 to 7, the panel consisted of sociologists; and finally, between August 14 and 16, we discussed the status of history in the Latin American field—and, rather obliquely, Latin American literature as it relates to the social sciences. On the days between these panel meetings, the core members of the summer seminars met to consider what they had read and heard. The names of the members of the panels are listed in an Appendix to this volume. We thank them all.

The authors of the papers presented in this book had the benefit of notes taken at the various sessions. The editor has incorporated suggestions from the discussions whenever he has felt they were useful. In addition, several members of the panels prepared short working papers or memoranda which extended the coverage of the prepared papers, corrected a point of view, or brought additional concepts to bear on the subject of discussion. We want to thank Richard N. Adams, Fred P. Ellison, William S. Barnes, L. A. Costa Pinto of the University of Brazil (not present), Samuel P. Huntington, Joseph Grunwald, James O. Bray, and Wayne H. Holtzman for their written statements.

Each of the papers included in this volume evaluates critically the present status of our knowledge of Latin America in a particular discipline of the social sciences. Not all these studies are of the same scope. This is as it should be; each discipline has a different history in the Latin American field (and elsewhere), each poses distinctive problems, and each has a different self-image. The authors were asked to review for the Latin American area the history of research in his discipline, to appraise present trends, and to point to significant opportunities for future research. All of them, with varying emphasis and focuses, have generally carried out this plan. The editor, in an introductory paper, has attempted to provide a framework for the studies of individual social science disciplines and to point out the special needs and opportunities of the various disciplines as they concern Latin America.

It must be noted that in general all of the papers are written from the North American point of view; it is almost as if we had asked, "What do we know about Latin America?" All the authors except Carlos Massad, a Chilean trained in Chile and in the United States, are from the United States. Although throughout this volume the stress is on the research and writings of U.S. scholars on Latin America, Latin American and European scholars are frequently mentioned. This is especially true for such fields as sociology and economics, in which there have been important developments in recent years in Latin America and in which there are still relatively few U.S. specialists. This U.S. bias of the present volume is, we hope, to be corrected in the future in a conference to be sponsored by the Joint Committee on Latin American Studies, at which Latin American social scientists will be asked to react to the present papers from their points of view. One of the papers in this volume focuses to a large extent upon land reform. This is not by chance. As stated above, it was decided in planning these summer seminars to hold one panel on a current problem of pan-Latin American importance. The paper prepared for discussion was that by Kenneth L. Karst. He was asked to survey the field of legal studies as well as the legal aspects of land reform.

It had become apparent to all of us by this time that we had neglected geography, one of the most important and experienced disciplines in Latin American studies. James J. Parsons agreed to undertake to survey the status of this discipline as it concerns Latin America. Mr. Parsons did not have the benefit of panel discussions, although his paper has been read by colleagues. We thank him especially for undertaking this important task and for having caught so well the point of the seminar.

Each paper in this volume is the responsibility of its author. Most of them have had the record of the panel discussions, and sometimes written statements from seminar and panel participants, which they have often incorporated in one form or another into their papers. It hardly seems necessary to make acknowledgments for contributions by panel members to each paper. Yet, several authors wish to express their gratitude to individuals who were not part of the meetings. James Parsons wishes to thank Hilgard O'Reilly Sternberg, who read his paper and provided several important addenda. Stanley J. Stein wishes to record his thanks for the criticism and suggestive revisions of Barbara Stein, who is herself an historian. Carlos Massad is indebted to Solon Barraclough, Robert T. Brown, Juan del Canto, and John D. Strasma for comments and contributions. The editor wishes to express his appreciation to Ariane Brunel and to Cecilia Roxo Wagley for editorial and bibliographical assistance.

CHARLES WAGLEY

Columbia University, 1964

Contents

Contents

1. Introduction

CHARLES WAGLEY

Never before has knowledge of Latin American societies been so important to the United States. In Latin America there are over 200 million people living in twenty nations. Their numbers increase each year as Latin America undergoes one of the most severe population explosions in the modern world. At the present rate of population growth, there would be 300 million Latin Americans by 1975 and over 600 million by the end of this century—twice as many as North Americans. The future of these Latin American nations and of these rapidly expanding peoples is crucial to our way of life.

Latin American nations are struggling for economic, political, and social modernization. In the mid-twentieth century they are undergoing many of the social and economic changes that took place in the United States in the late nineteenth century. Despite their current problems, Brazil, Chile, Colombia, Mexico, and Venezuela have experienced truly phenomenal economic advances in the last generation. Except for such countries as Mexico, Costa Rica, and Uruguay, Latin American nations seem to be almost perpetually unstable politically. But the political instability of the mid-twentieth century is very different from that of the "palace revolution" era of the nineteenth century. Today, Latin American revolutions are symptoms of profound and rapid social and economic change. New social classes and economic groups are emerging in many Latin American nations and are making new demands. Traditional relationships among social classes and individuals are vanishing, and new patterns of behavior and new institutions are slowly taking form. Meanwhile, large masses of people are left in a social limbo—supported neither by the traditional society nor by the emerging institutions of a new Latin America.

What political institutions will take form in Latin America in the next generation or so? Latin American nations might develop liberal democratic systems both analogous to and different from our own. They might also fall into chaos and adopt totalitarian regimes of one kind or another. The future of Latin America is thus important to our own security. Cuba illustrates dramatically the danger, both real and mythical, which a neighboring unfriendly government under an avowedly Communist regime represents to the people of the United States. Although formal diplomatic relations with our Latin American neighbors are cordial enough and although we are bound to them through the Organization of American States, it must be said that many Latin Americans do not look upon the United States as a friendly and protective neighbor. We are still looked upon as the "Colossus of the North," and the fear of Yankee imperialism, both economic and political, is still a reality in Latin America. Latin American nations are willing to accept our aid, but they are equally determined to free themselves from what they see as U.S. domination. Latin American nations are eager to industrialize and to free themselves from dependence on imports bought from income deriving from the export of raw materials. They are emotional in their desire to own and exploit their public utilities and natural resources. Latin American nations nowadays are taking an independent position in the UN, in the OAS, and in other international forums. There has even been talk of a Latin American bloc which would exclude the United States. Now, more than ever before, we must work closely on an egalitarian basis with Latin American countries. More than ever before, we need their votes and their support.

In many ways, Latin America is no less important to us than Asia, Africa, or even Europe. We should maintain our financial aid and technical assistance programs to the area. We must support those forces in Latin America which promote economic, social, and political progress by peaceful and democratic means. We must work with Latin Americans on their own terms to help them in the education of their people, the training of technicians to build up their industry and exploit their natural resources, and the over-all modernization of their societies. In order to co-operate with Latin Americans, we must know what they are like and what social, economic, and political problems they face. Knowledge of Latin American societies should be available to our decision-makers on the many levels of government, of business, and of private foundations. Policy-makers, diplomats, technicians, administrators, and others involved in extending United States cooperation to Latin America need a thorough grounding in the nature of Latin American society and culture. Better information on Latin America should be available to the public through newspapers and other mass media. Latin America should be studied in our schools, for the study of the history and problems of America is parochial if it fails to consider the other twenty republics whose experience in the New World is similar and yet so different from our own.

Unfortunately, we are still rather poorly informed about Latin America. Few newspapers, radio and television stations, or magazines have adequate coverage of Latin American affairs. Popular books often do little more than confirm the public in their suspicion that outrageous confusion prevails in Latin America. In our elementary and secondary schools, there are occasional courses in geography or social studies that devote some fleeting hours to Latin America. Latin American studies have been offered for many years in a number of universities and colleges, but it is generally agreed that they have often been taught on a rather superficial level. There is no doubt that Latin America has been neglected by the public, by policy-makers, by our own government, and by educational institutions in the last three decades. Latin America has also been neglected by our scholars, who in the end must provide the basic data for academic and public consumption. As much as Africa, Latin America has been in many ways a "dark continent."

This situation is now changing. There is a new public interest in Latin America, stimulated by a realization of its importance to our own national interests. The National Defense Education Act supports the study of Spanish and Portuguese and of Latin American society. The Alliance for Progress has increased the flow of foreign aid to Latin America and has dramatized the importance of the region to us. Private foundations have supported research and study on Latin America and the development of universities in the area. Our U.S. universities are now developing and improving their programs of Latin American studies. Many advanced graduate students and mature scholars have "discovered" Latin America and are now preparing to carry out research and teach on this highly strategic and interesting area. In the hope that a group of social scientists with a long-term concern with and considerable knowledge of Latin America might foster this rather belated interest, we have tried in this volume to provide a background for social science research and study on Latin America. Our studies are addressed primarily to students and scholars, but perhaps they may be of interest to policy-makers, administrators, technicians, and others who are eager to learn more about Latin America—and perhaps even to the public at large.

Latin American Studies in the United States: Background

It should be said at once that U.S. scholars have never ignored Latin America. In fact, there is a long but somewhat tangential tradition of Latin American studies in the United States.[1] The recent active interest in Latin America on the part of the scholarly community is not opportunistic, nor is it entirely a reflection of the growing political importance of the region. In the nineteenth century, a series of U.S. historians, explorers, naturalists, and travelers visited, studied, and wrote about Latin America. To mention just a few, there were Prescott's classic *History of the Conquest of Mexico* (1843) and *The Conquest of Peru* (1847), Stephens' celebrated volume on Yucatan (1841), and Herndon and Gibbon's report on their expedition down the Amazon river system from Peru (1853–54). The delightful and insightful *Life in Mexico* by Frances Calderón de la Barca, the American wife of the Spanish ambassador to Mexico, was first published in 1843. For Brazil, there were the well-known books by Kidder (1845) and the later volume by Kidder and Fletcher (1857), which ran through seven editions in ten years. Between 1870 and 1877, Squier published his geographic and ethnographic monographs on Peru and several Central American countries, and in 1878–79, Bandelier issued his famous study of the social organization and land tenure of the ancient Mexicans. An excellent account of

[1] See Bernstein (1961) for an excellent survey of the study of Latin America in the eighteenth and nineteenth centuries.

travel on the Amazon written by Louis and Elizabeth Agassiz was published in 1869, and a highly informative book on northern Brazil by Herbert H. Smith appeared in 1879. These are but a few of the U.S. students of Latin America in the nineteenth century.

In addition, there were U.S. scholars and scientists who were perhaps less well known to the general public but who contributed to our basic knowledge of Latin America and to the progress of scholarship in Latin America itself. Charles Hartt, who had taught at Vassar College and Cornell University, became the Director of the National Museum of Brazil; he wrote on Brazilian geology and ethnology. To give another example, there was John Casper Banner, who spent seven years (1874–81) in Brazil and later returned there three times for shorter periods. His maps and his scientific publications were important contributions to Brazilian studies; and later, as President of Stanford University, he established the first library on Brazil and the first center of Brazilian studies in the United States.

Most of these scholars (the great Prescott was an exception) had long and direct experience in Latin America. They had little patience with the general lack of knowledge in the United States about the region, and they were critical of those scholars who interpreted Latin America from afar or who gathered data on quick trips. Bandelier's criticism of the work of Daniel Brinton shows this quite clearly. Toward the end of the nineteenth century, Brinton was professor of American archaeology at the University of Pennsylvania and wrote widely on Central American linguistics, mythology, and prehistory, largely on the basis of library research. Bandelier had these strong words to say about Brinton's work, most of which is totally forgotten today:

> He is a very worthy, active, and industrious man, but only a reader and writer. American aboriginal history has never entered into his flesh and bone through practical experience.
> So it is the case with many; they gaze at things from an easy chair, invite the nation before them into an elegant study, and when he is seated (after they have washed, combed and perfumed him), they question him, carefully noting what he has to say. In this manner, they study Ethnology! [Quoted in Bernstein 1961: 137.]

Bandelier's complaint heralds a controversy that will be mentioned repeatedly in this book, namely, the difference of opinion between those scholars who believe in long-term intimate knowledge of a culture and a society and those who believe that theories developed elsewhere may be tested and applied in short visits or even from afar.

U.S. students of Latin America in the nineteenth century benefited enormously from the earlier and perhaps more thorough research and exploration carried out in the area by Europeans. Until the beginning of the nineteenth century, even European studies of Latin America, except for the numerous sixteenth- and seventeenth-century Spanish and Portuguese chronicles, tended to be bookish and done in archives. But when in the early nineteenth century the Spanish and Portuguese relaxed their strict travel controls and when later the nations of Latin America achieved independence, European explorers and scholars came to study the area on the spot. The field studies of Alexander von Humboldt between 1799 and 1804 provided basic data on the geology and geography of a large portion of Latin America. He was followed by a long series of expeditions whose reports contained not only information on the natural environment but also much data about the conditions and ways of life of the Latin American peoples. These were not quick trips to collect a few specimens, but often extended journeys lasting for several years. For example, Maximilian, Prince of Wied-Neuwied, spent two years in Brazil (1815–17) with a staff of naturalists. Auguste de Saint-Hilaire was in Brazil from 1816 to 1822, and Alcides d'Orbigny traveled from 1826 to 1833 in Argentina, Brazil, Chile, Paraguay, Peru, and Bolivia. Then, of course, there was Darwin's famous voyage of the *Beagle* from 1831 to 1836. The expedition of William H. Edwards to the Amazon Valley in 1846 attracted the attention of two well-known British naturalists who later followed him: Alfred Russell Wallace and Henry Walter Bates, whose book *The Naturalist on the River Amazons* (1875) is a classic in the Latin American field. Then, there were the expeditions led by the French cartographer and naturalist, Francis de Castelnau. From 1843 to 1847, he traveled across the continent from east to west and then from south to north—up the La Plata River system into the Amazon River system. These were but a few of the nineteenth-century European efforts to learn something of the new nations of Latin America.

Such studies were not, of course, without economic and political motivations.

The nineteenth-century studies of Latin America by U.S. scholars were, with some rare exception, weak and marginal to the main stream of our intellectual life. In the early nineteenth century, the United States was too busy acquiring territory and exploring its own West to be interested in the study of other new and poorly known nations. Despite the early announcement of the Monroe Doctrine in 1823, the importance of Latin America to our own security was not felt strongly until the end of the century. Our science and our scholarship were still in their early phase of development, and they were strongly bound to European tradition. We knew little of our fellow Americans.

In the latter part of the nineteenth century and in the early years of this century, Latin American studies began to attract the attention of a few of our scholars, especially historians. Their work concentrated on the colonial period of Latin American history, for their basic concern seems to have been the Spanish expansion in the New World and the history of those parts of our own country which were once Spanish. Few studies were devoted to the Latin American countries themselves and especially few to their hectic but fascinating early years of independence. Prime examples of these early historical studies of Latin America are the voluminous works of Hubert H. Bancroft on the Pacific states of the United States, on Mexico, and on Central America. Other historians of this period who worked on Latin America were Bernard Moses, Edward G. Bourne, Percy Alvin Martin, and William R. Sheperd. In the first two decades of this century, a small group of anthropologists, including Carl Lumholtz, Fredrick Starr, and Max Uhle, also did research in Latin America.

The interest of U.S. social scientists was still focused on their own society. Geographers studied our environment. Anthropologists recorded the ethnography of the North American Indian tribes before their culture disappeared. In political science, sociology, and economics, little of importance was published in the United States on Latin America. There were already centers of study and research for the area, such as those at the University of Texas and at Stanford University, and there were a few well-known authorities on the area. It was not until the 1920s and

1930s that a group of outstanding scholars on Latin America appeared in the United States.

In history, such men as Herbert E. Bolton, J. Fred Rippy, Arthur P. Whitaker, Clarence Haring, Roland Dennis Hussey, Lewis Hanke, Frank Tannenbaum, and others who will be mentioned by Stanley Stein in this volume, began to publish important contributions. *The Hispanic American Review* was founded in 1918, suspended in 1922, and revived in 1926. Since that time it has continued to publish excellent articles and reviews on Latin American history under a distinguished series of editors.

In geography, Isaiah Bowman continued his work and other outstanding geographers such as Carl Sauer, Preston James, Clarence Jones, G. M. McBride, and Donald Brandt have carried out research and have written on Latin America. Their work is required reading for anyone seriously interested in the area.

In anthropology, the same two decades saw a similar expansion of research on Latin America. This was the period when Alfred Kidder, George Vaillant, William Duncan Strong, J. Eric Thompson, Junius Bird, and other archaeologists began their research in Latin America. In ethnology, the area attracted such scholars as Alfred Tozzer, Elsie Clews Parsons, Ralph L. Beals, Alfred Métraux, John Gillin, Robert Redfield, Sol Tax, Melville J. Herskovits, Oliver La Farge, and Ruth Bunzel—all of them scholars who were not only Latin Americanists but also leaders in their professions.

The publication of James Bryce's *South America* in 1914 called attention to Latin America in the English-speaking world, but it was not until a decade later that studies on Latin American political systems by U.S. scholars began to appear. Many of these were by historians, but others were by political scientists, identified by Merle Kling in this volume as "traditionalists." Little was published in these two decades in sociology or economics. In fact, until the 1940s these two disciplines hardly contributed to the study of Latin America in the United States, which remained the province of geographers, anthropologists, and historians.

The Good Neighbor Policy of Franklin D. Roosevelt did much to stimulate Latin American studies. A Convention for the Promotion of Inter-American Cultural Relations was signed by the American republics in 1936. In 1938, the U.S. Department of State created its Division of Cultural Relations, which concentrated primarily on Latin America. In the same year, an Inter-Departmental Committee on Cooperation with the American Republics, which included representatives of thirteen Federal agencies, was established. In 1940, the Office of the Coordinator of Inter-American Affairs was formed, with Nelson D. Rockefeller as its head. All these governmental moves had important repercussions in the academic world. Public and foundation funds became available for the study of Latin America, and there were greater opportunities for U.S. scholars to study in Latin America. Various scholarly committees were formed to stimulate Latin American studies. Among them was the Joint Committee on Latin American Studies of the American Council of Learned Societies and the Social Science Research Council, first founded in 1942. Robert Redfield was the first chairman of this committee and Wendell C. Bennett was its executive secretary. In 1943, the committee consisted of ten members, including such well-known scholars as W. Rex Crawford, Earl J. Hamilton, Lewis Hanke, Clarence Haring, Irving Leonard, and George Vaillant. In addition, there were subcommittees on Personnel, Publication, and Research, on which served such men as Henry Grattan Doyle, George Kubler, William Duncan Strong, Arthur Whitaker, Miron Burgin, Russel Fitzgibbon, René d'Harnouncourt, William Schurz, Carlton Sprague Smith, Julian H. Steward, Ralph L. Beals, Melville J. Herskovits, Frances V. Scholes, Robert C. Smith, and T. Lynn Smith. The roster of the Joint Committee was a veritable "all-star cast" of Latin American experts.

For a short time, the Joint Committee published a journal-news bulletin, *Notes on Latin American Studies*. Leonard (1943) carried out for the Committee a survey of the status of Latin American studies in North American universities. His general conclusions sound strangely contemporaneous. He notes "a general lack of personnel in Latin American studies thoroughly equipped by the mastery of the techniques of their discipline, adequate foreign residence and sufficient command of languages." He also feels that, "With notable exceptions, Latin American studies do not seem to have attracted scholars of first-rate ability" (Leonard 1943: 45). And he writes:

The disciplines in their Latin American aspects most widely taught in the humanities were: languages, literature, and history; of the social sciences: anthropology, archaeology, and geography. Other disciplines are but slightly or incidentally developed, and in many institutions are entirely neglected (*ibid.*, p. 46).

There have been many developments since 1942, but the same basic conclusions were reached in 1963 by the seminars and panels which led to this volume.

During World War II, many U.S. scholars served in one way or another in Latin America, and their later studies benefited from this experience. Many young men got their first taste of Latin American culture while they were stationed at U.S. military or naval bases in the region. Scholars became cultural or economic attachés in U.S. embassies. Others served in strategic wartime programs such as that to increase wild-rubber production in the Amazon Valley or in one of the bilateral health or agricultural programs of the Institute of Inter-American Affairs (the successor to the Office of the Coordinator of Inter-American Affairs). As a result of the Good Neighbor Policy, the Smithsonian Institution created the Institute of Social Anthropology, which stationed archaeologists and social anthropologists in Mexico, Peru, and Brazil, where they were attached to local universities and research institutions. This organization published an important set of monographs on Latin America in the years just after the war (cf. Beals 1946; Foster 1948; Brandt 1951; Pierson 1951).

At the end of World War II, it seemed that Latin American studies in the United States were improving. And in fact a series of important research projects were carried out in the region, such as the studies of the Tarascan-speaking region of Mexico by anthropologists, geographers, historians, and others (Wagley 1948: 11–12) and the study of Puerto Rican communities and national culture by Steward *et al.* (1956).

Thus, in the mid-1940s Latin Americanists were optimistic about the future of their field. In 1947 a national conference was sponsored and organized by the Committee on World Area Research of the Social Science Research Council, which in a sense can be considered the "kick-off" for postwar area studies in the United States. The panel on Latin America had this to say:

The members of the Latin American panel needed no introduction to each other since many of them had worked together for many years on the Joint Committee on Latin American Studies or on similar area-type committees. This is but one factor that has made the Latin American area a focus for interdisciplinary study. Latin Americanists, by interest or by historical accident, have been organized for years. Numerous Latin American specialists in many disciplines are found in United States institutions of higher learning, area programs have been carried out, and reports published. Many of the problems which face specialists in other areas have been temporarily resolved or shelved in the Latin American field. The panel members, therefore, felt justified in limiting their discussions largely to field research problems (Wagley 1948: 39).

These may well have been "famous last words"; at best, they were not very realistic. In the following decade, Latin American studies did not improve as expected but rather in some ways became stagnant as compared with the study of other foreign areas. The war had made the public and the scholars of the United States fully aware of the importance of Russia, China, Japan, Indonesia, India, and the Middle East. We were shocked by the paucity of experts on the history, geography, ethnology, economics, sociology, politics, and "exotic" languages of these areas. Political and social events in all these regions subsequent to World War II doubly emphasized their importance and our painful ignorance. Then, when the European colonies in Africa began one by one to gain their independence, this complex part of the world came into the limelight. It was natural that government, private foundations, and public and private universities should promote teaching and research on these strategic areas.

Centers for the training of specialists and large research programs dealing with the Soviet Union and Eastern Europe, Southern Asia, the Far East, the Middle East, and Africa were founded at various universities. Fellowships were awarded to outstanding graduate students for study and research in these areas. Libraries were improved. Mature scholars were granted funds for travel and research. This was a real "breakthrough" in the United States. It established area studies as an integral part of the curriculum in many of our universities. It put an end to the parochialism of U.S. scholars and established once and for all the comparative approach in the social sciences.

Yes, throughout this exciting revolution, Latin American studies languished. True, a certain number of well-trained scholars carried on their research, and each year there were a limited number of recruits to the body of Latin American specialists in the social sciences and humanities. But financial support to institutions of higher learning and to individual scholars was small as compared with that which was available for other areas of the world. Latin America was specifically omitted from some graduate student fellowship programs. The Joint Committee on Latin American Studies, so promising in 1942–43, was disbanded in 1947 and was not re-established until 1959.

Writing in 1957 after the optimistic statement of the Latin American panel of the National Conference on Area Studies, Bryce Wood provided a clear statement of the reasons for the moribund state of Latin American studies in the United States. I shall quote his survey at some length:

> In the first place, after 1939, when the agencies of the federal government discovered the resources of scholarship to be an arm of policy and hitherto lonely scholars found themselves unwontedly besieged by officials desiring knowledge to buttress national power, the Latin Americanists came under less pressure than were specialists on nearly all other world areas. Latin America, unlike any other major area, has never contained a center of political or military power that threatened the United States, nor has it in the past hundred years been directly and immediately in danger of falling under the political or military control of a dangerous enemy of the United States. To be sure, Germany, Japan and the Soviet Union in turn have carried on propaganda campaigns against the interests of the United States in Latin America, but here, as elsewhere, the fifth column has not been truly menacing unless the other four columns were close on its heels. The attention of government officials, and it must be admitted, of the ablest humanists and social scientists has been attracted to the centers of hostile power, or more recently to areas on the fringes of the centers of such power, rather than to the countries of Latin America which rest within the shelter of the United States navy and air force as much as does the United States itself.
>
> Further, since the Nicaraguan intervention of 1926, there have been no "great debates" in the United States about policy toward Latin America. The Good Neighbor Policy has not been the subject of partisan dispute, except for rival claims of credit for its authorship; in the absence of alleged "disasters" as in China, or "blunders" as at Yalta, there have been no Congressional investigations and no unveiling of the documentary record of policy toward Latin America. That policy has consequently offered an appearance of placid virtue that has lacked dramatic appeal to more than a very few research men in the universities.
>
> In speaking of governmental pressures on universities for the development of area programs, it is of some importance to distinguish the intensity and the character of pressure exerted by different agencies. By

far the strongest demand has been made by the armed services, which until recently have possessed ample financial resources for making contracts for training of personnel. The funds possessed by the Department of State, like those available to other civilian agencies, have been relatively small. Further, the principal concern of the armed services during the war and afterwards, was with language training, particularly at elementary and intermediate levels, while that of the civilian agencies was with a much broader area training that included advanced language skills, but concentrated on understanding of whole societies. The weight of the defense establishment's pressures for language training was felt mainly by centers for study of the Far East, Southeast Asia and Europe, rather than by the Latin American centers.

It is in this connection that the second factor limiting the development of Latin American studies may be noted. Latin America lacks official languages that are either challenging because they are exceptionally difficult, or intriguing because they are exotic. The most readily observable item of an area specialist's equipment is his linguistic ability, and North Americans fairly quickly learn to "converse," and to read newspapers in Spanish or Portuguese. At the same time, there developed, and to some extent persists an unfortunate assumption held in official circles that equates linguistic competence with economic, political and social expertise with respect to a foreign area. Therefore, it has been hard to down the fallacy that an economist or political scientist who brushed up his high school Spanish thereby was justifiably accorded the status of Latin American area specialist (Wood 1957: 5–7).

This was the general state of Latin American studies in the United States when Richard Nixon traveled to Latin America and faced angry mobs, when Fidel Castro seized power in Cuba, and when President Kennedy announced the Alliance for Progress. Our government, our public, our universities, and our scholars came alive to the fact that Latin America was of utmost strategic importance to our national interest. The day was over when there could be

in the public sphere, and to some extent in government, business, and university circles—a condescension toward the people, institutions, and cultures of Latin America that, however, compounded with amusement and protectiveness, reflects a special feeling of superiority different from that expressed toward peoples in other regions" (Wood 1957: 20).

Social scientists, not unlike the general public, have discovered Latin America in the last three or four years. Scholars of outstanding competence have been attracted to do research in Latin America not only because of its strategic importance to national policy but because it offers an excellent laboratory for the study of a rapidly changing social system. In the last few years, there has been a veritable fever to develop social science research and competence on Latin America. There is much to overcome. Our present knowledge of this important area is embarrassingly poor. The number of trained specialists on the region is still small in relation to our academic and governmental needs.

We do not, however, begin our studies of Latin America or our promotion of their excellence on a *tabula rasa*. We have a long tradition of Latin American research in the United States which goes back to the nineteenth century or even earlier. This tradition has been marked by sudden spurts and declines of interest. It is to be hoped that Latin American studies will now be established firmly and permanently as an important aspect of our national intellectual life. In this atmosphere of renewed urgency, our seminar met in 1963 at Stanford, California.

Latin American Studies in the United States Today

The present status of each social science in the Latin American field is a reflection of its history. The strongest disciplines—anthropology, geography, and history—are those with the longest traditions in Latin American studies. It is precisely in these fields that Latin Americans themselves have made important contributions that have provided a basis and a stimulus for North American scholars. These are the disciplines most widely taught in our Latin American area centers and institutes, both on the undergraduate and on the graduate level. On the other hand, the study of political science, economics, sociology, and law in relation to Latin America is relatively recent, and there are fewer specialists in these fields in the United States. A recent survey of 27 universities regarded as having the most extensive course offerings on Latin America showed that they all offered courses in anthropology and history, while 24 offered courses in government, 22 geography, 18 in economics, and only 7 in sociology (Minnich and Saunders 1964). To look at it in another way, these 27 universities offered a total of 660 semester hours of courses in Latin American history, 290 semester hours of anthropology, and 167 semester hours of geography. They offered 229 semester hours of political science on Latin America, 153 hours of economics, and only 42 hours of sociology (*ibid.*). The number of courses and semester hours in government and economics is surprising, but then these are well-established subjects in the curricula of our universities and one wonders if such courses are not improvised to meet student demand.

One of the reasons that sociology, political science, economics, and law are poorly developed in regard to Latin America is that prerequisites for research have generally been lacking. Basic statistics and statistical series were not available for economists and sociologists. To Latin Americans, sociology consisted until recently of the theories of *pensadores* ("thinkers," or armchair philosophers). Political science as an objective discipline simply did not exist. Legal studies were concerned with the codified law. To a certain extent, there was no point of contact between these disciplines as they were understood in the United States and in Latin America. The meager development of these fields of study did not derive merely from the lack of basic data and supporting studies by Latin Americans. It lay more in the nature of these disciplines themselves than in the difficulties involved in studying the region. Until recently, these social sciences were mainly creatures of Europe and the United States. Their techniques and methods of research were geared to European and U.S. societies. Only in the last decade or so have scholars in these disciplines turned to the study of Asia, Africa, and Latin America and developed a comparative perspective.

Furthermore, the lack of interest in Latin America (and other foreign areas) on the part of economists, political scientists, and sociologists is also a result of their own self-image as social scientists. In their fundamental preoccupation with methodology and theory, they tend to view themselves—more than historians, geographers, or even anthropologists—as universalists. Their methods, theories, and models, developed from studies made in Europe and the United States, have generally been regarded as universally applicable. These theories and models could be tested and refined by further research in those areas of the world where basic quantitative data were available, so they saw no reason to do research on regions where the paucity of data kept them from developing their scientific theory. A Ph.D. candidate could contribute to economic, sociological, or political theory more easily by a study of New Haven, Connecticut, than by a laborious study of Mendoza, Argentina. This way of thinking has been especially true of economists, but in a more limited way it has also applied to sociologists and political scientists.

As a result of this professional self-image, the greatest professional rewards have come to those working in the central core of these disciplines—those doing research on the society of the United States and on the methodology and theory to be derived from such data. Area specialists have been considered as marginal and thus as "second-class citizens" in their disciplines. Until recently, professional rewards have not accrued to economists, sociologists, or political scientists who have spent years immersing themselves in foreign cultures and foreign languages. It was only when the economics of development became an important field, when sociologists became interested in underdeveloped societies, and when political scientists began to broaden the range of the comparative approach, that Latin America became a rewarding field of study for scholars in these disciplines.

In contrast, in anthropology, history, and the environmental sciences there is a tradition of comparative research limited in time and space. The anthropologist works in his tribe or peasant village, the historian within an epoch and a nation, and the geographer on a given place at a given time. Fredrick A. Olafson, in a paper presented to our seminars, made this point clearly:

> While anthropology is by no means a theoryless discipline, its focus of interest seems traditionally to have been strongly descriptive or "idiographic" in the way that history's is; and it is therefore entirely normal and even the expected thing for an anthropologist to study the institutions and social practices of a particular society and to do so with a minimum advance commitment to any set of theoretical assumptions. The same is true of legal scholarship, whether the latter is conceived of as the internal analysis of other legal systems or as the study of the way legal institutions function in a particular society. It also applies in a very obvious way to environmental studies which *ex hypothesi* deal with particular environments.

It is not surprising, then, that scholars in these disciplines have been more amenable to long-term dedication to foreign-area studies in general and to the study of Latin America in particular.

Thus, historians interested in Latin America, although they are few and have seldom gained the professional recognition granted their colleagues working with U.S. or European data, have long held a "Conference on Latin American History" during the annual meetings of the American Historical Association. Historians working in the Latin American field have been able to support and publish a journal for over forty years. Their work can hardly be called marginal to their discipline. Likewise, the recognition granted to such geographers as Carl Sauer, Preston L. James, and other working in the Latin American field indicates that they have contributed to the basic theory of their discipline.

It is perhaps in anthropology, however, that Latin Americanists have made the most important contributions to the basic theory of their discipline. Redfield's *The Folk Culture of Yucatan* (1941) is surely one of the most influential books in social anthropology in the twentieth century. It set off a series of critical discussions among anthropologists and other scholars in the Latin American field, and it has influenced research and theory on other areas of the world. Likewise, Steward's theories of cultural evolution (cf. Steward 1955) and his concepts regarding the study of complex societies (Steward 1950) were based primarily on Latin American data. The work of such anthropologists as Ralph L. Beals, George Foster, Sol Tax, Evon Vogt, Richard N. Adams, Oscar Lewis, Eric Wolfe, Allan R. Holmberg, and others too numerous to mention has contributed both to a substantive knowledge of Latin America and to the basic theory of anthropology. All these scholars have been granted full professional recognition for their work. In anthropology, the fact of being a confirmed Latin Americanist has led not to "second-class citizenship" but to basic contributions and fruitful careers.

This does not mean that everything is in order in the Latin American segments of these disciplines. There are broad gaps in the data, and there is still a lack of well-trained personnel. Many of the needs and potentialities involved are pointed out in the chapters that follow by James J. Parsons, Stanley J. Stein, Arnold Strickon, and Kenneth L. Karst and need not be discussed here. But it must be said that research and teaching on Latin America in the fields of history, geography, anthropology, and law needs strengthening if we are to have an adequate knowledge of the area.

The other social sciences which contribute to our knowledge of Latin America are developing rapidly. In Latin America there is a "new" sociology devoted to objective, quantitative, empirical research in contrast to the armchair theories of the *pensadores;* the trend is discussed by Rex Hopper in this volume. These Latin American sociologists are being joined by an increasing number of North American colleagues. Sociologists of the stature of Wilbert E. Moore, Alex Inkeles, Robert Havighurst, J. Mayone Stycos, Kingsley Davis, Joseph A. Kahl, and a few others have already done research in Latin America, while others are now preparing to do so.

The number of political scientists now working on Latin American data and using modern methodology is exceedingly small, as Merle Kling points out in this volume. There are, however, a number of young men, either candidates for the Ph.D. or recent recipients of the degree, who are now entering the Latin American field. To these political scientists we should add the sociologists, both in the United States and in Latin America, who are interested in the sociology of politics.

The increasing importance of the economics of development, the activities of international organizations and development banks, the programs of the Agency for International Development, and the increasing number of university-sponsored research programs on Latin America have brought numerous senior economists into contact with the area. They have taught at Latin American universities, served as advisers to goverments and to international organizations, and participated in the planning of economic development programs. Few of these men, however, have a long-term commitment to Latin American studies. Rather, most of them are dedicated to some special field such as the economics of development, finance, taxation, or agricultural economics. Yet, out of their experience with dual or multiple economies and with the economic systems of underdeveloped nations, some economists have come to see the value of a thorough and intimate knowledge of the society and culture of the region in which they worked. They realize that many of their techniques and methods of research and some of their basic theory must be adapted and even modified in terms of Latin American conditions. Young economists and advanced graduate students have discovered the research and career possibilities which exist in the Latin American field. Thus, the time may not be far off when this important discipline will have personnel sufficiently grounded both in knowledge of the area and in methodological skills to participate more fully in Latin American area studies.

At present, the shortage of personnel in sociology, political science, and economics with a thorough knowledge of Latin America, a command of methodological skills, and fluency in Spanish and Portuguese is especially acute. They are much needed in the academic world, and universities hoping to build up their Latin American programs compete for a handful of outstanding men. This shortage of personnel is especially crucial, for these disciplines are precisely the ones most concerned with policy-oriented and operations research which is aimed at reaching decisions in social, political, and economic situations. Thus, government, international organization, and independent research organizations compete with universities for economists, sociologists, and political scientists competent in the Latin American field. It is most certain that the increased importance of Latin America, the research opportunities to be found in the region, and the expanded career potential will attract scholars of outstanding ability in the years to come.

Research Possibilities and Research Needs

There are important gaps in our knowledge of Latin America in all the social sciences, and in some disciplines serious and objective research has just now begun. Each of the chapters in this volume attempts in part to indicate the possibilities and the needs of a particular discipline. It would be repetitious to describe these possibilities and needs here. Yet, there are a group of research topics and fields which were singled out repeatedly by the various panels. Some of them lend themselves to study by several disciplines, while others actually demand interdisciplinary research. The very fact that these topics and fields of inquiry were mentioned by scholars in various disciplines indicates their high priority in Latin American studies.

Without any attempt to establish relative priority or to be exhaustive, some of these areas of research are listed below. Studies were recommended in the following areas:

1. Land tenure systems.
2. Power structures at all levels of Latin American societies.

3. The ideology, changing composition, and role of elite groups in individual countries.
4. The dimensions, ideology, and role of the middle sectors of one or more Latin American societies.
5. The role of education in political and economic modernization.
6. The process of decision-making in various Latin American contexts.
7. Nationalism in its various forms.
8. The process of political socialization, including the assimilation of Indians and peasants into a dominant national society.
9. New groups, such as Protestant sects, voluntary organizations, and interest groups, which are appearing in Latin American societies.
10. Latin American political parties in one country.
11. Latin American revolutions.
12. Large agricultural establishments such as haciendas, plantations, and estancias.
13. The rapid process of urbanization and of rural-urban migration.
14. Inflation and the social tensions engendered by it.
15. The "dual" economies of many Latin American nations.
16. The processes at work and the trends in Latin American demographic growth.
17. Latin American national character and national self-images.
18. The economic balance between various sectors of the Latin American economies (for example, industry versus agriculture).

The mere listing of such broad fields of inquiry (and many might be added) leads immediately to a number of questions. How is such research to be implemented? What is the most strategic unit of study—the area as a whole, a subarea, a nation, a region within a nation, or a local community? What are the conditions in Latin America which act as barriers against such research? These and many other more specific questions were discussed by the various panels and by our core seminar group—and they will require even further study.

An important question for students of Latin America is the appropriate unit or units within which research can be organized and carried out effectively. Obviously, the unit of research depends on the problem to be studied, and the same general problem can often be studied in terms of different units. For example, studies of economic integration could be studied in terms of Latin America as a whole or in terms of the Central American Republics. Likewise, rural-urban migration may be studied as a pan–Latin American phenomenon or in terms of one country or in terms of one metropolitan center and its rural zones. In general, however, many of the Latin American specialists at our panel meetings and seminars seemed to agree that the nation was the largest effective unit of research. One of the participants spoke of "the myth of Latin America." "Each country," he added, "has to be treated in its own right. The region is not homogeneous." Far too often students of Latin America have bitten off more than they could chew. Books on Latin American history, geography, politics, or economics which attempt to encompass Latin America as a whole are apt to be vaguely general and full of qualifications, or else they neglect important countries.

Recently, in comparing the problems involved in the study of Latin America and Asia, Dore (1963: 13) made this point forcefully:

Students of Asia tend to be more narrowly specialized. There are a few who take Southeast Asia as their oyster, some who bestraddle China and Japan, but confine their research to only one society. By contrast, one hears of Latin Americanists, but not of Bolivianists or Peruvianists. . . . It is not easy for any one man to know enough about so many different societies, and the attempt to be comprehensive may lead to a diffusion of energy—to quick survey of formal structure rather than detailed analysis of process. . . . The predicate of any sentence beginning say "Students in Latin America" is likely to be so general, so vague, so hedged with qualifications as to be neither informative nor useful.

In the present stage of development, Latin American social science needs descriptive and analytical studies based on original research about individual nations. We need, for example, studies of the history of Colombia since independence, of the process of urbanization in Brazil, of the Peruvian elite, of the Mexican middle class, and of many other aspects of a national society. Furthermore, in the larger countries there is a need for regional and local studies in all the social sciences. Studies like those in the economics of the Brazilian northeast by Robock (1963) and Hirschman (1963) provide a depth of detail and analysis which make them extremely valuable to all students of Latin America. To cite another example, Stein's history of the community of Vassouras in the Paraíba Valley, Brazil, during the rise of the coffee planters (1957) demonstrates the importance of research limited in time and space to the understanding of national history. In the same sense, the numerous community studies by sociologists and social anthropologists, although too often focused on Indians or peasants, offer detailed description and analysis of the way of life of limited sectors of Latin American society. They have implications far beyond the local scene. We need more research and analysis of other sectors of Latin American society, such as the study by Whiteford (1960) of social stratification in a Mexican and Colombian city, as well as studies of parts of cities such as that carried out by Pearse (1961) in a *favela* (shantytown) of Rio de Janeiro. We need regional and local studies by political scientists, sociologists, and other social scientists in order really to understand Latin American societies.

Such concrete and highly specific research need not be limited to a spatial unit such as a region or a community. Instead, an institution or a nonlocalized corporate group could be the unit for research. A study of one Latin American political party would give us more insight into Latin American political process than a dozen superficial generalized accounts. Studies are needed along the lines of the book by Cochran and Reina (1962), mentioned by Strickon, of large-scale Latin American industrial enterprises. Kling's short study, *A Mexican Interest Group in Action* (1961), indicates a type of research project that might be undertaken usefully in various countries of Latin America and on a variety of interest groups. Latin American studies have suffered for too long from the superficiality evidenced in the traditional area-wide histories, surveys of Church and state relations, chronicles of political events throughout the continent, and other generalized accounts. Needed are specific and concrete pieces of original research upon which to build more valid generalizations and frame new hypotheses.

This should not be taken to mean that social science studies on Latin America should be entirely empirical, should avoid general theory, and be highly limited in scope. As stated above, certain fields of research, such as studies of voting behavior, population trends, or inflation, demand a national basis. Even so, localized and limited research is needed to help us interpret and evaluate quantitative data and national trends. The sample survey carried out by Stycos *et al.* (n.d.) in four Peruvian communities, each representing a "type" (i.e., capital city, small city, mestizo coastal town, and highland bilingual village), indicates a fruitful approach. In this case, the sample surveys were coordinated with analyses of national census data so that they could be interpreted on a nationwide basis. In turn, the surveys helped to interpret the census data. In view of the paucity of nationwide quantitative data, the presence of multiple or dual economies, and the fact that in many countries a large proportion of the people live marginally to modern society, many social scientists will have to depend upon local studies and sample surveys for their data.

Despite the need for national and local research, Latin America offers an excellent field for internal comparison. With their common Iberian tradition and their colonial experience under Spain (except for Brazil), Latin American nations share a basic set of social institutions and even of behavior patterns and values (cf. Gillin 1947). Yet, as mentioned earlier, they differ strikingly from one another—in physical environment, in the composition of their populations, and in their historical experience both before and after independence. They offer a unique opportunity to seek the causal connections among the environmental, historical, and cultural variables. As Dore (1963: 13–14) puts it,

Latin America does provide excellent opportunities for the kind of comparative sociology that seeks to arrive at generalizations about causal connections of the type: "X is likely to lead to Y, other things being equal." It is obvious that one has a better chance of arriving at such generalizations with fair confidence if other things *are* as equal as possible. It is in this respect that Latin America offers a promising field. Its societies do have so many points of similarity that an examination of their differences might yield new information about the way those differences are interrelated. Thus, for instance, Latin America is an excellent place to study say, the relation between levels of literacy and the political role of labor unions; between the size of the professional middle-class and the strength of liberal democratic parties; between the real extent of racial and cultural differences and the political or social importance attached to such differences; between the type of land tenure and the political involvement of peasants and so on. Economists have used such methods in a purely statistical way, for instance, in seeking a correlation between inflation and the rate of economic growth; there is still not enough systematic collection of data to enable sociologists or political scientists to use the same technique effectively.

Such comparative studies, it would seem, might best be undertaken within certain subregions of Latin America if it is desired that "all things be equal" to the highest possible degree. For example, the highland countries of Central and South America, with their large Indian populations, offer one such group of nations. Another broad area of relative similarity includes the tropical lowlands of northern Brazil, Venezuela, Colombia, and the West Indies, which share a slave-plantation–monoculture tradition. Still another subregion might be Argentina, Uruguay, and Chile, where in different degrees European immigrants have played such an important role (cf. Wagley 1957). On the other hand, if contrast or difference is sought in framing a research problem, then countries or localities in the different subregions might be selected for study.

Another comparative view would be gained through a typology of Latin American nations based on historical and functional criteria. An example is the typology used by Germani in his study of social stratification in Latin America (1962). He points out that Latin American societies range from traditional structures with clearly separated strata to industrial ones whose many strata are neither clearly separated nor readily identifiable. Using criteria and indices such as the size of the middle class, the degree of urbanization, the degree of literacy, and the number of university students per 1,000 inhabitants, he sets groups of Latin American nations along a scale ranging from the traditional to the industrial type of stratification. Thus, Argentina, Uruguay, Chile, and Costa Rica are grouped together as those nations which most closely approach the industrial type, Mexico and Brazil come next, and Cuba, Colombia, and Venezuela third, while Panama, Paraguay, Peru, Ecuador, El Salvador, Bolivia, Guatemala, Nicaragua, the Dominican Republic, and Haiti have retained to the highest degree their traditional class structure (Germani 1962: 148ff.). Such classification of Latin American societies can often be more useful than a classification by subregions, for they allow comparisons between countries that are at about the same stage of economic development and social modernization. One might ask, for example, what the similarities or differences are in the form of nationalism in, say, Argentina and Chile, which are roughly in the same stage of modernization; or one might ask the same question regarding Argentina and Peru, which are at opposite ends of the traditional-industrial spectrum. Or, one might frame a question as to the similarities and differences between the recent revolutions in Cuba and Bolivia, which are not only in different subregions of Latin America but in different stages of modernization.

In regarding Latin America as a unit for research, the subject of international relations at once comes to mind.[2] It was not found feasible to provide a separate chapter in this volume on research in international relations, but it must be pointed out, however briefly, that this is an important and much neglected field of social science research. Actually, the study of the relations among American states falls within the scope of several disciplines, notably history, political science, and economics, and it is likely to be neglected by all. It also includes three subfields: relations among the Latin American states themselves, bilateral relations between the United States and the various Latin American republics, and the treaties, institutions, and attitudes that have come to be called the "inter-American system."

The diplomatic and military history of the Latin American nations has been given little attention by North American scholars. There is a paucity of materials, the archives of Latin American foreign offices are difficult of access, and memoirs of Latin American diplomats are scarce and often unenlightening. There are few studies of the nineteenth-century conflicts among Latin American nations, again with outstanding exceptions such as Box (1927) and Burr (1962). Scholars in the United States have left almost untouched the three chief Latin American conflicts of this century, namely, the Chaco War between Bolivia and Paraguay, the dispute over Leticia between Peru and Colombia in 1932, and the Marañón struggle between Ecuador and Peru, which continues today, since Ecuador refuses to accept the "settle-

2 The editor is indebted to Bryce Wood and Robert N. Burr for preparing the basic notes for the following paragraphs on the study of inter-American relations.

ment" of 1942. The principal specialized works in this connection are those by Cooper (1934) and by Zook (1960). Given this lack of interest in the drama of Latin American conflict and war, it is not surprising that the more homely arts of peace among Latin American nations have been neglected by North American scholars.

The subject of bilateral relations between the United States and Latin American countries has, of course, received more attention. The literature on the subject prior to World War II was reviewed by Bemis (1943) and updated by Mecham (1961). The subject of United States relations with Latin American nations since the turn of the century has been studied by, among others, Munro (1964), Whitaker (1954), and Wood (1961). Students of U.S. policy toward Latin America have an advantage over those working on the policies of Latin American countries. The publication of the extensive documents contained in the so-called *American Republics* volumes through 1942 in the series entitled *Foreign Relations of the United States* (U.S. Government Printing Office) and the existence of excellent bibliographical tools such as Bemis and Griffin (1935) provides data not available elsewhere. In addition, publications on the relations of the United States with Latin American republics are reviewed annually in the *Handbook of Latin American Studies* (University of Florida Press).

The attempts of the American nations to keep the peace and further their mutual interests through the OAS and through hemispheric treaties is the subject of a large number of publications, most of which consist of official documents of the OAS itself and of the U.S. Government or the Alliance for Progress. There is a new and expanding literature by U.S. scholars on the experience of the OAS since 1948, such as Thomas and Thomas, Jr. (1963), Berle (1962), and Dreier (1962). The periodical literature and the government reports on this aspect of inter-American relations are abundant but demand study by scholars.

The social science aspects of inter-American relations are in need of development. There is a great need for the study of political relations among Latin American nations and of those nations' foreign policies. Their economic relationship since 1946, for example, the politics of the various coffee agreements, are not well understood. Another problem of inter-American rela-

tions which is of great current importance and sensitivity is the
changing role of U.S. business enterprises in Latin America.
Then, there is the question of inter-American security, including
the political as well as the military aspects of hemispherical defense. The OAS should be studied as an institution that could
exert economic and political pressure on its member states, not
just as a legal institution. The study of inter-American relations
is an important part of Latin American studies and adds another
dimension to this research.

Finally, something should be said about the advantages and
disadvantages of social science research in Latin America. Both
the pros and the cons derive from the historical and social characteristics of the area itself. Despite all its Indian and African
traditions, Latin America is fundamentally an extension of
Europe. The African slaves transported to America were torn
from their communities and arrived as an almost societyless
group of individuals. In countries where there was a dense aboriginal population, the Spanish were able to transform the Indians within a century or so into reasonable replicas of European
peasants and to impose upon them Iberian institutions and customs. This was a feat of "directed social and cultural change"
on a scale seldom equaled in the modern world. Latin American
nations have adopted governmental forms, constitutions, and
ideologies borrowed from Europe or the United States. For over
400 years, Latin America has been an offspring of Europe.

This fact has its advantages and disadvantages. First, it means
that the national languages are Spanish, Portuguese, and French.
Such languages hardly pose as much of an obstacle to research as
do Chinese, Japanese, Hindi, Arabic, or the African languages.
Furthermore, it means that the U.S. or European social scientist
is working with a set of institutions with which he is already
familiar, at least in their normal aspects. Yet this familiarity with
the European-derived institutions leads to a basic misunderstanding of Latin America. The similarity tends to be formal and
superficial. In the 400 years since Europeans settled in the New
World, Latin American nations have profoundly modified,
adapted, and reinterpreted European customs and institutions.
A Latin American constitution may read like its U.S. counter-
part, but it does not function in the same way. Latin American
courts may follow the formal procedure of French courts, but the

outcome is different. Latin American economic systems are formally patterned after Western capitalism, but in reality there are important structural differences and dual economic systems which bedevil economic theorists. The Europeanness of Latin America can be deceptive.

One great advantage for social scientists who are doing research in Latin America derives from this European heritage. Despite the large numbers of illiterates in many countries, Latin America has a literate tradition. The educated elite have written about themselves and their countrymen for centuries. Today, there are hundreds of universities and other institutions of higher learning and many specialists in the social sciences. Thus, the U.S. scholar who wishes to do research in Latin America has a backlog of written materials in a European language and the possibility of collaboration with his Latin American colleagues. Each year there is an increase in the output of serious social science studies by Latin Americans and in the quality of cooperative research between U.S. and Latin American scholars.

At the same time, Latin America suffers from poverty, illiteracy, political instability, inflation, food shortages, lack of educational facilities, and a multitude of other serious social and economic problems. These concerns are reflected in the research and theory of Latin American social scientists, which focus upon practical immediate political and policy problems. Latin American social scientists are interested almost exclusively in social and economic change. Their economists are apt to accuse their North American colleagues of overemphasizing equilibrium rather than economic development. And a Chilean sociologist has stated: "Some sociologists in North America seem to think that a society that is changing is destroying itself, but we consider that unless our societies are in process of change, they are destroying themselves" (Wood and Wagley 1961: 41).

The presence of so many urgent social and economic problems in Latin America means that the social sciences are in great demand as useful instruments for change. Social scientists are sought as planners, administrators, politicians, and teachers. But, in turn, this situation has its drawbacks. It means that social science is drawn inevitably into politics, into polemics, and into rapid surveys for immediate use. Social science runs the danger of losing its objectivity. The U.S. scholar who does research in Latin

America is not immune to this influence. If he is an intelligent and sensitive person, he learns to think and feel with his Latin American colleagues. He can share their exhilarating feeling of being useful in a dynamic and rapidly developing society. He can also feel the pinch of being forced to work on operational problems in a "ten minutes to midnight" atmosphere. In any case, he will learn that Latin America provides the well-trained and original social scientist with an opportunity to break new ground, both substantively and theoretically, as well as to contribute to the welfare of millions of our neighbors to the south.

BIBLIOGRAPHY

Agassiz, Louis, and Elizabeth C. Agassiz
   1867 A journey in Brazil. Boston and New York. (Later edition, 1896.)
Bandelier, Adolf F. A.
   1878 On the distribution and tenure of land, and the customs with respect to inheritance, among ancient Mexicans. Salem, Mass.
   1879 On the social organization and mode of government of the ancient Mexicans. Salem, Mass.
Bates, Henry Walter
   1875 The naturalist on the river Amazons. London and Boston. 3rd ed.
Beals, Ralph L.
   1946 Cheran: a Sierra Tarascan village. Washington, D.C., Smithsonian Institution.
Bemis, Samuel Flagg
   1943 The Latin American policy of the United States. New York.
Bemis, Samuel Flagg, and G. G. Griffin
   1935 Guide to the diplomatic history of the United States. Washington, D.C., Government Printing Office.
Berle, Adolph
   1962 Latin America: diplomacy and reality. New York, Council on Foreign Relations.
Bernstein, Harry
   1961 Making an inter-American mind. Gainesville, Fla.
Box, Pelham, H.
   1927 The origins of the Paraguayan war. Urbana, Ill.
Brand, Donald
   1951 Quiroga: a Mexican *municipio*. Washington, D.C., Smithsonian Institution, Institute of Social Anthropology. No. 11.
Bryce, James
   1914 South America.
Burr, Robert N.
   1962 The stillborn Panama congress: power politics and Chilean-Columbian relations during the war of the Pacific. Berkeley and Los Angeles.
Calderon de la Barca, Frances
   1843 Life in Mexico. (New edition 1954.)

Cochran, Thomas C., and Ruben E. Reina
1962 Entrepreneurship in Argentina culture: Torcuato di Tella and S.I.A.M. Philadelphia.
Cooper, Russell M.
1934 American consultation in world affairs. New York.
Daniels, Josephus
1947 Shirt-sleeve diplomat. Chapel Hill, N.C.
Dore, Ronald P.
1963 Some comparisons of Latin American and Asian studies with special reference to research on Japan. Social Science Research Council, Items 17: No. 2 (June).
Dreier, John C.
1962 The Organization of American States and the hemisphere crisis. New York, Council on Foreign Relations.
Edwards, William H.
1855 A voyage up the river Amazon, including a residence at Pará. London.
Foster, George M.
1948 Empire's children: the people of Tzintzuntzan. Washington, D.C., Smithsonian Institution, Institute of Social Anthropology. No. 6.
Germani, Gino
1962 Política y sociedad en una época de transición: de la sociedad tradicional a la sociedad de masas. Buenos Aires.
Gillin, John
1945 Moche: a Peruvian coastal community. Washington, D.C., Smithsonian Institution, Institute of Social Anthropology. No. 3.
1947 Modern Latin American culture. Social Forces 25: 243–48.
Herndon, William L., and Gardner Gibbon
1853–54 Exploration of the valley of the Amazon. (Part I by Lt. Herndon, Washington, D.C., 1853. Part II by Lt. Gibbon, Washington, D.C., 1854.)
Hirschman, Albert
1963 Journeys toward progress: studies of economic policy-making in Latin America. New York.
Kidder, Daniel P.
1845 Sketches of residence and travels in Brazil. Philadelphia and London.
Kidder, Daniel P., and James C. Fletcher
1857 Brazil and the Brazilians. Philadelphia.
Kling, Merle
1961 A Mexican interest group in action. Englewood Cliffs, N.J.
Leonard, Irving
1943 A survey of personnel and activities in Latin American aspects of the humanities and social sciences at twenty universities of the United States. Notes on Latin American Studies, No. 1 (April): 7–46.
Mecham, J. Lloyd
1961 The United States and inter-American security, 1889–1960. Austin, Texas.
Minnich, R. Herbert, and John V. D. Saunders
1964 Latin-American content courses at selected American universities, 1963–1964. Gainesville, University of Florida, Latin American Language and Area Center.

Munro, Dana G.
1964 Intervention and dollar diplomacy in the Caribbean, 1900–1921. Princeton, N.J.

Pearse, Andrew
1961 Some characteristic of urbanization in the city of Rio de Janeiro. *In* Urbanization in Latin America, Philip M. Hauser, ed. UNESCO.

Pierson, Donald
1951 Cruz das Almas: a Brazilian village. Washington, D.C., Smithsonian Institution, Institute of Social Anthropology. No. 12.

Prescott, William H.
1843 History of the conquest of Mexico with the life of the Conqueror Hernando Cortes, and a view of the ancient Mexican civilization. Boston. 3 vols.
1847 The conquest of Peru.

Redfield, Robert
1941 The folk culture of Yucatan. Chicago.

Robock, Stefan H.
1963 Brazil's developing northeast. A study of regional planning and foreign aid. Washington, D.C., The Brookings Institution.

Smith, Herbert H.
1878 The Amazon and the coast. New York.

Squier, Ephraim G.
1853 Observations on the archaeology and ethnology of Nicaragua. American Ethnological Society, Transactions 3: 85–158.

Stein, Stanley J.
1957 Vassouras: a Brazilian coffee county, 1850–1900. Cambridge, Mass.

Stephens, John Lloyd
1841 Incidents of travel in Central America, Chiapas, and Yucatan. New York. 2 vols.
1860 Incidents of travel in Yucatan. New York.

Steward, Julian H.
1950 Area research: theory and practice. New York, Social Science Research Council. Bulletin 63.
1955 Theory of culture change: the methodology of multilinear evolution. Urbana, Ill.

Steward, Julian H., *et al.*
1956 The people of Puerto Rico: a study in social anthropology. Urbana, Ill.

Stycos, J. Mayone, Allan G. Feldt, and George C. Myers
n.d. The Cornell international population program.

Thomas, Ann Van Wynen, and A. J. Thomas, Jr.
1963 The Organization of American States. Dallas, Texas.

Wagley, Charles
1948 Area research and training: a conference report on the study of world areas. New York, Social Science Research Council. Pamphlet No. 6.
1957 Plantation–America: a culture sphere. *In* Caribbean studies: a symposium, Vera Rubin, ed. New York, Institute of Social and Economic Research, pp. 3–13.

Whitaker, Arthur P.
1954 The Western hemisphere idea. Ithaca, N.Y.

Whiteford, Andrew H.
    1960   Two cities of Latin America: a comparative description of social classes. Beloit, Wis., Logan Museum of Anthropology. Beloit College.
Wood, Bryce
    1957   Latin American studies in the United States. (Unpublished memorandum.)
    1961   The making of the good neighbor policy. New York.
Wood, Bryce, and Charles Wagley
    1961   The social sciences; parochial or cosmopolitan? Reflections on the inter-American conference on research and training in sociology. Social Science Research Council, Items 15: No. 4 (December).
Zook, David H., Jr.
    1960   The conduct of the Chaco War. New York.

2. The Contribution of Geography to Latin American Studies

JAMES J. PARSONS

Geography stands as an independent field of inquiry by virtue of its concern with the place-to-place variation of the earth's surface and its human societies and the causes and consequences of this variation. It is unique as to point of view, of which the map is an effective mirror. Man's evaluation of the relative habitability of the earth, in good part a cultural judgment, is expressed through the uneven distribution of population and such material marks of his occupancy as houses, cities, factories, roads, farmsteads, and fields—and these features and their distributions are the raw material of most geographical investigation. The understanding of why and how people live where they do and the nature and durability of man's relationship with and dependence upon the physical environment are major themes within geography.

Although geography's organizing principle is spatial, as that of history is chronological, the manner in which a contemporary landscape has evolved cannot be understood without the perspective of time. The historical orientation of geography has been especially pronounced in the Latin American field, where the lines of history are deeply etched on the land and its people. Indeed, the interests of cultural anthropologists, historians, and geographers have often fused in Latin American studies, as in investigations of the origins, spread, limits, and modifications of culture traits or cultural complexes, until the distinction between them often becomes blurred. Much of geography's strength stems from its flexibility—its ability to work with materials from both the physical and social sciences from its own distinctive and integrating point of view.

For its relative lack of concern for theory, its neglect of methodological innovation, its wariness of broad generalizations, and its past tendencies to be satisfied with "mere description," geography of late has been chided by some of its own and passed by unrecognized by others. There are many misconceptions of what geography is, even its confusion with "geology" or the not infrequent assumption that it is little more than the study of place names, the proving of "influences" of the environment on human activity, or gazeteerlike description.

Most geographical work transcends the boundaries of the social sciences, drawing on the ideas, field techniques, and observations of natural science. It considers the whole wherever possible in terms of mapped distributions and the interrelationship of physical phenomena, cultural attitudes, and economic activities. As a bridge between the natural and the social sciences, but with its own distinctive set of problems, the field of geography has a unique opportunity to contribute to the fuller understanding of man's place in nature, especially through its emphasis on empirical relationships and on the application of spatial and ecologic thinking to the human use of the earth. Potentially it has important contributions to make to scientific programs concerned with land utilization, food production, water supply, industrial development, urban and regional planning, and natural resources conservation. It may equally be concerned with man's attitudes about the earth and his attachments to the local character of places. The appreciation and enjoyment of landscapes for their own sake, and a naive curiosity about the arrangement of things in space, has attracted many workers to geography. So too has the "conservation ethic," a concern for the husbanding and protection of the earth against man's destructive exploitation and despoiliation. The engineering of economic and social development in itself, the provision of resources for an expanding world population at rising levels of living, if not a geographical goal, may nevertheless have profound geographical consequences.

Traditionally geography has been committed strongly to direct field observation. This could well be its unique challenge and its opportunity. Nowadays, with new techniques and the proliferation of the printed word, more and more scholars are doing their work in the office or laboratory, well removed from contact with the countryside and the enormously difficult task of analyzing complex reality. Indeed, the provision of trained field workers, sensitive to both culture and environment and willing to get their boots muddy, may be one of geography's more important contributions to scholarship generally and to area studies in particular.

Scholarly geography is placing more emphasis on problems, concepts, ideas, and techniques today than ever before. Yet the world of scholarship still properly looks to geography for information about places and will doubtless continue to do so. The term "geography" means "writing about the earth," by which the Greeks understood "describing the earth." Good regional description, as much art as science, is likely to be useful to scholars of the future long after the theories and models toward which so much of contemporary social science is geared have been forgotten or have been enshrined as quaint relics of another era. Although the facts the geographer perceives must be examined, labeled, and perhaps measured with care and accuracy, the presentation of these facts involves personal choice, taste, and judgment. The reading of the landscape, the interpretation of scenery, whether for its own sake or for some specific end, involving as it does the intricate interplay of its physical and cultural elements, is in a manner comparable to art or music appreciation, a legitimate subject of humanistic inquiry. The sympathetic editor of *Landscape* magazine (1951) once put it this way:

The manner in which the environment is exploited, the attitude toward nature as she manifests herself in that environment, is a culture trait second to none in importance. The human landscape is the visible sign of that attitude. It is in the interpretation of that landscape that ecology falters, and where human geography comes into its own. Skeptical of "scientific" laws, aware of the enormous diversity among human groups, disdaining no discipline in its effort to understand the man-made environment, it does much to bring together and to moderate the various professions which have undertaken to study man and his habitat. More than anything else, perhaps, human geography is a way of looking at man and the world; it is a new word for humanism. If so, we must see to it that . . . its qualities become generally diffused [among other disciplines], ecology taking over its human concern, its earthier aspects being absorbed by the social sciences.

Such interpretive insight depends on long and intimate familiarity with place, language, and culture. This is the first requisite of the "area specialist," whether in Latin America or elsewhere, but especially so of the geographer.

In recent years quite another direction has come to geography, an abstract and mathematical concern for space and space-distance relations, centering on the search for verification of observation and the search for generalizations and laws through systems analysis, spatial and simulation models, and the methods, concepts, and approaches of the physical sciences applied to economic and cultural data. William Warntz (1959), perhaps representative of those striving to bring the subject more in line with the more theoretically oriented social sciences, has called for "a macroscopic geography aimed at developing concepts at a more meaningful level of abstraction so as to make possible the understanding of the whole economic system and to provide a conceptual framework into which to put the micro-descriptions." In this macroscopic analysis and especially through the application of gravity and potential models in which earth variables are purposefully disregarded, he has envisioned a step towards "the forging of a theory of human society [that] can be greatly aided by finding regularities in the aggregate." Others complain that this is hardly geography's responsibility. Labeling this doctrine "the new teleology of the equilibrium and functional concepts," Lukerman and Porter (1960) conclude that, if this is the level of abstraction that geography is searching for, "the seventeenth century lies dead ahead."

The lively ferment in contemporary geography cannot but have its effect on Latin American studies. As elsewhere the winds of change blow strongly within geography, yet what Sauer called the subject's "lingering sickness," a consequence in part of its work being too much ruled "not by inquisitiveness but by definitions of its boundaries," cannot be said to have been entirely eradicated. While extricating itself from the quagmire of pedagogy, it runs the risk of splintering today into quantitative economic geography, historical-cultural geography, and physical geography, with limited communication between the segments. Geographers working in foreign areas, however, may be less affected by this treatening schism than those working in North America and Europe.

In Latin America the absence of reliable statistical data has in the past restricted sharply the amount of work possible by the quantitative approach. This is also the reason for the generally poorly developed level of economic geography, in which the new techniques have been primarily employed. It might be claimed that the vogue for statistical correlations is most evident among those with the least field exposure. It is best developed among economic geographers working within the North American and European framework, a part of the larger movement within the social sciences generally. The use of statistical inference in climatic and vegetation studies has been of long standing, but it has not attracted attention to the same extent as its more recent application in economic geography. Among its practitioners there are confidence and high hope for such mechanistic approaches to the understanding of reality. Planning and development agencies, sometimes seduced by the easy confidence of figures and formulas, provide increasingly ready markets for their wares. Attempts to make economic geography increasingly generalized and predictive are certain to continue, and we may confidently predict that Latin America will provide the frame of reference for more of these studies in the future (see *Latin American Congress on Regional Science,* Caracas, 1962).

The geographic method is clearly no more the monopoly of geographers than is their particular point of view. Much work in Latin America done by nongeographers has a strong geographic character to it, and the borrowing back and forth between geography and neighboring fields is inevitably a continuing matter. This survey, however, has for obvious reasons, been confined to the work of persons who have been identified professionally and explicitly with geography as a separate research discipline.

The Work of European Geographers

The opening up of the New World by Europeans was a geographical achievement. The first geographers were the explorers and navigators who first defined the limits of the New World. The early chroniclers, including Columbus himself, Oviedo, Las Casas, Martyr, Bernal Díaz del Castillo, Pero Vaz de Caminha, Fernão Cardim, and Pedro de Magalhães Gandavo, gave a strong geographical flavor to their works. In the following years many geographical reporters, serving in a semi-official capacity, reported in detail to the Crown on the character of the new lands across the sea and the people who inhabited them. Garcilasso de la Vega, Vásquez de Espinosa, Francisco Hernández, and their like conveyed admirably precise knowledge of the varied nature of the Americas to their peninsular readers. These chroniclers' accounts are still of great interest for their esthetic qualities as well as for their utility in reconstructing the past distributions of population, crops, and vegetation from which the extent and direction of subsequent changes can be measured. In particular the *Relaciones geográficas,* detailed accounts of the various parts of the Indies ordered made by the Crown in the 1570s and again in the late eighteenth century, hold a wealth of geographical information of great interest and utility, even to the student of contemporary Latin America. A systematic survery of the known *Relaciones* for Mexico and Central America is currently being prepared by Howard Cline for the forthcoming *Handbook of Middle American Indians.* For South America the best source remains Jiménez de la Espada's introduction to Volume I of his *Relaciones geográficas de Indias* (1881).

Beginning with Alexander von Humboldt's celebrated travels to the New World (1801–04), the nineteenth century saw an extraordinary extension of our geographical knowledge through the accounts of the great European naturalists and travelers. Humboldt, acclaimed the father of modern scientific geography, set the pattern for precise observation and analysis, with maps, which gave rise to the incomparable literature, at once scientific and literary, of such men as Appun, Boussingault, Darwin, Belt, Squier, D'Orbigny, and Agassiz. Nothing comparable exists from the present century, perhaps in part because travelers' descriptions have somehow come to be considered "unscientific" by modern "science." Whatever the reason, our understanding of Latin American today is incomparably the poorer. In Latin America, more than most parts of the world, field observation, language facility, an eye for country, and a sympathy for the countryman's values and way of living has remained a *sine qua non* of geographical research.

Geography as a scholarly discipline originated in Germany. From Humboldt to the present there has been a strong tradition of foreign travel and study among the German geographers. The lure of the New World tropics has been especially compelling to them. In the temperate regions of South America and in highland Central America, German colonization and settlement have further encouraged intensive local field investigations, much as Japanese attention is currently beginning to be similarly attracted by Japanese agricultural colonies in Bolivia and Brazil. Many of the leading figures in German geography have contributed in a major way to the literature of Latin American geography. Humboldt set the pattern more than 150 years ago. Hettner (1859–1941), a major figure in scientific geography in Germany over a long and productive life, did significant fieldwork in the Colombian Andes in his early years (Hettner 1888, 1892), as did Sievers (1887, 1888) in Venezuela and Colombia, Passarge (1933) in Venezuela, and Wagner (1856, 1861, 1876) and Sapper (see Termer 1956 for bio-bibliography) in Central America. Wagner's observations on the migrations of organisms (1868), forgotten for nearly 100 years, have recently been receiving new and respectful attention from zoologists and other students of evolution; Hanno Beck, Humboldt's biographer, is currently working on Wagner's papers. Sapper spent the longest period in the field. He lived in Guatemala from 1888 to 1900 and traveled the length and breadth of the volcanic highlands of Central America and southern Mexico on foot. From this period alone his extensive bibliography contains 87 titles (Termer 1956), and he continued to publish extensively on the physical, cultural, and economic geography and ethnology of the area for another thirty years, while he was professor of geography at several different German universities. In the same tradition a surprising number of the key figures in post-World War I German or German-language geography have done major work in Latin America. The list would include Credner, Haberland, Helbig, Hueck, Kinzl (Austria), Klute, Kühn, Maack, Maull, Otremba, Pfeifer, Rawitscher, Schauffelberger (Switzerland), Schmieder, Schmithüsen, Termer, Troll, Waibel, Wilhelmy, and, among the younger generation, Blume, Gierloff-Emden, Lauer, Sandner, and Zimmermann. Several of these men have held appointments at universities in the United States and in Latin America and a few have established residence in Latin America. Their influence has been considerable. If their work has had a common focus, it has been on agricultural colonization and settlement, on the one hand, and land forms and biogeography on the other, with special emphasis on man's modification of the soil and of the vegetative mantle. Such a focus, it may be noted, is very close to that of Humboldt and equally so to that of the Berkeley geographers, who, especially under the influence of Sauer, have given the principal impetus to work in cultural and historical geography in Latin America in this country.

French contributions to the geographical literature on Latin America have likewise been of considerable substance, beginning a century ago with Elisée Reclus. In the past thirty years French geographers have confined their efforts chiefly to Brazil—Deffontaines, Dion, Dresch Gourou, Martonne, Monbeig, Pardé, Rochefort, Ruellan, Sermet, and Tricart, among others, have done significant work there based often on extended field observations. The French islands of the West Indies have been a second focus of interest (Revert 1949; Lasserre 1961). In Chile Borde has recently played an influential role in the establishment of a land tenure studies program in the Instituto Geográfico. The University of Cuyo at Mendoza, Argentina, has had an exchange program with Bordeaux; similar links between French geographical institutes and Bahia, São Paulo, and Bogotá either exist or are planned.

German university ties have been especially close at Córdoba and Tucumán (Schmieder, Czajka, Hueck) and in Chile (Schmieder, Lauer, Schmithüsen, Weischet). What is remarkable is the relative lack of research by Europeans in Mexico and the lack of academic ties of any sort with French or German geographers.

Geographical work by other Europeans in Latin America has been meager. The British geographers, save for a few exceptions (Ogilvie 1922; Butland 1957; Haggett 1961, 1963; Cole 1959, 1960; Crossley 1961), have been concerned with their own back yard and the former colonies, as have the Italians. Agustin Codazzi, the Italian immigrant engineer-geographer who mapped and described Venezuela and Colombia in the early nineteenth century, is still much revered in those countries, but he had little influence beyond their borders. The geographical literature emanating from Spain and Portugal on their former New World colonies has been notably meager save for the work of an occasional political refugee, such as Vila in Venezuela or Rubio in Panama.

The Latin American Geographers

Geography as a university subject and a research field is but weakly developed in Latin America. Traditionally it has been linked with history and anthropology. The geographical societies are most commonly combinations of academies of arts and letters and exclusive social clubs. Some are of venerable age, such as the Sociedad Mexicana de Geografía e Estadística, which was founded in 1833 and which is the oldest geographical society in the Americas. The geographical journals, of which there is no shortage—there are at least ten in Brazil alone—not uncommonly deal in nongeographical themes. Although there is no shortage of contributions, recourse to precise personal observation and rigorous interpretative explanation is more the exception than the rule. To this, Brazil and Chile, especially, are partial exceptions. The government geographical institutes are in most cases primarily mapping and surveying organizations, although some may occasionally support geographical research relating to urban problems, land use, and agricultural colonization.

In Brazil, where European influence has been the strongest, there are university departments of geography at Rio de Janeiro (Sternberg), at São Paulo (Azevedo, França, Müller, and others), at Bahia (Santos), at Recife (Melo and Osorio), and at Curitiba (Maack), among others. Sternberg is widely known both for his work on Brazilian economic development and for his handling of the successful International Geographical Union Congress at Rio de Janeiro in 1956 and the excursion guidebook and other publications of the Congress. His ties with both continental and North American geographers have been numerous and close. At the University of São Paulo a series of visiting French geographers, beginning with Deffontaines in 1934 and Monbeig between 1935 and 1947, have much influenced geographical thought, especially in the direction of the French school of regional geography. Among North American geographers in Brazil, the work and influence of James and his students have been particularly noteworthy. The federal government's Conselho Nacional de Geografía, manned by geographers, has played an active research role, especially in resources inventories and interior colonization. The Centro de Pesquisas de Geografia do Brasil is the research center for the geography of Brazil at the Universidade do Brasil in Rio de Janeiro. In addition to research papers, it publishes bibliographies on the geography and cartography of Brazil.

European and American geographers have also had substantial influence in Chile. The list of visitors would include several

North Americans, beginning with Jefferson and McBride and including Keller, MacPhail, Martin, and Thompson among the younger generation. The Instituto Geográfico of the Universidad de Chile, founded by Fuenzalida in 1954, is a full-time research organization with sections in physical, human-historical, regional geography and planning, and biogeography and a geochemical laboratory. There is no professional curriculum in geography, however, except at the Instituto Pedagógico.

Elsewhere in Latin America resident geographers are relatively few. In Mexico, as in Argentina, the orientation of geography is chiefly toward the preparation of secondary and normal school teachers rather than researchers, although some substantive work is being done both at the National University and at the Escuela Normal Superior. For a recent review of Mexican developments, one may be referred to the recently initiated Anuario de Geografía (Universidad Nacional Autónoma de Mexico, 1961). In Peru, government and UNESCO development programs have employed foreign geographers in some numbers. Some of these have produced significant research studies, especially relating to agricultural and fisheries progress and potentialities. Although there is little academic geography in Colombia, most of the professional anthropologists and sociologists there (Duque, Reichel-Dolmatoff, Fals Borda, the Pinedas) have a strong geographical orientation. The German-born and trained geographer Guhl, a long-time resident of Bogotá, has been conspicuous for his long list of contributions in the field of land use and land tenure in different parts of Colombia. The Ford Foundation is considering support, through Guhl, to plans for the establishment of a department of geography within the National University. In the Instituto Geográfico "Agustin Codazzi," currently being reorganized, "Geographical Studies" has been the smallest and least active section.

In Puerto Rico extensive use has been made of geography and geographers in the islands development program, partly through the influence of Picó, president of the Development Bank, and the U.S. geographer, Hanson, propagandist for "Operation Bootstrap," and adviser and confidant to Governor Muñoz Marin. The Puerto Rico Land Classification Survey (1949–51), directed by Jones of Northwestern University in cooperation with the

Puerto Rican government, produced a 1:10,000 map of physical characteristics and land use, using a fractional field notation method based directly on aerial photographs and on some 12 Ph.D. dissertations, all concerned with the rural economy of the island, by U.S. geography graduate students who participated in the program. But it seems to have left no lasting impact on Puerto Rican geography and not more than 4 of the 19 Americans who participated have continued to work actively in the Latin American field.

The Puerto Rican program remains, however, the only major cooperative effort of its kind to have been undertaken in Latin America. It is represented in the literature by two monographs (Proudfoot 1952; Jones and Picó 1955) and several descriptive papers on land use and commodity production. The only parallel of which the author is aware is the currently developing land use survey of central Chile, organized through the Instituto Geográfico there and taken over and enlarged by the AID program. It is employing the I.G.U. land-use classification code with data taken from large-scale field maps and air photos, the resulting maps to be used in conjunction with planning and land reform programs.

In Cuba, too, for better or for worse, geography has been a handmaiden to change. Professional contributions of Cuban geographers have always been numerous and substantial, for example, Marrero (1950), and the Massips (1942). A geographer, Nuñez de Jimenez (1959), has directed the Cuban Land Reform program of the revolutionary Castro government.

Along with their local geographical journals, Latin American geographers have found a further outlet for their work in the *Revista Geográfica,* the organ of the Section on Geography of the Pan American Institute of Geography and History (PAIGH). The PAIGH itself, although designed to promote and coordinate research, has been principally an administrative agency. Its Consultations on Cartography have been perhaps its most important geographical achievements, along with the *Revista.* A Commission on Natural Resources and Land Use Classification and Working Groups on Climatology, Population Mapping, and Urban Geography have also been active. A recent shift of focus to support geographic analysis for regional development is said to have been more enthusiastically supported by U.S. than by Latin American delegates.

U.S. Geographers and Latin America

Academic geography at the university level is somewhat less well developed in the United States than in Canada, Great Britain, continental Europe, or the Soviet Union. At a few important private institutions, including Harvard and Stanford, it is at present not formally represented. Its strength has been in the great state universities, its orientation as much toward professional preparation for employment in government, business, and industry as in education. Of the 3,200 members of the Association of American Geographers, probably not more than half are in academic appointments, a large share of these in teacher's colleges. The pool of research geographers, by the broadest definition, may not exceed 500 persons. Membership figures for other comparable professional organizations in related fields include the American Historical Association (10,000), the American Political Science Society (12,000), the Geologic Society of America (4,000), and American Anthropological Association (3,500).

Of the 1,768 American geographers listed in the 1961 Handbook-Directory of the A.A.G., 9 percent (161 persons) professed a "research or professional interest" in some part of Latin America. Of these latter perhaps 70 had published significant monographs or articles on a Latin American theme or area. A rough count established that a similar 9 percent of the Ph.D. theses written in geography at U.S. universities between 1906 and 1962 (a total of 1,065 degrees were awarded) have been on Latin American topics; the figure is 13 percent for the period 1952–62. The proportion appears to have been close to constant for many years. Of the 75 Foreign Field Research Program fellowships awarded by the National Academy of Sciences–National Research Council from the Office of Naval Research (Geography Branch) funds since the program's inception, mostly to geography Ph.D. candidates, 21 (or 28 percent) have been for fieldwork in some part of Latin America or the West Indies. The ONR Geography Branch has in addition supported some dozen different field projects in Latin America during the past decade, including such topics as coastal vegetation and morphology, climatic change in southern Chile, physical geography of the Guiana coast, and regional studies of the Caribbean margins, the Pacific lowlands of Colombia, the southwest coast of Mexico, the Guajira Peninsula, and the Sinú Valley of Colombia.

As measured by Ph.D. degrees granted in geography, geographical research in Latin America has been rather notably concentrated at a few institutions. At the University of California at Berkeley, for example, 25 of a total of 55 Ph.D. theses accepted had been on Latin American (or West Indian) topics through mid-1963. Comparable figures for some of the major graduate geography schools are shown in Table 1. The influence of a few

Table 1. NUMBER OF PH.D. THESES IN GEOGRAPHY, THROUGH MID-1963

University	Theses in Latin American geography	Total geography theses
California (Berkeley)	25	55
Northwestern	18	76
Clark	16	172
Chicago	8	129
Florida	6	12
Syracuse	6	35
Wisconsin	5	73
Johns Hopkins	4	20
California (Los Angeles)	4	27
Illinois	4	32
Columbia	4	35
Michigan	4	96
Texas	3	3
Washington	2	54
Louisiana State	1	17
Indiana	0	14

individual scholars is strongly reflected in this distribution, especially Sauer at Berkeley, James at Syracuse, Jones at Northwestern (to which he went from Clark in 1943), Crist at Florida, and Brand at Texas. Of the Berkeley theses all but two have dealt with Mexico, Central America, or the Caribbean margins; all the Syracuse theses, on the other hand, have been on South American topics; all of Texas' on Mexico; and 12 of Northwestern's 18 on Puerto Rico, reflecting the 1949–51 Cooperative Land Classification Program between the university and the Puerto Rican government. The emphasis at each of these institutions (except Northwestern) has been on historical and cultural geography, a fact which has strongly influenced the bent of U.S. geographical scholarship in Latin America. This is well exemplified by California's *Ibero-Americana* monograph series, founded in 1932 by Sauer and Kroeber, in which 12 of the 46 volumes to date have been by geographers, the remainder by colleagues working on the margins of the field, with active concern for human ecology, demographic and economic history (Cook, Borah, Simpson). For an extended and appreciative review of this series by a French historian, see Chaunu (1961). The *University of California Publications in Geography* has included another 17 separate papers and monographs on Latin American topics; others have appeared on ONR reports of more limited distribution. Tropical biogeography, especially the study of man's modification of the natural vegetation, has also received considerable attention from the Berkeley group; economic and political geography, in contrast, are scarcely represented.

The Significance of Tropicality

From a geographical point of view one of the most important characteristics of the Latin American environment is its predominant tropicality. The successes and failures of different societies in their attempts to cope with the warm wet lands of low latitudes (*tierras calientes*) has logically attracted the attention of numerous geographers. A host of erroneous impressions and deeply rooted misconceptions are held by mid-latitude man about the tropical world. The fragility of tropical nature is insufficiently appreciated. Here, as Gourou (1961), Pendleton (1950), and others have pointed out, problems of soil fertility and soil exhaustion, of human disease and dietary deficiency, take on special characteristics quite unfamiliar to mid-latitude observers (see also Pacific Science Association 1957).

Some of the most fundamental problems of the humid tropics are related to the question of tropical soils. Their fragility may be comparable to that of the tropical forest. Once they are destroyed, their reconstitution may be impossible. The high temperatures and intense rains bring about a rapid decomposition of organic matter and, as a result, rapid weathering, a high rate of carbon dioxide production, an acid soil reaction, destruction of the soil structure, dispersion and leaching of colloids and bases, and finally impeded drainage.

Whether the native systems of shifting agriculture, basically an adaptation to the fast rate of tropical soil depletion, can be significantly improved upon on old rain-forest lowland soils is by no means proven. The introduction of tree crops and African pasture grasses and legumes, of slow-release pelletized fertilizers, and of new systems of land preparation and cultivation hold out substantial promise, but the answers will be slow in coming in.

Migratory agriculture, known in Mexico as *tonanmil* or *tlacolol,* has its rationale. It has permitted the maintenance of the fertility of soils for centuries in regions of low population density. What is necessary is to find a system of permanent cultivation that will maintain the soil's fertility. There is some evidence that pre-Columbian Americans knew more about some of these matters than does contemporary man. In recent years major development projects, supported by heavy capital investment and often undertaken in an atmosphere of urgency, have been undertaken in many tropical American lowlands, as in the Baixada Fluminense of Rio de Janeiro, the Rio São Francisco Valley, the Peruvian Amazon, the Artibonite of Haiti, and Mexico's Papaloapan, Grijalva-Usamacinta, and Tecalcatepeque basins. The documentation of their successes and failures and their economic and ecologic consequences should add immeasurably to our understanding of the potentialities of tropical lowlands generally (e.g., Winnie 1958).

We still know little about the adaptability of mid-latitude or highland man to the lowland tropics, or even of the extent to which climate may condition the energy and ambitions of native peoples there. It is clear that, given sufficient capital and sociopolitical stability, modern technology can ameliorate climatic stress and control disease. The promise of the eventual harnessing of a part of the intense solar energy received in tropical latitudes for energy lies in the more distant future, but it is a promise with enormous overtones and implications.

Some archeologists have recently been increasingly concerned with the limiting effect of the tropical environment on cultural evolution, at times invoking a modified form of the same environmental determinism upon which geographers earlier turned their backs. The time seems ripe for a thorough review of the role of tropicality in human history. Few themes could have more significance for Latin America, especially at this time when industrialization and economic development are being held out as the panaceas for the problems of the entire non-Western world, a world that to a remarkable degree lies within the tropical latitudes.

Drought and Topography

Moisture deficiency and seasonal drought pose problems second only to those of tropicality to man in Latin America. Northern Mexico, the north coast of Venezuela and Colombia, the coast of Peru and Chile, the northeast of Brazil, and Patagonia are all lands of stress with special qualities and distinctive problems of human adjustment to limited water supply. A UNESCO Arid Lands Commission conference at Buenos Aires in September, 1963, was focused on these problems. It seems clear that a deeper understanding of climatic variability and ways of adapting to it offers one of the more promising avenues open to inquiring geographical climatologists. A few, like Aschmann (1959, 1960) and Aubert de la Rüe (1957), have been concerned with cultural adaptations to aridity; the more strictly climatological studies are considered in the last pages of this report.

A further characteristic of Latin America is the extent of its rugged topography, which frequently presents formidable barriers to trade and commerce precisely in those areas of highest population concentrations. While the resulting cultural compartmentalization may have stimulated social evolution in an earlier time, there seems little doubt that in the commercial world of today the Andes and their Central American extensions have presented substantial physical barriers to economic development. The airplane can only partially neutralize the costs of the steep and tortuous ascents and descents that characterize the land way, especially in the Andean states. The unbroken cordillera, knifed by deep *quebradas*, that hugs the western side of the continent provides an amelioration of the lowland tropical climate and often superior volcanic-ash soils which have made it the preferred settlement area, but it is also an area inordinately subject to the hazards of earthquakes, volcanic eruptions, soil erosion, landslides, and floods. Human misuse of the land can leave it an eroded skeleton in shockingly short order. A look at the state of Tlaxcala in central Mexico today, as compared with the account of it by Bernal Díaz, or a study of the several sites occupied by the Central American capitals, plagued with earthquakes and ash falls, will convince the most skeptical. Outside the volcanic zones, the mountains have been the source of mineral wealth, of course, but they also have posed barriers to trade and to economic and cultural integration that are greater than any part of Europe or North America have ever known.

Regional Studies in Latin America

The regional geography of Latin America as a whole has been admirably summarized in James's *Latin America,* now in its third edition (1959). Although designed as a text, this 942-page study is noteworthy not only for its comprehensiveness but also for its numerous original maps and geographical interpretations. Brazil, so often slighted, is here given special attention. Schmieder's two slim volumes, *Mittelamerika* (1934) and *Südamerika* (1932), recently revised (Schmieder 1962), are less encyclopedic but with a stronger bias towards physical and historical geography. Denis' *Amerique du Sud,* Volume XV of the *Geographie universelle,* and Jones's *South America* (1930) were other earlier statements and interpretations. Platt's *Latin American Countrysides and Regions* (1943) represents an experiment in microregional sampling, an outgrowth of a school of geographical thought that flourished in the U.S. Middle West in the 1930s.

There is an impressive bulk to the regional descriptive accounts of the Latin American landscape, mostly to be found scattered through the numerous European geographical journals and to a lesser extent those of the United States and Brazil. These accounts by professional geographers have as frequently been focused on physical geography (geomorphology) as on cultural and economic landscapes or problems. This has been especially true of the work of the French and Germans, with whom the physical side of the subject has retained its full vigor. These accounts can perhaps best be savored by consulting the regionally organized *Research Catalogue* of the American Geographical Society; they are also indexed in the monthly *Current Geographical Publications* of the same organization. They range from the pedestrian to the brilliant, from the purely descriptive to the problem-oriented and thematic. The 1956 International Geographical Union Congress in Brazil, in particular, had the effect of turning the eyes of many geographers to the South American continent, as had the earlier and continuing ties with academic geography in Europe.

Among the outstanding country geographies, some of encyclopedic proportions are those of Denis (1922) and Kühn (1927, 1933) on Argentina, Vila (1960) on Venezuela, Marrero (1950) on Cuba, Pittier (1912, 1942) and M. Wagner (1856, 1944) on Costa Rica, Vivó (1958) and Tamayo (1962) on Mexico, Picó (1951) on Puerto Rico, McBride (1936) on Chile, Raimondi (1879–1940) and Romero (1961) on Peru, and Termer (1936–41) on Guatemala. A selected list of regional studies might include Alexander (1958) on Margarita Island; Helbig (1959, 1961) on northeast Honduras and the Río Grijalva Basin, Chiapas; West (1957) on the Pacific lowlands of Columbia; Crist (1937, 1952) on the Venezuelan Llanos and the Cauca Valley; Gourou (1949–50) on the Brazilian Amazon; Butland (1956) on Southern Chile; Termer (1954) on Yucatán; Pfeifer (1939) on Sonora and Sinaloa; Guhl (1951, 1957) on northern Colombia; Sterling et al. (1955) on the Venezuelan Andes; Waibel (1933) and Vivó (1959) on Chiapas; P. Wagner (1958) on Nicoya; Schweigger (1959) and Reparaz (1958) on coastal Peru; Sternberg (1956) on the Amazon island of Careiro; Monbeig (1952) on São Paulo, Brazil; and Brand (1960) on southwest Mexico.* The excursion guidebooks published in connection with the 1956 International Geographical Union Congress in Rio de Janeiro, in a total of more than 2,000 pages, summarized much new work on Brazilian man-land relations for the first time in the English language. The several volumes of regional essays on Brazil published in recent years by the Conselho Nacional de Geografía are also worthy of note. Preparation of a two-volume report (published in 1955) on the geography of the Paraná–Uruguay basin by the Associação dos Geógrafos Brasileiros was a new milestone. For the first time in Brazil a government agency (the Paraná–Uruguay Basin Interstate Commission) enlisted the cooperation of the professional geographers' (nongovernmental) organization in laying the

* Parsons' excellent study (1949) of the Antioqueño highlands (Colombia) should be added to this list (ed. note).

groundwork for regional economic planning. Shorter interpretative essays that have stood as classics of a sort are Sauer's "Personality of Mexico" (1941) and "Middle America as a Culture
Historic Location" (1959), Higbee's "Of Man and the Amazon"
(1951), Sternberg's "Agriculture and Industry in Brazil" (1955),
and James's "Trends in Brazilian Agricultural Development"
(1953). One might add, too, several of the papers on Latin America by French geographers that have appeared in the *Cahiers
d'Outre Mer*.

The persistence of the past, the survival of Indian, African, or
colonial Iberian ways, has profoundly influenced the manner of
living and thinking and the rate of cultural change everywhere
in Latin America except in the temperate southern part of South
America. This cultural conservativeness, bolstered by an isolation and compartmentalization enforced by topography or climate, is reflected in many ways in the cultural and economic
landscape—in house types, field boundaries, land tenure, agricultural systems, town patterns, and communications routes.
The shaping of these landscapes, a cumulative process in which
each stage conditions the next, has been of central concern to a
substantial share of the geographers who have worked in Latin
America. Schmieder (1927, 1929), Hueck (1928), Sauer (1932,
1948), West (1949, 1952), Parsons (1949, 1952), Monbeig (1957),
Aschmann (1959), Pfeifer (1952), Brand (1960), and Lauer (1961)
provide examples of attempts to reconstruct past landscapes or to
trace the processes at work in their modification through time.
All reflect a similar concern for cultural particularism and local
adaptations to particular sets of environmental conditions. So,
too, do such studies of culture elements as West and Armillas
(1950) and Schilling (1939) on the Mexican *chinampas*, Spencer
and Hale (1960) and Guzman (1962) on agricultural terraces,
Bruman (1944) on the culture history of vanilla, Daus (1948) on
transhumance, West (1959), on ridge, or *era*, agriculture, and
Rubio (1950) and Fuson (1964) on rural house types.

There have long been close links between anthropology and
geography in Latin America, perhaps because both have tended
to depend so much more on fieldwork than the other social
sciences. Not a few scholars, especially in Germany, have divided
their work between archeology and ethnology on the one hand
and geography on the other—Schultze-Jena, Haberland, Sapper,

Trimborn, and Termer fit into this category, as do Sauer, Brand, Arnold, and Aschmann among the U.S. geographers. The significance of geomorphology, soils, and ecology to archeologic reconstruction makes the cooperation between these fields of particular importance, and its maintenance is clearly much to be desired. In U.S. geography, however, only a corporal's guard has shown such inclination in recent years, perhaps in part because of a slackening of interest in physical geography, as anthropologists have increasingly moved into the breach.

A concern for *Der Gang der Kultur über die Erde* has led Sauer and some of his students, especially, into the vastly complicated and speculative puzzle of New World prehistory, including the evidence for the existence of seaworthy craft capable of trans-Pacific voyages (Edwards 1960), the antiquity and route of peopling of the Americas (Sauer 1944, 1956), and the origin and dispersal of domesticated plants and animals (Sauer 1950, 1952). Pre-Columbian cultural patterns, as interpreted from archeologic and ecologic evidence (Sauer and Meigs 1927; Sauer and Brand 1932; Sauer 1935) and from early Spanish exploration and mission activity (Sauer 1948; Meigs 1935), have also attracted substantial attention. Culture element exchange in postcontact times between Asia and Mexico's west coast has drawn the attention of Bruman (1944) and Guzman-Rivas (1960).

Sauer has emphasized in particular the significance of the geographical position of Central America as a corridor and as a crossroads in terms of the migrations of plants, of animals, and of man and his culture traits (Sauer 1959). He suggests that perhaps nowhere in the world has there been so narrow, long, and significant a land passageway. He calls for its study as such, with the most accurate identifications of its elements of culture and of the total range of distribution of each and thus of whatever may be learned of their appearance and movements in actual time as opposed to inferred or imagined stages. Such a task has been initiated by Sauer himself in connection with domesticated plants and animals and by Driver and Massey (1957), two anthropologists who studied with him, in their distributional studies of culture traits. In the same context Sauer has emphasized the potential of distributional studies of items of archeology and ethnology for the knowledge and consideration of far connections of culture, the mobility of peoples, and the communication of ideas beyond the sheltering limits of the so-called culture areas.

Contemporary culture spheres and their geographical delineation have recently concerned other American geographers. Augelli (1962), Lowenthal (1960), and Parsons (1954), among others, have considered the contrasts between Caribbean and mainland cultures, the former with generally Negroid or part-Negro components, the latter with Indian or mestizo. Zelinsky (1949) has initiated a study of the distribution of Negro population in Latin America (see also Murphy 1939). The larger problem of African culture elements in the New World has chiefly attracted the attention of cultural anthropologists such as Herskovits, Ramos, Aguirre Beltrán, and others.

Studies in Agricultural Colonization and Settlement

Geographical research in Latin America has given special attention to the process of agricultural colonization and settlement. The opening of new lands, whether the grasslands of the pampas, the irrigated oases of northern Mexico, the forested parklands of southern Chile, the steep ash slopes of the Colombian cordillera, or the fastnesses of the Amazon basin, has been one of the most persistent themes in recent geographical inquiry. This interest can be traced back at least forty years, when Isaiah Bowman initiated a research project, under the auspices of the American Geographical Society, designed to identify and describe the pioneer zones of the world from which substantial increase in the world's food supply might be expected to be derived. In the studies resulting from this project, *The Pioneer Fringe* (1931) and *The Limits of Land Settlement* (1937), tropical South America loomed large. Jefferson (1921, 1926) and McBride (1936) dealt in part with similar themes in the temperate southern end of the continent.

Modern colonization and settlement presents a striking example of the modification of the landscape by human agency. The experience of European settlers within the lower latitudes has been the object of concern of Augelli, Bruman, Dozier, Eidt, Krause, Monbeig, Otremba, Pfeifer, Rothwell, Schmieder, Waibel, and Wilhelmy, among others. A team of Japanese geographers is reportedly studying the experiences of Japanese agricultural settlers in Brazil. Tigner (1963), working both in Japan and in Bolivia, has presented a thoughtful analysis of the Ryukuans in the latter country and is extending the study to Brazil. In general, however, recent works have tended to be concerned with smaller areas and particular closely knit ethnic groups.

In contrast to the southern lands, nineteenth- and twentieth-century immigration into northern South America and Middle America has been relatively insignificant. In these areas research attention has been focused more on internal settlement by nationals, facilitated by modern highway construction, especially a downslope movement from the highlands into the relatively empty and often rainier *tierras calientes* or, in Brazil, into the interior heartland of Goiás, Mato Grosso, and Amazonia. The whole matter of agricultural colonization and the cultural and environmental conditions that have determined its successes and failures call out for careful attention (Stewart 1963). It is peculiarly amenable to comparative geographical analysis, to the blending of field observation and mapping, and to historical and ecological inquiry and interpretation. A brilliant example of this sort is the recent work of Sandner (1961) in Costa Rica. It also has been a focus of particular attention for a group at the University of Florida working with Crist.

Examination of the natural and institutional barriers to frontier expansion involves an understanding of soil and water relationships, land tenure and taxation, cultural attitudes, and economics. The obstacles of climate and topography, health hazards, and transportation difficulties and the failure to integrate land settlement schemes with economic and social development plans have all hindered the settlement of the vast unoccupied areas of the continent. Yet the myth of the vast unoccupied frontier persists, above all in Brazil. The most successful immigrant farming groups have been the Japanese market gardeners near São Paulo (Holzmann 1959), or the closely knit ethnic-religious groups, whether Italian, German, Dutch, Polish, Latvian, or Mennonite, but the diffusion of Old World attitudes and skills to the native populations has often been disappointingly slow. Waibel (1950), for example, saw the German immigrant as competing with the ill-paid Brazilian *caboclo* and eventually and irresistibly being pulled down to his level of living. Others have been more impressed by the contributions of immigrant groups to the technology and general level of living and to the persistence among them of Old World attitudes, culture traits, and settlement features like linear and rectangular village and field forms and systems of crop and land rotation.

Unplanned and haphazard settlement of free land is being replaced by organized colonization schemes, supported by governments, private land companies, or foreign companies. Each has its distinctive structural characteristics, its visual manifestations, and its causal factors. Modern agricultural colonists generally require capital, large-scale investments in housing, land-clearing, transportation, and equipment, as well as money to purchase clothing and the other manufactured items that have become necessities of modern life. Where subsistence is no longer an acceptable end, the production of cash crops becomes a major concern. This requires good local communications, especially farm-to-market roads; but roads, adequate financing, and sound management are not enough, for the land must be suitable and of the sort that will support permanent tillage. No less than the total ecology of the area and of man's place within it is involved. The matter is particularly important in tropical lowlands of Af and Aw* climate, where soils are often leached and sterile or rapidly become so with the clearing of the original forest and the exposure of the surface horizons to accelerated rates of tropical weathering. Land classification and land potential surveys have yet to be made for most of tropical America. Even population maps showing where people live are few and unsatisfactory, although an I.G.U. committee, headed by James, is currently preparing 1:1,000,000 population maps of South and Central America. A group of geographers at the Universidad Nacional Autónoma de Mexico (1962) has been mapping Mexican population shifts. Zelinsky has a population mapping project under way for Central America and the West Indies, and Nunley has made an impressive contribution on a micro scale for Costa Rica, as has Guhl for Colombia, but the study of the population geography of South America remains in its infancy. The

---

* In the Köppen classification, A climates are those in which during the coldest month the temperature does not fall below 64.4 degrees Fahrenheit. Subdivisions of A climates include Af—places that have abundant rain in all seasons. In Aw climates the dry season is prolonged or is not compensated by the rains of the rainy season (ed. note).

truth is that our knowledge of the local environment of the so-called "developing countries" and of what kinds of land in what areas offer the best opportunities for successful settlement is abysmal.

Burgeoning highland populations, the sanitary revolution, and improved communications that link the frontier zones with older settled areas have all contributed to the often spectacular new waves of settlement that are converting dense forests into fields and pastures at unparalleled rates. The downslope movement from the overcrowded Andean highlands into the Amazonian Oriente over a 3,000-mile front from Venezuela to Bolivia has attracted the attention of several geographers, including McBride and McBride (1944), Tosi (1960), Eidt (1962), Crist (1937), Guhl (1956), Drewes (1958) and Crossley (1961). Generalizations regarding the potentialities of these tropical lowlands are difficult and often misleading, but in general the poor lateritic soils of the higher interfluves cannot be expected to support permanent agricultural settlement except possibly one based on some sort of tree-crop agriculture, in which the physiognomy and micro-ecology of the forest is maintained. Along the rivers, where the soils are better, seasonal flooding may be at one time a boon, and again a limiting factor. Where well-marked dry seasons and lower rainfall make land preparation easier and the soils better, conditions tend to favor the eventual alteration and degradation of the soils and vegetation to savanna conditions.

Tosi, in a recent study (1960) of the ecologic life zones of Peru, describes the high optimism and subsequent failures of colonization schemes in the rain-drenched Oriente. Ignorance of the limitations imposed by climate and topography, he argues, has been at the root of past failures. Only a few merchants and land speculators have profited from most of these projects. The prosperity of such highly publicized colonies Tingo María or Quince Mil on new roads into the *tierra caliente* are held to be fictitious. Tingo María (elevation 1,800 feet), for example, depends more on its strategic location on the Lima-Pucallpa road than on the surrounding countryside. Despite much favorable publicity, its twenty-five-year history has been one of repeated crises and failures. Although it was surveyed for agricultural development more than fifteen years ago, there is said to be not a single commercial venture in the area from which returns have been adequate to cover the investment. The land along the road is described as abandoned and without permanent population, save for a few road maintenance crews. Perhaps such lands should better be left in a national forest reserve. The massive assault on the tropical forest at the LeTourneau colonization scheme on somewhat better lands on the Pachitea River near Pucallpa should be watched with special interest, for here is an opportunity under almost controlled laboratory conditions to observe the effect of massive forest clearings on soil structure and soil productivity.

In Brazil it has been argued by Sternberg, James, and others that intensification of agriculture in the older settled areas closer to the coastal metropolitan markets will be more rewarding than continuation of attempts to extend the already long life lines into the far interior, as in Mato Grosso or Goiás. But, as the establishment of the new capital of Brasilia on the sterile red *campo cerrado* lands at the water divide between the Tapajos and the São Francisco well illustrated, the lure of the west is persistent, however unrealistic. It will continue to be reflected on the changing population map of Brazil for many years to come.

Increasingly, arguments are being heard that colonization of the marginal lands may be weakening, rather than strengthening, the fabric of many economies, that already too many people may be trying to wrest a living from the land, that the products of agriculture are in relatively low demand, and that an extension of the amount of cultivated land only worsens the market condition of the small farmer, as do all measures to keep the farm population from declining. In Colombia, for instance, the drastic proposal of Lauchlin Currie's *Operación Colombia* would have increased the population of the 12 largest cities 44 percent in two years, moving the small-farmers from the slopes to the cities and putting the flat lands of the Magdalena Valley and the coast under large-scale mechanized cultivation. The presumptions of such projections are imposing—that employment can be found in the cities for these massive numbers and that the tropical lowlands are in fact generally suitable for large-scale mechanized farming operations on a continuing basis. Fundamental knowledge on the last point, in particular, calls clearly for geographical and ecological research in the *tierras calientes* at a much augmented intensity.

Archeology and historical documentation have thrown much light on pre-Columbian population distributions. They prove conclusively that extensive areas both in the *tierras calientes* and in the high Andes, until recently unpeopled, once supported significant numbers of men. Studies of Indian population geography at the time of the Conquest, and its modification under the impact of Europeans, have been the subject of numerous monographs in the *Ibero-Americana* series. Its contributors, whether geographers or not, have been strongly influenced by Sauer. His *Aboriginal Population of Northwest Mexico* (1935), a brilliant example of the manner in which field observation and archival research can be brought to bear on a single problem, was the model for numerous later works. The historical ethnographies of the Berkeley geographers, such as Kniffen (1931), Meigs (1939), McBryde (1945), West (1948), and Pennington (1963) are also relevant. [See also Schmieder (1930), Sapper (1936), Termer (1950), Zimmermann (1958), Eidt (1959), and Denevan (1963).] Some of these were by-products of the Institute of Social Anthropology of the Smithsonian Institution, which during and immediately after World War II played a significant role in bringing geographical and anthropological thinking closer together.

The Neglect of Economic and Political Geography

Contrasting with the considerable emphasis on historical and cultural studies by geographers in Latin America has been the weak development of work in contemporary economic geography. This is the more remarkable in view of the major revitalization of this field that has occurred within the United States in recent years, in part through the introduction of new and more rigorous methods of regional economic analysis. The broad sweep of problems associated with Latin American population growth and economic development has, with a few exceptions, been left largely to the economists, engineers, and politicians.

Some of this neglect reflects an obeisance to the extraordinary mark of the past on contemporary society and landscape in Latin America, some to the relative paucity of economic data available for analysis. Apparently once an intimate feel for the country and a language competence have been attained, the geographer in Latin America is particularly susceptible to being diverted to cultural and historical themes. Even among Latins themselves little of the work being done is of an economic or applied nature, a situation sharply in contrast with that found, for example, in anthropology. The qualities of human geography are much more and other than the things that get enumerated and made available for quantitative processing. Yet one cannot but be impressed with the paucity of even descriptive economic studies or studies of the causes and consequences of uneven distributions of population, not to mention the absence of any efforts to seek such principles and probability statements as may derive from the austerely spatial approach of the new school of quantitative economic geographers.

The neglect of the phenomenon of urbanization by students of Latin America generally and by geographers in particular has been striking. As the organizational center of human society, exercising powerful influences on the use of surrounding space, and as a geographical phenomenon of interest for its own sake, whether in terms of historical evolution, lay-out and morphology, or internal and external linkages, the Latin American city offers a multitude of significant and unexplored geographical themes. This neglect is the more remarkable in the face of an extensive literature on urban evolution and morphology in other parts of the world. Stanislawski's essay on "Early Spanish Town Planning in the New World" (Stanislawski 1947), the survey of South American cities by Wilhelmy (1952), and the four-volume study of São Paulo by Azevedo and his Brazilian colleagues (Azevedo 1958) are among the principal landmarks in the field. A useful contribution is the volume *Aspectos da geografia Carioca* (Associação dos Geógrafos Brasileiros 1962) published as the outcome of a series of public lectures dealing with different aspects of the city of Rio de Janeiro, and organized in 1958 by the Rio de Janeiro chapter of the Association of Brazilian Geographers. A recent study on the process of absorption by greater Rio de Janeiro of one of its suburbs in the Baixada Fluminense has been carried out by Soares (1962).

An occasion for the study of urban geography arises from the annual meeting of the Associação dos Geógrafos Brasileiros. The

Association meets during the winter or dry season holidays for a week or ten days in a different locality, usually a smallish town. Members, gathering from various parts of the country, are bent not so much on listening to papers as on dedicating themselves as a body to a research project in the field. Splitting up into several field parties, some undertake the study of the surrounding countryside, while others remain to study the urban geography of the town chosen as headquarters. Subsequently discussed, and edited, the materials gathered during the meeting are published by the Association. In this way, a number of studies of urban geography have taken shape.

The food supply studies of Minas Gerais and Fortaleza by Webb (1959, 1961) have suggested one of many fruitful directions for future inquiry. A considerable number of studies of particular cities can be listed (James 1933; Martonne 1935; Rubio 1950; Borde 1954; James and Faissol 1956; Czajka 1959; Brisseau 1963), but most of these are of a historical-descriptive character and of modest compass. Smaller places have received somewhat more attention (Deffontaines 1937; Martonne 1938; Stanislawski 1950; Brand 1951; Carmin 1953), but such widely discussed concepts as the central place theory and the economic base * seem to have found no application to date anywhere in Latin America. The only analytical study of urban function and form known to the writer is that of the central business district of Monterrey, Mexico, by Megee (1958).

Contributions to general agricultural geography in Latin America have been almost wholly of a descriptive nature (Jones 1928–30; U.S. Department of Agriculture 1958). There have been numerous analyses of agricultural systems in particular areas, as, for example, Chile (Almeyda Arroyo 1927), the Spanish West Indies (Gerling 1938; Credner 1943), Brazil (James 1953), Tucumán (Hueck 1953), El Salvador (Lauer 1956), Guadeloupe (Hoy 1962), and Haiti (Wood 1963). Enjalbert (1948) has consid-

---

* The *central place theory* is a theory of economic location suggested by Christaller. In essence, the theory postulates that service, or trade, centers tend to be dispersed over the countryside in a hexagonal pattern, given a uniform economy and a uniform topography.

The money that enters a city allows one to formulate its *economic base*. This is expressed by an *index of basic activity:* the ratio of basic economic activities to a city's total employment (ed. note).

ered the characteristics of European agriculture in temperate South America.

Most topical or commodity studies have been studies of plantation export crops within restricted areas, as Russell (1942), Jones and Morrison (1952), Guhl (1953), Gerling (1954), Moral (1955), Parsons (1957), and Chardon (1961). The plantation system in the New World awaits a geographical analysis in depth, though Gerling (1954), Rubio (1959), and others have considered it in local areas. A Chilean geographer has recently done a substantial analysis of the historical geography of the Chilean wheat export trade (Sepulveda 1956). The livestock industry has received scant attention (but see Deffontaines 1957a, 1957b, 1962; MacPhail 1963), and the forest products industries virtually none.

The economic geography of mining has been little better off, save for the outstanding historical studies of West on Parral (1949), the Chocó (1952), and Honduras (1959), and Rudolph (1963) on the Chuquicamata copper operation and its impact on the Atacama desert area. Venezuelan petroleum has been the subject of two different German studies (Otremba 1954; Wilhelmy 1954), but curiously no North American geographer seems to have touched it. The location of manufacturing industry has been considered chiefly in the form of case studies (e.g., Kennelly 1954–56; Butler 1960).

Land tenure studies in Latin America have been more in the domain of economists and sociologists than that of geographers, despite the early classic works of McBride on Mexico (1923) and Chile (1936). The appearance of a recent group of monographs on Chilean land problems, however, suggests that this situation may be changing (Alaluf 1961; Baraona 1961; Borde and Gongora 1956; Martin 1960). Case studies of communal land ownership (*ejidos*), *minifundismo, latifundismo,* Indian *resguardos* and such offer attractive themes of inquiry to the geographer. Everywhere in Latin America the hand of the past lies heavily on the land (see, e.g., Crist 1952), so that economic criteria in planning must always be strongly conditioned by cultural and historical considerations. The operation of the Mexican and Guatemalan land reforms has recently been examined briefly by geographers (Jensen 1958; Pearson 1963), but most of what is known about the pressing problem of land in Latin America is to be found either in government reports or in the work of a handful of economists, where the regional and ecologic points of view are often lost from sight.

There is an almost total absence of descriptive case studies of transportation and its effects on cultural and economic evolution in Latin America, whether by geographers or others. Partial exceptions to this may be represented by Snyder (1962), Bassols (1959), Labasse (1957), and Rothwell (1960). Statistical data on interregional traffic flow and relative costs of movement of different goods by different means are almost entirely lacking. Although the crucial role of transportation in economically underdeveloped countries is widely recognized, generalizations about the nature and mechanics of economic flows, the role of the "route," market accessibility, the relationship of air transport in economic development, the bus as a transporter of men and goods, etc., will have limited meaning until a great deal more spadework has been done in understanding of actual situations within limited areas. It is perhaps time for a geographer to take hold of the Mexican or Brazilian trucking system, of the Amazon river trade, of air transport in Brazil, of Chile's road and rail competition, of Colombia's Quindío Road or the new Magdelena Valley Railroad, to put them in their proper historical, geographical, and economic context. Such studies might eventually lead to generalizations of significance about the role of transportation in nonindustrial economies.

Political geography, a field intensively tilled by many North American and European geographers elsewhere, has almost no representation in the literature on Latin America. This can hardly be explained by any lack of political tension or awareness in the area. The flamboyancy and instability of Latin American politics has generally been more associated with military or left-wing extremism than with the resources or boundary disputes with which geographers have generally been concerned. The principal contributions of significance to the general literature of political geography have been on historical rather than contemporary themes (Stanislawski 1947; Termer 1943; Vidal de la Blache 1902). The significance of the size and shape of nations and their provincial subdivision, the nature and function of boundaries (mostly passing through sparsely settled areas), the geography of voting habits, of political awareness, and of civil disobedience and *violencia,* along with many other themes, re-main to be seriously considered from the geographical point of view.

Social scientists, long preoccupied with social and political man, are showing signs of increasing awareness of the physical environment as an element of cultural evolution. Increased rec-ognition of man's role in changing the face of the earth (Thomas, ed., 1956) is coupled with renewed concern with possible en-vironmental limits on culture growth, especially within the rainy tropics (Wilbert, ed., 1962). The ecology of tropical farming, an issue of prime significance to the problems of culture history and economic development in Latin America, has become a major concern of a growing number of cultural anthropologists who, perforce, are adopting the geographical point of view. Blaut (1961), reviewing the relationships of the biophysical environ-ments to tropical land use patterns, has objected that the pessi-mistic views of Gourou, Pendleton, and others regarding tropical soils may not be wholly justified. Here again local geographical conditions, deviations, and exceptions are of crucial importance. The older generalization that soil exhaustion forces land aban-donment in shifting-field (*milpa*) agriculture is being modified, and grass and weed invasion, insect infestation, and cultural tra-dition are being suggested as often being of at least equal im-portance. Yet at the same time there is increasing evidence from many directions that where increased population pressures force the shortening of the fallow period, a progressive impoverish-ment of the second growth (*rastrojo*) may lead eventually to savanna (*campo*) conditions and ecologic disaster (Budowski 1956, 1958).

Ecologic Balance versus Environmental Deterioration

Recent development programs in Latin America have been directed largely toward economic development. To the planners this is likely to mean drastic rises in productivity and in the in-centive to consume. Emphasis on the immediate political means of change easily diverts attention from the long-term conse-quences, the increased pressures on resources, and increased rates of extraction. Yet the physical environment on which the Latin Americans depend for food, water, shelter, and fiber has been taking a dreadful beating in many places. Vogt (1963) has recently called attention again to the alarming rate of environmental deterioration in Mexico and El Salvador. "These are matters of moment to North Americans," he writes, "whether or not they are interested in conservation. They create humanitarian problems. And by contribution to human illfare they [eventually] . . . take on a political dimension."

In Mexico three-quarters of the country is considered to have suffered some degree of soil erosion. Somewhat more than half of El Salvador's total area was judged fifteen years ago to be composed of worn-out soils—thin, rocky, and rarely fertile. Since then the country's population has increased some 30 percent. In the Venezuelan Andes the situation is in some areas acute. Silting of reservoirs, due to ecological ignorance and failure to protect watersheds, is a major problem in most semi-arid areas, as in northern Mexico and in the dry northeast of Brazil. Such matters are but little understood by the politicians and decision-makers or even by many engineers. Rainfall variability may be more important to an average *campesino* or *caboclo* than economic aid in much of Latin America.

Vogt, in his plea for greater ecological and geographical understanding, quotes Rodolfo Brena Torres, Governor of the state of Oaxaca, Mexico:

The problem of land here is acute. Lack of foresight started the destruction of the forests that covered the state in the 18th century; the lands stripped of their vegetation were eroded by wind and rain, leaving this desolate landscape, sad to look at and even sadder from an economic aspect—since there remain regions so dead that one can get nothing useful from them. The population increase makes the situation more distressing and in the face of the impossibility, for a great part of the population, to satisfy here the necessities for existence, it has no alternative but to emigrate to other places, at times on a temporary basis as when the braceros go to work in the United States, or at other times to settle in Mexico City or in neighboring states.

This is blunt talk. Studies such as that of Cook (1949) on soil erosion and population in Central Mexico suggest that such environmental deterioration can be traced well back into pre-Conquest times. That it was not more accelerated by the introduction of European livestock and farming techniques can be attributed to the abrupt decline of human population (and cultivated acreage) in the sixteenth century (Cook and Borah 1960; Simpson 1952).

The wide lack of understanding of agricultural and, even more, ecological matters in Latin America, results in a neglect of them in educational and governmental structure.

The economists and planners [Vogt argues] are largely city-oriented, urban-trained and committed to the symbol-manipulation, whether of money or statistics, that is economics' tool. Few of them are knowledgeable in geography, still less in biology and ecology. They seem rarely to get into the back-country. They have developed sophisticated techniques that, unfortunately, disregard the realities of runoff, plant successions, soil structure, pleistocene waters, and many other facts and processes with which man must live. . . . The industrialization the economists so effectively promote is an important conservational tool insofar as it reduces pressure on the land; yet the dependence of industry itself on a favorable ecological balance is commonly overlooked. Ecologically triggered disaster, which may find a forerunner in political explosions, lie not many years or decades ahead for much of Latin America.

Histories of land use in such countries as Mexico, which should give us a clearer picture of the changes in land productivity since the early sixteenth century, are one of the urgent tasks Vogt envisages for geographers. Such studies as those by Brand, Denevan, Gordon, James, Lauer, Schmieder, Sternberg, Vivó, Wagner, and West may point the way, but a great deal remains to be done, particularly by way of comparative works and the analysis of processes through which soil-water and soil-vegetation relationships operate and are altered through time.

Physical Geography

An important contribution of geography to area studies is the bringing of natural history into human affairs. The study of man's modification of the plant cover of the earth has been pursued by numerous American and European geographers in Latin America (Schmieder 1927; Berninger 1929; Parsons 1955; Budowski 1956, 1959; Gordon 1957; Denevan 1961; Harris 1962; Wagner 1962; Johannessen 1963).

The use of vegetation as a key to land use and settlement potentialities has been especially reflected in the growing literature on the *campo cerrado* question in Brazil and the more general question of the origin of tropical grasslands, both by ecologists and by geographers with an ecologic orientation (Arens 1959; Waibel 1948; Cole 1959, 1960; Hueck 1957, 1959; Rawitscher 1948). The appropriation of wild plants by man has been the concern of others (Pennington 1958, 1963; Johannessen 1957).

Although plant geography is a field more cultivated by botanists and ecologists than geographers, the last have on occasion made significant contributions to it in Latin America (e.g., Dansereau 1950; Frenguelli 1941; Schmithüsen 1956, 1960; Soares 1953; Hueck 1959, 1961). Some, like Pittier and Dansereau, have operated as both botanists and geographers, thus bringing new insights into both fields of inquiry. In the same way animal geography has tended to be the domain of the zoologists, although man's use of wild game and fish has tended to come within the range of concern of geographers (Gordon 1957a, 1957b; Bennett 1962; Parsons 1962; Sapper 1936).

Climatologic studies by geographers in Latin America have been relatively limited in number and scope. Outstanding is the descriptive account and statistical analysis of Middle American and South American climates in the two volumes of the Köppen-Geiger *Handbuch,* but it is now some thirty years old. Special attention has been given to the arid margin tension zones by Freise (1938), Martonne (1940), Duque (1951), Ives (1949), Shreve (1944), Petersen (1956), Schweigger (1959), and Trewartha (1961. Sternberg (1951, 1957) has made special reference to climatic extremes and their effect on man and the land. In Argentina significant work has been done by Prohaska (1961a, 1961b), while Wallén (1955, 1956) has considered rainfall variability in Mexico, and Troll (1959) the vertical distributions of mountain climates. Lauer's length of dry season study (1952), comparing South America with Africa, has been widely commented upon. Paleoclimatic themes have been pursued by Wilhelmy (1954), Auer (1956), Arnold (1957), and Heusser (1960), among others. In the Caribbean area most of the climatologic work has been done by meteorologists working through the U.S. Weather Bureau, although Blume (1962) has recently considered rainfall variability and intensities in the area. Hydrologic studies include those by Rudolph (1936), Monheim (1956), Sioli (1957), Reparaz (1958), and Pardé (1962), but the more important work has been done by engineers working through government agencies, especially in Mexico. (See especially the periodical *Ingeniera Hidraúlica*.) Initial reconnaissance observations on the Amazon involved gauging the river at high and low stage and the collection of water and sediment. Samples were completed in December, 1963, under the direction of Sternberg as a joint project of the U.S. Geological Survey, the Centro de Pesquisas de Geografía do Brasil, and the Directorate of Hydrography and Navigation of the Brazilian Navy.

Acclimatization of man to tropical lowland climates has been considered by Lee (1957) and Price (1939), among others, while Monge's study (1948) of acclimatization in the high Andes is another well-known approach to a similar problem, mostly from the historical point of view. The related field of medical geography has attracted some recent attention (e.g., Slutsky 1960), and seems likely to continue to do so.

The study of land forms on geomorphology has been a traditional concern of geographers, whether as existing surface features that provide the stage for human history, or in terms of their structure, process, and stage from which the operation of the laws of nature on the earth can be traced. The complexities of the Andean structure have attracted the attention of numerous well-known geographers (Hettner 1892; Bowman 1916; Ogilvie 1922; Schmieder, 1926; Kinzl 1950). So, too, have coastal forms, including terraces, reefs, and beaches, especially in the Caribbean region (Brand 1957–58; Russell 1959; Vann 1959; Gierloff-Emden 1959; Alexander 1961; Barrett 1962; Tuan 1962; Stoddard 1962; Vermeer 1963). The studies of Sapper (1902, 1925) and Termer (1936) in Central American vulcanism paid much attention to the significance of volcanoes to man. Marbut (1926), Pendleton (1950), James (1952), Wilhelmy (1957, 1958), and Haggett (1961), among others, have been concerned with landforms and soils in terms of human occupance. Others, such as Maull (1924), Ruellan (1944), Martonne (1940), Czajka (1958), Hammond (1954), and King (1956), have been concerned with the physical features of the landscape on their own terms.

Maps and Mapping

A survey of geographical contributions to Latin American studies would not be complete without some mention of the map as the representation of the earth's surface. The production of the map has come to be increasingly an engineering concern, but the content and nature of the map is often shaped by the geographer's judgment, its production by his initiative.

The American Geographical Society's 1:1,000,000 map of Latin America, in 107 sheets, with contour lines and layer coloring, remains the finest map coverage of the area as a whole (*Geographical Review* 36: 1–28). Although there has been a modest program of revision and updating, many of the sheets are now unsatisfactory. The *Atlas do Brasil* (1960) is a valuable publication of the Conselho Nacional de Geografía, a federal agency. Air photography, especially, has opened up the prospect of precise mapping in even the most inaccessible parts of the continent. The ambitious mapping program of the Interamerican Geodetic Survey, a cooperative venture of the U.S. Coast and Geodetic Survey and the various Latin American countries, is resulting in the publication of superior large-scale maps at 1:25,000 or 1:50,000 for an increasing number of areas. The program is a continuing one involving the expenditure of many millions of dollars. Although these maps are being printed in the United States, distribution has been only through the local country mapping agencies.

The Natural Resources Unit of the OAS is currently publishing indices of map and air photo coverage for each of nineteen Latin American countries with the aim to facilitate planning for natural resource development and general geographic research. The prototype of these index atlases, on Colombia, appeared in limited edition in October, 1963. This work is being directed by North American and Latin American geographers.

Among privately prepared maps, Erwin Raisz's exquisitely detailed *Land Form Map of Mexico* and the *Atlas of Cuba* by Raisz and Canet are perhaps outstanding. Air photography, in particular, has come to be a major new tool for geographical research. Mapping of land use and land tenure directly onto photographs has been carried on successfully in Chile and Guatemala, giving promise of breaking a major bottleneck in economic planning—the lack of accurate cadastral surveys. Foreign investigators have often experienced difficulty in the past in obtaining access to the photographs, which are often held under military supervision. This situation, however, seems to be easing.

The scope of geography is vast. It is not without significance that Alexander von Humboldt, often called the last universal man, is also commonly described as the Father of Modern Geography. To a degree greater than that of the other social or physical sciences, it has been dominated by pedagogy. Leighly (1963) has recently written of it:

In the absence of an accepted pattern of scholarly activity, differences in intellectual qualities among the practitioners of geography are more conspicuous than in more standardized fields of learning. If the pedestrian mind appears more heavy-footed here than elsewhere, the first-class mind finds room for longer and higher flights.

Latin America is the closest and most accessible of the tropical areas of the world for North Americans, and it is bristling with problems for the alert and inquiring geographer. One still somehow tends to live closer to nature here, and his powers of observation and perspective on natural history and man's place within it are correspondingly sharpened by the diversity and complexity of the natural setting. In the past most geographical work in Latin America has been concerned with the description and historical explanation of phenomena and with the uniqueness of place and culture. The emphasis on understanding the past and present landscapes is likely to continue, but there is opportunity, too, for much greater contributions by geographers to natural resource management, planning, and development, especially through the introduction of spatial and ecological thinking in the social sciences. But the subject's strength will derive in the end not from any handmaiden role it may play to the social sciences and to planning, but from its own inherent values and its contributions to the understanding of the earth as the home of man and the appreciation of its infinite variety and diversity for its own sake and on its own terms.

BIBLIOGRAPHY

Alaluf, David
    1961   Problemas de la propriedad agrícola en Chile. Schriften des Geographishen Institut Universitat Kiel 19: No. 2.
Alexander, Charles S.
    1961   The marine terraces of Aruba, Bonaire, and Curaçao. Annals, Association of American Geographers 51: 102–23.

Alexander, John
1963 Economic geography. Englewood Cliffs, N.J.

Almeyda Arroyo, Elias
1957 Geografía agrícola de Chile. Santiago, Chile.

Arens, Karl
1959 O cerrado como vegetação oligotrófica. Comptes Rendus, XVIII Congrès Internationale de Géographie, Rio de Janeiro, 1958. Vol. I: 308–19.

Arnold, Brigham A.
1957 Late Pleistocene and recent changes in land forms, climate and archeology in central Baja California. University of California Publications in Geography 10: 201–318.

Aschmann, H. Homer
1959 The central desert of Baja California. Ibero-Americana 42: 282.
1960. Indian pastoralists of the Guajira peninsula. Annals, Association of American Geographers 50: 408–18.

Associação dos Geógrafos Brasileiros (Secção Regional do Rio de Janeiro)
1962 Aspectos da geografia carioca. Rio de Janeiro, 284 pp.

Aubert de la Rüe, Edgar
1957 Brésil aride: la vie en la caatinga. Paris.

Aubreville, André
1961 Étude écologique des principales formations végétales du Brésil et contribution à la connaissance des forêts de l'Amazonie brésilienne. Nogent-sur-Marne, Centre Technique Forestier Tropical, 268 pp.

Auer, Vaino
1956 The Pleistocene of Fuego-Patagonia. I. The ice and interglacial ages. Annales Academiae Scientiarum Fennicae (Helsinki), Series A, No. 45.

Augelli, John P.
1958a Cultural and economic changes of Bastos, a Japanese colony on Brazil's Paulista frontier. Annals, Association of American Geographers, 48: 3–19.
1958b The Latvians of Varpa, a foreign colony on the Brazilian pioneer fringe. Geographical Review 48: 365–87.
1962 The rimland-mainland concept of culture areas in Middle America. Annals, Association of American Geographers, 52: 119–29.

Azevedo, Aroldo de (ed.)
1958 A cidade de São Paulo; estudos de geografia urbana. São Paulo. 4 vols.

Baraona, Rafael, Kimena Aranda, and Roberto Santana
1961 Valle de Putaendo: estudio de estructura agraria. Instituto de Geografía, Universidad de Chile, Santiago.

Barrett, Ward
1962 Emerged and submerged shorelines of the Dominican Republic. Revista Geográfica (Rio de Janeiro) 30 (No. 56): 51–77.

Bassols, Batalla, Angel
1969 Consideraciones geográficas y económicas en la configuración de las redes de carreteras y vias ferreas en México. Revista Geográfica (Rio de Janeiro) 24 (No. 50): 5–42.

Bennett, Charles F., Jr.
1962 The Bayano Cuna Indians, Panama: an ecologic study of livelihood and diet. Annals, Association of American Geographers, 52: 32–50.

Berninger, Otto
1929 Wald und offenesland in Sud-Chile seit der spanische eroberung. Stuttgart.
Blaut, James
1961 The ecology of tropical farming systems. Revista Geográfica (Rio de Janeiro) 28 (No. 54): 47–67.
Blume, Helmut
1962 Beiträge zur Klimatologie Westindiens. Erdkunde 16: 271–89.
Borde, Jean
1954 L'essor d'une capitale: Santiago de Chile. Les Cahiers d'Outre-Mer 7: 5–24.
Borde, Jean, and Mario Góngora
1956 Evolución de la propriedad rural en el Valle del Puangue. Santiago, Instituto de Sociología, Universidad de Chile. 2 vols.
Bowman, Isaiah
1916 The Andes of southern Peru. New York, American Geographical Society.
1931 The pioneer fringe. New York, American Geographical Society. Special Publ. 13.
Bowman, Isaiah (ed.)
1937 Limits of land settlement. New York, Council on Foreign Relations.
Brand, Donald D.
1951 Qurioga: a Mexican municipio. Washington, D.C., Smithsonian Institution, Institute of Social Anthropology. No. 11.
1957–58 Coastal study of southwest Mexico. Dept. of Geography, University of Texas, Austin. 2 vols.
1960 Coalcomán and Matines del Oro, an ex-districto de Michoacán, Mexico. The Hague.
Brazil, Conselho Nacional de Geografia
1960 Atlas do Brasil. Rio de Janeiro.
Brisseau, Janine
1963 Les "barrios" de Petare; faubourgs populaires d'une banlieue de Caracas. Les Cahiers d'Outre-Mer 16 (No. 61): 5–42.
Bruman, Henry J.
1944 The Asiatic origin of the Huichol still. Geographical Review 34: 418–27.
1948 The culture history of Mexican vanilla. Hispanic American Historical Review 28: 360–76.
1958 Post-war agricultural colonization in Brazil. Final report, ONR Contract Nonr 233 (03), Department of Geography, University of California, Los Angeles (mimeographed).
Budowski, Gerardo
1956 Tropical savannas, a sequence of forest felling and repeated burnings. Turrialba 6: 23–33. Turrialba, Costa Rica.
1959 The ecological status of fire in tropical American lowlands. 33rd Congreso Internacional de Americanistas, San José, 1958. Vol. I: 264–78.
Butland, Gilbert J.
1957 The human geography of southern Chile. London, Institute of British Geographers. Publication 24.
Butler, Joseph L.
1960 Manufacturing in the Concepción region of Chile. NAS–NRC Foreign Field Report 7. Washington, D.C.

72 James J. Parsons

Carmin, Robert L.
1953 Anapolis, Brazil: regional capital of an agricultural frontier. University of Chicago, Dept. of Geography. Research Paper 35.

Carter, Douglas B.
1955 The water balance of Lake Maracaibo Basin during 1946–53. Drexel Institute of Technology, Laboratory of Climatology, Publications in Climatology 8: 209–27.

Chardon, Roland
1961 Geographic aspects of plantation agriculture in Yucatán. NAS–NRC Foreign Field Report 11. Washington, D.C.
1963 Hacienda and ejido in Yucatán: the example of Santa Ana Cucá. Annals, Association of American Geographers, 53: 174–93.

Chaunu, Pierre
1961 Une histoire hispano-Américaniste pilote; en marge de l'oeuvre de l'école de Berkeley. Revue Historique 124: 339–68.

Cole, Monica
1959 The distribution and origin of the savanna vegetation with particular reference to the "campos cerrados" of Brazil. Comptes Rendus, XVIII Congrès Internationale de Géographie, Rio de Janeiro, 1958. Vol. I: 339–45.
1960 Cerrado, caatinga, and pantanal: distribution and origin of the savanna vegetation of Brazil. Geographical Journal 76: 169–79.

Cook, S. F.
1949 Soil erosion and population in central Mexico. Ibero-Americana, Vol. 34.

Cook, S. F., and Woodrow Borah
1960 The Indian population of central Mexico, 1531–1610. Ibero-Americana, Vol. 44.

Credner, Wilhelm
1943 Typen der Wirtschafslandschaft auf den Grossen Antillen. Petermanns Mitteilungen 89: 1–23.

Crist, Raymond E.
1937 Étude géographique des Llanos du Venezuela occidental. Grenoble.
1952 The Cauca valley, Colombia: land tenure and land use. Baltimore.

Crist, Raymond E., and Ernesto Guhl
1956 Pioneer settlement in eastern Colombia. Smithsonian Institution Annual Report, 391–414.

Crossley, J. Colin
1961 Santa Cruz at the cross-roads: a study of development in eastern Bolivia. Tijdschrift voor Economische en Sociale Geographie 52: 197–206.

Currie, Lauchlin
1961 Operation Colombia. A national economic and social program. Bogotá (mimeographed). (Also in Spanish.)

Czajka, Willi
1958 Estudos geomorfológicos no nordeste brasileiro. Revista Brasileira de Geografia 20: 135–78.
1959 Buenos Aires als Weltstadt. In Zur Problem der Weltstadt, J. H. Schultze, ed. Berlin, pp. 158–202.

Dansereau, Pierre
1950 Ecological problems of southeastern Brazil. Scientific Monthly 71 (No. 2): 71–84.

Daus, F. A.
1948 Transhumación de montaña en Neuquen. Annales Sociedad Argentina de Estudios Geográficas, pp. 383–426.
Deffontaines, Pierre
1937 Mountain settlement in the central Brazilian plateau. Geographical Review 27: 394–413.
1938 The origin and growth of the Brazilian network of towns. Geographical Review 28: 379–99.
1957a Routes et foires a bétail en Amérique latine. Revue de Géographie Alpine 45: 659–84.
1957b L'introduction du bétail en Amérique latine. Les Cahiers d'Outre-Mer 10: 5–22.
1962 Contribution à la géographie pastorale de l'Amérique. Latine. Centro de Pesquisas de Geografia do Brasil, Curso de Altos Estudos Geográficos 3, Rio de Janeiro.
Denevan, William
1961 The upland pine forests of Nicaragua, a study in cultural plant geography. University of California Publications in Geography 12 (No. 4): 251–320.
1963 Additional comments on the earthworks of Mojos in northeastern Bolivia. American Antiquity 28: 540–45.
Dozier, Craig
1956 Northern Paraná, Brazil; an example of organized regional development. Geographical Review 46: 318–33.
Drewes, Wolfram U.
1958 The economic development of the western montaña of central Peru as related to transportation. Andean Air Mail and Peruvian Times, supplement, Lima.
Driver, Harold E., and William C. Massey
1957 Comparative studies of North American Indians. Transactions, American Philosophical Society, 47: 165–456.
Duque, J. G.
1951 Solo e água no polígono das sêcas. Fortaleza, Brazil.
Edwards, Clinton R.
1960 Sailing rafts of Sechura: history and problems of origin. Southwestern Journal of Anthropology 16: 368–91.
Eidt, Robert
1959 Aboriginal Chibcha settlement in Colombia. Annals, Association of American Geographers 49: 374–92.
1962 Pioneer settlement in eastern Peru. Annals, Association of American Geographers 52: 255–78.
Enjalbert, Henri
1948 L'agriculture europééne en Amérique du Sud. Les Cahiers d'Outre-Mer 1: 149–82, 201–28.
Fabila, Alfonso, et al.
1955 Tlaxcala: tenencia y aprovechamiento de la tierra. Mexico, Centro de Investigaciones Agrarias.
Freise, Friedrich W.
1938 The drought region of northeastern Brazil. Geographical Review 28: 363–78.
Frenguelli, Joaquin
1941 Rasgos principales de fitografía argentina. Revista Museo de La Plata, N.S., Sección Botánica, 3: 65–181.

Fuson, Robert H.
1964 House types of central Panama. Annals, Association of American Geographers 54: 190–208.

Gerling, Walter
1938 Wirtschaftsentwicklung und Landschaftswandel auf den West-indischen Inseln Jamaika, Haiti, and Puerto Rico. Freiburg.
1954 Die plantagen wirtschaft des Rohrzuckers auf den grossen Antillen; ein Beitrag zur Agrargeographie der Tropen. Mitteilungen des Geographischen Gesellshaft, Würzburg, Vol. 2.

Gierloff-Emden, Hans G.
1959 Die Küste von el Salvador. Acta Humboldtiana, Vol. 2, Wiesbaden.

Gordon, B. LeRoy
1957a Human geography and ecology in the Sinú country of Colombia. Ibero-Americana, Vol. 39.
1957b A domesticated wax-producing scale insect kept by the Guaymí Indians of Panama. Ethnos (Stockholm), 36–49.

Gourou, Pierre
1949–50 Observações geográficas na Amazônia. Revista Brasileira de Geografia 11 (No. 3): 355–408; 12 (No. 2): 171–250.
1961 The tropical world: its social and economic conditions and its future (trans. by E. D. Laborde). London. 3rd edition, revised.

Guhl, Ernesto
1952 Ambiente geográfico-humano de la costa del Atlántico, Colombia. Revista Geográfica 1: 139–72.
1953 El aspecto económico-social del cultivo del café en Antioquia. Revista Colombiana de Antropología 1: 197–257.
1957 Panorama geo-económico del departamento de Antioquia. Economia y Estadística (Bogotá) 13: 5–89.

Guzman, Louis E.
1956 Farming and farmlands in Panama. Dept. of Geography, University of Chicago. Research Paper 44.
1962 Las terrazas de los antiguos Mayas montaneses. Revista Interamericana de Ciéncias Sociales 1: 398–406.

Guzman-Rivas, Pablo
1960 Geographic influences of the galleon trade on New Spain. Revista Geográfica (Rio de Janeiro) 27 (No. 53): 5–81.

Haggett, Peter
1961 Land use and sediment yield in an old plantation tract of the Serra do Mar, Brazil. Geographical Journal 127: 50–62.
1963 Regional and local components in land-use sampling: a case study from the Brazilian "Triângulo." Erkunde 17 (1/2): 108–14.

Hammond, Edwin H.
1954 A geomorphic study of the Cape region of Baja California. University of California Publications in Geography 10: 45–112.

Hanson, Earl Parker
1960 Puerto Rico, land of wonders. New York.

Harris, David R.
1962 The invasion of oceanic islands by alien plants: an example from the Leeward Islands, West Indies. Transactions Institute of British Geographers 31: 67–82.

Helbig, Karl M.
1961 Das Stromgebiet des oberen Rio Grijalva: eine landschaftstudie aus

Chiapas, Südmexico. Mitteilungen Geographischer Gesellshaft Hamburg 54: 7–274.

1959 Die Landschaften von Nordost-Honduras; auf Grund einer geographischen Studienreise im Jahre 1953. Petermanns Mitteilungen, Ergänzungsheft 268.

Hettner, Alfred

1888 Reisen in den columbianischen Anden. Leipzig.

1892 Die Kordillera von Bogotá. Petermanns Mitteilungen, Ergänzungsheft 104.

Heusser, Calvin J.

1960 Late Pleistocene environment of the Laguna de San Rafael area, Chile. Geographical Review 50: 555–77.

Higbee, E. C.

1951 Of man and land in the Amazon. Geographical Review 41: 401–20.

Holzmann, Gustav

1959 Die japanischen Siedler in Brasilien. Mitteilungen Osterreicher Geographischer Gesellschaft 101: No. 3.

Hoy, Don R.

1962 Changing agricultural land use on Guadeloupe. Annals, Association of American Geographers 52: 441–54.

Hueck, Kurt

1953 Urlandschaft, Raublandschaft und Kulturlandschaft in der Provinz Tucumán in nordwestlichen Argentinien. Bonner Geographische Abhandlungen, Vol. 10.

1957 Sobre a orígen dos campos cerrados do Brasil. Revista Brasileira de Geografía 19: 67–81.

1959a Die Ursprünglichkeit der brasilianischen "Campos Cerrados" und Neue Beobachtungen an ihrer Südgreuze. Comptes Rendus, XVIII Congrès International de Géographie, Rio de Janeiro, 1958. Vol. I: 319–31.

1959b Bosques secos de la zona tropical y subtropical de la America del Sur. Boletim, Instituto Forestal Latino Americano (Mérida, Venezuela) 4: 1–49.

1961 Die Wälder Venezuelas. Hamburg.

Ives, Ronald

1949 Climate of the Sonoran desert region. Annals, Association of American Geographers 39: 143–87.

James, Preston E.

1933 Rio de Janeiro and São Paulo. Geographical Review 23: 271–98.

1952 Observations on the physical geography of northeast Brazil. Annals, Association of American Geographers 42: 153–76.

1953 Trends in Brazilian agricultural development. Geographical Review 43: 301–28.

1959 Latin America. Maps by Eileen W. James. New York. 3rd edition.

James, Preston E., and S. Faissol

1956 The problem of Brazil's capital city. Geographical Review 46: 301–17.

Jefferson, Mark

1918 Rainfall in Chile. New York, American Geographical Society.

1921 Recent colonization in Chile. New York, American Geographical Society.

1926 The peopling of the Argentine Pampa. New York, American Geographical Society.

Jensen, G. Granville
    1958   The ejido in Mexico: an agrarian problem. Yearbook, Association of Pacific Coast Geographers 20: 7–16.
Jimenez, de la Espada
    1881–97   Relaciones geográficas de las Indias. Madrid. 4 vols.
Johannessen, Carl
    1957   Man's role in the distribution of the corozo palm (Orbignya spp.). Yearbook, Association of Pacific Coast Geographers 19: 29–33.
    1963   Savannas of interior Honduras. Ibero-Americana, Vol. 46.
Jones, Clarence
    1928–30   Agricultural regions of South America, Economic Geography 4: 1–30, 159–86, 267–94; 5: 109–40, 277–307, 390–421; 6: 1–36.
    1930   South America. New York.
Jones, Clarence, and Paul C. Morrisson
    1952   Evolution of the banana industry of Costa Rica. Economic Geography 28: 1–19.
Jones, Clarence, and Rafael Picó (eds.)
    1955   Symposium on the geography of Puerto Rico. Río Piedras, P.R.
Kennelly, R. A.
    1954–56   The location of the Mexican steel industry. Revista Geográfica 14: 51–80; 15: 105–29; 16: 199–213.
King, Lester C.
    1956a   A geomorfologia do Brasil oriental. Revista Brasileira de Geografia 18: 147–256.
    1956b   A geomorphological comparison between eastern Brazil and Africa (central and southern). Quarterly Journal of the Geological Society (London) 112: 445–74.
Kinzl, Hans
    1950   Cordillera Blanca (Peru). Innsbruck.
Kniffen, Fred B.
    1931   The primitive cultural landscape of the Colorado delta. University of California Publications in Geography 5: 43–66.
Köppen, Waldimir, and Rudolph Geiger
    1930–32   Handbuch der Klimatologie, II G, II H. Berlin.
Kühn, Fritz
    1927   Argentinien: handbuch zur physischen Landeskunde. Breslau.
    1933   Grundriss der Kulturgeographie von Argentinien. Hamburg.
Krause, Anemarie
    1952   Mennonite settlement in the paraguayan Chaco. University of Chicago, Dept. of Geography Research Paper 25.
Labasse, Jean
    1957   La vie de relation en Colombia. Annales de Géographie, November–December.
Landscape; magazine of human geography
    1951   [Editorial.] Santa Fe, New Mexico. Vol. I.
Lassarre, Guy
    1961   La Guadeloupe; étude géographique. Bordeaux. 2 vols.
Latin American Congress on Regional Science
    1962   [Papers.] Caracas.
Lauer, Wilhelm
    1952   Humide and aride Jahreszeiten in Afrika und Südamerika und ihre Beziehungen zu den Vegetationsgürteln. Bonner Geographische Abhandlungen 9: 15–98.

1956 Vegetation, Landnutzung und Agrarpotential in El Salvador. Schriften des Geographischen Instituts Universität Kiel 16: No. 1.
1961 Wandlugen im Landschaftsbild des südchilenischen Seegebietes seit Ende der spanischen Kolonialzeit. *In* Beiträge zur Geographie der Neuen Welt, W. Lauer, ed. Schriften des Geographischen Instituts Kiel 20.

Lee, Douglas H. K.
1957 Climate and economic development in the tropics. New York, Council on Foreign Relations.

Leighly, John (ed.)
1963 Land and life; a selection from the writing of Carl Ortwin Sauer. Berkeley and Los Angeles.

Lowenthal, David
1960 Population contrasts in the Guianas. Geographical Review 50: 41–58.

Lukermann, Fred, and P. W. Porter
1960 Gravity and potential models in economic geography. Economic Geography 50: 493–504.

Maack, Reinhard
1962 Neue Forschungen in Paraguay und am Río Paraná: die Flussgebiete Monday und Aracay. Die Erde 93: 4–48.

McBride, George M.
1923 The land systems of Mexico. New York, American Geographical Society.
1936 Chile: land and society. New York, American Geographical Society.

McBride, George M., and M. A. McBride
1944 Peruvian avenues of penetration into Amazonia. Geographical Review 34: 1–35.

McBryde, Feliz Webster
1947 Cultural and historical geography of southwest Guatemala. Washington, D.C., Smithsonian Institution, Institute of Social Anthropology. No. 4.

MacPhail, Donald
1963 Puerto Rican dairying: a revolution in tropical agriculture. Geographical Review 53: 224–46.

Marbut, Charles F.
1926 The soils of the Amazon basin in relation to agricultural possibilities. Geographical Review 16: 414–42.

Marrero, Levi
1950 Geografía de Cuba. Havana.
1964 Venezuela y sus recursos. Caracas.

Martin, Gene E.
1960 La división de la tierra en Chile central. Instituto de Geografía, Universidad de Chile, Santiago.

Martonne, Emmanuel de
1935 Buenos Aires: étude de géographie urbaine. Annales de Géographie 44: 281–304.
1940 Problèmes morphologiques du Brésil tropical atlantique. Annales de Géographie 49: 1–27, 106–29.

Massip, Salvador, and Sarah E. y Salque de Massip
1942 Introducción a la geografía de Cuba. Havana.

Megee, Mary
1958 Monterrey, Mexico: internal patterns and external relations. University of Chicago, Dept. of Geography Research Paper 59.

Meigs, Peveril
  1935 The Dominican mission frontier of Lower California. University of California Publications in Geography 7: 1–232.
  1939 The Kiliwa Indians of Lower California. Ibero-Americana, Vol. 15.
Monbeig, Pierre
  1952 Pionniers et planteurs de São Paulo. Paris.
Monge, Carlos
  1948 Acclimatization in the Andes. Baltimore.
Monheim, Felix
  1956 Beiträge zur Klimatologie und Hydrologie des Titicacabeckens. Heidelberger Geographische Arbeiten, Vol. 1.
Moral, P.
  1955 La culture du café en Haiti. Les Cahiers d'Outre-Mer 8: 233–56.
Morrison, Paul C., and Jorge León
  1951 Sequent occupance, Turrialba Central District, Costa Rica. Turrialba 1: 185–98 (Turrialba, C.R.).
Murphy, R. C.
  1939 Racial succession in the Colombian Chocó. Geographical Review 29: 461–71.
Nunley, Robert E.
  1960 The distribution of population in Costa Rica. NAS–NRC Foreign Field Report 8. Washington, D.C.
Nuñez Jimenez, Antonio
  1959 Geografía de Cuba, adaptada al nuevo programa revolucionario de bachillerato. Havana. 2nd ed.
Ogilvie, A. G.
  1922 Geography of the central Andes; and handbook to accompany the La Paz sheet of the map of Hispanic America on the millionth scale. New York, American Geographical Society.
Otremba, Erich
  1954 Entwicklung und Wandlung der Venezolanischen Kulturlandschaft unter der Herrschaft des Erdöles. Erdkunde 8: 169–88.
  1958 Die landwirtschaftlichen Betriebsgormen in Venezuela und das Problem der Agrarkolonisation durch Europäer. Wirtschaftliche Veröffentlichungen Deutsches Institut für Landerkunde (Leipzig) 15/16: 5–50.
Pacific Science Association
  1957 Climate, vegetation and rational land utilization in the humid tropics. Proceedings, Ninth Pacific Science Congress, Bangkok, Vol. 20.
Pardé, Maurice
  1962 Crues remarquables de rivières sud-brasiliennes et uruguayennes. Revue Géographique des Pyrénées et du Sud-Ouest 33: 5–47.
Parsons, James J.
  1949 Antioqueño colonization in western Colombia. Ibero-Americana, Vol. 32.
  1952 The settlement of the Sinú valley of Colombia. Geographical Review 42: 67–86.
  1954 English-speaking settlement in the western Caribbean. Yearbook, Association of Pacific Coast Geographers 16: 3–16.
  1955 The Miskito pine savanna of Nicaragua and Honduras. Annals, Association of American Geographers 45: 36–63.
  1957 Bananas in Ecuador, a new chapter in the history of tropical agriculture. Economic Geography 33: 201–16.

1962 The green turtle and man. Gainesville, Fla.

Passarge, Siegfried
1933 Wissenschaftliche Ergebnisse einer Reise im Gebiet des Orinoco, Caura und Cuchivaro im Jahre 1901–1902. Hamburg.

Pearson, Ross
1963 Land reform, Guatemala style. American Journal of Economics and Sociology, April, pp. 225–34.

Pendleton, Robert H.
1950 Agricultural and forestry potentialities of the tropics. Agronomy Journal 42: 115–23.

Pennington, Campbell D.
1958 Tarahumar fish stupefaction plants. Economic Botany 12: 95–102.
1963a Medicinal plants utilized by the Tepehuán of southern Chihuahua. América Indígena 23: 31–47.
1963b The Tarahumar of Mexico; their environment and material culture. Salt Lake City.

Petersen, Georg
1956 Estudios climatológicos en el noroeste peruano. Boletín, Sociedad Nacional Minera y Petroleo (Lima) 48: 3–112; 49: 2–55.

Pfeifer, Gottfried
1939 Sinaloa und Sonora: Beiträge zur Landeskunde und Kulturgeographie des nordwestlichen Mexico. Mitteilungen des Geographischer Gesellschaft Hamburg 46: 289–460.
1952 Brasiliens stellung in der kulturgeographischen Entwicklung den Neuen Welt. Erdkunde 6: 85–103.
1962 Brasilien als Entwicklungsland; Beobachtungen im Hinterland von Rio, in Espírito Santo, Minas Gerais, Goiás und Amazonien. Westfälische Geographische Studien 15: 125–94.

Picó, Rafael
1950 The geographic regions of Puerto Rico. Río Piedras, P.R.

Pittier, Henri
1912 Kostarika, beiträge zur orographie und hydrographie. Petermanns Mitteilungen, Ergänzungsheft 175.
1942 Capítulos escogidos de la geografía física y prehistórica de Costa Rica. San José, Museo Nacional. 2nd ed., revised.

Platt, Robert S.
1943 Latin America, countrysides and united regions. New York.

Price, A. Grenfell
1931 White settlers in the tropics. New York, American Geographical Society.

Prohaska, Frederico
1961a El problema de las sequías en la región semiárida pampeana y la sequía actual. Republicade Argentina, Instituto de Suelos y Agrotecnia, Publ. 71.
1961b Las características de las precipitaciones en la región semiárida pampeana. Republicade Argentina, Instituto de Suelos y Agrotecnia, Publ. 72.

Proudfout, M. J. (ed.)
1952 The rural land classification program of Puerto Rico. Northwestern University Studies in Geography, Vol. 1.

Raimondi, Antonio
1879–1940. El Perú. Lima. 5 vols.

Rawitscher, Felix K.
1948 The water economy of the vegetation of the "campos cerrados" in southern Brazil. Journal of Ecology 36: 237–68.

Reparaz, G. de
1958 La zone aride du Perou. Geografiska Annaler 40: 1–62.

Revert, Eugène
1949 La Martinique: étude géographique et humaine. Paris.

Roche, Jean
1959. La colonisation allemande et le Rio Grande do Sul. Paris, Institut des Hautes Etudes de l'Amérique Latine.

Romero, Emílio
1961 Geografía económica del Perú. Lima. 3rd ed.

Rothwell, Stuart C.
1957–59 The old Italian colonial zone of Rio Grande do Sul, Brazil. Revista Geográfica 20: 22–54; 21: 1–21; 23: 89–101; 24: 67–108.
1960 Ports and hinterlands of Rio Grande do Sul State, Brazil. Dept. of Geography, University of Miami, Coral Gables, Fla.

Rubio, Angel
1950a La ciudad de Panamá: biografía, funciones, diagnosis, paisaje. Panama, Banco de Urbanización y Rehabilitación.
1950b La vivienda rural panameña. Panama, Banco de Urbanización y Rehabilitación.

Rudolph, William E.
1963 Vanishing trails of Atacama. New York, American Geographical Society.

Ruellan, Francis
1944 A evolução geomorfológica da Baía de Guanabara e das regiões vizinhas. Revista Brasileira de Geografia 6: 445–500.

Russell, Joseph A.
1942 Fordlandia and Belterra rubber plantations on the Tapajós river, Brazil. Economic Geography 18: 125–45.

Sandner, Gerhard
1961 Agrar-Kolonisation in Costa Rica. Siedlung, Wirtschaft und Socialgefüge an der Pioniergrenze. Schriften Geographischen Instituts Universität Kiel 19: No. 3. (Spanish edition published by Instituto Geográfico de Costa Rica, San Jose, 1962–64, 2 vols.)

Sapper, Karl
1902 Die geographische Bedeutung der Mittelamerikanischen Vulkane. Zeitschrift Gesellschaft für Erdkunde Berlin 37: 512–36.
1925 Los volcanes de la América Central. Halle.
1936a Geographie und Geschichte der indianischen Landwirtschaft. Ibero-Amerikanen Studien Vol. 1. Hamburg.
1936b Bienenhaltung und Bienenzucht in Mittelamerika und Mexico. Ibero-Amerikanische Archiv 9: 183–302.

Sauer, Carl O.
1932 The road to Cíbola. Ibero-Americana, Vol. 3.
1935 The aboriginal population of northwest Mexico. Ibero-Americana, Vol. 10.
1941 The personality of Mexico. Geographical Review 31: 353–64.
1948 Colima of New Spain in the sixteenth century. Ibero-Americana, Vol. 29.
1950 Cultivated plants of South and Central America. In Handbook of South American Indians, Julian H. Steward, ed. Vol. 6: 487–543.

1952 Agricultural origins and dispersals. New York, American Geographical Society.
1959 Middle America as a culture historical location. 33rd Congreso Internacional de Americanistas, San José, 1958, Vol. 2: 115–22. San José, Costa Rica.

Sauer, Carl O., and Donald D. Brand
1932 Aztatlán: prehistoric Mexican frontier on the Pacific Coast. Ibero-Americana, Vol. 1.

Sauer, Carl O., and Peveril Meigs
1927 Site and culture at San Fernando de Velicatá. University of California Publications in Geography 2: 271–302.

Schilling, Elisabeth
1939 Die schwimmenden Gärten von Xochimilco. Ein einzigartiges Beispiel altindianischer Landgewinnung in Mexico. Schriften Geographische Institut Universität Kiel 9: No. 3. Kiel.

Schmithüsen, Josef.
1956 Die räumliche Ordnung der chilenischen Vegetation. Bonner geographische Abhandlungen, Vol. 17.
1960 Die Nädelholzer in den Waldgesellschaften der südlichen Anden. Vegetatio 9: 313–27.

Schmieder, Oscar
1926 The East-Bolivian Andes south of the Río Grande or Guapay. University of California Publications in Geography 2 (No. 5): 85–210.
1927 The Pampa, a natural or culturally induced grassland? University of California Publications in Geography 2 (No. 8): 255–70.
1928 The historic geography of Tucumán. University of California Publications in Geography 2 (No. 12): 359–86.
1929 The Brazilian culture hearth. University of California Publications in Geography 3 (No. 3): 159–98.
1930 Settlements of the Tzapotec and Mije Indians, Oaxaca, Mexico. University of California Publications in Geography 4: 1–184.
1932 Landerkunde Südamerikas. Leipzig and Vienna.
1934 Landerkunde Mittelamerikas. Leipzig and Vienna.
1962 Landerkunde der Neue Welt. I. Mittel- und Südamerika. Stuttgart.

Schweigger, Edwin
1947 El litoral peruano. Lima, Compañía Administradora del Guano.
1959 Die Westküste Südamerikas im Bereich des Peru-Strom. Heidelberg.

Sepulveda, Sergio
1956 El trigo chileno en el mercado mundial; ensayo de geografía histórica. Informaciones Geográficas (Lima), pp. 6–133.

Shreve, Forrest
1944 Rainfall of northern Mexico. Ecology 25: 105–33.

Sievers, Wilhelm
1887 Reise in der Sierra Nevada de Santa Marta. Leipzig.
1888 Venezuela. Hamburg.
1913 Die Cordillerenstaaten. Berlin and Leipzig. 2 vols.
1914 Reise in Peru and Ecuador ausgeführt 1909. Munich and Leipzig.

Simpson, Lesley Byrd
1952 Exploitation of land in central Mexico in the sixteenth century. Ibero-Americana, Vol. 36.

Sioli, Harold
1956 Über Natur und Mensch in brasilianischen Amazonasgebiet. Erdkunde 10: 89–109.

82   James J. Parsons

Sioli, Harold
1957   Beiträge zur regionalen Limnologie des Amazonasgebietes. Archiv für Hydrobiologie 53: 161–222.

Slutsky, H.
1960   An ecological study of total mortality among Guatemala preschool children with special emphasis on protein malnutrition and kwaskiokor. NAS–NRC Foreign Field Report 6, Washington, D.C.

Snyder, David E.
1962   Commercial passenger linkages and the metropolitan nodality of Montevideo. Economic Geography 38: 95–112. (Also in Spanish.)
1964   Alternative perspectives on Brasilia. Economic Geography 40 (No. 1): 34–45.

Soares, Lúcio de Castro
1953   Limites meridionais e orientais da área de ocorrência da floresta amazônica em território brasileiro. Revista Brasileira de Geografia 15 (No. 1): 2–122.

Soares, M. T. de Segadas
1962   Nova Iguaçú: Absorção de uma célula urbana pelo Grande Rio de Janeiro. Revista Brasileira de Geografia 24 (No. 2): 155–256.

Spencer, J. E., and G. A. Hale
1961   The origin, nature, and distribution of agricultural terracing. Pacific Viewpoint (Wellington) 2: 1–40.

Stanislawski, Dan
1947a   The political rivalry of Patzcuaro and Morelia, an item in sixteenth century political geography of Mexico. Annals, Association of American Geographers 37: 135–44.
1947b   Tarascan political geography. American Anthropologist 49: 46–55.
1947c   Early Spanish town planning in the New World. Geographical Review 37: 94–105.
1950   The anatomy of eleven towns in Michoacán. Latin American Studies 10. University of Texas, Austin.

Sterling, Henry (ed.)
1955   Problemas económicos y sociales de los Andes Venezolanos. Caracas, Consejo de Bienstar Rural. 2 vols.

Sternberg, Hilgard O'Reilly
1951   Floods and landslides in the Paraíba valley, December 1948; influence of destructive exploitation on the land. Comptes Rendus, XVI Congrès Internationale de Géographie, Lisbon, 1949, pp. 335–64.
1955   Agriculture and industry in Brazil. Geographical Journal 21: 488–502.
1956   A água e o homem na várzea do Careiro. Rio de Janeiro. Map supplement.
1957   Land use and the 1957 drought in Ceará. Proceedings, 17th International Geographical Congress, Washington, D.C., 1952, pp. 672–82.
1959   Geographic thought and development in Brazil. The Professional Geographer 11 (No. 6): 12–17.

Stewart, Norman R.
1963   Foreign agricultural colonization as a study in cultural geography. The Professional Geographer 15 (No. 5): 1–5.

Stoddart, David R.
1962   Three Caribbean atolls: Turneffe Islands, Lighthouse Reef, and Glover's Reef, British Honduras. Atoll Research Bulletin 87, Washington, D.C.

Tamayo, Jorge L.
1962 Geografía general de México. 2nd ed. Mexico. I and II: Geografía física; III: Geografía biológica y humana; IV: Geografía económica.

Termer, Franz
1936 Zur Geographie der Republik Guatemala. I: Physischen Geographie; 1941 II: Kultur- und Wirtschaftsgeographie. Mitteilungen des Geographischer Gesellschaft Hamburg 44: 89–275; 47: 7–262.
1943 Die ethnischen Grundlagen der politischen Geographie von Mittelamerika. Zeitschrift des Gesellschaft für Erdkunde Berlin, pp. 148–71.
1950 La densidad de población de los Imperios Mayas como problema arqueológico y geográfico. Sociedad Mexicana de Geografía y Estadística, Boletin No. 70: 211–39.
1956 Carlos Sapper, explorador de Centro América (1866–1945). Annales de Sociedad Geográfica y Histórica Guatemala 29: 55–130.

Thomas, William L., Jr. (ed.)
1956 Man's role in changing the face of the earth. Chicago.

Tigner, James L.
1963 The Ryukyuans in Bolivia. Hispanic America Historical Review 43: 206–29.

Trewartha, Glenn
1961 The earth's problem climates. Madison, Wis.

Tosi, Joseph A., Jr.
1960 Zonas de vida natural en el Perú. Boletin Technico 5, Proyecto 39, Programa de Cooperación Técnica, Instituto Interamericana de Ciéncias Agrícola de OEA. Lima.

Troll, Carl
1959 Die tropischen Gebirge. Bonner geographische Abhandlungen, Vol. 25.

Tuan, Y-Fu
1962 A coastal reconnaissance of central Panama. California Geographer 3: 77–96.

Union Géographique Internationale
1959–61 Comptes Rendus, XVIII Congrès International de Géographie, Rio de Janeiro, 1956. 4 vols.

U.S. Department of Agriculture
1958 Agriculture Geography of Latin America. U.S.D.A. Miscellaneous Publication 743.

Universidad Nacional Autónoma de Mexico. Instituto de Geografía
1961 Anuario de Geografía, Vol. 1.
1962 Distribución geográfica de la población en la república mexicana. Mexico City.

Vann, John
1959 Landform-vegetation relationships in the Atrato delta. Annals, Association of American Geographers 49: 345–60.
1963 Developmental processes in laterite terrain in Amapá. Geographical Review 53: 406–17.

Vidal de la Blache, Paul Marie Joseph
1902 La rivière Vicente Pinzon, étude sur la cartographie de la Guyane. Paris.

Vila, Pablo
1960 Geografía de Venezuela. I. Geografía física. Caracas.

Vivó, Jorge
1948 Geografía de México. Mexico City.

Vivó, Jorge
1958   La conquista de nuestro suelo: estudio sobre los recursos naturales de México. Mexico City.
1959   Estudio de geografía económica y demográfica de Chiapas. Mexico City.
Vogt, William
1963   Comments on a brief reconnaissance of resource use, progress and conservation needs in some Latin American countries. New York, The Conservation Foundation.
Wagner, Moritz
1856   Die republik Costa Rica in Central Amerika. Leipzig.
1861   Beiträge zu einer physisch-geographischen skizze des Istmus von Panama. Petermanns Mitteilungen, Ergänzungsheft 5.
1868   Die Darwinische theorie und das migrationsgesetz der organismen. Leipzig.
1870   Naturwissenschaftliche reisen im tropischen Amerika. Stuttgart.
Wagner, Philip L.
1955   Parras, a case history in the depletion of natural resources. Landscape, Summer, pp. 19–28.
1958   Nicoya, a cultural geography. University of California Publications in Geography 12 (No. 3): 195–250.
1962   Natural and artificial zonation in vegetation cover: Chiapas, Mexico. Geographical Review 52: 253–74.
Waibel, Leo
1939   White settlement in Costa Rica. Geographical Review 29: 529–60.
1943   Place names as an aid to the reconstruction of the original vegetation of Cuba. Geographical Review 33: 376–96.
1948   Vegetation and land use in the Planalto Central of Brazil. Geographical Review 36: 529–54.
1950   European colonization in southern Brazil. Geographical Review 40: 529–47.
1955   Die europäische Kolonisation Südbrasiliens. Colloquium Geographicum (Bonn). Vol. 4.
Wallén, Carl Christian
1955   Some characteristics of precipitation in Mexico. Geografiska Annaler 37: 51–85.
1956   Fluctuations and variability in Mexican rainfall. American Association for the Advancement of Science, Publication 43: 141–55.
Warntz, William
1959   Progress in economic geography. In New viewpoints in geography, P. James, ed. 29th Yearbook of the National Council for the Social Studies. Washington, D.C., pp. 54–75.
Webb, Kempton E.
1959   Geography of food supply in central Minas Gerais. NAS–NRC Foreign Field Report 4, Washington, D.C.
1961   Problems of food supply in Brazil. Journal of Interamerican Studies 3: 239–48.
West, Robert C.
1948   Cultural geography of the modern Tarascan area. Washington, D.C. Smithsonian Institution, Institute of Social Anthropology, No. 7.
1949   The mining community in northern New Spain: the Parral mining district. Ibero-Americana, Vol. 30.
1952   Colonial placer mining in Colombia. Baton Rouge, La.

1957 The Pacific lowlands of Colombia, a negroid area of the American tropics. Baton Rouge, La.

1959a Ridge or *era* agriculture in the Colombian Andes. 33rd Congreso Internacional de Americanistas, San José, 1958. Vol. 1: 279–82. San José, Costa Rica.

1959b The mining economy of Honduras during the colonial period. 33rd Congreso Internacional de Americanistas, San José, 1958. Vol. 2: 767–77. San José, Costa Rica.

West, Robert C., and Pedro Armillas

1950 Las chinampas de México. Cuadernos Americanos 50: 165–82.

Wilbert, Johannes (ed.)

1961 The evolution of horticultural systems in native South America, causes and consequences. A symposium, Caracas, Sociedad de Ciencias Naturales "La Salle."

Wilhelmy, Herbert

1941 Die deutschen Siedlungen in Mittelparaguay. Schriften des Geographischen Instituts Universität Kiel 11: No. 1.

1949 Siedlung im südamerikanischen Urwald. Hamburg.

1952 Südamerika im Spiegel seiner Städte. Hamburg.

1954a Curaçao, Aruba, Maracaibo: eine ölwirtschaftliche Symbiose. Akademie für Raumforschung und Landesplanung Abhandlungen 28: 275–302.

1954b Die klimamorphologie und pflanzengeographie Entwicklung des Trockengebietes am Nordrand Südamerikas seit dem Pleistozän. Die Erde 3: 244–73.

1957a Eiszeit und Eiszeitklima in den feucht tropischen Anden. Petermanns Mitteilungen, Ergänzungsheft 262: 281–310.

1957b Das Grosse Pantanal in Mato Grosso, Abhandlungen Deutscher Geographentag Würzburg, pp. 45–71.

1958 Umlaufseen und Dammuferseen tropischer Tieflandflüsse. Zeitschrift für Geomorphologie 2: 27–54.

1963 Die La Plataländer, Argentinien, Paraguay, Uruguay. Braunschweig.

Winnie, W. W., Jr.

1958 The Papaloapan project, an experiment in tropical agriculture. Economic Geography 34: 227–48.

Wood, Harold A.

1963 Land, land use, and settlement, a geographical investigation of the Departement du Nord. Toronto.

Zelinsky, Wilbur

1949 Historical geography of the Negro population of Latin America. Journal of Negro History 34: 153–221.

Zimmermann, Josef

1958 Studien zur Anthropogeographie Amazoniens: die Wirtschaftsraum Santarém. Bonner Geographische Abhandlungen 21, Bonn.

3. Latin American Historiography: Status and Research Opportunities

STANLEY J. STEIN

Among the disciplines that have been focused upon Latin America in the nineteenth and twentieth centuries, history has attracted the largest number of scholars and achieved the greatest volume of output. Within the field of history, the period drawing the most scholarly attention has been the colonial, from pre-Conquest to the beginning of the independence movements (1810), or if one accepts a modern tendency to call the immediate post-independence decades "neocolonial," to the middle of the nineteenth century (1850–70). Broad scholarly interest in the post-1850 years, the "national" or "modern" period, is largely a phenomenon of the last twenty-five to thirty years. Such are the conclusions drawn from recent surveys of Latin American historiography.[1]

The Colonial Period, 1450–1850

Interest has not been spread evenly over the four colonial centuries. Historians have tended to cluster their studies around three colonial eras: (1) discovery, Conquest, and settlement to roughly 1570: (2) the antecedents of independence movements, 1763–1810; (3) the anti-colonial surge against Iberian imperialism and the decades of postwar adjustment, 1810–50. The reasons for this distribution of time-interest are fairly clear. Nineteenth-

[1] The references for this paper are only suggestions. The following have been consulted in preparation for this survey: Gibson and Keen (1947: 855–57), Cline (1959), Simpson (1949), Barager (1959: 588–642), Potash (1960: 383–424), Griffith (1960), Naylor (1962), Zavala (1962), Griffin (1961), Gibson (1958), Whitaker (1961a), Burgin (1947), Mosk (1949).

century scholars in the United States and Latin America were naturally interested in the origin of their New World cultures, partly from the natural bent of historians to seek the beginnings of a process, partly from their viewpoint of the whole colonial experience. Latin American scholars, such as Bustamante, Alamán, Orozco y Berra, García Icázbalceta, Varnhagen, Barros Arana, and Amunátegui, often examined the colonial period, and in particular the sixteenth century, because they wished to extol or deprecate the colonial heritage.[2] North American scholars from Irving and Prescott to Bancroft and Bourne looked to the era of discovery and conquest with the romantic "nostalgia for the Hispanic past," or, as in the case of Winsor, Fiske, and Thacher, because they saw in nineteenth-century Latin America the survival of colonial institutions and values or because of Spanish contacts on the rim or approaches to the continental United States (Gibson and Keen 1957: 855–57). While nineteenth-century U.S. historians limited their attention to discovery, Conquest, and exploration, their Latin American counterparts also wrote about the bloody and dramatic debacle of Iberian colonialism, the wars of independence, origins, evolution, and end. From 1910 to 1922 centennial ceremonies commemorating the independence movements reinforced this aspect of Latin American historiography. By 1918, U.S. scholars had produced a few outstanding monographs on the colonial period, Prescott's *History of the Conquest of Mexico* (1847), Bancroft's *History of Mexico* (1883–88), Bourne's *Spain in America* 1904), Priestley's *Gálvez* (1916), and Haring's *Trade and Navigation* (1918), not to mention the bibliographical tools of Shepherd (1907), Robertson (1910), Bolton (1913), Hill (1916), and Chapman (1919).[3]

The founding of the *Hispanic American Historical Review* (1918) helped establish Latin American history as a field of professional activity among U.S. scholars of Latin America. The next two decades were a period of "concentration, specialization and elaboration" (Gibson and Keen 1957: 860–61) leading to the publication of monographs on colonial political institutions and economic, intellectual; and literary history textbooks; and

[2] See particularly Bustamante (1829, 1836), Alamán (1844–49, 1849–52), Orozco y Berra (1880, 1938), Garcia Icázbalceta (1886, 1858–66), Varnhagen (1854–57, 1871), Barros Arana (1874, 1884–1902), Amanátegui (1862).

[3] See also Keniston (1920), Jones (1922), Gibson and Keen (1957: 858–59)

Bolton's controversial hemispheric view of historical development, "The Epic of Greater America" (1933, 1939). After 1940 the growth of scholarly interest in the recent, i.e., nineteenth-century, origins of Latin American problems detracted from the formerly overriding emphasis upon colonial history. None the less, in quality, theme, and synthesis, there has been in fact a renaissance in colonial studies. Pre-Conquest and Conquest periods in Meso-America and Andean America have been re-examined and reinterpreted;[4] neglected aspects of the sixteenth and seventeenth centuries have been illuminated by studies of demography and social, economic, and intellectual history and by analyses of political theory and institutions;[5] there has been more interest in economic and intellectual developments of the eighteenth century.[6] Certain institutions and social forms—*encomienda*, the hacienda, peonage, mestization, Indian aristocracy —have been traced through the colonial centuries and beyond.[7] Particularly promising have been essays in comparative colonial history in which authors of monographic studies have tried to look beyond the particular to broad historical patterns (Chamberlain 1954; Mauro 1961: 571–85). It is not surprising to note that since 1940 broad syntheses of the colonial period by Haring (1947), Diffie (1945), and Picón-Salas (1944) have appeared. On a more limited scale, Chaunu (1955–60), Arcila Farías (1946), and Mauro (1960) have focused upon economic aspects and Borah (1956) on sixteenth-century institutions. Finally, a number of scholars have stressed economic and social aspects of the independence movements in general, as well as the over-all significance of the movements in such areas as Mexico and Argentina (see Griffin 1949, 1962; Humphreys 1950, 1952).

In sum, it is evident that although colonial historians have

[4] Especially useful from this point of view are Armillas (1951, 1962), Rowe (1946), Morley (1956), Thompson (1954), Palerm (1955).

[5] Important for this subject are Cook and Simpson (1948), Borah and Cook (1963), Gibson (1952), Kubler (1946), Cline (1949), Chevalier (1952), Marchant (1942), Rowe (1957), Zavala (1943a), Hanke (1949), Leonard (1949), Miranda (1952), Gibson (1948), Borah (1956), Góngora (1951), Parry (1957).

[6] About this subject see Hussey (1934), Smith (1944, 1948), Céspedes del Castillo (1945), Arcila Farías (1950), Levene (1927), Whitaker (1941), Howe (1949), Whitaker, ed. (1942), Lanning (1940).

[7] On this subject see Zavala (1943b), Mörner (1960), Konetzke (1946: 7–44, 215–37), Gibson (1955, 1960), Kubler (1952).

broken new ground and ably synthesized the growing monographic literature, lacunae are numerous. First of all, colonialists are testing colonial codes against colonial practice. The most
notable gap concerns the "formative" seventeenth century, when
many enduring colonial institutions, it is now argued, were
forged (Simpson 1949: 189–90; Gibson and Keen 1957: 862).
Other gaps are those institutions and attitudes that characterized
the eighteenth century and endured into the nineteenth. Griffin's article (1949) on the economic and social aspects of the era
of independence has suggested that the conflict accelerated "evolutionary" rather than "revolutionary" change. Scholars interested in modern Latin America, the decades following 1850, have
an unparalleled opportunity to bridge the late colonial and
early modern periods (1750–1850) by examining such institutions as hacienda and plantation, mestization, family structure,
and elitism; the relationships among economic development,
demographic growth, and the desire for economic liberty and
social mobility; the varying patterns and consequences of independence movements in Mexico, Argentina, and Brazil; and the
factors insuring continuity of colonial rule in Cuba and Puerto
Rico.

The Modern Period, 1850 to the Present

Sustained interest in the historiography of modern Latin
America has been largely the result of U.S. political and economic expansion, the economic crises of the 'thirties, the stresses
and strains of World War II, and the problems of economic
growth, social change, and political stability since 1945. The
problems of the student of the modern period are, however, far
more complex than those of the colonialist. The colonial era has
unity of time, a beginning and an end; colonial Latin America
was subject to uniform codes of law, in theory applied throughout the colonies; the materials and tools of research are, relatively speaking, well organized and accessible; and change occurred almost imperceptibly after 1570. Consequently, the task
of the colonial historian is relatively simple when compared with
that of the historian of modern Latin America, who must deal
with twenty different states, scattered sources, and the absence of
tools of research and who must respond to a rapidly changing

pattern of contemporary events raising new questions about a very superficially known past. Whereas colonialists are checking their syntheses by examining the specific operation of institutions at local levels, students of the modern period have yet to make the detailed national studies to justify syntheses. It is not intended to deprecate the useful syntheses proposed by Humphreys (1946), Mosk (1948), Bernstein (1952), Worcester and Schaeffer (1956), Johnson (1958) and Griffin (1961), but merely to point out how much there remains to be done on the historiography of modern Latin America and how weak are the bases of our generalizations.

Obviously one difficulty in synthesis and generalization is the complexity of Latin American history in the modern period.[8] The complexity may be traced to a number of related factors: (1) the shortened perspective; (2) the increase in the size of the literate population, and the corresponding increase in publications dealing with historical themes; (3) the shift from political, military, and diplomatic to economic, social, and intellectual history, which make great demands on the training of scholars and their ability to integrate; (4) the dispersal of manuscript sources and the absence of catalogues of manuscript and printed collections; (5) the varying impact of external phenomena—the fluctuations of a world market, two world wars, and post-1945 international tensions; and (6) the overriding dedication of Latin American scholars to national historical questions.

It is possible, however, to indicate certain historiographical trends in the treatment of modern Latin America. Although Whitaker's *Latin American History since 1825* limits its discussion to materials available in English, its topical organization suggests the principal trends among both U.S. and Latin American scholars. With some fusion of Whitaker's major categories, the broad trends are (1) greater interest in social, economic, and intellectual history, supplementing the traditional politico-military-diplomatic focus; (2) within the still paramount political emphasis, the theme of democracy versus dictatorship and the issue of the state versus clericalism; (3) a broad conception of

[8] As Griffin (1961) has phrased it, "For the national period the plethora of data is overpowering. . . . More important . . . is the rapidity of historical change and the more exact knowledge available as to how and why these changes occurred."

international relations going beyond diplomatic exchanges between the United States and individual Latin American republics to include Latin America's involvement in the United Nations and the Latin American process of economic development in an international context.

These trends require further elaboration. Professionalization of the historian's craft is occurring among both U.S. and Latin American scholars, and Latin American scholars' output naturally exceeds that of their U.S. colleagues. The appearance of excellent scholarly journals has acted as both a stimulus and a response to the growth of the community of scholars in the social sciences.[9] Despite the publication of several heuristic syntheses covering Latin America as a whole, such as Johnson's politico-social view of the middle classes and politics in his *Political Change in Latin America* (1958), Prebisch's *The Economic Development of Latin America and Its Principal Problems* (1950), Zea's pioneer study of *The Latin America Mind* (1963), and Beal's "Social Stratification in Latin America" (1953), the principal contributions have been made in nationally oriented studies. In the largely neglected specialization of intellectual history there have appeared the studies by Ramos (1934), Zea (1944), and Romanell (1952), the Brazilian studies of Cruz Costa (1956) and Miguel Pereira (1952), and the Argentine studies of Martínez Estrada (1933) and Romero (1946). Historically oriented economists have made the most significant contributions to economic history in the form of highly original essays: Pinto's *Chile: Un caso de desarrollo frustrado* (1958) and Furtado's *The Economic Growth of Brazil* (1963). Finally, the outstanding contributions to historiography have been either single-volume national studies, such as Cline's *The United States and Mexico* (1953) and *Mexico: Evolution to Revolution* (1962), Rennie's *The Argentine Republic* (1945), and Whitaker's brief *The United States and Argentina* (1954), or the multivolume series organized by Cosío Villegas for Mexico (1955–63), Buarque de Holanda for Brazil (1960–), Levene for Argentina (1936–50), and Guerra y Sanchez and associates (1952) for Cuba. Few will cavil with the statement

9 For example, *Revista de historia de America* (Mexico), *Historia Mexicana*, *Trimestre Economico* (Mexico), *Revista de história* (São Paulo), *Revista de historia* (Buenos Aires), *Revista de Indias* (Madrid), *The Americas* (Washington, D.C.).

that the volumes in the *Historia moderna de Mexico,* prepared under the editorship of Cosío Villegas and the auspices of the Colegio de Mexico, constitute the most notable historical publications of the last decade in Latin American historiography.

No doubt the complexity of modern Latin American history and the corresponding difficulty of synthesis are also partly due to the fact that the clusters of topics that interest historians vary from country to country. As recent historiographical articles on the history of modern Mexico, Brazil, and Argentina indicate, only in the broadest of senses are the historical "questions" of these countries comparable.[10] Scholars of Argentine history have debated the age of Rosas, the *Unicato* and the revolution of 1890, the trajectory of Radicalism—party, personalities, and program—the Revolution of 1930, and the Peron era. Brazilianists have re-examined the last four decades of the monarchy, the origins of the republic, abolitionism and the process of integration, and the Vargas "revolution" (1930–45). For the Mexicans the questions have turned on the Reforma, the Díaz era, and the Revolution to 1940 and on the evolution of Mexico's liberal tradition. As might be expected, the authors of the historiographical articles differ on lacunae. Potash recommends analyses of Mexico's local and regional electoral processes in 1867 and 1871, the role and function of the *jefe politico,* the utilization of hacienda and factory records for economic history, dispassionate biographies of leading political figures of the revolution, the roots of nationalism, and nineteenth-century Mexican conservatism. Barager urges specialists to study the Argentine "agrarian revolution" after 1880, immigration (1870–1914) and urbanization in a "socio-political framework," trade unionism, and social welfare organizations. Even from this brief review it is clear that the leading areas of historiographical interest and production are Mexico, Brazil, and Argentina and that scholars' interests, and lacunae awaiting treatment, vary markedly. Equally manifest is the fact that the historians whether colonialists or students of the modern period are specialists in the history of one, or at most, two areas, on the basis of which they risk generalization and heuristic syntheses (see Dore 1963). Perhaps the most ambitious synthesis of this type, continental rather than Latin American in

10 On this subject see Potash (1960), Stein (1960), Barager (1959).

scope, is Griffin's *The National Period in the History of the New World: An Outline and Commentary* (1961). Based upon preliminary outlines of collaborators in the program of the history of the New World, Griffin's periodization, skillful weighting of extra continental, continental, and regional phenomena, and judicious bibliography render the volume a godsend to textbook writers and a boon to the research-oriented seeking the macrocosm in the microcosm.

Research Opportunities

This summary review of Latin American historiographical trends of the near and distant past comes at an appropriate moment. In the first place, the historian heeding the precepts of what was once termed the "New History," an interdisciplinary and multicausal view of the historical process, can and indeed must now call upon research tools, analytical approaches, and the findings of scholars in allied disciplines—economics, sociology, anthropology, psychology, art, and literary history—in unraveling the complexity of modern, i.e., post-1850, Latin America's historical evolution. Probing for the economic and social roots of political instability since the onset of the great depression, perceptive social scientists examining Latin American phenomena have implicitly and explicitly forced historians to modify what was until then a generally purblind adherence to the tradition of political, military, diplomatic, and bad biographical history. A start in this direction has been made, but historians have a long road to travel. In the second place, the decade since the end of the Korean conflict has undoubtedly been one of great transition in the evolution of Latin America as remnants of the "old," or "neocolonial," order crumble swiftly under rising pressure from hitherto submerged, unrecognized, and neglected classes. Visible are the vestiges of obsolescent tradition as well as the spearheads of change. Historians now have an unparalleled opportunity for a multilateral approach to their craft, by developing tools of research (guides to historical literature, specialized bibliographies, and catalogues of manuscript and printed source materials) and through improved graduate training. Above all, this historical moment of almost cataclysmic change in Latin America obliges the historian to isolate the key problems and issues of contemporary developments and to subject them to macro- as well as microanalysis—in effect to do what the craft has always considered its ideal, to eschew antiquarian interests and to reinterpret the past that is relevant. No doubt historians differ on what is relevant, and consensus among historians diverges from generation to generation. The relevance of the past to the present is a personal matter, to be sure, and the following tasks for the Latin American historian today in both national and international perspective and in terms of a broad research "design" have the merit only of suggestive probes in a limited number of areas.

MEXICO

Mexico's pre-Conquest background of high Stone Age cultures, phases of the Conquest, its economic importance to Spain in the eighteenth century, its bitter drawn-out civil war for independence, and its turbulent history of modernization since the 1850s have produced perhaps the most voluminous body of historical literature. To the historian of modern Mexico, the Revolution of 1910 is the great watershed of Mexican history and the first social revolution of modern Latin America. First of all, the historian must raise the broadest question, why was there a great upheaval in Mexico in 1910 rather than in so comparable an Indo-American area as Peru? In evaluating the independence struggle, what relative weight should be given to (1) Mexico's relatively close communications with the countries bordering on the North Atlantic and Caribbean basins; (2) the economic expansion of Mexico at the end of the eighteenth century, the stagnation of the Peruvian economy, and the Spanish government's readiness to make in Mexico a last-ditch stand against anti-colonialism; and (3) the relative "openness" or mobility of Mexican society, the spirit of nationalism, and the early emergence of Mexican insurgent leadership? (See McAlister, 1963.) In Mexico this conflict apparently forged an abiding Hispanophobia and an attempt to expel Spaniards judged to be security risks, i.e., whose loyalty to the republican regime was questionable in the 1820s. Hispanophobia may have led to broader criticism and rejection of Spanish traditions inherited from colonial times, whereas republican Peru seems to have kept a Hispanophile tradition. In sum, historians have to ransack archives in the search for mate-

rial on the struggle against Spanish hegemony as a social movement. Beyond doubt, however, the independence movement laid
the basis for the deep liberal-conservative cleavage that apparently subsided in the 1880s, after Mexico's mid-century liberal
surge associated with the figure of Juárez had swept conservatives
from political, if not from social and economic, power. Curiously, historians on both sides of the border have failed to assess
the impact of the Mexican-U.S. war that preceded the Reforma
and which may have induced the liberals to modernize to prevent further dismemberment. Research on Mexico's neocolonial
decades from 1821 to 1867 must go beyond Cosío Villegas' (1955:
I, 45–107) introduction to post-1867 developments, Potash's pioneer economic study of the Banco de Avío (1959), Chávez Orozco's analysis (1938), and the political treatment of Scholes' *Mexican Politics under the Juárez Regime* (1957).

To what may be conceived as the background of the Mexican
revolution of 1910, perhaps the first stage in Mexico's modernization, or what Cosío Villegas has termed the Porfiriato (1876–
1910), historians have devoted considerable attention. Admirably
detailed as are the numerous studies available, they have left
unanswered certain key questions.

It must be recalled that in justifying the Mexican revolution,
muckraking liberal historians have peopled the Mexican cos-
mography with an underworld of Porfirio Díaz, José Limantour,
Bernardo Reyes, and others, involved in a vast conspiracy to exploit the Indian masses. No one denies the facts of exploitation,
yet historians may more profitably investigate this and related
aspects as part of a stage of modernization of an underdeveloped
area, as a syndrome of agricultural change, early industrialization, mobilization of unskilled rural and urban labor, social mobility, and pragmatic liberalism whose tenets did not include
economic democracy (see Bazant 1960). Since Diaz and his associates were products of the Reforma and never repudiated the liberal tradition, Hale has questioned Reyes Heroles' interpretation
that "Porfirism . . . is not a legitimate descendant of liberalism"
(Hale 1963: 460). Historians must re-examine the stage in the development of Mexico's nineteenth-century liberalism that produced the pleiade of the Reforma and then evolved into the
Porfirian oligarchy which abandoned the earlier emphasis upon
political liberalism for rapid economic growth. Assuming that

the major characteristic of the Porfirian decades was growth rather than stagnation, treatments of agrarian problems of that era are inadequate. What happened to the confiscated landed property of the Roman Catholic Church, urban and rural, after 1859? More specifically, who obtained what, how much, where? Analyses of the Mexican hacienda before 1910 have emphasized its "semifeudal" aspects, its reliance upon minimal capital inputs, extensive cultivation, and labor immobility (Tannenbaum 1929). On the other hand, it is now becoming evident that certain agricultural sectors—for example, those producing *pulque* near railroads or the Morelos and Puebla sugar *ingenios*—were modernizing rapidly. Was the modernization of the sugar sector of Morelos and Puebla agriculture principal element of social disequilibrium there and consequently an explanation of the intensity of Indian peasant revindications under Zapata after 1910 (Chevalier 1961: 66–82)? Did Mexican peasants revolt in 1910 because their standards of living as well as level of aspirations were significantly or measurably higher than those of their counterparts in Peru? It may be concluded that in 1910 Díaz' authoritarian handling of the political process sparked a revolution because Mexican society was far more "open" than that of Indo-America, because (1) the struggle for independence and the Reforma were more than political upheavals; (2) wage labor in Mexican mining, consumer industry, and railroad construction siphoned labor from isolated rural communities and haciendas, thereby undermining the traditional hacienda complex; and (3) landowners and mine operators, too, were dissatisfied with the Porfiriato's post-1907 fiscal policy (Rosenzweig Hernandez 1962: 519–24; Vernon 1962).

Regardless of how historians interpret the Porfiriato's decades, no one questions the role of the Revolution in accelerating modernization by destroying the hacienda, the core institution of "semifeudal" Mexico. The revolution has been characterized as lacking ideology, as a response to intermittent pressures that force revolutionary govrenments to respond in piecemeal, pragmatic fashion with the sole goal of social betterment for all Mexicans whether they be the new elite, the middle classes, the "transitional" groups (Cline 1962: Chap. XI), or the rural and urban underdogs who constitute the human material of the "culture of poverty" (Lewis 1959). Some Mexicans now argue that there were purposeful currents in their Revolution and that its success in toppling the Porfiriato came from a marriage of convenience, so to speak, a pragmatic collaboration among dissatisfied elements of a small but vocal middle class and an oppressed peasantry (Flores Olea *et al.* 1959). This interpretation opens the way to a series of hitherto neglected aspects of the Revolution. First, what lessons may students of Latin American agrarian reform learn from (1) the Madero administration's efforts to institute a moderate program of land reform through full compensation for selected haciendas or (2) the proposals of liberals such as Luís Cabrera to maintain the hacienda while granting hacienda workers ownership of subsistence plots (*pegujales*)—neither of which succeeded? Next, what was the long-term influence of U.S. government policy upon the course and duration of agrarian reform and indeed upon the Mexican Revolution itself? Still unevaluated is Tannenbaum's provocative thesis of 1933 that "fear of the United States" had led the Mexican government after 1917 to avoid confiscation of large estates, thereby "protracting" the Revolution. Was this, rather, one of the results of a moderate middle-class orientation, of the Bucareli treaties that "put a complete stop to the Revolution," or of Ambassador Morrow's friendship with President Calles (Tannenbaum 1933: 172; Castañeda 1963: 403)? More to the point, what was the background of the decision to nominate Cárdenas for the presidency in 1933? Little has been published on the ideological cross currents sweeping Mexico between 1930 and 1934. In many respects, the most radical phase of the revolution came two decades after its outbreak, in the six years of the Cárdenas administration (1934–40), when the spine of the hacienda complex was finally shattered by massive, albeit hasty, land redistribution. This was a radical solution, but was it socialistic? Was the ideology of the Cárdenas government basically compounded of New Deal–type reform, in which the state would act merely as a balance wheel, creating opportunities for all interest groups and favoring none? The ideological premises of the Cárdenas regime would then not differ markedly from those of the Vargas government in Brazil, the Aprista movement in Peru, or the Chilean popular front—all contemporaneous.

There is no disagreement that immediately following the end of the Cárdenas administration the incoming administration chose to de-emphasize radical agrarianism and to put its human and natural resources behind industrialization. Still subject to debate is whether this decision terminated the Mexican revolution. Awaiting historical investigation are careful analysis of how the great decision to industrialize was made and whether it was at this crucial point or in the last years of Cárdenas regime that middle-class interests and orientation came to predominate over those of the Mexican peasantry and industrial workers. Without employing the terminology of economic or social class, Cline (1962: Chap. III) has contended that the direction of the revolution changed after 1940, and he has termed this latter phase the era of the "institutional revolution."

At this point, historical perspective and insight indicate that the "institutional" phase of the revolution is analogous to liberalism under the Porfiriato when the political elite rationalized that the returns of economic growth would seep downward and that authoritarian political practices within the form of the Constitution of 1857 were required to mold a favorable climate for domestic and foreign investment. Certainly this has been done in Mexico since 1940, as is evidenced by the statistics of the growth of volume and value of output, urbanization, private and public investment, and the industrial labor force. Economic historians have yet to assess the role of government planning and investment and the relative contributions of private U.S. and Mexican investors to industrialization since 1940. Has the state been the principal motor of economic growth? In a society of revolutionary traditions how has Mexican industrial labor been made to accept a reduced slice of the national income pie? What is the significance for the history of labor in Mexico of the career of the secretary-general of the CTM, Fidel Velázquez, now a senator? Finally, what lessons may be drawn from two major phases of the revolution, anticlericalism and agrarian reform, in the light of the contemporary resurgence of clerical influence and the twin phenomena of renewed concentration of agricultural properties and millions of landless peasants?

BRAZIL

It is difficult to define what is most relevant to the historian today reviewing the history of Brazil of approximately the past century, far more so than in the case of Mexico. Mexico's history can be written in terms of dramatic upheavals against entrenched conservatism: liberation from Spanish tutelage, the Reforma and anticlericalism, the Revolution. Similar mass movements of wide and deep repercussion do not seem to have punctuated Brazilian history; their absence supports those who hold that its history is monotonous (Marchant 1951: 37–51; Morse 1962: 159–82). This may be traced to the continuity of Brazilian conservatism, to an oligarchy whose temper has been "more restrained, its techniques less brutal," [11] to a frequently cited national spirit of providential compromise, or merely to the fact that neither Brazilians nor foreigners have produced a large corpus of historiographical literature. Cynics may dismiss the problem by citing space, "windows" on the Atlantic coast, and fertility rates. Whatever the causes, the historian must still account for Brazil's high rate of sustained economic growth accompanied by relative political stability (or continuity) since 1850.

Historians must test what is perhaps the most general theory of Brazilian evolution, a tradition of determined yet intelligent conservatism which has known when and where to yield to pressures for change. Independence from Portuguese colonialism came late, twelve years after the Argentine May revolution, after the spectacular military campaigns of Bolívar and San Martín. It was a relatively bloodless movement, almost a *coup d'état,* despite bloody episodes in Pernambuco and Baía; it left intact plantations, livestock, mining installations, and human lives and human property, namely, chattel slaves. Just as republican Mexico preserved and indeed expanded from colonial times its major rural labor institution, debt slavery, or peonage, independent neocolonial Brazil maintained zealously chattel slavery. Rodrigues (1961) argues cogently that in 1822 Brazilian slaveholders accepted an independent monarchy primarily to insulate themselves from British pressure on the Portuguese metropolitan government to abolish the African slave trade. To pursue further the political role of slavery in neocolonial Brazil, were the unity as well as the monarchical institutions of the huge Brazilian land mass preserved despite sectional uprisings (many with republican overtones) because slaveholders gave massive support to a mon-

11 On this subject see Lambert (1953: 70–77, 118–36), Lipson (1956: 183–84). On the Brazilian conservative tradition and the "social dilemma," see Fernandes (1963: 31–71).

archy promising the maintenance of aristocracy and privilege and of the "contract between masters and slaves"?

Williams (1930: 313–336), Tannenbaum (1947), Elkins (1959), and Freyre (1945: 49, 1959: 79), among others, have claimed that Brazilian (and by extension Hispanic American) slavery was more humanitarian than the U.S. variety. Only Boxer (1963) has offered a dissident view. Perhaps the bases of such comparisons should be reviewed judiciously, for analysis requires the use of comparable criteria, such as (1) phase of agricultural development, whether expanding or stagnating, and the corresponding role of slave labor; (2) size, function, and location of plantations as well as the labor force utilized; (3) availability of a slave labor supply. Have modern students of slavery, like colonial historians, confused the humanitarianism of legal codes with the raw hell of practice? It is also premature to believe that Brazilian emancipation was unaccompanied by violence. Was slavery abolished in 1888, as the monarchy was in 1889, because the Brazilian elite finally recognized that semifeudal or neocolonial institutions impede economic growth at a certain historical juncture? Understandably the apparently peaceful integration of Negroes and non-Negroes in post-abolition Brazilian society has intrigued U.S. scholars tracing the persistence of the Ku Klux Klan and of Jim Crowism. Recent studies suggest that Negro freedmen and their descendants in Brazil until recently stayed at the lowest, most unskilled occupation levels, abandoning to the more skilled and more market-oriented immigrant laborers the better employment opportunities (Fernandez 1960; Ianni 1962; Wagley, ed., 1952). An explanation may perhaps be found in (1) the tradition of miscegenation in the lowest strata of Brazilian colonial and neocolonial society and the formation of a large body of free colored artisans and (2) consequently the relative lack of friction in incorporating freedman into the rural and urban labor force (Cardoso 1962: Chap. VI, 299–305). Is it verifiable that lacking a tradition of communal landholding as existed in pre-1910 Mexico, Negro freedmen in Brazil accepted their new role as wage laborers or sharecroppers instead of forming a *Jacquerie,* as some have characterized the early phases of the Mexican revolution?

Normano and others have noted that waves of economic specialization—dyewood, sugar, gold, cotton, coffee, rubber, ferrous ores—have highlighted Brazil's economic history.[12] Is the secret of Brazil's social evolution, rather than revolution since 1850, the succession of internal economic frontiers of enterprise in coffee, cacao, sugar, and cotton cultivation, supplemented by recurrent attempts at economic diversification? For example, what is the significance of the "big spurt" of growth, 1850–64, when investment was redirected from the profitable slave trade into the infrastructure of development—turnpikes, coach lines, railroads, urban services (gas, sewage, illumination, trolleys), portworks, textile mills, iron foundries, and banking and insurance companies? After the rate of growth had slumped in the 1880s, the new republican regime in the 1890s almost immediately on taking control stimulated new economic sectors in industry to create sectors of allegiance to republican rather than imperial institutions. Here historians have noted but not investigated an effort to accelerate the "Anglo-Saxonization" of Brazil, using not only Great Britain but also the United States as prototypes (Freyre 1949: 447–51). Should the historian introduce into this model of socio-economic growth the hypothesis that the slow but uninterrupted growth of the Brazilian economy until 1930 was in no small measure due to the influx of millions of immigrants between 1880 and 1934, whose rearing, education, skills, and levels of aspiration were subsidized by the European countries of origin and who provided a market for Brazilian industrial output? Thus, when the Vargas regime in the 1930s sought frantically to stabilize the national economy during the great depression, when overseas markets for Brazil's raw materials production slumped disastrously, it attempted to preserve a small but promising industrial sector-in-being. How this decision was made historians still must speculate, although ample documentation exists in ministerial archives. Did a comparable situation of incipient stagnation trigger the decision after 1954 to sustain the rate of growth and levels of employment despite the dangers of domestic inflation and the inelasticity of demand for Brazil's traditional exports? Is Furtado's hypothesis accurate, namely, that the policy of massive state intervention of the past decade has liberated Brazil's economy from the bottleneck of terms of

[12] On this subject see Normano (1935), Furtado (1963), Simonsen (1937), Prado (1942, 1945).

trade and capacity to import—in effect, placing Brazil at the level of self-sustained industrialization (Furtado 1961: Chap. VI)? How was this decision made? As a result of pressure-group politics, rather than via the political parties, if Lipson's hypothesis about the political process is correct (Lipson 1956)?

On reflection, it appears that the Vargas administration of 1930–45 was the great watershed in the history of modern Brazil. Wagley (1960: 177–230) has described the decades since 1930 as "the Brazilian revolution," and Bello (1956) and Werneck Sodré (1958) have also supplied provocative syntheses of the period. But these remain products of intelligent speculation until detailed monographic studies materialize. For example, unless the term "revolution" is employed only to indicate a more rapid rate of change within the existing structure, the historian must question its use to describe the Brazil's transformation since 1930. Unlike Mexico, where a massive redistribution of income was tried through agrarian reform, no similar phenomenon occurred in Brazil. Small and medium-sized holdings have increased, yet, as Sternberg (1955: 488–502) states, the traditional agricultural pattern of large estates and extensive agriculture has remained the dominant feature of the agrarian structure. How has the political influence of the 2 percent of the population active in agriculture, controlling 75 percent of total farm area, been preserved as the electorate expands? Since agricultural interests have resisted rising rural wage levels, how has there been created a larger domestic market for increased industrial output? Has the process of capital accumulation for the industrial investment of nineteenth-century Europe been repeated in Brazil, that is, by keeping to a minimum the rate of increase of real wages? In other words, the whole post-1930 period constitutes a serious lacuna of Brazilian historiography and a major field of inquiry for the economic historian.

Yet to be clarified is the ideology of the revolts in the decade preceding the October revolution, as well as that of the civilian and young military officers (*tenentes*) in 1930. Did the ideology of *tenentismo* only reflect interests and aspirations of the still small Brazilian petty bourgeoisie whence the *tenentes* were recruited?[13] Were the goals of 1930 a desire to democratize the po-

[13] On this subject see Mello Franco (1931), Barbosa Lima (1933), Santa Rosa (1933), Lins de Barros (1953), Werneck Sodré (1958: 204–13).

litical process inherited from the monarchy, to destroy the political power of regional oligarchies composed of rural magnates (the "colonels") (Leal 1948) who administered the politics of the monarchy and of the "old republic" of 1889, and to terminate the bipolar domination of the national government by the vested interests of São Paulo and Minas Gerais? To guarantee continuity of policy and orderly transmission of power, the Mexican revolutionaries engineered in the late 'twenties a remarkable instrument of political manipulation, a powerful one-party system, or what Cline has termed "single-party democracy." Why did Vargas' solution develop as a variety of creole corporativism (the New State) with legislation emanating from the executive office, with governmental censorship of communications media, with military support, and without elections (1937–45)? Via advanced codes of social legislation, however, the Vargas administration gave to the submerged masses of the interior and especially to the urban industrial laborers a sense of recognition and of participation that the old republican regime had failed to impart. Yet, while the Mexican single-party device survived with periodic adjustments, the apparatus of the New State collapsed when the military ousted Vargas in 1945. Was this a belated postwar liberal reaction to an authoritarian or creole fascist regime, or was its motivation the fear that Vargas' late flirtations with Communism foreshadowed radicalization of his regime? On the other hand, should the sustained and vigorous development of a multiparty political system since 1946, despite the suicide in office (1954) of a re-elected Vargas and the strain of an unexpected presidential resignation in 1961, lead historians to seek in the orderly constitutional processes of the slaveholding monarchy (in Oliveira Torres' nomenclature, the "crowned democracy") the roots of contemporary Brazilian political practice (Oliveira Torres 1957; Freyre 1959)? Or is the assumption of orderly constitutional processes the misinterpretation of a political process vacillating between authoritarian tradition and profound federalism? Should the origins of the present "prerevolutionary" political situation be sought in the tensions since 1946 between federalism and the presidency, between electorate and political parties, and in the fact that pressure groups have forced decisions by direct action rather than via formal political parties lacking either ideology or program? Or is the present situation largely the product of an electorate that has mushroomed from 1.5 million (1933) to 15.5 million in 1954 (Lipson 1956)? Why has the Brazilian military establishment, unlike the Argentine military since 1945, apparently maintained the role of guardian rather than overlord of the political process (Johnson 1964)?

One final comment needs to be made about the related themes of economic growth through forced-draft industrialization, the appearance of many characteristics of an "open" or permeable social structure, and the seemingly peaceful evolution of modern Brazil. The industrial and agricultural heartland of south central Brazil, marked by relatively high indices of literacy, per capita income, and political participation, has indubitably widened the gulf separating it from the generally depressed areas of the north and northeast. Has the heartland functioned for at least a century as an internal frontier, a sector of opportunity, an escape valve of social discontent? At one time, planters of the north and northeast sold their slaves to south central planters when they recognized it was uneconomic to utilize their services; periodic droughts have sent waves of wretched and penniless *flagelados* formerly by river boats and coastal steamers, now by truckloads, to work in the fields and farms of south central Brazil. Has such internal migration, historians may hypothesize, averted until now serious social conflict in the depressed areas? It is evident, too, that the industrializing sectors have gained by tapping an apparently inexhaustible and highly elastic labor supply eager to work at low, i.e., near subsistence, wages (W. A. Lewis 1963: 406–10). Furtado (1962) has declared that industrial labor in the heartland constitutes a sort of Brazilian labor "aristocracy" resistant to revolutionary blandishments. Similarly, has the heartland generated enough economic opportunity so that the extended families of former agrarian and commercial elite groups have been able to participate in new enterprise, financial, distributive, industrial? With "room at the top," so to speak, has the elite accepted newcomers from the middle classes and presumably some middle-class values and aspirations? Is Lipson (1956) correct in his diagnosis that "instead of a transfer of power to the mass of the population" over the past century there have been in Brazil only periodic internal arrangements "and a relatively slight extension of the circle of privilege"? If so, this contrasts markedly with the situation in Colombia, according to

Beals (1952–53). In Colombia, lack of economic opportunity at the elite level has forced many of its members down into the middle-class occupations, fastening their value orientation upon numerically weak middle groups and siring a rigid political system whose salient characteristic is violence. Indeed, is it plausible for diplomatic historians to assume that the current emergence of an independent, hence unpredictable, Brazilian foreign policy, as well as the unquestioned Brazilian paternity of the Alliance for Progress in Kubitschek's Operation Pan America, reflect the predictable pressures of a rapidly changing society and economy?

ARGENTINA

In the post-1850 history of Mexico and Brazil, the historian finds a series of progressive surges either smashing or steadily eroding traditional institutions. In the post-1930 decades, moreover, and especially since the end of World War II, the major strains may be logically diagnosed as symptomatic of generalized growth, i.e., broad-scale industrialization, literacy campaigns, social mobility, and the search for and even the achievement of a measure of democratic political consensus. In Latin American diplomacy, he notes a new constellation of leadership, that of Brazil and only slightly behind, Mexico, replacing the once undisputed hegemony of Argentina from 1889 to 1936. But when the historian turns to post-1930 Argentina, he observes that its great twentieth-century watershed, the Peron era from 1945 to 1955, was a postwar phenomenon, a belated Argentine radicalism in a hemisphere consolidating rather than initiating revolutionary changes. In contrast with Mexican and Brazilian experimentation and modernization of the 1930s, Argentina offers what Whitaker (1954: 62–65) has called an era of "conservative restoration." As the historian maps the salient features of the contemporary Argentine landscape, he locates generalized stagnation, political fragmentation, and a society deeply divided against itself. While these symptoms are indisputable, the roots of the Argentine paradox have yet to be satisfactorily unraveled (Whitaker 1961b: 103–12).

Are the roots to be found in the nature of the revolt against Spanish colonial rule, as Acevedo (1957) and Barreiro (1955) believe, or in the unitary-federal schism that yawned in the decade of unitary experiment, the 1820s, associated with the figure of Bernardino Rivadavia? Or in the almost twenty-five years of authoritarian nationalist control of the right-wing federal, Rosas, whose career and action have always remained the subject of scholarly and not so scholarly debate? Rosas' ouster in 1852 seemed to have inaugurated a unitary-federal compromise, the mechanics of which have not been clarified. Was this compromise, reminiscent of the Brazilian era of reconciliation between liberals and conservatives (1850–68) and Mexican liberalism under the Porfiriato, an agreement between the rural and urban oligarchies that political fratricide dammed the flow of foreign capital and labor to a capital-scarce and labor-scarce Argentine economy? Alberdi's *Bases* (1852) and *Sistema económico y rentístico* (1854) would thus foreshadow the later appeal of positivism's order and progress. Such a compromise may have sired the patrician liberalism of the *Unicato* which dominated the Argentine polity and economy from 1880 to 1916 and, after Radicalism's brief interregnum under Irigoyen, was resurrected from 1930 to 1943. Both the republican revolution in Brazil (1889) and the Mexican revolution (1910) destroyed political systems unresponsive to the pressures of change. Why, the historian must ask, did violence in Argentina during 1890 (the *Noventa*) topple an administration but leave intact the political system of the Unicato and spawn parties of protest, Socialist and Radical (*Revista de Historia* 1957)?

Prior to the Peronist decade, Radicalism provided the Argentine masses with an ideology, a party, and a charismatic leader— none of which have historians carefully examined. Once in power, it was torn by factionalism, weakened by opportunism, corroded by corruption. As a form of Argentine progressivism with its emphasis upon political democracy, it seemed to aggregrate a variety of interest groups, despite or perhaps because of the ambiguity of its ideology and the turgidity of its leader's oratory. Del Mazo has published a useful but far from impartial study of Radicalism. Historians should supply an objective balance-sheet of program and realizations, and critical biographies of Irigoyen and Alvear (Del Mazo 1952; Gálvez 1940). Equally superficial is our knowledge of anarcho-syndicalism and socialism in Argentina. Why, for example, has Argentine socialism failed to generate mass appeal? [14] Irigoyen's and Radicalism's fall have been attributed to Irigoyen's senility, the corruption of party hacks, and the great depression (Rennie 1945). Others have theorized that Irigoyen's attempts to barter Argentine foodstuffs for Soviet crude oil led conservatives to engineer with the military the revolution of 1930 (*Revista de Historia* 1958).

It was during the conservative restoration that there surfaced tendencies that Argentines and non-Argentines had long thought moribund: militarism, clericalism, elitism, and overt manipulation of the political process. The historian may ask if the economic foundation of reaction in the 1930s was Argentine conservatives' faith in traditional dependence upon hitherto successful beef and grain export sectors on the assumption that Great Britain and other European customers would sustain the Argentine economy indefinitely. Or was it characteristic of a government run by and for agrarian and ranching interest groups to overlook the dangers of a massive rural exodus to the Buenos Aires megalopolis, to underestimate the pressures for diversification through industrialization, for unionism and social welfare legislation, and to defraud systematically the restless urban and rural masses at the polls (Weill 1944; Palacio 1955; Puiggrós 1956; Galletti 1961)? Was the political foundation of the restoration the conservatives' skill in wooing the collaboration of right-wing elements among the Radicals in the *concordancia* or, as some prefer to term it, the *contubernio?*

Obviously this is not the place to review the literature on the Peron era (see Barager 1959; Hoffmann 1956, 1959). However, two major questions may be appropriate. First, is it plausible to assume that between 1943 and 1945 segments of the Argentine middle classes joined urban labor and sectors of the military to overthrow an incompetent, reactionary conservative regime? If so, what were the promises of Peronism to the middle classes? This line of reasoning suggests that in 1955 the middle classes,

[14] Potash, who has been investigating the Argentine military after 1920, argues that "socialism as an imported ideology that stressed rationality, internationalism, and principle rather than romanticism, nationalism, and personalities seemed somewhat un-Argentine to the lower-class mind. A contributing factor was its deep-seated and doctrinaire anti-clericalism, which, outside Buenos Aires and a few other areas, was a self-imposed kiss of death" (Letter, Amherst, Mass., August 23, 1963).

fearing radicalization of the Peronist regime, chose to abandon it and joined sectors of the military and remnants of the still influential oligarchy to overthrow it. How, then, did that favorite target of Peronist vituperation, the oligarchy, preserve itself during the Peronist decade? Because, for all the rhetoric, Peronism never considered seriously agrarian reform? Given the mass appeal of Peronism's "social justice," why did the urban masses accept so docilely the ouster of Peron?

In the second place, what are the key factors in the long-term stagnation of the Argentine economy? During the last three years of the Peron regime, the rate of economic growth dropped, presumably through Peronist authoritarian ineptitude. Yet how is the historian to account for subsequent stagnation? By defects in the national character, as Fillol (1961) proposes? By an alliance of privileged landholding and industrial groups pursuing intransigently a policy of economic liberalism no longer adequate for Argentine conditions (Portnoy 1961)? By a large middle class unwilling to accept governmental controls, divided in its aspirations, ready to yield political decision-making to "military officers, and powerful business, banking and landowning groups" in order to stave off the political participation of the urban masses (New York *Times* 1963; Germani 1960, 1962)? Or does the trajectory of Argentine twentieth-century evolution imply that a large amorphous middle class in crisis will, as the European middle classes did in the interwar decades, turn to charismatic demogogues, clericalism, anti-Semitism, the parody of its former democratic traditions, and militarism?

Understandably modern Latin American militarism has drawn scholars' attention in recent years. Avoiding the problem of definition of varieties of militarism, it is obvious that militarism is no novel phenomenon in Latin American history.[15] However, its virulence in Argentina, presumably one of the most modernized republics, requires full-scale historical case study. There it cannot be dismissed as the product of nonprofessionalism; the Argentine military have not shown strong expansionist tendencies, and aggressive neighbors in recent times have not threatened Argentina's territorial integrity. How then does the historian explain the creation of a military caste in an "open" society? To general-

15 About this subject see Lieuwen (1960), McAlister (1960, 1961), Johnson (1962, 1964), Potash (1961), Wyckoff (1960).

ize that militarism may follow "in the event of a serious political or economic crisis" in Argentina or anywhere, only begs the question: Why have Argentine civilian governments collapsed repeatedly since 1930 leaving to the military the role of constituting a "coalition government with groups of officers substituting for political parties" (McAlister 1961; Potash 1961)? Does the Argentine experience indicate that the military remain a bulwark in Latin America for the existing structure of society, except where total defeat in revolutionary movements has reformed them as in Mexico after the revolution and Cuba since 1959?

CUBA

Until 1959, historians saw little in the development of Cuba to indicate that it would become the scene of Latin America's second major social upheaval of the twentieth century, and the first socialist republic of the western hemisphere. Its isolation, its military garrison, its role as refugees' haven during the anti-colonial upheaval against Spanish rule, and—the historian may speculate—the enjoyment of *de facto* free trade from 1808 onward, insulated it from the changes sweeping over Latin America, 1808 to 1824. With Puerto Rico, it remained a Spanish colony. With Brazil and the U.S South, it formed part of "plantation America" (Wagley 1960b) in the nineteenth century, producing for export coffee, sugar, and tobacco with forced labor, African Negroes. On three occasions between 1868 and 1959 Cuban revolutionaries were embittered and disillusioned by their meager results, first during the Ten Years' War (1868–78), then in the struggle against Spain (1895–98) ending in the Platt Amendment, and finally the mass, bloody uprising that toppled Machado and led to the failure of the nationalist regime of Grau San Martín (Corbitt 1963). From the perspective of five years of Cuban revolution it may be argued that the lessons of these abortive movements as well, perhaps, as those of the Mexican and Guatemalan revolutions of the twentieth century made Castro and his collaborators—all historically minded and highly literate —intractable, unbending, and uncompromising where principle was involved.

Two major clusters of Cuban problems will engage the historian for some time. With that perverse insight historians generally obtain from hindsight rather than foresight, it can be seen that in the past half-century of Cuban history there have cropped up all the ingredients of a massive revolutionary explosion. The first major question for historians concerns, therefore, not the isolation of the factors contributing to the revolutionary explosion but rather the combination of factors, external and internal, that destroyed the Batista regime in 1958, entrusted the modernization of Cuba to the 26 of July movement and led to the tragic estrangement of Cuba and the United States. What forces led the Batista regime in the 1950s to what appears to have been the generalized alienation of almost all sectors of Cuban society? The idiosyncrasies of Batista and Castro? Or should the historian take a broader perspective and exhume the conflict suggested by Jenks (1928) in "the efforts of Cuba to reconcile nationality with the persistent penetration of alien enterprise and capital"? Much suggestive material will be found in the publications of Guerra y Sanchez (1927, 1935), Buell (1935), Thomson (1935–36), Portell Vilá (1938–41), Roig de Leuchsenring (1935, 1960), Nelson (1950), Hunter (1951), and Smith (1960), to name only a few, as well as in hitherto untouched manuscript materials in government and business archives in the United States and Cuba.

The second problem-cluster luring the historian—determination of the critical phases of the revolution since 1959, assessment of the factors involved in decision-making, evaluation of the consequences, domestic and foreign—will demand of the profession the maximum powers of source criticism, objectivity, perspective, and synthesis. For a long time to come the historian will have to learn to live cheek by jowl with the polemicist, for the crucible of modern social revolution is more conducive to the pyrotechnics of polemic than to the practice of the historian's craft. In Mexico and Bolivia the basic reform surge, agrarian reform, led to parcelization of large estates. In Cuba, on the contrary, there developed a rapid transition from the privately owned to the state-owned plantation, bypassing the phase of peasant agriculture. Is the historian to explain this phenomenon by a century of large-scale heavily capitalized agriculture which transformed large segments of the rural population into a plantation proletariat, gave Cuba one of Latin America's highest per capita income levels, and made it one of the most literate nations of the area (Sweezy and Huberman 1960: Chap. X; Seers 1964: Chap. I)? In the second place, given the presence of a powerful, modernized bourgeoisie, by Latin American standards at any rate, why did this social segment lose its influence over the revolutionary process, unlike the Mexican bourgeoisie after 1910? Because Castro resolved to betray his class, or because the revolutionary leadership in the spring of 1959 sensed in the Cuban bourgeoisie only another exploiting group, eager to nationalize foreign property and enterprise for their private use? Mexicans deny any clear ideological formulation in their revolution, and most observers of the Cuban scene argue that in January, 1959, the 26 of July movement had no well defined ideology, that it was then only a "national revolutionary" movement with only a common enemy to destroy, but no social and political program for the period of revolutionary reconstruction. Accepting this assumption, historians must then explain the rapid transition from revolutionary eclecticism of "liberty with bread and without terror" in January, 1959, to the proclamation of a socialist Cuba two years later. One school of interpretation argues that Castro arrived at this proclamation because he had to accept from Cuban Communists the elements he lacked, "disciplined and experienced cadres, the ideology and the international support to switch revolutions . . . " (Draper 1962: 57), while the opposing interpretation stresses external rather than internal pressures and contends that the revolutionaries "alienated from the West, in need of economic aid, and military and political support, . . . were to seek new friends" (Zeitlin and Scheer 1963: 142). Ultimately, of course, the historian of modern Latin America will have to address himself to the broader problem of the Cuban Revolution's contributions to the general theory of revolution in the twentieth century.

Some Broad Trends and Research Designs

This highly subjective review of lacunae in modern Latin American historiography should illustrate what is meant by the rich diversity and complexity of historical phenomena in that area. It should indicate that at specific epochs since roughly 1750 major foci of interest have drawn scholars' attention: the struggle for political independence and commercial liberty against Luso-Spanish overlordship, the search for new principles of authority and a viable economic base in neocolonial decades, the anticlerical crusades to eliminate the political role of ecclesiasticism, the integration of the Latin American and the world economy after 1850, the rise of the middle classes, the awakening of the masses, and in most recent times the quest for indigenous response to the problems of economic growth through industrialism. Above all, the survival of conservatism or traditionalism almost everywhere leads historians and social scientists to re-assess the taproots of its resilience.

After the United States it is Latin America that has had political independence longer than any once colonial area. By comparison with most areas of Asia and Africa, Latin America is not backward, although pockets of comparable human misery certainly exist in both rural and urban areas. Yet Latin America since the 1820s, and especially since 1850, has not achieved a large measure of economic autonomy; hence, many of its scholars and intellectual community refer to their colonial past *and* present, to the imperialist tradition of Great Britain and latterly of the United States. Historians must recall that newly emergent areas of Africa and the Near and Far East have not turned for guidance to Latin America. Is this because they discern in this area the institutions, values, and resistance to change that they desire ardently to abandon? In the quest for the foundations of conservative tradition, what should the historian examine? The hacienda and the plantation? The crossing of the elite groups from agriculture to distribution, banking, and heavy industry? The unexpected plasticity of the Church? The example of foreign corporations? The military? In short, is there a broad framework for the investigation of general and specific aspects of conservatism?

Ever since Bolton (1939) assayed a broad interpretation of the frontier as a unifying factor in the development of the western hemisphere, historians have been circumspect in floating new trial balloons of synthesis. Whitaker (1951: 73) has proposed as a "unifying idea" that Latin America's experience be viewed as part of the common experience of the Atlantic Triangle, of Europe, Anglo-, and Latin America. In the quest for methods of fusing "liberty with justice," the individual and society, and in common European roots Griffin (1951: 122–23) perceives a common hemispheric theme. An economist drawn to the historical origins of contemporary phenomena, Mosk (1948) points to the integration of the Latin American with the industrializing economy of Western Europe and the United States after 1850, to the outflow of raw materials in return for the inflow of consumer goods, capital goods, technology, investment, and skills.[16] By extrapolation students of the modern period may profit from the study of colonial demographic variations whose magnitude Borah, Cook, Simpson, and Kubler have been painstakingly documenting, but whose wide ramifications for Latin American history as a whole await fuller elucidation. What is common to all such approaches is their complementarity, not their exclusivism. They are scattered vantage points overlooking a vast canyon of unexplored or partially explored human experience.

It is perhaps through the prism of economic growth and related political and social aspects, i.e., via economic and political history, that historians may find the most satisfactory overview at this historical juncture. Have the principal instruments of modernization been technological innovations, the railroad, the steamship, and the electric generator, which have undermined isolation at both international and intranational levels? Or the secular trend in terms of trade, adversely affecting Latin America's capacity to import, and thereby impelling the area to abandon the international division of labor, to diversify rather than emphasize agricultural specialization, as Prebisch (1950) insists? [17]

The economic historian may hypothesize that there have been two principal stages in Latin American history since the late fifteenth century. Western Europeans brought commercial capitalism, but its effects were limited. Beside a Europe-oriented sector, there remained a large traditional precapitalist, or subsistence, sector creating a "dual economy" and, of course, two cultures, urban and rural (Mosk 1954: 3–26). Accelerated economic integration between 1850 and 1914 expanded the market-oriented agricultural sectors, encroaching upon the precapitalist sectors. With the movement toward industrialism, whose Latin American origins before World War I may be presumed in Mexico and Brazil, the second stage appears, the capitalist-industrial phase, which has had so varied an impact, political, social, cultural, and ideological, and which wars and depression have in-

---

[16] Bolton's interpretation as well as the articles by Whitaker, Griffin, and Mosk may be found in Hanke, ed. (1964).

[17] See also the exposition of Prebisch's theory of Latin American underdevelopment in Baer (1963: 144–61). Prebisch's original manifesto should be compared with his recent reflections (1963) on the problems of Latin American development.

tensified. Modernization under the capitalist-industrial system is no reversible process, but it might well be argued that in historical perspective it has not severed Latin America from the principal social legacy of its colonial heritage, in Gibson's words (1963: 389), "the rigid class system, which neither the revolution for independence nor any of the subsequent revolutions successfully destroyed, and which is only now being partially modified."

Thus, the Latin American historian must undertake that reinterpretation every generation of historians faces, he must re-examine prejudices, premises, hypotheses, implicit or explicit, in the light of unfolding reality. He may do this as an individual scholar, ready to turn to the resources of allied disciplines when necessary, or as participant in a research team. He must constantly review the broad issues and generalizations of Latin American history and test them at all levels, preferably at the local level—village, municipal, state, provincial, or departmental —searching for primary materials. In the study of hemispheric diplomacy, he must obtain a comprehensive background in the domestic foundations of the Latin American republics' foreign policy (Wood 1961). So closely related is the contemporary world that the historian examining relevant issues of the past is drawn inevitably to the main currents of his craft as practiced anywhere. But whatever his area of interest or specialization, the Latin American historian will sooner or later find that he must come to grips with the tenacity of conservatism—the persistent flexibility of traditionalism, whether his theme be hacienda, plantation, or mine, peddler, moneylender, or commercial or mortgage bank, factor or importer, enterprise of indigenous entrepreneurs or branch factory of foreign firms, the problem of the domestic market and capital accumulation or international trade, capital flows and the amortization and servicing of public and private debt, the church as bulwark of the past or instrument of social change, the military as professional core, as modernizing agent, or as instrument of social and political immobility.

But enough of research opportunities and grand designs. Historians, to work!

BIBLIOGRAPHY

Acevedo, Edberto Oscar
1957   El ciclo histórico de la revolución de mayo. Seville.

Latin American Historiography 115

Alamán, Lucas
1844–49 Disertaciones sobre la historia de la república mexicana. Mexico City. 3 vols.
1849–52 Historia de Méjico. Mexico City. 5 vols.
Alberdi, Juan Bautista
1852 Bases y puntos de partida para la organización política de la república argentina. Buenos Aires.
1854 Sistema ecónomico y rentístico de la confederación argentina según su constitución de 1853. Valparaiso.
Amunátegui, Miguel Luís
1862 Descubrimiento y conquista de Chile. Santiago, Chile.
Arcila Farías, E.
1946 Economía colonial de Venezuela. Mexico City.
1950 Comercio entre Mexico y Venezuela. Mexico City.
Armillas, Pedro
1951 Tecnología, formaciones socioeconomicas y religión en Mesoamerica. *In* Civilizations of ancient America, selected papers of the International Congress of Americanists, Vol. I. Chicago.
1962 The native period in the history of the New World. Mexico City.
Baer, W.
1963 La economía de Prebisch y de la CEPAL. Trimestre Economico 30: 144–61.
Baltra Cortes, Alberto
1961 Crecimiento económico de América Latina. Santiago, Chile.
Barager, J. R.
1959 The historiography of the Rio de La Plata area since 1830. Hispanic American Historical Review 39: 588–642.
Barbosa Lima Sobrinho, A. J.
1933 A verdade sobre a revolução de 1930. Rio de Janeiro.
Barreiro, José P.
1955 El espíritu de mayo y el revisionismo historico. Buenos Aires.
Barros Arana, D.
1874 Los antiguos habitantes de Chile. Santiago, Chile.
1844–1902 Historia general de Chile. Santiago, Chile. 16 vols.
Bastos, Abiguar
1946 Prestes e a revolucão social. Rio de Janeiro.
Bazant, J.
1960 Tres revoluciones mexicanas. Historia Mexicana 10: 232.
Beals, Ralph
1952–53 Social stratification in Latin America. American Journal of Sociology 58: 327–39.
Bello, J. M.
1956 História da república (1889–1945). (Addenda, 1945–54.) São Paulo.
Bernstein, Harry
1952 Modern and contemporary Latin America. New York.
Bolton, Herbert E.
1913 Guide to materials for the history of the United States in the principal archives of Mexico. Washington, D.C.
1933 The epic of greater America. American Historical Review 38: 448–74.
1939 Wider horizons of American history. New York.
Borah, W. W.
1956 Representative institutions in the Spanish empire in the sixteenth century. III: The New World. The Americas 12: 246–57.

116 Stanley J. Stein

Borah, W. W., and S. F. Cook
1963 The aboriginal population of Central Mexico on the eve of the Spanish conquest. Ibero-Americana, Vol. 45.

Boxer, Charles R.
1963 Race relations in the Portuguese colonial empire, 1415–1825. London.

Buarque de Holanda, Sergio (ed.)
1960– Historia geral da civilização brasileira. São Paulo.

Buell, R. L.
1935 Problems of the new Cuba. Report of the Commission on Cuban Affairs. New York.

Burgin, Miron
1947 Research in Latin American economics and economic history. Inter-American Economic Affairs 1: 3–22.

Bustamante, Carlos Maria de
1829 Historia del emperador Moctheuzoma, Xocoyotzín. Mexico City.
1836–38 Notas y suplemento. In A. Cavo, Los tres siglos de México durante el gobierno español hasta las entrada del ejercito trigarante. Mexico City. 4 vols.

Cardoso, Fernando Henrique
1962 Capitalismo e escravidão no Brasil meridional. São Paulo. Chap. 6, pp. 299–305.

Castañeda, Jorge
1963 Revolution and foreign policy: Mexico's experience. Political Science Quarterly 78 (September): 391–417.

Céspedes del Castillo, G.
1945 La avería en el comercio de Indias. Seville.

Chamberlain, Robert S.
1954 Simpson's The encomienda in New Spain and recent encomienda studies. Hispanic American Historical Review 34 (May): 238–40.

Chapman, C. C.
1919 Catalogue of materials in the Archivo General de Indias for the history of the Pacific Coast and the American Southwest. Berkeley, Calif.

Chaunu, Pierre, and Huguette Chaunu
1955–60 Séville et l'Atlantique (1504–1650). Paris. 8 vols.

Chávez Orosco, Luíz
1938 Historia económica y social de Mexico. Mexico City.

Chevalier, F.
1952 La formation des grands domaines au Méxique. Paris.
1961 Le soulèvement de Zapata. Annales. Economies. Sociétés. Civilizations. Vol. 16: 66–82.

Cline, H. F.
1949 Civil congregations of the Indians in New Spain, 1598–1606. Hispanic American Historical Review 29: 349–69.
1953 The United States and Mexico. Cambridge, Mass.
1962 Mexico: revolution to evolution, 1940–1960. London and New York.

Cline, H. F. (ed.)
1959 Latin American studies in the United States. Washington, D.C.

Cook, S. F., and L. B. Simpson
1948 The population of Central Mexico in the sixteenth century. Ibero-Americana, Vol. 31.

Corbitt, D. C.
  1963   Cuban revisionist interpretations of Cuba's struggle for independence. Hispanic American Historical Review 43 (August): 395–404.
Cosío Villegas, Daniel (ed.)
  1955–63   Historia moderna de México. Mexico City. 6 vols. Vol. I (1955): La República restaurada. La vida política, pp. 45–107.
Cruz Costa, João
  1956   Contribuição à historia das idéias no Brasil. Rio de Janeiro.
Del Mazo, Gabriel
  1952   El radicalismo. Buenos Aires.
Diffie, B. W.
  1945   Latin American civilization: colonial period. Harrisburg, Pa.
Dore, Ronald P.
  1963   Some comparisons of Latin American studies and Asian studies with special reference to research on Japan. Social Science Research Council, Items 17 (June): 13.
Draper, Theodore
  1962   Castro's revolution: myths and realities. New York, p. 57.
Elkins, Stanley
  1959   Slavery, a problem in American institutional and intellectual life. Chicago.
Fernandes, Florestan
  1960   Mudanças sociais no Brasil. São Paulo.
  1963   Reflexões sobre a mudança social no Brasil. Revista Brasileira de Estudos Políticos, No. 15 (January–July), pp. 31–71.
Fillol, T. R.
  1961   Social factors in economic development. The Argentine case. Cambridge, Mass.
Flores Olea, Victor, et al.
  1959   Tres interrogaciones sobre el presente y el futuro de México. Cuadernos Americanos, año XVIII, 102 (No. 1): 44–75.
Freyre, Gilberto
  1945   Brazil: an interpretation. New York.
  1949   República. In Manual bibliográfico de estudos brasileiros, Rubens Borba de Morais and William Berrien, eds. Rio de Janeiro, pp. 447–57.
  1959   New World in the tropics. New York.
Frondizi, Silvio
  1955–56   La realidad Argentina. Buenos Aires. 2 vols.
Furtado, Celso
  1961   Desenvolvimento e subdesenvolvimento. Rio de Janeiro.
  1962   Reflecciones sobre la pre-revolución brasileña. Trimestre Económico 29: 373–84. [Translated as Brazil: what kind of revolution? Foreign Affairs 41 (1963): 526–35.]
  1963   The economic growth of Brazil. Berkeley, Calif.
Galletti, Alfredo
  1961   La politica y los partidos. Buenos Aires.
Gálvez, Manuel
  1940   Vida de Hipólito Yrigoyen. Buenos Aires.
Garcia Icázbalceta, J.
  1858–66   Colección de documentos para la historia de México. Mexico City.
  1886   Bibliografía mexicana del siglo XVI. Mexico City.

118 Stanley J. Stein

Germani, Gino
1960 Política e massa. Revista brasileira de estudos políticos. Estudos sociais e políticos. Rio de Janeiro. No. 13.
1962 Politica y sociedad en una época de transición de la sociedad traditional a la sociedad de masas. Buenos Aires.
Gibson, Charles
1948 The Inca concept of sovereignty and the Spanish administration in Peru. Austin, Texas.
1952 Tlaxcala in the sixteenth century. New Haven.
1955 The transformation of the Indian community in New Spain. Cahiers d'histoire mondiale 2: 581–607.
1958 The colonial period in Latin American history. Washington, D.C.
1960 The Aztec aristocracy in colonial Mexico. Comparative Studies in Society and History 2 (January): 169–96.
1963 Colonial institutions and contemporary Latin America: Social and cultural life. Hispanic American Historical Review 43: 380–89.
Gibson, Charles, and B. Keen
1957 Trends of United States studies in Latin American history. American Historical Review 62 (July): 855–77.
Góngora, M.
1951 El estado en el derecho indiano. Época de fundación. Santiago, Chile.
Griffin, Charles C.
1949 Economic and social aspects of the era of Spanish-American independence. Hispanic American Historical Review 29: 170–87.
1951 Unidad y variedad en la historia americana. In Ensayos sobre la historia del nuevo mundo. E. McInnis, ed. Mexico City.
1961 The national period in the history of the New World. An outline and commentary. Mexico City.
1962 Los temas sociales y economicos en la época de la independencia. Caracas.
Griffith, W. J.
1960 The historiography of Central America since 1830. Hispanic American Historical Review 40: 548–69.
Guerra y Sánchez, R.
1927 Azúcar y población en las Antillas. Havana.
1935 La expansión territorial de los Estados Unidos a expensas de España y de los hispanoamericanos. Havana.
Guerra y Sanchez, R., et al.
1952 Historia de la nación cubana. Havana. 10 vols.
Hale, C.
1963 Liberalismo mexicano. Historia Mexicana 47: 457–63.
Hanke, Lewis
1949 The Spanish struggle for justice in the conquest of America. Philadelphia.
Hanke, Lewis (ed.)
1964 Do the Americas have a common history? A critique of the Bolton theory. New York.
Haring, C. H.
1947 The Spanish empire in America. New York.
Hill, R. R.
1916 Descriptive catalogue of the documents relating to the history of the United States in the Papeles Procedentes de Cuba. Washington, D.C.

Hoffmann, F.
1956 Peron and after. Hispanic American Historical Review 36: 510–28.
1959 Peron and after: Part II. Hispanic American Historical Review 39: 212–33.
Howe, Walter
1949 The mining guild of New Spain and its tribunal general, 1770–1821. Cambridge, Mass.
Humphreys, R. A.
1946 The evolution of modern Latin America. London and New York.
1950 Economic aspects of the fall of the Spanish American empire. Revista de Historia de America, pp. 450–56.
1952 Liberation in South America, 1806–1827. London.
Hunter, J. M.
1951 Investment as a factor in the economic development of Cuba, 1899–1935. Inter-American Economic Affairs 5 (Winter): 82–100.
Hussey, R. D.
1934 The Caracas company, 1728–1784. Cambridge, Mass.
Ianni, Octavio
1962 As metamorfoses do escravo: apogeu e crise de escravatura no Brasil meridional. São Paulo.
Jenks, Leland H.
1928 Our Cuban colony: a study in sugar. New York.
Johnson, John J.
1958 Political change in Latin America. Stanford, Calif.
1964 The military and society in Latin America. Stanford, Calif.
Johnson, John J. (ed.)
1962 The role of the military in underdeveloped countries. Princeton, N.J., pp. 91–129.
Jones, C. K.
1922 Hispanic American bibliographies. Baltimore.
Keniston, R. H.
1920 List of works for the study of Hispanic American history. New York.
Konetzke, R.
1946 El mestizage y su importancia en el desarrollo de la población hispano-americana durante la época colonial. Revista de Indias 7: 7–44, 215–37.
Kubler, George
1946 The Quechua in the colonial world. In Handbook of South American Indians, Julian H. Steward, ed., Vol. 2: 331–410.
1952 The Indian caste of Peru, 1795–1940. Washington, D.C.
Lambert, Jacques
1953 Le Brésil, structure sociale et institutions politiques. Paris.
Lanning, J. T.
1940 Academic culture in the Spanish colonies. New York.
Leal, V. N.
1948 Coronelismo, enxada, e voto. Rio de Janeiro.
Leonard, I.
1949 Books of the brave. Cambridge, Mass.
Levene, Ricardo
1927 Investigaciones acerca de la historia económica del virreinato del Plata. La Plata.
Levene, Ricardo (ed.)
1936–50 Historia de la nación argentina. Buenos Aires. 10 vols.

120   Stanley J. Stein

Lewis, W. Arthur
1963 Economic development with unlimited supplies of labor. *In* The economics of underdevelopment, A. N. Agarwala and S. P. Singh, eds. New York.
Lewis, Oscar
1959 Five families: Mexican case studies in the culture of poverty. New York.
Lieuwen, E.
1960 Arms and politics in Latin America. New York.
Lins de Barros, João Alberto
1953 Memórias de um revolucionário. Rio de Janeiro.
Lipson, L.
1956 Government in contemporary Brazil. Canadian Journal of Economics and Political Science 22: 183–98.
McAlister, Lyle
1960 The military in government. Hispanic American Historical Review 60: 582–90.
1961 Civil military relations in Latin America. Journal of Inter-American Studies 3: 341–49.
1963 Social structure and social change in New Spain. Hispanic American Historical Review 63: 349–70.
Marchant, Alexander
1942 From barter to slavery. Baltimore.
1951 The unity of Brazilian history. *In* Brazil: portrait of half a continent, A. Marchant and T. Lynn Smith, eds. New York.
Martínez Estrada, Ezequiel
1933 Radiografía de la pampa. Buenos Aires.
Mauro, Frederic
1961 México y Brasil: dos economías coloniales comparadas. Historia Mexicana 10 (April–June): 570–87.
1960 Le Portugal et l'Atlantique au XVIIè siècle. Paris.
Mello Franco, Virgilio
1931 Outubro, 1930. Rio de Janeiro.
Miguel Pereira, Lucia
1952 Cinquenta anos de literatura. Rio de Janeiro.
Miranda, J.
1952 Las ideas y las instituciones políticas mexicanas: primera parte, 1521–1820. Mexico City.
Morley, S. G.
1956 The ancient Maya. Stanford, Calif. 3rd ed.
Mörner, Magnus
1960 El mestizage en la historia de Ibero-America. Stockholm.
Morse, Richard M.
1962 Some themes of Brazilian history. South Atlantic Journal 61: 159–82.
Mosk, Sanford A.
1948 Latin America and the world economy, 1850–1914. Inter-American Economic Affairs 2: 53–82.
1949 Latin American economics: the field and its problems. Inter-American Economic Affairs 3: 55–64.
1954 Indigenous economies in Latin America. Inter-American Economic Affairs 8: 3–26.

Naylor, R. A.
1962 Research opportunities in modern Latin America: I. Mexico and Central America. The Americas 18: 353–65.

Nelson, L.
1950 Rural Cuba. Minneapolis.

New York Times
1963 [Editorial.] July 5.

Normano, J. F.
1935 Brazil: a study of economic types. Chapel Hill, N.C.

Oliveira Torres, J. C. de
1957 A democracia coroada (Teoria política do império). Rio de Janeiro.

Orozco y Berra, M.
1880 Historia antigua y de la conquista de Mexico. 4 vols.
1938 Historia de la dominación española en Mexico. Mexico City.

Palacio, E.
1955 Historia de la Argentina. Buenos Aires.

Palerm, A.
1955 The agriculture basis of urban civilization in Meso-America. In Irrigation civilization: a comparative study, Julian H. Steward et al., eds. Washington, D.C., pp. 28–42.

Parry, J. H.
1957 The sale of public office in the Spanish Indies under the Hapsburgs. Ibero-Americana, Vol. 37.

Picón-Salas, M.
1944 De la conquista a la independencia. Mexico City.

Pinto Santa Cruz, Aníbal
1958 Chile: un caso de desarrollo frustrado. Santiago, Chile.

Portell Vilá, H.
1938–41 Historia de Cuba en sus relaciones con los Estados Unidos y España. Havana. 4 vols.

Portnoy, Leopóldo
1961 Análisis critico de la economía argentina. Buenos Aires.

Potash, Robert A.
1959 El banco de avío de Mexico. Mexico City.
1960 The historiography of Mexico since 1821. Hispanic American Historical Review 40: 383–424.
1961 The changing role of the military in Argentina. Journal of Inter-American Studies 3: 571–77.
1963 Personal communication. Amherst, Mass., August 23.

Prado Caio, Jr.
1942 Formação do Brasil contemporâneo. Colônia. São Paulo.
1945 Historia econômica do Brasil. São Paulo.

Prebisch, Raúl
1950 The economic development of Latin America and its principal problems. United Nations, Dept. of Economic Affairs (ECN 12/89 Rev. 1).
1963 Towards a dynamic development policy for Latin America (ECN 12/680 April 14, 1963); Política (Mexico) 4: No. 75 (June 1).

Puiggrós, Ricardo
1956 Historia crítica de les partidos políticos argentinos. Buenos Aires.

Ramos, Samuel
1934 El perfil del hombre y de la cultura en México. Mexico City.

Rennie, Ysabel F.
1945 The Argentine Republic. New York.
Revista de Historia [Argentina]
1957 La crisis del 90. Buenos Aires. No. 1.
1958 La crisis de 1930. Buenos Aires. No. 3, pp. 3, 59, 70–71.
Robertson, J. A.
1910 List of documents in Spanish archives relating to the history of the United States. Washington, D.C.
Rodrigues, José Honório
1961 Africa e Brasil: outro horizonte. Rio de Janeiro.
Roig de Leuchsenring, E.
1935 Historia de la enmienda Platt: una interpretación de la realidad cubana. Havana. 2 vols.
1960 Cuba no debe su independencia a los Estados Unidos. Havana, 3rd edition.
Romanell, P.
1952 Making of the Mexican mind. Lincoln, Neb.
Romero, José Luís
1946 Las ideas políticas en Argentina. Mexico City.
Rosenzweig Hernandez, Fernando
1962 El proceso político y desarrollo económico de México. Trimestre Económico 29: 519–24.
Rowe, John Howland
1946 Inca culture at the time of the Spanish conquest. In Handbook of the South American Indians, Julian H. Steward, ed., Vol. 2: 183–330.
1957 The Inca under Spanish colonial institutions. Hispanic American Historical Review 38: 155–99.
Santa Rosa, Virginio
1933 O sentido do tenentismo. Rio de Janeiro.
Scholes, W. V.
1957 Mexican politics under the Juarez regime, 1855–1872. Columbia, Mo.
Seers, Dudley (ed.)
1964 Cuba, the economic and social revolution. Chapel Hill, N.C.
Shepard, W. R.
1907 Guide to the materials for the history of the United States in Spanish archives. Washington, D.C.
Simonsen, Roberto C.
1937 História econónica do Brasil, 1500–1820. São Paulo. 2 vols.
Simpson, Lesley B.
1949 Thirty years of the Hispanic American Historical Review. Hispanic American Historical Review 29: 188–204.
Smith, R. F.
1960 The United States and Cuba: business and diplomacy, 1917–1960. New York.
Smith, R. S.
1944 The institution of the consulado in New Spain. Hispanic American Historical Review 24: 61–83.
1948 Sales taxes in New Spain, 1575–1770. Hispanic American Historical Review 28: 2–37.
Stein, Stanley J.
1960 Historiography of Brazil. Hispanic American Historical Review 40: 234–78.

Sternberg, Hilgard O'R.
1955 Agriculture and industry in Brazil. Geographical Journal 121: 488–502.
Sweezy, P., and L. Huberman
1960 Cuba: anatomy of a revolution. New York.
Tannenbaum, Frank
1929 The Mexican agrarian revolution. New York.
1933 Peace by revolution. New York.
1947 Slave and citizen. The Negro in the Americas. New York.
Thompson, J. Eric
1954 The rise and fall of Maya civilization. Norman, Okla.
Thomson, C. A.
1935–36 The Cuban revolution. Foreign Policy Association, Reports, No. 11: 250–76.
Varnhagen, F. A. de
1854–57 História geral do Brasil. Rio de Janeiro. 2 vols.
1871 História das lutas com os holandezes no Brazil. Vienna.
Vernon, R.
1962 The dilemma of Mexico's development. Cambridge, Mass.
Wagley, Charles
1960a The Brazilian revolution: social change since 1930. In Social change in Latin America today, [by] Richard Adams et al. New York, pp. 177–230.
1960b Plantation America: a culture sphere. In Caribbean studies: a symposium, Vera D. Rubin, ed. Seattle, 2nd edition, pp. 3–12.
Wagley, Charles (ed.)
1952 Race and class in rural Brazil. Paris, UNESCO.
Weill, Felix
1944 The Argentine riddle. New York.
Werneck Sodré, Nelson
1958 Introdução à revolução brasileira. Rio de Janeiro.
Whitaker, Arthur P.
1941 The Huancavelica Mercury mine. Cambridge, Mass.
1951 The Americas in the Atlantic triangle. In Ensayos sobre la historia del nuevo mundo, E. McInnis, ed. Mexico City.
1954 The United States and Argentine. Cambridge, Mass.
1961a Latin American history since 1825. Washington, D.C.
1961b The Argentine paradox. Annals, American Academy of Social and Political Science 334: 103–12.
Whitaker, Arthur P. (ed.)
1942 Latin America and the enlightenment. New York and London.
Williams, M. W.
1930 The treatment of Negro slaves in the Brazilian empire: a comparison with the United States. Journal of Negro History 15: 313–36.
Wood, Bryce
1961 The making of the good neighbor policy. New York.
Worcester, D. E., and W. G. Schaeffer
1956 The growth and culture of Latin America. New York.
Wyckoff, T.
1960 The role of the military in contemporary Latin American politics. Western Political Quarterly 13: 745–62.
Zavala, Silvio
1943a New viewpoints on the Spanish colonization of America. Philadelphia.

Zavala, Silvio
     1943b   Orígenes coloniales del peonaje en México. Trimestre Económico 10:
           711–48.
     1962   The colonial period in the history of the New World. (Abridgment
           by Max Savelle.) Mexico City.
Zea, Leopoldo
     1944   Apogeo y decadencia del positivismo en México. Mexico City.
     1963   The Latin American mind. Translated by James H. Abbot and
           Lowell Dunham. Norman, Okla.
Zeitlin, M., and R. Scheer
     1963   Cuba: tragedy in our hemisphere. New York.

4. Anthropology in Latin America

Generally considered a social science, anthropology—through its various subdisciplines of physical anthropology, linguistics, archeology, and ethnology—is also a historical science, a biological science, and one of the humanities. In all these roles, anthropology has long found in Latin America a major source of data and often a focus of interest as well. To most anthropologists the concept of area studies and the role of the area specialist within the larger discipline represent no departure from the traditions of the field.

This apparently diverse collection of specialties within a common tradition is held together by a concern, sometimes implicit rather than explicit, with culture—its history, its regularities, its interplay with the rest of nature, its evolution, and its role in the emergence and evolution of the biological organism Homo sapiens. That part of the world lying to the south of the Rio Grande presents to the anthropologists a multitude of cultures and peoples, living and dead, for description, analysis, and comparison.

All the traditional subdisciplines of anthropology are critical to the concern with the "phenomena of man" in the Latin American area. Yet many anthropologists who have done research in the area are not concerned with Latin American society and culture per se. The aboriginal peoples of Middle, Central, and South America were no more "Latin American" than were the men of Altamira cave "Spanish." Physical anthropologists, drawing their sample from Latin American populations, have done important work in, for example, population genetics (Layrisse 1959; Newman 1960; Salzano 1957; Allen *et al.* 1952), physiology (Hammel 1960a, 1960b; Monge 1952), and biometrics and somatology (Newman 1953, 1962). The feedback, however, from work in the biological aspects of anthropology into Latin American studies is indirect. Similarly anthropological linguistics tends to be indirectly related to an understanding of Latin American culture. The analysis and classification of the Indian languages of Middle, Central, and South America (McQuown 1955; Greenberg 1960) is critical as an analytical tool in attempting to reconstruct the aboriginal occupation of what is now Latin America and the differentiation of cultures within it. Such linguistic classifications also play an important role as a control in comparative studies of the aboriginal peoples of the area. Of course, millions of people still speak aboriginal languages and the growth of aid, development, and research programs which deal with communities of non-Spanish speaking peoples in Latin America has recently led to the placing of Quechua (spoken in Peru) and Nahuatl (spoken in Mexico) in the catalogues, respectively, of Cornell University and the University of Chicago.

The work of archeologists in Mexico, in Central America, in highland South America, and even in the regions beyond the realm of the complex native civilizations contribute in an important way to our understanding of the modern scene. The long-term history of the millions of American Indians who inhabited the New World before the arrival of the Europeans is as much a part of the history of Latin America as that of Europe. Archeology has provided a major source of data concerning the history and evolution of the aboriginal peoples of the New World. With notable exceptions archeology has tended to concentrate upon those areas of Middle, Central, and South America which were the seats of the civilizations of the pre-Columbian New World. There is, however, a growing interest in the archeology of those areas which never developed great political, artistic, and architectural traditions (see, for example, Meggers and Evans 1963). The reconstructed history, ethnology, and evolution of such areas as northern Mexico, the Amazon Basin, or southern South America are of perhaps less interest from a layman's point of view than are the great ruins of the Valley of Mexico or of the highlands of Guatemala or Peru. They are of equal importance to anthropology, however, and to its concern with the history and development of the cultures of the New World.

The problem of the settlement of the New World, the differentiation of cultures within it, and the variables involved in the emergence of the high civilizations of the area demand an approach that is not concerned with individual cultures or sites as its primary focus. As the archeologists themselves are well aware, a wider temporal and geographic net is required. Those archeological investigations which went beyond and before the Inca Empire and its immediate precursors and dealt with wider areas and dug their way back to the earliest appearance of man in the regions of concern had the greatest influence both on our understanding of the cultural history of South America and on anthropology in general. Such work was of particular importance in understanding the emergence of the state in South America (Bennett 1948; Bennett and Bird 1949; Strong and Evans 1952). The value to history and theory of attempting to deal comprehensively with data relating to relatively large cultural areas over long periods of time can be paralleled in Middle America.

A major source of data for the anthropologist concerned with New World cultural history is, of course, direct historical evidence where it is available. I will not enter here into a discussion of ethnohistory in Latin America (see Adams 1962), except to note that such history does not replace the more traditional sources of time depth in anthropological studies, such as distribution studies, archeology, and comparative linguistics. Rather, written history must be integrated into a model which includes the data and analysis of these other techniques. All contribute to the data which must be correlated and organized into some sort of comprehensive theoretical or historical model by those anthropologists whose area of interest is that of the aboriginal cultures of southern America.

The present paper stresses the work carried out in the Latin American area in the field of cultural anthropology and, within this, especially social anthropology. It is this subdiscipline of anthropology which contributes most directly to our knowledge of contemporary Latin America. Furthermore, I have imposed certain limitations upon myself, chiefly because of considerations of time, space, and personal interests. There is a vast literature which dates back to the sixteenth century by such authors as Sahagun, Las Casas, and Soares de Souza, which is of inestimable anthropological value. In this paper, however, I shall restrict my comments to work done in the twentieth century by people who were consciously doing research in cultural anthropology and were trained in this field. I shall be dealing chiefly with South America (excluding the Guianas), but significant contributions based upon work done elsewhere in Latin America will be included. In general, I shall limit myself to work by social anthropologists with some few exceptions. This is a difficult limitation for anthropological research. Any complex culture demands data and draws upon concepts from a wide diversity of disciplines. Thus, the social anthropologist working in Latin America makes use of background information from geography, history, economics, sociology, political science, and the humanities. The content which anthropology derives from these other fields is to some degree discussed in the other papers of this symposium.[1] The focus of the following discussion is very narrowly anthropological.

The balance of this paper is thus devoted to the consideration of research on the cultures of the people who inhabited what we today call Latin America, both those cultures which were there prior to the Conquest period and those which developed after the arrival of the European and persist today.

Studies of Aboriginal Cultures

Until the second decade of the twentieth century, there were few anthropological studies of the living people of Middle America and of the western highlands of South America. What data existed came from travelers and naturalists; instead, anthropological interest focused in these regions on archeological investigations of pre-Conquest civilizations. It was in the lowland regions of the Amazonian tropical forest, in the Chaco, and in Tierra del Fuego that the first important field investigations of South American aboriginal cultures began. These lowland re-

---

[1] The amount of such information that must be controlled by the modern social anthropologist often seems staggering. It was even suggested during the conversations at Stanford that the *area* specialist in anthropology be replaced by the *national* specialist. Such a formal recognition of national specialization would tend to put a parochial stamp on a field whose philosophical basis has always stressed the rejection of such parochialism and emphasized quite the opposite value. Although such narrow specialization should certainly not be held up as an ideal, the need to know the nation exists, as do national specialists, *de facto* if not *de jure*. Such specialization exists, however, based upon a broader comparative knowledge of cultures outside the nation of specialization within Latin America as well as outside the area as a whole.

gions of South America provided one of the largest "reservoirs" remaining in the world of primitive societies (that is, societies not directly involved in state organization and with a social structure based primarily upon kinship). The most important early research was carried out by European ethnologists such as Steinen (1894), Schmidt (1905), Kock-Grünberg (1909–10), Krause (1911), Nordenskiold (1924), Baldus (1931; 1937), Métraux (1937, 1946), Gusinde (1937), and Nimuendaju (1942, 1946). It was not until the 1930s that North American cultural anthropologists began to work in lowland South America in any great numbers. Then, such studies as that of the Barama River Caribs (Gillin 1936), of the Kaingang of South Brazil (Henry 1941), of the Siriono of lowland Bolivia (Holmberg 1950), of the Trumai of central Brazil (Murphy and Quain 1955), of the Tapirape (Wagley 1940, 1943), and of the Tenetehara of northeastern Brazil (Wagley and Galvão 1949) began to appear. From then to now, field research has increased in volume by North American anthropologists, and they have been joined by highly trained South Americans. This more recent research deals with problems of social structure, cultural history, acculturation, ecology, and religion and in at least one case with the restudy of a tribe that had been studied in the early 1930s (Leeds 1960, 1961, 1962; Santa Cruz 1960; Wilbert 1958; Crocker 1961; Maybury-Lewis 1956, 1960; Carneiro 1956–58, 1961; Dole 1956–58; Murphy, 1957, 1958, 1960).

Until the period of World War II the vast majority of ethnological field work was concerned with the description and analysis of tribal and subtribal peoples. The literature on these people is massive (see O'Leary 1963) and is in many European languages. By the late 1930s the large amounts of data on the aboriginal peoples of South and Middle America—ethnological, linguistic, archeological, and historical—had reached what seemed to many to be unmanageable proportions. It was necessary that some attempt at collation be made (Gillin 1940). The result was the publication, between 1946 and 1950, of the *Handbook of South American Indians,* under the editorship of Steward (1946).

The original organizing principle for the *Handbook* was the concept of the culture area, a geographic region occupied by similar cultures. Similarity of culture, in practice, usually meant similarity of culture traits. The approach, even in its application to South America, was not new. As early as 1917 Wissler had attempted to apply the concept of the culture area, originally developed to order the data on North American Indians, to the Indians of South and Middle America. Nor did the publication of the *Handbook* put an end to such attempts to organize South American cultural materials in regional categories (Murdock 1951a, 1951b; Steward and Faron 1959). The importance of the *Handbook* lay in more than the fact that huge masses of ethnographic, archeological, linguistic, and historical materials were collated region by region and group by group. Rather it was in the study of South American cultural history and anthropological theory in general that its great contribution was made.

In its early stages the *Handbook* had organized its data regionally. Volumes were devoted to those cultures which inhabited more or less contiguous areas and tended to resemble each other on the basis of trait distributions. As the material began to grow, however, it became apparent that the similarities and dissimilarities among the Indian cultures of South America correlated not only with regional differences but also along other dimensions as well. There were typical clusters of complexes relating to such variables as physical environment, technology, population density, and social structure. These complexes seemed to the editor to fall into a limited number of specific "types" of cultures. These "types" then became the new basis of analysis of the *Handbook* materials.

These cultural "types" were defined by their structural features. The patterns of human groupings and institutions that appeared repeatedly in spite of differences or similarities in the particulars of culture content. These structural "types" in turn correlated strongly with the major environmental regions of the continent. In the fiords and islands of the southernmost tip of the continent and up through the grasslands of the pampas the occupying peoples at the time of the conquest had been simple hunters and gatherers. Their societies were organized by the simplest of kinship institutions. These were the *marginal* cultures. North of these were large areas inhabited for the most part by semisedentary village horticulturalists. Their social organization, though still based primarily upon kinship, was a good deal more complicated than those of the hunters and gatherers. These were the *tropical forest* cultures. In the northern part of the continent and extending out into the islands of the Caribbean were the multicommunity confederacies. These were marked by class structure, overlaying that of kinship, and also by a full-time professional priesthood. This was the culture type of the *circum-Caribbean*. Finally, centering in the western highlands, were the great state-organized peoples, culminating in the Inca Empire.

This organization of the ethnographic, historical, and archeological data suggested to Steward a cultural-historical approach to the continent. It also suggested the evolutionary stages in the development of South America cultures. Through this it shed comparative light on cultural evolution and on the emergence of the state elsewhere in the world. These reconstructions and conceptualizations, although shown to be inadequate in some particulars in the years since they were initially presented, did raise questions of a wider scope than the concern with particular societies.

In the attempt to collate data on a continent-wide basis, questions of a very fundamental nature had to ask: What is the nature of cultural evolution? What are the basic parts of culture and what aspects of culture are of lesser importance? What is the state and what preconditions are necessary for its appearance out of nonstate organizations? What is the relation between culture and environment and between a particular culture and its environment? What began simply as an attempt to organize a large body of materials ended as a fundamental contribution to the study of the nature, definition, and evolution of culture. The experience of the *Handbook* in having to formulate basic definitions, problems, and hypotheses when dealing with multiple cultural units spread over both time and space became a fundamental interest of cultural anthropology in Latin America in the years following the publication of the *Handbook*.

The aboriginal cultures of South America still present a challenge to the social anthropologist. Only New Guinea, South America, and a handful of other places still have tribal peoples relatively untouched by the expansion of the West. The remaining primitive groups are rapidly disappearing, and it is increasingly urgent that the few remaining groups of central Brazil, the Guianas, Venezuela, lowland Colombia, and Ecuador which are relatively unacculturated be studied. Furthermore, there are tribal groups which have maintained their identity as sociocultural units but have been profoundly influenced by modern

Latin American culture. Studies of these groups provide us excellent laboratories of social and culture change.

Studies of Post-Conquest Latin American Cultures

As Service (1955) has pointed out, the kinds of social systems
which developed in the New World in the period beginning with
the Conquest were to a large degree conditioned by the kind of
native society and culture the Iberians found in a particular
region. Considering the cultural variations within Spain at the
time of the Conquest, a remarkably homogeneous culture and
policy were introduced by the Iberians into the New World
(Service 1955; Foster 1960). Where there were goods or resources
wanted by the Conquerors and a manageable supply of labor
needed to produce these things, the Indians left a mark on the
post-Conquest society and culture that remains for all to see.
Elsewhere the aboriginal peoples died of disease or were killed,
to be replaced by African slaves (where masses of labor were
needed) or only by Europeans where the need for labor was not
so acute.

As the post-Conquest culture developed over time, several types
of cultures emerged and continued to take form in response to
changes in international, national, and regional developments.
On the one hand, some aboriginal peoples managed to retain
their independence of the controls of the Iberian colonizers or
their nineteenth- and twentieth-century heirs. Such groups were,
for the most part, to be found in the Amazon basin and the surrounding lowlands. These groups provided the subjects for the
"classic" ethnologies which were mentioned above.

Another kind of culture developed during the initial period
of contact when the Indian or African was integrated into a
European-imposed socio-cultural system. What emerged from
this period of initial contact varied with local conditions. The
cultures varied in type from gaucho patterns associated with the
spread of the livestock pattern on the pampas to the emerging
Afro-Iberian patterns in the slave plantations in the north coastal
areas of the continent to the reintegration of highland Indian
communities into the Iberian political organization.

Later changes in the Latin American social system, both economic and political, also produced their characteristic types of

communities and cultures but did not necessarily replace those already existing. These older types, however, did adapt to newer conditions. This process of emergence of new types of cultures from major changes in the total social system continues. The industrial revolution is undoubtedly bringing forth types of groups, communities, and cultures that were previously unknown in Latin America.

In the rest of this paper there is a classification of Latin American cultures which is implicit in the previous paragraphs. There are three categories or types of cultures (for purpose of this paper) in Latin America. These are

1. *Tribal or aboriginal,* those cultures and social groups which are, except for the most tenuous of ties, independent of the nation-state economically and politically and whose internal organization is primarily in terms of kinship roles and institutions; they are treated above.

2. *Traditional Latin America,* those cultures and social groups which emerged historically from colonial and early republican Latin America.

3. *Modern Latin America,* those cultures and social groups which have emerged and are emerging because of the Industrial Revolution in Latin America.

TRADITIONAL LATIN AMERICAN CULTURES

The interest of cultural and social anthropologists in the traditional Latin American culture rather than in the aboriginal or tribal cultures of the area may be said to have begun in the late 1920s and in the 1930s. Even then the work of anthropologists was strongly influenced by a concern with the native culture of the area. This is true of the pioneer study by Gamio and his associates (Gamio 1922) on Teotihuacan, although they used quantitative methods of sociologists. This primary concern with the aboriginal cultures was also manifested in the pioneering work of Parsons (1936), who was primarily concerned with Indian (i.e., pre-Conquest) elements in the culture of the town of Mitla and in separating these from Spanish accretions. She was not concerned with describing and analyzing a functioning social system, although she gave us a graphic picture of her community.

Redfield's early study (1930) of the town of Tepoztlan in

Morelos (Mexico) was an attempt to apply the concepts of sociology and functionalist social anthropology to the description and analysis of a community which was part of a modern complex society. Redfield's approach was, as compared with his later work, unsophisticated. Redfield was primarily concerned with the Indians of the town and the continuity of an Indian culture. The study lacked an appreciation of the complexity of intra-village relationships and the relationships of the various segments of the community to the outside world and especially to the national capital (see Lewis 1951). To a large degree Redfield used his data in much the same way as it might have been handled had Tepoztlan been a primitive settlement somewhere in the jungle. Instead Tepoztlan was a town neck-deep in a twenty-year-old revolution. This fact was recognized by Redfield only in his consideration of *zapatista* folklore.

From a distance of thirty-three years it is easy to dwell on the conceptual and methodological shortcomings of Redfield's study of Tepoztlan. Its historical importance, however, lay in what it did rather than in what (we later learned) it did not do. It opened contemporary Latin American culture as a field of anthropological endeavor.

The lack of sophistication in these early works on Latin American cultures was not immediately corrected, nor was it absolutely necessary to do so. Anthropological interest in South and Middle America was still primarily concerned with archeology and with the remaining primitives. For example, in an article in which he surveyed the cultures of the Tropical Forest area of South America, Gillin (1940) dealt with the aboriginal peoples of this area and with classic ethnological problems. Only in the last few pages of his article (under the heading "Applied Anthropology") did Gillin turn to a consideration of nontribal peoples of this region. Even so he noted that these latter were of less interest to the anthropologist than were the tribal peoples. Gillin's reason for recommending the study of the "modern" peoples of the tropical forest at all was that the aborigines were becoming assimilated to the various national cultures and in a short time would have disappeared. Anthropology was still oriented to the study of "primitive" peoples.

One of the problems which faced the anthropologists who

turned to the study of contemporary cultures in Latin America
(or anywhere else, for that matter) at this time was the lack of
method, theory, and problem. To a large degree anthropology,
and especially its North American variety, was primarily historical in its concerns. It saw as its chief function the reconstruction of the history of the primitive world through the study of
the distribution and diffusion of cultural traits. The study of
historical problems by such techniques was of very little interest
when such problems could be dealt with to a large degree by
direct appeal to historical sources. The training of anthropologists at North American universities in the 1930s was less concerned with theory and the analysis of socio-cultural systems than
it was with a solid grounding in the comparative analysis of material culture and a few institutional standbys such as kinship.
Such training would ill prepare the fieldworker for the problems
he would face in the analysis of a modern Latin American community. It was to a large degree the influence of the British social anthropologists and their concern with total social systems
that began to reorient American anthropology in the direction
of complex communities in the range of anthropological concerns.

Whatever concern anthropolgy had with complex cultures, at
least through the 1930s, was with the impact that they had on the
aboriginals who came into contact with them. Although in theory
the concept of acculturation (Redfield, Linton, and Herskovitz
1936) was equally concerned with the impact of the aboriginal on
the colonizer, the focus was in fact almost always on the aboriginal group. In the acculturation study the position of the complex culture was marginal to an understanding of the aboriginal,
which remained the center of attention.

Serious anthropological interest with Latin American cultures
can be said to date from the late 1930s with the work of Redfield
and his associates in Yucatan (Redfield 1941; Redfield and Villa
Rojas 1934; Villa Rojas 1945; Hansen 1934). The field studies
carried out by Redfield, Villa Rojas, and Hansen were parts of
a regional study of Yucatan. The larger regional study dealt not
only with the pre-Conquest and contemporary culture of Maya
Indians but also with the region's biological (Shattuck 1930;
Steggerda 1932) and historical (Chamberlain 1948; Roys 1943;

Scholes 1937) aspects. The whole regional study was coordinated and supported by the Carnegie Institution of Washington, which also published most of the resulting monographs.

Redfield, Villa Rojas, and Hansen carried out field studies of four Yucatecan communities which ranged in size and complexity from Merida, the commercial and political capital of the state of Yucatan, to a relatively isolated small refuge community in the jungles of Quintana Roo. Without entering at this time into a discussion of their methods and analysis, suffice it to say that they dealt with these cultures in their own terms. Here were not "primitives" confronted with "civilization" but rather living systems which, before anything else, had to be understood in their own terms and in terms of the region to which they all belonged. It was no longer Indian *versus* Spanish, but rather comparison among a number of varieties of Latin American culture.

The publication of Redfield's *Folk Culture of Yucatan* (1941) may be taken as a convenient historical marker for the start of intensive anthropological work with traditional Latin American culture. In fact, however, a number of field studies were going on in Middle America at about the same time, which indicated that the discipline as a whole was, in fact, moving in this direction. Many of these studies were carried out among Maya-speaking groups in the Guatemalan highlands, but the workers ultimately found themselves involved with the problem of placing the "Indian" communities in larger regional, national, class, and historical perspectives. As with the workers in Yucatan, they began with particular Indian communities but ended with the consideration of varieties of Latin American culture. The works of Tax (1953), La Farge (1940), Bunzel (1952), and Wagley (1941, 1949) were among the first in a veritable flood of studies of Maya communities that still continues.

The concept of regional specialization is not new to anthropology. Many anthropologists have long been Middle American or South American specialists. It was not until the eve of World War II, however, that anthropologists became concerned about Latin American culture per se, and the appearance of Latin American specialists began to crystallize out of the more traditional ethnographic matrix. The catalyst was the interest in Latin America expressed by the New Deal prior to and during the war—the so-called "Good Neighbor Policy." There can be little doubt, I think, that the continuing interest of cultural anthropology in Latin American culture is connected with the increasing awareness of the American government and public with the underdeveloped nations in general and those of Latin America in particular.

With the coming of World War II the U.S. government inaugurated a number of programs aimed at cultural cooperation among the American republics. One of the results was the production of the *Handbook of South American Indians,* which has been described earlier, by the Bureau of American Ethnology of the Smithsonian Institution with the cooperation of the U.S. Department of State. As part of this program of cooperation, the Institute of Social Anthropology of the Smithsonian Institution was established. It published a number of monographs dealing with Latin American cultures. Some of these studies involved the cooperation of Latin American (and especially Mexican) scholars as well as the training of students from both the host nation and the United States.

Some of the research published by the Institute of Social Anthropology dealt with aboriginal peoples in South America (Holmberg 1950; Oberg 1949). Most of the publications, however, such as the work of Beals (1946), Brand (1951), a cultural geographer, Foster (1948), Tax (1953), Gillin (1947), and Pierson (1951), dealt with cultures that were intimately involved historically and structurally with the larger societies in which they were located. The people who lived in some of these communities did not even speak the national language, while others were peasants speaking the national language (Spanish or Portuguese) and identified with the nation although the historical source of their culture was the early period of Indian-Iberian contact. The content of such cultures, material or institutional, was comprehensible only in terms of that contact. The changes that they were experiencing was comprehensible only as part of the changes which their respective national societies were undergoing.

Government sponsorship of research in anthropology in Latin America was obviously motivated by national interest. In an increasingly complex world there was a "need to know" about these countries whose policies and activities were of direct and immediate concern to the United States. Although direct government support was withdrawn in the years following the war, the "need to know" increased rather than decreased. The increasing support in recent years for anthropological research from both public and private sources reflects this growing need to know about Latin America at the grass-roots level.

In the years following the war, anthropological interest in Latin American culture increased. After World War II, the proportion of articles and book reviews in the *American Anthropologist* devoted to contemporary Latin America as against native South and Middle America was reversed. Articles or book reviews on the aboriginal cultures of the area became relatively rare, while articles and reviews devoted to research on peoples involved in the complex socio-political systems of Latin America were most frequent. This phenomenon, of course, was not limited to the Western Hemisphere, but was part of a growing social anthropological concern with complex societies all over the world.

In the study of communities which were part of complex societies (or in dealing with problems which had to be researched in such communities), the anthropologist was faced with new methodological problems. His traditional methods, developed in his studies of small and nonliterate societies, were no longer completely adequate to describe and analyze a Yucatecan city or a Brazilian sugar plantation. To a large degree a primitive tribe could be viewed as an isolated universe. Within this universe the anthropologist could with some confidence become expert in the economics, political organization, technology, religion, and philosophy of "his" people. In the more complex situations which the anthropologist began to face in modern social systems, he no longer had the universe even potentially within his ken. Effective decisions which could have a profound effect upon the people being studied might not be made by them at all and very likely were not. Much of the knowledge that the ethnographer might gain by observation and interrogation in a primitive community had to be obtained in a complex society from sources and from experts who were little concerned with the problems of the anthropologist. The expert might inform the fieldworker about what was involved in the signing of a sugar agreement in London. It was up to the anthropologist to see the significance of these outside factors to village baptism, marriage, politics, or kinship organization.

As late as 1949 Gillin found it necessary to remind some of his colleagues that peoples involved in modern cultures have written histories and are involved with formal political institutions which are themselves sources of information on the culture under study. Redfield, in his *Folk Culture of Yucatan* (1941), for all practical purposes ignored history and the presence of the Mexican state in his analysis of Yucatecan culture. He depended upon comparisons among the four communities which he and his associates had studied to determine trait (including institutional complexes) distributions on the peninsula. These distributions were used, in turn, to write what was, in effect, a history of Yucatecan society and culture. This method was similar in many ways to the distribution analysis and reconstructed history used by anthropologists when trying to convert spatial distribution into historical depth in dealing with societies that had no written histories. In so doing, however, Redfield missed the plantation system in Yucatan, which had in fact been one of the major, if not the major, determinant of the development of Yucatecan culture since the time of the Spanish conquest (Strickon 1965).

The problem of relating small communities to the national systems of which they are a part has been one of the major themes in much of the social anthropological work in Latin America. This problem, of course, has two faces. The first is the question of the effect of the nation on the community. The second is the question of what kind of light is shed on the history, structure, and function of a nation-state by studies which are carried on in relatively small rural communities. Small communities, at least so far, have been the location of most anthropological research in Latin America. For the anthropologist qua anthropologist, the second question may be less pressing than the first. The study of a Tarascan marketplace or a kinship network in the Argentine countryside may be of interest to anthropologists for technical and theoretical reasons which have little if any bearing on the nations in which the studies occurred or for Latin American culture in general. If any broader understanding of the nation or the area can be achieved, beyond the insights gained into the problem isolated by the researcher, it can be considered a fortunate and unanticipated boon. The nation and the community may set the boundaries within which the phenomenon is investigated, but they are not the objects of study.

If the concern is with a total social system, however, even if that system is a small community, then the problem of what the unit of investigation represents in terms of the nation must be faced. What aspects of the nation are revealed by the community or culture under investigation? In such a situation the anthropologist is operating not only as an anthropologist but also as a variety of Latin American area specialist, and the data and analysis of other disciplines must be integrated into his own analytical model (Steward 1950; Arensberg 1954, 1961).

The People of Puerto Rico: A Study in Social Anthropology, by Steward (1956) and his associates (Robert Manners, Sidney Mintz, Elena Padilla-Seda, Raymond Scheele, and Eric Wolf), represents the first concerted and integrated attempt to describe and analyze a whole complex cultural system in Latin America from an anthropological point of view. The fieldworkers operated within a common theoretical system and collected comparable data. The communities chosen for study were seen as samples representing types of communities which were historically and ecologically significant in contemporary and historical Puerto Rico. These communities included small independent farmers, a modern privately owned sugar plantation, a government-owned sugar plantation, and a traditional type of plantation system. These communities were seen as emerging from the various political, economic, and ecological changes which Puerto Rico had undergone in the course of its history.

Each of the communities was analyzed in terms of both its internal structure and its relations to the larger society. Each of the analysts used a common set of categories for their data, and their analyses also depended upon the use of common variables. Both the categories and the variables in turn were determined by the researchers' emphasis on economic and ecological variables as major determinants of culture.

The situations in the particular communities, both at the time of the field study and in the historic past, were related to the policies of the great metropolitan powers, first Spain and then the United States, which controlled the island. There thus was developed a structural network which related ways of life in particular classes and communities to local conditions, to the island as a whole, and finally to the world outside the island. This was further reinforced by a consideration of some of the institutions and subcultures which were islandwide in distribution and which, therefore, cut across local systems.

As is too often the case with the work of anthropologists, *The People of Puerto Rico* is weak in its study of urban groups. Scheele studied the upper class in San Juan, but it was less thoroughly integrated into the general analysis than were the rural community studies. There is also relatively little material in the study on other urban groups and social classes. In spite of its weaknesses, however, *The People of Puerto Rico* remains a model, though one which must be expanded upon and refined, for the sort of work that still remains to be done in most of Latin America.

For some parts of Latin America the studies already extant could be used to give as complete a picture of the interplay between history, ecology, community, class, region, and nation from a developmental and structural point of view as Steward's carefully planned study. This would require reanalyzing the data in a large number of articles and monographs in terms of some common set of variables and categories. These might be similar to those used in Puerto Rico or might differ, depending upon the interests and orientation of the analyst. For a large part of Latin America, however, the data already on library shelves could not so serve. Anthropologists have been drawn to Latin America for a legion of independent studies. These range in focus from child-rearing to planned culture change. The data these separate studies provide are not always comparable.

Information on the varieties of Latin American culture is unfortunately uneven. It tends to be concentrated both geographically and in terms of the kinds of cultures and social groups upon which research has concentrated. Anthropologists have tended to concentrate upon those communities, cultures (or subcultures), and groups which emerged early in the contact, colonial, and republican periods. They have tended to avoid those which have emerged from more recent developments.

COUNTRY AND REGIONAL STUDIES

In the following pages I shall attempt a survey, of South America, of some of the work already published describing traditional Latin American culture. The following pages do not attempt, or begin to approach, bibliographical comprehensiveness. Even within the limits set, the bibliography for Middle America is at least as large as that for South America. What will be discussed are studies dealing with nontribal peoples who can be seen as sharing, to various degrees, in Latin American culture. The emphasis is on anthropological materials (i.e., done by anthropologists), although other materials will be dealt with as required.

Brazil. Of all the nations of South America, Brazil, perhaps, has received more anthropological attention (within the limits defined above) than any other. The wealth of material is not only due to the interest Brazilian culture has roused in foreign scientists but also to the work in their own country of Brazilians of the highest professional caliber.

Even in the case of Brazil, however, where studies from almost every major region are available, anthropologists have tended to focus upon the area to the north of Rio de Janeiro (Wagley 1952).

In terms of subject matter there was, for many years, a concentration upon "the Negro in Brazil" and a comparison, implicit or explicit, with the status of the Negro in the United States.[2] This area of study was first represented by a major publication in 1942 with the appearance of Pierson's *Negroes in Brazil: A Study of Race Contact at Bahia.* The "Negro in Brazil" also provided a fertile ground for the study of African survivals in the New World. Work on this type of problem tended to center upon the lower-class religious cults with their strong African content (Landes 1947; Costa Eduardo 1948; Bastide 1960).

By the early 1950s a number of publications reflected a shift in anthropological interest in Brazil away from the relatively circumscribed subject of "the Negro" and toward a wider investigation of social systems. This shift is best represented by the cooperative effort, headed by Wagley and Azevedo, between Columbia University and the Fundação para o Desenvolvimento da Ciência na Bahia. This involved a number of field studies carried out in the state of Bahia. The separate studies were imbedded in regional, national, and historical matrices (Wagley 1952,[3] 1953;

---

[2] One wonders why another phenomenon, the massive assimilation of European immigrants into southern Brazil, Uruguay, and Argentina has not generated comparable comparative studies with the United States.

[3] This work ("Amazon Town") was not itself a result of the Columbia-Bahia Project. Its results, however, were to a large degree integrated into the findings of the project.

Hutchinson 1957; Harris 1956). The area studied, however, was one which had played its crucial role in the evolution of the modern nationality and state of Brazil in the past. At the time of the study it was no longer a "key economic area."

Studies of the northern parts of Brazil gained much from the large bodies of historical materials which had been collated in categories meaningful for anthropological analysis. The work of Freyre (1956, 1963) comes immediately to mind. On a stage comparable in size with that usually dealt with by the field anthropologist, Stein's (1957) book, *Vassouras: A Brazilian Coffee County, 1850–1900,* is a model of its kind. It is an ethnology reconstructed from historical sources. In its descriptive and analytical categories it is comparable in almost every respect to a modern ethnography. It provides historical depth to contemporary studies of the area (Greenfield 1963) and also provides a comparative check on plantation studies in so far as there is a difference along the variable of crop produced, that is, coffee, as against most studies, which have been concerned with sugar-producing plantations. Also of value to an understanding of northern Brazil, owing to its common involvement with Negro slavery in the New World and the sugar plantation, is much of the work done on the historical and economic aspects of these phenomenon in the Caribbean (Williams 1944; Elkins 1959; Mintz 1961).

Southern Brazil, perhaps because of its lack of involvement with the "Negro in the New World," its "Europeanness," and the fact that it is a relatively recent emergent as a critical area in the evolving Brazilian economy, society, and polity, did not receive the attention that the North did. There were few studies of the region south of Rio de Janeiro. Those studies in the area that were done (Willems 1947, 1953; Pierson 1951) tended to be of communities that were relatively isolated and not involved in, or only marginally involved in, the massive changes in the South which were crucial to the transformation of Brazil.

It is not surprising that it has been Brazilian scholarship which has turned to the South. It is here, more than in any other single part of the nation, that Brazil is feeling the impact of the Industrial Revolution. Here are the studies concerned with the immigrants of diverse European and non-European backgrounds, the industries, the slums, the cattle ranches, and the explosively growing cities. This is still a new area (in terms of anthropological research going on within it), and most of the material on it is still scattered in articles, pamphlets, and other short works (Azevedo 1961; Willems 1948; 1958; Silva 1954; Laytano 1952; Barcelos 1951; Smith 1951). The classical study by Willems (1946) is still the best work on German acculturation; the recent works by Cardoso and Ianni (1960) on race relations and the community provides new insights into Brazilian sociology.

Peru. After Brazil Peru has had more anthropological research devoted to it than any other country in South America. If archeological and ethnohistorical materials were included in this survey, Peru would easily be the most studied area in South America. Brazil attracted anthropological interest by its large African population and in the remaining groups of tribal Indians. The attraction of Peru lay in its magnificent archeological remains and its large Indian "peasantry." The Peruvian Indian population provided the base of great civilizations before the coming of the Spanish. After the conquest it was the base upon which Spain built her own empire in the highlands. The system that developed in the highlands grew out of the interaction between Spanish needs and policies and the pre-existing social and cultural base. This contrasts strongly with Brazil, where the Indians were assimilated or killed off and for the most part replaced by a completely new population.

The degree to which the aboriginal population of the western highlands retained their old traditions and way of life varied widely. There are still Indian communities which own their land in common and speak Quechua or Aymara as their chief language. These felt their greatest impact (until very recently) of Spanish culture during the colonial period. At the other extreme is the vast majority of the population of Peru. This group, although heavily Indian biologically, is culturally Latin American.

Relatively few studies deal with "Indian" communities in Peru. They tend, rather, to concentrate upon those communities which, to varying degrees, have shed their native languages as well as many of the institutions, beliefs, values, and material traits that are symbolic of the Indian. They became a part of the national system. The survey carried out by Tschopik, *Highland Communities of Central Peru* (1948), included some small villages of Quechua speakers. Some of the preparatory work for the

Vicos Project (see below) dealt with Indian communities which served as a labor pool for capital-extensive haciendas in the Peruvian highlands (Holmberg 1960; Stein 1961; Fried 1962).

Most of the field studies in Peru have been of communities of *mestizos,* people who, though possibly genetically Indian (and more usually Indian and European genetically), are Spanish speakers, use the European rather than the Quechua technological kit, and are to a greater or lesser degree directly involved in the social, economic, and political life of the Peruvian nation and state. Adams (1959) in his study of the Andean community of Muquiyauyo, combined field and ethnohistoric research to trace the shift of this community from the Indian to the Peruvian category. Other studies have considered *mestizo* communities in highland and coastal Peru. These range in type from independent "indigenous" communities to urban slums (Gillin 1947; Faron 1960; Hammel 1962; Soler Bustamente 1954).

One of the most significant anthropological efforts in Peru is the Vicos Project sponsored by Cornell University with the cooperation of the Peruvian government. The project was directed by Holmberg. The Vicos Project was an attempt to restructure a Peruvian Indian hacienda community from a position of semi-serfdom into a functioning part of the national society. This project represents perhaps the most intensive effort ever made by applied anthropology on the community level.

In this attempt to apply anthropological and other social science theories, techniques, philosophy, and values to practical application, many problems had to be faced in practice which normally would have been only analytical. The relations of the Indian community to the national upper-class groups which had originally owned the hacienda that Cornell took over had to be described and analyzed. Relations within the community, within the neighborhood, and to the national state had to be plotted. The meaning of all this in terms of the behavior and expectations of the *Vicosinos* themselves had to be determined. Following this it was necessary to introduce the changes or, more accurately, to motivate the *Vicosinos* to do so and then to learn what impact these changes had on the community. The Cornell-Peru Project has resulted in a number of articles (Holmberg 1960; Holmberg and Dobyns 1962; Dobyns, Monge, and Vasquez

1962; Lasswell 1962) and monographs. (The latter have been mentioned earlier.) As of this moment there has been no definitive descriptive, analytical, and evaluative publication on the project. When it does come, it will undoubtedly represent a major contribution to anthropology and to Latin American studies in general.

Colombia. Colombia is represented by a mere handful of studies. These, though, are of a high quality. The work of the Reichel-Dolmatoffs (1961) and Fals Borda (1955, 1959) deal with rural *mestizo* villages of the traditional type usually studied by anthropologists. Fals Borda's study of Saucio does deal with *la violencia*, the constant guerrilla warfare associated with traditional political cleavages in Colombian politics (although according to some it may be in the process of becoming associated with revolutionary political movements). The study of Saucio thereby relates this community to one of the major problems of the Colombian polity. More recently Fals Borda, Gutzman, and Umaña published *La violencia en Colombia* (Gutzman 1962).

In a modest but stimulating little study, which I think represents a portent of things to come in Latin American anthropology, Whiteford (1960) tackles the city, a subject which anthropologists have tended to avoid. His book, *Two Cities of Latin America: A Comparative Description of Social Classes*, compares Queretaro, Mexico, with Popayan, Colombia. The former is a city increasingly involved in a modern industrial economy; the latter is nonindustrial and has a social system as traditional as its economy. Whiteford's study is primarily concerned with the different patterns of stratification, which in turn are related by the author to the different economic and technological bases of the two cities. In this work the objects of study are social groups and categories of people. The cities themselves merely provide the larger social and economic matrix within which these people function.

Bolivia, Ecuador, and Venezuela. These three countries are practically *terra incognita* as far as studies of their contemporary culture is concerned. Parsons' study (1945) of the Indian village of Peguche is to a large degree concerned, as was her study of Mitla in Mexico, with traditional ethnology. It is weak on information relating to economics, social structure, and politics. Also dealing with the same Ecuadorian Indian community is the photographic study of the Otavalo Valley by Collier and Buitron (1945).

Bolivia is represented by the work of La Barre (1948) in his study, *The Aymara Indians of the Lake Titicaca Plateau, Bolivia*. Patch has done considerable research in Bolivia but has published only on economic, social, and political matters (Patch 1960). Bolivia still lacks a range of monographic publications which would provide a sample of types of ecological adaptation, cultural and class variations, and historical emergents that must characterize various subcultures in Bolivia as they do in any complex society.

Venezuela is, for all practical purposes, untouched by the anthropologist. With the exception of some ethnographical survey material along the Venezuelan-Colombian border (Sociedad de Ciencias Naturales La Salle 1953), there is little published material by anthropologists on the traditional Latin American culture of Venezuela.

Paraguay, Chile, Argentina, and Uruguay. We turn now to an area which, as a whole, has received less anthropological attention vis à vis its contemporary culture than any other part of South America. This region has been called "Euro-America" to contrast it with the areas sometimes termed "Mestizo America" and "Afro-America." Geographically "Euro-America" may be said to begin in southern Brazil and to extend west and south from there to include all the states of the southern tier of South America—Paraguay, Uruguay, Argentina, and Chile.

This area lacks many of the characteristics which have traditionally attracted anthropological interest. It is lacking in impressive archeological remains. It is throughly European biologically and culturally. During the war, when much research was begun elsewhere in Latin America, this part of South America was politically aloof and was not involved in cooperative programs with the U.S. government. With the exception of Paraguay, the pre-Conquest populations contributed little genetically to the present population. Except for isolated traits, the pre-Conquest cultures contributed little to the present way of life. This is apparently true even of Paraguay, according to Service (1954b), in spite of its retention of Guarani as a second language.

Southern South America is also the area of the cattle ranch

rather than the plantation. The ranch, lacking the huge labor requirements of the sugar or coffee plantation, never became involved to any significant degree with the slave trade and with the problem of the African in the New World. Finally, much of this area has witnessed during the last century a massive European immigration. The man on the land is not the Indian peasant but rather the European farmer and cowboy.

Of the four nations in Euro-America, Paraguay has fared best at the hands of the anthropologist. The Services' *Tobati* (1954b) and a first-rate ethnohistorical work by E. Service, *Spanish-Guarani Relations in Early Colonial Paraguay* (1954a), are basic works for Paraguay. The latter work is significant because of the importance of this period for the study of acculturation (both Spanish and Indian) in Paraguay, and for the development of what was to become the culture of the contemporary society. It is also important because it sheds light on the colonial problems of the southern tier of South American nations. These problems were quite different from those of Brazil or the western highlands (Service 1955). The only other published work by an anthropologist on Paraguay are two very brief reports on a Mennonite colony in the Chaco (Hack 1958, n.d.).

Little work has been done on the modern culture of Chile by anthropologists. Faron's study (1961) of the Araucanian Mapuche deals with a group which, while retaining a certain amount of structural cohesion and group identity, seems, at least to this reader, to be more Chilean than Indian. The Mapuche are integrated into the Chilean political and economic system. Faron argues, however, that while adopting much that is Chilean, the Mapuche are not like the Chilean farmers among whom they live. Unfortunately we now know more about the Araucanian Indians than we do about Chilean farmers. There is little basis for judging similarities or dissimilarities between the two groups. Titiev (1951), who briefly studied a group of Araucanian Mapuche other than the one dealt with by Faron, sees them as retaining little that is distinctive vis à vis the surrounding Chileans.

The only other anthropological study in Chile (excluding other works dealing with the Araucanians) is based upon a brief ethnographical survey. The community dealt with is located near the Bolivian and Argentine frontiers. It is described as being an Indian community. The people, however, are Spanish speakers and they are probably more akin to what are called *mestizos* in the highland areas (Mostny 1954).

The "folk culture" of Argentina, that of the *gaucho*, has attracted a great deal of attention from Argentine scholars. This interest, however, has been literary and folkloric rather than in the realm of the social sciences (see, for example, Nichols 1942 for a review of this type of material). There are no published anthropological studies of Argentine communities, although one article discusses a limited aspect of social structure in a Pampean cattle-grazing community (Strickon 1962).

The work of Cochran and Reina (1962), like that of Whiteford in Colombia, is something of a pioneering effort in Latin American anthropology. The book, *Entrepreneurship in Argentine Culture: Torcuato di Tella and S.I.A.M.*, is essentially a study of the growth of a large-scale industrial enterprise (the senior author is an economic historian) and its relation to the changing structure and economy of Argentine society. Their study considers the internal organization of the company, relations, both kinship and nonkinship, among the owners and top managers, the values of the management, how these latter points effect policy decisions of the company, and finally relations of the management to the workers. Reina unfortunately was not able to perform a full-scale study of the corporation management. The material that this study provides, however, points the way to the kinds of data that are needed if anthropology is to study complex cultures at their centers rather than at their peripheries.

Uruguay is an anthropological blank. As in the case of Argentina, there is a good deal of literary and folkloric interest in the *gaucho*. There are no anthropological descriptions and analyses of Uruguayan communities nor use of Uruguayan cultural materials to exemplify theoretical anthropological problems. Some data on Uruguayan rural life is provided, as it is in the rest of Latin America, by the work of geographers and rural sociologists (Vidart 1955).

In terms of mere geographical coverage, it is apparent that much remains to be done in South America. Aside from Brazil and Peru, no South American nation is represented by more than a handful of professional studies. In a few cases there are none at all. Some of these countries, Argentina, for example, are regionally complex, and an adequate sample of class, ethnic, and regional variations would require studies comparable in number and scope to those available for Brazil or Peru. Even these latter two nations have large descriptive gaps to be filled.

The problem of large descriptive holes for whole nations exists also in Middle and Central America. In these areas the majority of studies are concentrated in Mexico and Guatemala. Even in these two countries, there is a strong emphasis on "Indian" communities. Central America has been the location of relatively little research on contemporary Latin American culture. Adam's survey (1957) of Panama, Nicaragua, Guatemala, El Salvador, and Honduras, although it covers the area, seems most useful when it discusses areas, chiefly in Guatemala, for which there are available depth studies to support the survey material.

The gaps in geographical coverage are no more serious than the gaps in the types of cultures or subcultures. There has been a marked predilection for research in the communities which are isolated, which are "traditional," and which represent a way of life on the verge of disappearance. Where is the social anthropological study of the Venezuelan oilworker, the Bolivian tin-miner, the Argentine tenant farmer? The lack of studies of various urban groups very obviously represents a major descriptive gap. There are also great gaps in the kinds of historical and economic studies which provide invaluable, and necessary, supporting data for the anthropologist. There is no economic, political, and social analysis of the history of the livestock industry comparable, for example, to Williams' study of sugar in the Caribbean. The same can be said in reference to the mining industry in the western highlands. Who has reconstructed the way of life and the social system of the nineteenth-century cattle *estancia* of Brazil, Uruguay, or Argentina? Who has given us the kind of detailed "ethnohistory" of a "cow county" or a mining county that Stein has given us for a "coffee county"?

Classifications of Latin American Cultures

The field data which the various ethnographic studies have collected are, of course, meaningless without some theoretical framework into which they can be fitted. It is the theoretical framework, in fact, which determines the kinds of data to be collected. In terms of the numerous particular studies the problem and the theoretical outlook vary widely. Beyond the problem investigated in the field research is the problem of correlating and synthesizing the data collected in a way that is relevant for the area as a whole. The vast majority of syntheses of Latin American cultural data has been typological or taxonomic, beginning with Redfield's work on Yucatan.

The establishment of any sort of taxonomic system requires the identification of criteria to be used in assigning the unit of interest (be it biological organism, culture, or anything else) to one taxonomic category as against another. It is obviously necessary as well for all those who use a taxonomic system (that is, who organize materials in terms of categories) to agree upon the significant criteria. Finally, although it is possible to set up taxonomic systems *pour le sport*, that is, with no particular purpose in mind, generally such systems are techniques used to organize data for analysis in terms of some underlying theory. The relationship between modern biological taxonomic systems and the theory of evolution represents a classic case of this sort of relationship between the selection of significant criteria, taxonomic categories, and underlying general theory.

There have been two basic taxonomic systems used to categorize Latin American culture by anthropologists, each using two different but overlapping sets of criteria. In neither case have all the implications of the systems been spelled out, nor have the relationships between the categories always been made explicit.

The earliest typological system was that of Redfield (1941, 1947), his concept of the "folk-urban continuum." The folk-urban typology has only one explicitly defined category, the folk society. In his description of the folk society, Redfield did not make quite clear whether by this he meant a primitive society (that is, one based primarily upon face-to-face relationships and structured by kinship) or something other. The existence of the category "folk society" implies as well a second category, "nonfolk society." Redfield, however, opposed the category "folk society" with the concept of "urban society." This class, unlike its opposite, was never explicitly defined by Redfield. Its characteristics were presumed to be the opposite of those of the "folk society." Both of these categories were conceived of in essentially Platonic terms. It was not believed that any society would fit the models exactly. Any specific society would be assigned, then, not to any specific typological category but rather somewhere along a continuous distribution between the two archetypes. If nothing more can be said for such a typological "system," it does represent a way of organizing the data in a way that is "close to nature." Few if any "natural distributions" are discontinuous. Discontinuities are imposed by the analyst on a more or less continuous distribution of phenomenon by stressing some criteria over others for some theoretical reasons of his own.

The continuous distribution with which Redfield dealt was a function of the criteria he used and the theoretical basis (of, perhaps, lack of one) which underlay the folk-urban construct. Redfield in his selection of criteria did not stress some aspects of culture over others. He dealt with a summary of all parts of culture, a *gestalt,* as it were, a "way," or "style of life." The use to which this construct was put was, in terms of the particular Yucatecan study from which it developed, historical. Implicitly, however, it was also moral and judgmental. Its analytical value was limited.

Redfield's work set off a series of discussions which attempted to clarify the concept of "folk" (Redfield 1941, 1947; Miner 1952; Foster 1953, to name but a few). But since neither the categories, the criteria, the underlying theory, nor the use to which the construct was to be applied were agreed upon or ever clearly stated, the outcome of these discussions could not help but be vague and uncertain. Whatever the ultimate value of the folk-urban construct, however, it did serve an important purpose. It provided a new framework in which to place a growing number of studies.

The second taxonomic "system" which has been used to organize Latin American data to some degree also grew out of the discussions of the folk-urban continuum. It is not the work of one man but rather represents the thinking, often more or less independent, of a number of authors. There is no agreed upon term for these typologies and categories. It is even possible that some of the authors would resent being placed together with others under a single rubric. In any event, it seems to me that they can be lumped together in many ways. For ease of discussion I shall refer to them as a whole as the "evolutionary" typology. Some of the particular authors would deny that their categories have evolutionary implications; and, in fact, such implications are often implicit.

Unlike the "way of life" criteria upon which Redfield based his typology, the "evolutionary typology" tend to stress economic and structural criteria as that which determines membership in a taxonomic class. Implicitly, at least, the typologies (or single types) are evolutionary or, at least, historical. The implication, or statement, is that one type develops out of another. The assumption is also that what makes for change between one category and another are modifications in the larger social, economic, and political matrices in which the particular units under consideration are imbedded.

It is interesting that most of these classifications into which, potentially, all of Latin American culture could be included had, like Redfield's concepts, grown out of research which had not been limited to a particular community, but which had attempted to describe and analyze large regions or even whole nations.

Several of the more sharply delineated constructs which have tended to replace that of Redfield grew, directly or indirectly, out of the work of Steward and his associates in Puerto Rico. Working within an evolutionary and structural framework provided by Steward (1951), they defined a series of structural types. These were seen as emergent societies resulting from the changing structure of the great commercial and industrial centers of the Western world. The value of these types lay in fact that they clearly delineated the criteria for membership. Furthermore, the criteria used fitted in with the general theoretical position of the authors vis à vis culture in general. The criteria were economic and structural. Their theory held that the interplay between technology, environment, and economy was central to an understanding of society and culture. These typologies had a further value in so far as they pointed up the kinds of broader relationships in which the small community is involved and so forced the fieldworkers to look for these relationships in his own work.

The types as delineated obviously had implications beyond those areas of the Caribbean or Latin America from which the authors had drawn the data to exemplify the types (Mintz 1953; Wolf 1955, 1957; Wolf and Mintz 1957). If the criteria for the various categories was structural and ecological, it was, in theory free of the particular content and tradition through which the relationships were expressed. This being so it becomes possible, and even imperative, that societies drawn from different traditions but characterized by similar structural complexes be compared (Wolf 1957).

Overlapping somewhat with the taxonomic categories created by Steward, Wolf, and Mintz, are those submitted by Wagley and Harris (1955) and by Adams (1956) for Latin America. Whereas the types developed by the Puerto Rican project had a number of independent categories, those presented by Wagley and Harris and by Adams more closely approached a taxonomic *system*. These two latter schema, like that which developed out of the Puerto Rico Project, emerged from the attempt to deal with large and complex cultural phenomenon. The Wagley and Harris typology grew out of the Bahia-Columbia Project, while that of Adams derived from his Central American survey.

The Wagley-Harris and Adams categories are not completely comparable. Adams stresses content differences between his categories to a greater degree than do Wagley and Harris, who weigh structural factors more heavily. Adams goes into much greater detail in reference to the aboriginal groups and also sets up categories based upon differing cultural traditions among the nonaboriginals. The Wagley-Harris system, on the other hand, has a single category that includes all the aboriginal cultures. Wagley and Harris, therefore, effectively set aboriginal cultures outside their universe of discourse. Their typology concentrates on structural criteria and is not concerned with ethnic variation among the contemporary peoples of Latin America.

When dealing with those cultures and categories which are the chief concern of this article, it is clear that the Wagley-Harris and Adams categories represent those two well-known breeds of taxonomists, the "lumpers" and the "splitters." Adams' categories could be reduced to those of Wagley and Harris, while their categories could be easily subdivided into the ones that Adams discusses. The similarities between the two schemes far outweigh their dissimilarities. Similarly, the categories defined by Steward, Mintz, and Wolf would fit easily into the typologies produced by Wagley and Harris and by Adams.

The categories that various authors have arrived at—various types of peasantries, various kinds of plantations systems, urban and rural proletariats, etc.—do not always isolate equivalent units. At times the taxonomic categories are socioeconomic classes (urban and rural proletariats). Other categories describe "types" of communities (closed corporate peasant communities). Still other categories represent institutional complexes (corporate and family plantations). Still other categories represent combinations of types of communities and social classes (metropolitan elites). In any event, all these categories attempt to define the major structural and economic-ecological central feature of "the type." They then attempt to see to what extent other features, such as values and material traits, cluster around these central structural features. The value of such typologies, aside from the sheer convenience of a framework within which to organize materials, could be improved if the reasons for the typologies, the units of analysis, and the criteria used could be more rigorously defined.

Even as they stand, however, these typologies of Latin American culture are useful in that they describe a network of relationships associated with certain central features in the culture or subculture. If the central features change, then it should be possible to predict the effect of this change across the range of cultural phenomenon. This assumes, of course, that the change is in the direction of a "type" who defining characteristics and internal structure are already known.

The typologies have other benefits. Attempts to set up categories which among them will include all the various subunits of Latin American culture serve to direct attention to the great gaps in our current knowledge of the range and varieties of this culture. The most obvious typological gaps relate to the various categories of people that reside in the cities, both provincial and metropolitan, and those areas (urban or rural) which are central to the massive economic changes occurring today in Latin America. Most of the data collected about such people by anthropologists have been collected informally and not as a result of specific research.

Problems for Future Research

First and most obvious is the need for descriptive studies. It is upon accurate description and measurement that any science ultimately depends. For anthropologists who are concerned with Latin American culture the description of the varieties of that culture are of some value in themselves. Description for the sake of description could reach a point of diminishing returns, but the areas of descriptive needs in Latin America—regional, national, and typological—are such that this danger is, for the moment, academic.

Description, however, is a function of the theoretical and problem kit which the researcher carries with him into the field or library. What is to be described will vary with the problem and interests of the particular anthropologist. One of the great contributions of anthropology, however, is that while a particular kind of problem may elicit certain kinds of data, there is always the assumption that social facts are related to each other in numerous and complex ways. One of the problems of the field worker is to describe and analyze these connections. The structure and content of the society being investigated is not assumed but described. Whether, for example, a market system exists is not decided upon the assumption that all people seek to economize, nor is it based on the physical presence of a market place. It is based on the kind of relationships and expectations that exist among people or groups when goods are being transferred.

Description is most obviously lacking for those ways of life which have emerged and are emerging from the presence of the industrial revolution in Latin America. This is no excuse, however, to ignore those types of cultures which are more traditional anthropological subjects. The Indian communities of Middle America and western South America are of interest for a multitude of theoretical and historical reasons. Furthermore, the impact of massive social change that is in process in the nations of which these communities are a part is perhaps most dramatically and clearly seen in such Indian villages. The response which the semi-isolated village must make to those changes are the most drastic kinds of readaptation. Under such circumstances, what is involved is to a large degree the emergence of a new kind of society and culture. It is in such "isolated" situations as are found in these traditional kinds of communities that the effect of planned programs of change can be most clearly observed.

Although such communities should remain the subject or the site for further research, it is also clear that such traditional objects of anthropological research are not central to the massive changes which are straining the traditional fabric of Latin American society.

It is interesting that when anthropologists are asked to take a look at contemporary national systems in Latin America, they all stress the importance of categories of people which center on metropolitan areas; they are especially concerned with the "middle class" (Council on Foreign Relations 1960). To study such systems, they must incorporate data and concepts derived from other disciplines into their own conceptual schemes. Anthropology in Latin America has been greatly influenced by the work of Latin American sociologists among their own urban populations. This growing concern with these people by anthropologists may be roughly dated from early in the 1950s with the appearance of *Materiales para el estudio de la clase media en la America Latina* (Crevenna 1950).

Having recognized the importance of various metropolitan and other "nontraditional" groups for the evolving culture of Latin America, it behooves anthropologists, I should think, to design research that will shed light upon them. Anthropological interest in these people has been in delineating them in typological categories. This kind of delineation has, of course, been done with traditional groups as well, but although when dealing with a peasantry, for example, we use a limited number of criteria in order to identify them, we know a great deal about their internal organization, material content, values, and beliefs. In a word, we know about the culture which correlates with the taxonomic criteria. Unfortunately, this cannot be said of the "nontraditional" taxa. We still know relatively little about them as organized groups; or, perhaps more accurately, we know little about the organized groups to be found within these categories. We do have good material on a few "modern types," such as workers on certain kinds of plantations. We have little or nothing on the factory worker, the miner, the oil-field roughneck, or the white-collar worker. There can be little question that such groups, as well as the urban middle and upper classes, are central to the changes that are now in process in Latin America.

There are some models before us in Latin America for the study of such categories and groups as Whiteford's work on stratification in Mexican and Columbian cities and the work of Cochran and Reina on an upper-class management group. Lewis has for some years been concerned with the lower class in Mexico City (Lewis 1952, 1959, 1961), although much of this work so far has been descriptive and biographical.

In the attempt to understand the culture of newly emerging groups in Latin America, it will probably be necessary to attack the problem at a number of levels. The focus of such studies might be such phenomena as immigration, regional or national development programs, or power structures. On the other hand, studies might focus on such groups as voluntary associations, occupational groups or categories, and others that we know are critical to the organization of urban peoples in other parts of the world. Similarly, kinship as a means of structuring economic and polital elites might come in for study. A critical group in the economic or political life of a community might be isolated as the focus of interest. Then the interconnections both within and without the community of this group could be traced. The community would not serve as the focus of interest. It would be merely the stage upon which we could see the myriad of connections (both within and without the locality) among the people, their organization, and various categories of cultural phenomenon. This is no revolutionary suggestion (see Wolf 1956), but the actual attempt to carry it into practice is yet to be made.

As anthropological interest begins to focus upon groups which are central to the functioning of a modern state, it is clear that anthropological concern with politics, labor unions, political parties, and large corporations will involve anthropology with other social science disciplines even more than it already is. This involvement will certainly require changes in anthropological method and technique at least as radical as that required when "peasantries" as well as primitives became an anthropological concern. The anthropologist will be even more involved in inter- or multi-disciplinary projects with other social sciences. And it will require anthropologists to deal with the data and concepts of other social sciences in a more sophisticated and detailed way than was necessary when the anthropologist's universe consisted chiefly of primitives and peasants. The reverse is also true. Anthropological concern with core groups in modern societies will presumably make the work of anthropologists even more relevant to the interests of the other social sciences in Latin America than it is now.

As anthropologists become involved with the study of groups central to the emerging industrial culture of Latin America, there can be little doubt that this work will be for the most part by individuals primarily concerned with a vast number of separate research problems and projects. This is as it should be. We should keep in mind, however, that in the past some of the most significant results produced by anthropology have been, directly and indirectly, the result of attempts to study large and complex phenomena. Many of these projects, such as the work of the Mexican office of the Institute of Social Anthropology in the 1940s and the Puerto Rican project, worked closely with Latin American scholars and institutions. They were also involved not only with research but also with the training of Anglo- and Latin American graduate students. The lesson of attempting the large effort, in addition to the small one, should not be forgotten. It has produced major results in a high proportion of cases where it has been tried, from the *Handbook of South American Indians* to the changes inaugurated at Vicos.

Anthropology is the study of man. In the past this definition was, *de facto,* the study of *primitive* man. Later it became the study of primitive and *peasant* man. Anthropology is now on the verge of dropping the qualifying adjective altogether.

BIBLIOGRAPHY

Adams, Richard N.
   1956   Cultural components of Central America. American Anthropologist
          58: 881–907.
   1957   Cultural surveys of Panama–Nicaragua–Guatemala–El Salvador–
          Honduras. Washington, D.C., Pan American Sanitary Bureau. Scien-
          tific Publications No. 33.
   1959   A community in the Andes: problems and progress in Muquiyauyo.
          Seattle.
   1962   Ethnohistoric research methods: some Latin American features.
          Ethnohistory 9: 179–205.
Allen, F. H., Jr.
   1958   Inheritance of the Diego (Di[a]) blood group factor. American Journal
          of Human Genetics 10: 64–67.
Arensberg, Conrad M.
   1954   The community study method. American Journal of Sociology 59:
          109–124.
   1961   The community as object and sample. American Anthropologist 63:
          241–64.

Azevedo, Thales de
1961 Italian colonization in southern Brazil. Anthropological Quarterly 34: 60–68.
Baldus Herbert
1931 Indianerstudien in nordöslichen Chaco. Forschungen zur Völkerpsychologie und Soziologie. Leipzig. Vol. XI.
1937 Ensaios de etnologia brasileira. São Paulo.
Barcellos, Fernanda A. V. F.
1951 As favelas; estudo sociológico. Niteroi, Livraria Universitária.
Bastide, Roger
1960 Les réligions africaines au Brésil: vers une sociologie des interpenetrations de civilisations. Paris.
Beals, Ralph L.
1946 Cheran: a Sierra Tarascan village. Washington, D.C., Smithsonian Institution, Institute of Social Anthropology. No. 2.
Bennett, Wendell C.
1948 A reappraisal of Peruvian archeology. Memoirs of the Society for American Archaeology, No. 4.
Bennett, Wendell C., and Junius Bird
1949 Andean culture history. New York, American Museum of Natural History. Handbook Series, No. 15.
Brand, Donald D.
1951 Quiroga: a Mexican municipio. Washington, D.C., Smithsonian Institution, Institute of Social Anthropology. No. 11.
Bunzel, Ruth
1952 Chichicastenango: a Guatemalan village. Publications of the American Ethnological Society, No. 22.
Cardoso, Fernando Henrique, and Octavio Ianni
1960 Côr e mobilidade social em Florianopolis. São Paulo.
Carneiro, Robert
1956–58 Extra-marital sex freedom among the Kuikuru indians. Revista do Museu Paulista 10: 135–42.
1961 Slash and burn cultivation among the Kuikuru. Anthropologica, Supplement II: 47–67.
Chamberlain, R.
1948 The conquest and colonization of Yucatan: 1517–1550. Washington, D.C., Carnegie Institution of Washington. No. 582.
Cochran, Thomas C., and Ruben E. Reina
1962 Entrepreneurship in Argentine culture: Torcuato di Tella and S.I.A.M. Philadelphia.
Collier, John, and Anibal Buitron
1949 The awakening valley. Chicago.
Costa Eduardo, Octavio da
1948 The Negro in northern Brazil: a study in acculturation. Monographs of the American Ethnological Society, No. 15.
Council on Foreign Relations
1960 Social change in Latin America today: its implications for United States policy. New York.
Crevenna, Theo. R. (ed.)
1950 Materiales para el estudio de la clase media en la America Latina. Publicaciones de la Oficina de Ciencias Sociales. Washington, D.C., Union Panamericana. 6 vols.
Crocker, W. H.
1961 The Canela since Nimuendaju. Anthropological Quarterly 14: 69–84.

Dobyns, Henry F., Carlos M. Monge, and Mario C. Vasquez
1962 Summary of technical-organizational progress and reactions to it. Human Organization 21: 109–15.
Dole, Gertrude E.
1956–58 Ownership and exchange among the Kuikuru indians. Revista do Museu Paulista 10: 125–33.
Elkins, Stanley M.
1959 Slavery. Chicago.
Fals Borda, Orlando
1955 Peasant society in the Andes: a sociological study of Saucio. Gainesville, Fla.
1959 Facts and theory of socio-cultural change in a rural social system. Bogotá, Universidad Nacional de Colombia, Departamento de Sociología. Monografías sociológicas, No. 2.
Faron, Louis C.
1960 The formation of two indigenous communities in coastal Peru. American Anthropologist 62: 437–53.
1961 Mapuche social structure: institutional reintegration in a patrilineal society of central Chile. Urbana, Ill.
Foster, George M.
1948 Empire's children: the people of Tzintzuntzan. Washington, D.C., Smithsonian Institution, Institute of Social Anthropology. Publication No. 6.
1953 What is folk culture? American Anthropologist 55: 159–73.
1960 Culture and conquest: America's Spanish heritage. Viking Fund Publications in Anthropology, No. 27.
Freyre, Gilberto
1956 The masters and the slaves. New York.
1963 The mansions and the shanties: the making of modern Brazil. New York.
Fried, Jacob
1962 Social organization and personal security in a Peruvian hacienda Indian community. American Anthropologist 64: 771–80.
Gamio, Manuel, et al.
1922 La población del Valle de Teotihuacan. Mexico City. 2 vols.
Gillin, John
1936 The Barama River Caribs of British Guiana. Cambridge, Mass., Papers of the Peabody Museum of Archaeology and Ethnology, Harvard University, Vol. 14, no. 2: 1–274.
1940 Some anthropological problems of the tropical forest area of South America. American Anthropologist 42: 642–56.
1947 Moche, a Peruvian coastal community. Washington, D.C., Smithsonian Institution, Institute of Social Anthropology. No. 3.
1949 Methodological problems in the anthropological study of modern cultures. American Anthropologist 51: 392–99.
Greenberg, Joseph H.
1960 The general classification of Central and South America languages. Acts of the International Congress of Anthropological and Ethnological Sciences. (Various places.)
Greenfield, Sidney M.
1963 Social change and labor commitment in southern Minas Gerais. Inter-American Economic Affairs 17: 29–58.
Gusinde, M.
1937 Die Feuerland Indianer. II. Die Yamana. Mödling bei Wien.

Gutzman Campos, German, Orlando Fals Borda, and Eduardo Umña Luna
  1962   La violencia en Colombia. Facultad de Sociología, Universid Nacional,
         Bogota. Monografias sociológicas No. 12.
Hack, H.
  1958   Primavera, a communal settlement of immigrants in Paraguay. Am-
         sterdam, Department of Cultural and Physical Anthropology, Royal
         Tropical Institute.
  n.d.   Die Kolonisation der Mennoniten im Paraguayischen Chaco. Amster-
         dam, Koninklijk Instituut fur Kulturelle und Physische Anthropolo-
         gie. No. 65.
Hammel, Eugene A.
  1962   Wealth, authority and prestige in the Ica Valley, Peru. Albuquerque.
Hammell, H. T.
  1960a Responses to cold by the Alacaluf Indians. Current Anthropology 1:
         146.
  1960b Thermal and metabolic responses of the Alacaluf Indians to moder-
         ate cold exposure. Wright Air Development Center, Technical Re-
         ports, No. 60-633.
Hansen, Asael T.
  1934   The ecology of a Latin American city. In Race and culture contacts,
         American Sociological Society. New York.
Harris, Marvin
  1956   Town and country in Brazil. New York.
Henry, Jules
  1941   Jungle people, a Kaingang tribe of the highlands of Brazil. New
         York.
Holmberg, Allan R.
  1950   Nomads of the long bow: the Siriono of eastern Bolivia. Washing-
         ton, D.C., Smithsonian Institution, Institute of Social Anthropology.
         No. 10.
  1960   Changing community attitudes and values in Peru: a case study in
         guided change. In Social change in Latin America today, Council on
         Foreign Relations. New York.
Holmberg, Allan R., and Henry F. Dobyns
  1962   The process of accelerating community change. Human Organization
         21: 107–09.
Hutchinson, Harry W.
  1957   Village and plantation life in northeastern Brazil. Seattle.
Koch-Grünberg, Theodor
  1909–10 Zwei Jahre unter den Indianern. Reisen in Nordwest-Brasilien
         1903/1905. Berlin. 2 vols.
Krause, Fritz
  1911   In den wildnissen Brasiliens. Leipzig.
La Barre, Weston
  1948   The Aymara indians of the lake Titicaca plateau, Bolivia. American
         Anthropological Association, Memoirs, No. 68.
La Farge, Oliver
  1940   Maya ethnology: the sequence of cultures. In The Maya and their
         neighbors. New York.
Landes, Ruth
  1947   The city of women. New York.
Lasswell, Harold D.
  1962   Integrating communities into more inclusive systems. Human Organ-
         ization 21: 116–24.

Layrisse, M. de, and Z. de Layrisse
1959   Frequency of the new blood group antigen Jsa among South American Indians. Nature 184 (supplement 9): 640.

Layrisse, M. de, and J. Wilbert
1961   Absence of Diego antigen: a genetic characteristic of early immigrants to South America. Science 134: 1077–78.

Laytano, Dante de
1952   A estância gaucha. Rio de Janeiro, Ministério da Agricultura, Serviço de Informação Agricola. Documentário da Vida Rural, No. 4.

Leeds, Anthony
1960   The ideology of the Yaruro Indians in relation to socio-economic organization. Anthropologica 9: 1–10.
1961   Yaruro incipient tropical forest horticulture. Anthropologica, Supplement II, pp. 13–46.
1962   Ecological determinants of chieftainship among the Yaruro Indians. International Congress of Americanists 34: 597–608.

Lewis, Oscar
1951   Life in a Mexican village: Tepoztlan revisited. Urbana, Ill.
1952   Urbanization without breakdown: a case study. Scientific Monthly 75: 31–41.
1959   Five families: Mexican case studies in the culture of poverty. New York.
1961   The children of Sanchez, autobiography of a Mexican family. New York.

McQuown, N. A.
1955   The indigenous languages of Latin America. American Anthropologist 57: 501–70.

Maybury-Lewis, D.
1956   Kinship and social organization in central Brazil. International Congress of Americanists 32: 125–35.
1960   Parallel descent and the Apinaye anomaly. Southwestern Journal of Anthropology 16: 191–216.

Meggers, Betty J., and Clifford Evans
1963   Aboriginal cultural development in Latin America: an interpretative view. Washington, D.C., Smithsonian Institution, Smithsonian Miscellaneous Collections. Vol. 146, No. 1.

Métraux, Alfred
1937   Études d'éthnographie Toba-Pilaga (Gran Chaco). Anthropos (Mödling/Wien) 32: 171–94, 378–401.
1939   Myths and tales of the Matako Indians. Etnologiska Studies (Göteborg) 9: 1–127.
1946   Myths of the Toba and Pilaga Indians. Philadelphia.

Miner, Horace
1952   The folk-urban continuum. American Sociological Review 17: 529–37.

Mintz, Sidney W.
1953   The folk-urban continuum and the rural proletarian community. American Journal of Sociology 59: 136–43.
1961   Review of Slavery, by Stanley M. Elkins. American Anthropologist 63: 579–87.

Monge M., Carlos
1952   Physiological anthropology of the dwellers in America's high plateaus. International Congress of Americanists 29 (No. 3): 361–73.

Mostny, Grete, *et al.*
1954 Peine, un pueblo Atacameño and other selections. Santiago, Chile, Museo Nacional de Historia Natural.
Murdock, George P.
1951a Behavior science outlines II.
1951b South American culture areas. Southwestern Journal of Anthropology 7: 415–36.
Murphy, Robert
1957 Intergroup hostility and social cohesion. American Anthropologist 59: 1018–35.
1958 Mundurucu religion. University of California Publications in Archaeology and Ethnology, No. 49.
1960 Headhunters' heritage. Berkeley, Calif.
Murphy, Robert, and B. Quain
1955 The Trumai Indians of central Brazil. Memoirs, American Ethnological Society, No. 34.
Newman, M. T.
1953 The application of ecological rules to the racial anthropology of the aboriginal New World. American Anthropologist 55: 311–27.
1960 Blood group systems in Latin American Indians. American Journal of Physical Anthropology, N.S. 18: 334–35.
1962 Evolutionary changes in body size and head form in American Indians. American Anthropologist 64: 237–57.
Nichols, Madeline W.
1942 The gaucho: cattle hunter, cavalryman, ideal of Romance. Durham, N.C.
Nimuendaju, Curt
1942 The Šerente. Los Angeles, The Frederick Webb Hodge Publication Fund.
1946 The eastern Timbira. Berkeley and Los Angeles.
Nordenskiöld, Erland
1924 The ethnography of South America as seen from the Mojos in Bolivia. Göteborg, Comparative Ethnographical Studies.
Oberg, Kalervo
1949 The Terena and Caduveo of southern Matto Grosso, Brazil. Washington, D.C., Smithsonian Institution, Institute of Social Anthropology. No. 9.
O'Leary, Timothy J.
1963 Ethnographic bibliography of South America. New Haven, Human Relations Area Files.
Parsons, Elsie Clews
1936 Mitla: town of souls. Chicago.
1945 Peguche: a study of Andean Indians. Chicago.
Patch, Richard W.
1960 Bolivia: U.S. assistance in a revolutionary setting. *In* Social change in Latin America today, Council on Foreign Relations. New York.
Pierson, Donald
1942 Negroes in Brazil: a study of race contact at Bahia. Chicago.
1951 Cruz das Almas: a Brazilian village. Washington, D.C., Smithsonian Institution, Institute of Social Anthropology. No. 12.
Redfield, Robert
1930 Tepoztlan: a Mexican village. Chicago.

1941 The folk culture of Yucatan. Chicago.
1947 The folk society. American Journal of Sociology 52: 293–308.
Redfield, Robert, and Alfonso Villa Rojas
1934 Chan Kom: a Maya village. Washington, D.C., Carnegie Institution of Washington. No. 448.
Redfield, Robert, Ralph Linton, and Melville J. Herskovits
1936 Memorandum for the study of acculturation. American Anthropologist 38: 149–52.
Reichel-Dolmatoff, Gerardo, and Alicia Reichel-Dolmatoff
1961 Aritama: the cultural personality of a Colombian mestizo village. Chicago.
Reynafarje, C.
1957 El factor Rh y otros grupos sanguineos. Anales de la Facultad de Medecina, Universidad Nacional de San Marcos 40 (No. 3): 573–84.
Roys, Ralph L.
1943 The Indian background of colonial Yucatan. Washington, D.C., Carnegie Institution of Washington. No. 548.
Salzano, F. M.
1957 The blood groups of South American Indians. American Journal of Physical Anthropology N.S. 15: 555–79.
Santa Cruz, A.
1960 Acquiring status in Guajiro society. Anthropological Quarterly 33: 115–27.
Scholes, F. V.
1937 The beginnings of Hispano-Indian society in Yucatan. Washington, D.C., Carnegie Institution of Washington. Supplementary Publication No. 30.
Service, Elman R.
1954a Spanish-Guarani relations in early colonial Paraguay. Anthropological Papers, Museum of Anthropology, University of Michigan, No. 9.
1954b Tobati: Paraguayan town. Chicago.
1955 Indian-European relations in colonial Latin America. American Anthropologist 57: 411–25.
Schmidt, Max
1905 Indianerstudien in zentral-brasilien. Erlebnisse und ethnologische Ergebnisse einer Reise in den Jahren 1900–1901. Berlin.
Shattuck, G. C.
1930 The peninsula of Yucatan, medical, biological, meteorological and sociological studies. Washington, D.C., Carnegie Institution of Washington. No. 431.
Silva, Zedar Perfeito da
1954 O vale do Itajaí. Rio de Janeiro, Ministério da Agricultura, Serviço de Informação Agrícola. Documentário da Vida Rural No. 6.
Smith, T. Lynn, and Alexander Marchant (eds.)
1951 Brazil: portrait of half a continent. New York.
Sociedad de Ciencias Naturales La Salle
1953 La region de Perija y sus habitantes. Publicaciones de la Universid del Zulia, Venezuela.
Soler Bustamante, Eduardo
1954 La agricultura en la communidad de San Pedro de Huancaire. Publicaciones, Universidad Nacional Mayor de San Marcos, Instituto de Etnologia 23: No. 9. Lima.

Steggerda, M.
1932 Anthropometry of adult Maya Indians; a study of their physical and physiological characteristics. Washington, D.C., Carnegie Institution of Washington. No. 434.
Stein, Stanley J.
1957 Vassouras: a Brazilian coffee county, 1850–1900. Cambridge, Mass.
Stein, William W.
1961 Hualcan: life in the Highlands of Peru. Ithaca, N.Y.
Steinen, Karl von den
1894 Unter den naturvölkern zentral Brasilien. Berlin.
Steward, Julian H.
1950 Area research, theory and practice. New York, Social Science Research Council.
1951 Levels of sociocultural integration. Southwestern Journal of Anthropology 7: 374–90.
Steward, Julian H., and Louis Faron
1959 Native peoples of South America. New York.
Steward, Julian H. et al.
1956 The people of Puerto Rico; a study in social anthropology. Urbana, Ill.
Steward, Julian H. (ed.)
1946 Handbook of South American Indians. Washington, D.C., Smithsonian Institution, Bureau of American Ethnology, Bulletin 143. 6 vols.
Strickon, Arnold
1962 Class and kinship in Argentina. Ethnology 1: 500–15.
1965 Hacienda and plantation in Yucatan: an historical-ecological consideration of the folk-urban continuum in Yucatan. America Indigena. In press.
Strong, William Duncan, and Clifford Evans
1952 Cultural stratigraphy in the Viru Valley, northern Peru: the formative and florescent epochs. New York.
Tax, Sol
1953 Penny capitalism: a Guatemalan Indian economy. Washington, D.C., Smithsonian Institution, Institute of Social Anthropology. No. 16.
Titiev, Mischa
1951 Araucanian culture in transition. Occasional contributions from the Museum of Anthropology of the University of Michigan, No. 15.
Tschopik, Harry, Jr.
1948 Highland communities of central Peru. Washington, D.C., Smithsonian Institution, Institute of Social Anthropology. No. 5.
Vidart, Daniel D.
1955 La vida rural Uruguaya. Montevideo, Ministerio de Ganaderia y Agricultura, Departamento de Sociología Rural. No. 1.
Villa Rojas, Alfonso
1945 The Maya of east central Quintana Roo. Washington, D.C., Carnegie Institution of Washington. No. 559.
Wagley, Charles
1940 World view of the Tapirape Indians. Journal of American Folklore 53: No. 210.
1941 Economics of the Guatemalan village. Memoirs, American Anthropological Association, No. 58.

1943 Xamanismo Tapirapé. Boletim do Museu Nacional, N.S. Anthro-
      pologia, No. 3, Rio de Janeiro.
1949 The social and religious life in a Guatemalan village. Memoirs,
      American Anthropological Association, No. 71.
1952 The folk culture of the Brazilian Amazon. *In* Selected Papers of the
      XXIXth International Congress of Americanists, Sol Tax, ed. Chi-
      cago, pp. 224–30.
1953 Amazon Town: a study of man in the tropics. New York.
Wagley, Charles, and Eduardo Galvão
1949 The Tenetehara Indians of Brazil. Columbia University Contribu-
      tions to Anthropology, No. 35.
Wagley, Charles, and Marvin Harris
1955 A typology of Latin American cultures. American Anthropologist
      57: 428–51.
Wagley, Charles (ed.)
1952 Race and class in rural Brazil. New York.
Whiteford, Andrew H.
1960 Two cities of Latin America: a comparative description of social
      classes. Beloit, Wis., Logan Museum of Anthropology, Beloit College.
Wilbert, J.
1958 Kinship and social organization of the Yekuana and Guajiro. South-
      western Journal of Anthropology 14: 51–60.
Willems, Emilio
1946 A aculturação dos alemães no Brasil. São Paulo, Cia, Editora Nacional.
1947 Cunha: tradição e transição em uma cultura rural do Brasil. São
      Paulo, Diretoria de Publicidade Agrícola, Secretaria da Agricultura
      do Estado de São Paulo.
1948 Aspectos da aculturação dos japoneses no Estado de São Paulo. São
      Paulo, Universidade de São Paulo, Faculdade de Filosofia, Ciências e
      Letras, Boletim 82.
1953 Buzios island: a Caiçara community in southern Brazil. Monographs
      of the American Ethnological Society, No. 20.
1958 Minority subcultures in Brazil. XXXI Congreso Internacional de
      Americanistas. Mexico, Universidad Nacional Autonoma de Mexico,
      pp. 877–84.
Williams, Eric E.
1944 Capitalism and slavery. Chapel Hill, N.C.
Wissler, Clark
1917 The American Indian. New York.
Wolf, Eric R.
1955 Types of Latin American peasantry. American Anthropologist 57:
      452–71.
1956 Aspects of group relations in a complex society: Mexico. American
      Anthropologist 58: 1065–78.
1957 Closed corporate peasant communities in Meso-America and Central
      Java. Southwestern Journal of Anthropology 13: 1–18.
Wolf, Eric R., and Sidney W. Mintz
1957 Haciendas and plantations in Middle America and the Antilles.
      Social and Economic Studies 6: 380–412.

5. The State of Research on Latin America: Political Science

MERLE KLING

Political research on Latin America resembles the area which is the object of its study. It retains underdeveloped and traditional features; it is under both internal and external pressures to modernize.

Little capital (funds, talent, or organizational experience) has been invested in political studies of Latin America, and as a result the returns have been relatively meager. Personnel with adequate training and appropriate technical competence have been in scarce supply, research techniques adapted to Latin American studies have been of a relatively primitive nature, and the level of productivity has been low. Political scientists conducting research on Latin America, like some landowners, have been reluctant to introduce advanced tools and machinery and to extend the intellectual acreage under cultivation—that is, to acquire new skills, to accept technical assistance, to encourage methods designed to diversify the crop of research findings, and to consider a redistribution of disciplinary properties. Political scientists specializing in Latin America have not reached, to borrow Rostow's familiar metaphor, the take-off stage. Like the large segment of the population functioning on the output side of Latin American political systems, they often have been content to play the role of consumers rather than creators of the newer conceptual products of modern political science. They therefore have enjoyed few of the rewards and exposed themselves to few of the hazards of participation in more recent experimental trends in political science.

With the aim of encouraging a program of political research

on Latin America, this paper will describe some of the studies
published in the past, analyze the nature of the current transitional phase in the evolution of political studies of Latin America, and point to some of the research opportunities and needs
in the field of Latin American political studies.[1]

Traditional Studies of Latin American Politics

Elements of traditional cultures inevitably survive in modernizing environments. The style of living of a single individual
may, indeed, incorporate both the heritage of an ancient Indian
community and the complex rituals of a modern industrialized
metropolis, for at a specific point in time the congeries of traditional values are not totally displaced by the distinctive patterns
of behavior attributed to a modern culture. Likewise, traditional
political studies of Latin America have not been relegated to an
abandoned past. They continue to be carried on by meticulous,
and sometimes sophisticated, research workers, and their contributions are not merely anachronistic and dysfunctional. Modern
political science does not discard its Indian heritage when it exchanges the *huaraches* of constitutional documents for the shoes
of IBM cards. And the same scholar, of course, may—even must
—wear the footgear of both intellectual cultures when he con-
ducts research. Neither chronological time nor personality completely differentiates the past from the present. Traditionalism in
political science, rather, is distinguished by its content and methods.

The accumulation of data has been the major preoccupation
of traditional political research on Latin America, the failure to
construct explanatory theory (on the basis of generalizations
derived from systematic observation) has been its major short-
coming, and the generous distribution of prescriptions for public
policies has been its major diversion. A general survey of political

[1] The fields of international relations, international organization, and international law, as they impinge upon the study of Latin American political
processes, are construed as falling outside the boundaries of this paper.
Accordingly, the paper omits comment upon such works as L. Lloyd Mecham,
The United States and Inter-American Security, 1889–1960 (Austin, Texas),
C. Neale Ronning, *Law and Politics in Inter-American Diplomacy* (New York,
1963), Bryce Wood, *The Making of the Good Neighbor Policy* (New York,
1961), and John C. Dreier, *The Organization of American States and the
Hemisphere Crisis* (New York, 1962).

literature might yield the same set of judgments for the entire discipline of political science, for the term "traditional" is not used in any pejorative sense. Rather, as indicated below, it indicates an approach often basic and necessary before other research can be carried out, and it reflects the status of the discipline of political science at the time most such studies were carried out. By the same token, the term "modern" does not connote any ideal approach to the problems of political science. It is used to suggest a more general awareness of the full range of methods and concepts that have come into the forefront in recent years, such as the comparative, the behavioral, and the quantitative or mathematical.

Since the days of James Bryce, political literature dealing with Latin America has been composed predominantly of an amalgam of reports of personal observations, commentary on the discrepancies between formal governmental structure and effective practice, speculative explanations (there has been a shift from a racial to an economic emphasis) of the "causes" of violence and instability, and expressions of regret that the Spanish conquerors neither personified nor propagated the democratic faith. Sometimes the data and opinions have been organized on a country-by-country basis, sometimes the chapters have been arranged topically and references to conditions in particular countries have been inserted for illustrative purposes (in a "for example" spirit), occasionally a monograph has been devoted to a single country or specialized topic. But boundary lines among journalism, history, law, and social science often have been blurred and value preferences liberally interlarded.

Although Bryce's (1926) work, originally published in 1912, did not inspire many political scientists to turn their attention to Latin America, it served as a recognizable antecedent, if not a prototype, for the general volumes on Latin American governments and politics that were published after World War II. Bryce's treatment was both topical and country by country. Despite his professed "curiosity to learn the causes which produced so many revolutions and civil wars in Spanish America" (p. xvii), he refrained from engaging in systematic political analysis or elaborate political reporting. He included chapters on the history and races of Latin America, he described in some detail geo-

graphical and social conditions in the seven South American republics that he had visited, and he concluded with "Some Reflections and Forecasts." While his lengthy sections on geography
sometimes resemble a travel guide and his misunderstanding of
concepts of race can only alarm a generation that has endured
Hitler, his perception of Latin American problems lingers on in
contemporary political science: after all, one of his chapters is entitled, "The Rise of New Nations"!

After World War I, political science in the United States became self-consciously cosmopolitan. It turned its attention to western Europe, eastern Europe, international relations, and the
League of Nations; but it could scarcely have displayed greater
indifference to the internal politics and governments of the Latin
American countries. Under the auspices of the Carnegie Institution of Washington, however, several monographs were published: specifically one on Argentina (Rowe 1921), on Brazil
(James 1923), on Peru (Stuart 1925), and on Bolivia (Cleven
1940). As the titles suggest, these studies were cast largely, though
not exclusively, in a legalistic framework. In addition, the interwar period was marked by the publication of Mecham's massive
study, *Church and State in Latin America* (1934), with its focus
indicated by its subtitle, *A History of Politico-Ecclesiastical Relations*. Also prior to active participation by the United States in
World War II, an issue of the *Annals* of the American Academy
of Political and Social Science was devoted to a symposium on
the topic, "Mexico Today" (1940). We search in vain, however,
for a comprehensive treatise on political conflict in a single Latin
American country or a textbook on the area written from the
perspectives of political science. Before World War II, it was left
largely to journalists and a few heterodox historians (since im-
mersion in Latin American colonial history has been the orthodox source of status awards for historical scholarship) to cope
with such dramatic political movements as the Mexican revolution.

Nor did political scientists vigorously respond to the stimuli of
official expressions of interest in Latin America on the part of the
U.S. government during World War II. By any standards the
scholarly yield of the war effort must be regarded as meager, yet
the analytical boundaries set by the Carnegie-sponsored studies

were enlarged. Stevenson (1942), utilizing documents and interviews (but, of course, not sample survey techniques), published a historical account of the Chilean popular front, which stressed the nature of party alignments. The same year saw the appearance of Macdonald's *The Government of the Argentine Republic*, which sought to describe party programs and electoral practices as well as governmental structure in the pre-Peron era. A volume on Brazilian government and politics (Loewenstein 1942), however, provoked a reviewer, perhaps unfairly, to complain that "only a political philosopher could have devoted a large and learned book to a constitution that does not exist except upon paper" (Tannenbaum 1943).

Only after World War II did the first more or less conventional textbook appear. In the absence of rich deposits of monographic literature susceptible to synthesis and analysis, Macdonald (1949) also may be regarded as a research contribution. Besides an opening chapter attempting to identify common features of Latin American political life (such as *caudillismo*), this volume, in a country-by-country sequence, described governmental institutions and reviewed party conflicts in the twenty Latin American republics. Except for its brief descriptive sections on the geography, economy, and general social structure of most Latin American countries and its historical synopses, Macdonald's textbook sought to shape Latin American materials into the familiar mold of textbooks on the government and politics of the United States.

Subsequent textbooks, such as Jorrin (1953), Pierson and Gil (1957), Davis (1958), and Stokes (1959), have assembled political data under such chapter headings as "The Executive Power," "The Legislature," "The Judiciary," "Political Parties and Elections," "Revolutions," "The Army," "Constitutional Developments," and "Municipal Government." They have commonly included lengthy chapters on education, demography, and economic development in Latin America. The authors frequently have compiled larger masses of data than Macdonald, sometimes have exploited the taxonomic potentialities of a topical organization, and sporadically have posed explanatory problems; but they have not exhibited a sustained concern for systematic political analysis. The presentation of data, ordered without special reference to explicit conceptual schemes, has been their chief preoccupation.[2]

Traditional studies of individual states have likewise retained a descriptive, historical, and normative focus. Such volumes as those by Stokes (1950), Fitzgibbon (1957), Tucker (1957), and Taylor (1960a) reflect diligent research and a capacity for the tenacious pursuit of elusive data. All these writers are sensitive to the limited clues to political behavior offered by the content of constitutional documents. Implicitly at least, they reveal a concern with problems of prediction. Nevertheless, large portions of these studies trace, in the spirit of the historian, the political and constitutional development of Honduras, Mexico, and Uruguay and describe, in the spirit of the lawyer, the formal procedures of government. They approach most closely some of the emphases of modern political science in their analyses of party organization and electoral practices. In conformity with the ethos of traditionalism they, of course, shun neither reification nor value judgments:

There is much to admire in both the structure and the functioning of Honduran government. . . . Authority without responsibility, however, is objectionable in both the theory and practice of government (Stokes 1950: 298, 300).

Thus far Uruguay has been made to seem, by and large, a paragon. There are debits to be recorded, however—fortunately neither numerous nor fatal (Fitzgibbon 1954: 271).

Mexico can be regarded as a developing democracy because of its representative governmental structure and its recent progress in the direction of responsibility to the people (Tucker 1957: 419).

In Uruguay,

The State clearly has promised more than it has been able to deliver. . . . Although its leaders know . . . that the State misuses the services of a shockingly large percentage of the productive population, there has been no slightest effort made to encourage either narrow or broad-scale improvement within the bureaucracy (Taylor 1960a: 156–57).

Among works primarily devoted to the synthesis and organization of data on a single Latin American country, Blanksten's

---

[2] An abridged version in this genre is illustrated by the works of Alexander (1962a) and Gomez (1960). The latter omits the usual chapters on social and economic factors.

Ecuador: Constitutions and Caudillos (1953a) is notable on at least three counts: its value judgments are inserted with extreme restraint, its literary style does not impose an obstacle for the reader, and its conclusion that in Ecuador "the Indian must die . . . in a cultural sense" (Blanksten 1953a: 176) anticipates a later stress among political scientists on cultural change as a corollary, if not a prerequisite, of political change.

The collection of constitutional documents with accompanying commentary is, I suppose, the most widely recognized manifestation of traditionalism in political science. This facet of traditionalism in Latin American studies is registered chiefly in Fitzgibbon's useful reference work, *The Constitutions of the Americas* (1948).[3] In addition, the legal documents, along with brief descriptions of their historical context, providing for the formal structure of Colombian governments from 1811 to 1945, have been brought together [4] by Gibson (1948).

Latin American scholars, as might be anticipated, have made contributions largely from the perspectives of public law. The academic structure of Latin American universities tends to assign the study of government to the law faculties, and political studies originating in Latin America accordingly incline in the direction of formal description of administration and constitutional exegesis. Falling into these categories are such works as Gonzalez Calderon (1930, 1931), Lazcano y Mazón (1942), Linares Quintana (1946), Miranda (1957), Mendieta y Nuñez (1942), Lopez Rosado (1955), Lanz Duret (1947), and Fabregat (1949).

When Latin American scholars have allowed their attention to wander from governmental institutions, they have not embraced empirical research. Their academic culture and tradition, rather, apparently has provided a congenial environment for speculative and philosophical excursions into nonlegalistic subject matter.

[3] Latin American Constitutions in English translation have also been collected by Peaslee (1950, 1956).

[4] The scope of Vanorden Shaw's study, *The Early Constitutions of Chile, 1810–1833* (1930), is indicated by the title. The 1853 constitution of Argentina and the 1891 constitution of Brazil, with brief historical introductions, are printed in Wallace (1894). The monograph by Amadeo (1943) concentrates on the role of the judiciary in the Argentine federal system before the Peron era. Scott (1951) discussed the Peron Constitution. Clagett (1952) acknowledges adherence to one standard of traditionalism when the author observes (p. 13): "It is not within the scope of the present work to go into any other aspects of the matter than legislation as it appears on the statute books."

The brief essay on political parties by Mendieta y Nuñez (1947) adheres to the format of an early phase of sociological and political thought, and U.S. students will recognize citations to Max Weber and R. N. MacIver. Echaiz (1939) reviews, without the distracting apparatus of footnotes, the development of Chilean parties in the context of Chilean history. The thick volume on *Los partidos politicos: Instrumentos de gobierno* (1945) by Linares Quintana approaches the study of political parties from the point of view of comparative law and comparative legislation. Political science as carried out by Latin Americans has been mainly oriented toward "filosofia" (Holt 1963) and formal legal studies.

Despite the current ubiquity of "readers"—books composed mainly of other people's writings—the legacy of traditional political science includes only one substantial book of readings in the Latin American field, *The Evolution of Latin American Government* (1951) by Christensen.[5] This volume probably accurately reflected the state of Latin American studies immediately following World War II. It did not seek to point instruction and research on Latin American politics in new directions. Incorporating selections chiefly from North American historians, sociologists, economists, and political scientists, the book foreshadowed the topically-organized textbooks of the next decade in both its form and its content. As compared with the Christensen volume, *Political Behavior* (1956), a book of readings edited by Eulau, Eldersveld, and Janowitz, enlarged the audience for the findings and methods of a more self-conscious and empirically-oriented political science and thus could influence at least somewhat the tilt of the research effort in American politics.

Concomitants of Traditionalism

Fastidious concern with methodology can frustrate students of the "substance" of Latin American politics and exasperate the harassed policy maker, for they demand "facts" and up-to-date analyses of political trends and events. Sets of conceptual premises, nevertheless, have consequences. Unavoidably they establish

[5] Kantor and Chang-Rodríguez (1961) have edited a textbook for students of Spanish that includes selections from prominent political figures in Latin America.

standards of relevance for research and interpretation of the political scene. What have been the consequences of traditionalism
for research on Latin American politics and government? What
generalizations can be made about the quantity and nature of
the products of traditional research in this field?

Initially, the positive contributions of traditional research
should be acknowledged. Thanks to the products of traditionalism, we have available studies in some depth of the formal governmental heritage of a number of Latin American countries.
The monographic studies of Honduras, Ecuador, Uruguay, and
Mexico illuminate the institutional environment of political conflict in these countries. Textbooks have made considerable quan-
tities of available facts readily accessible. Traditional studies have
richly documented such relevant characteristics of political behavior in Latin America as instability in the tenure of governmental personnel, *caudillismo,* and the dominance of the executive; and they have suggested and often stressed, especially since
World War II, that numerous cultural factors, both social and
economic in content, cannot be ignored by political scientists in
quest of an understanding of Latin American politics.

The yield of traditionalism, however, has failed to satisfy many
political scientists of varied conceptual persuasions and policy
makers of diverse partisan loyalties. In the first place, the rate of
obsolescence in traditional research is relatively high. Latin
American society is changing rapidly. Latin American political
regimes are often short-lived. The formal governmental structure of a nation, including the constitutional-legal bases of its
government, may change before a book is through the press. Research concentrating exclusively on the description of formal governmental structure in Latin America quickly can acquire a dimension that endows it with greater relevance to the historian
than the political scientist.

Second, scholarly productivity under conditions of traditionalism has been extremely low. Few political scientists have been
recruited into the Latin American field, and embarrassing gaps
in scholarship have persisted. Only recently have a handful of
young North American political scientists begun to specialize on
Brazil! In fact, as yet there is no book-length manuscript dealing
with Brazilian politics since the suicide of Vargas in 1954. And
this almost incredible gap exists despite popular forecasts that
Brazil, as a concomitant of its size, population, and social fer-

ment, is destined to exert significant weight in the international political conflicts of the future. Although Argentina regularly finds a place on lists of "advanced" and "important" countries in Latin America, no political scientist has completed a book-length study of Argentine politics since Peron was deposed in 1955.[6] Quite apart from questions of methodological elegance, political scientists have not provided us with comprehensive studies of countries in Latin America with prima-facie claims to our attention.

Third, traditionalism in Latin American political studies, as in other sectors of political science, has been characterized by conceptual vagueness and semantic ambiguity. Criteria for the inclusion or exclusion of data in particular studies often appear to reflect relatively casual interests of authors and some of the conventional categories of political science. What is the relationship between the geographical data, frequently introduced, and the manner in which the legislature operates (or, rather, does not operate)? Why does a volume on Mexican government include the sentence, "Petroleum was used for medicinal and specialized purposes by the Aztecs" (Tucker 1957: 251)? Traditionalism, in other words, does not appear to have imposed an obligation upon investigators to define specific problems and to offer explanations derived from the systematic correlation of pertinent evidence. In these studies relationships between one kind of data and another are assumed or asserted rather than demonstrated or verified.

Since, moreover, the vocabulary of the politics of the western world—sufficiently deceptive when the usage is confined to the world of its origin—has been transferred without purification to the study of Latin America, attempts at the kind of explanation that is directed toward prediction either do not take place or lead into an analytical cul-de-sac. For the designation of men and groups in Latin America as "democrats," "socialists," "fascists," "nationalists," and "communists" provides unreliable clues to their political behavior. If we are in search of indices to political action by groups in Latin America, the normative language of western political science serves the purpose of neither accurate description nor heuristic classification. The language identifies the groups of which the author approves and disapproves, but it

---

[6] Whitaker (1956), a historian, has analyzed the revolt against Peron and the nature and policies of the succeeding government in Argentina.

does not differentiate among the political interests in conflict or the decisions that will be made by those in a position to exercise power.

The main source of data for traditional research has been the written word. Political scientists anchored in traditional research methods have relied chiefly upon documents and books stored in libraries and acquired in foreign travel to provide them with the raw materials for their studies. In addition, they have drawn upon their observations while traveling in Latin America and have tapped residents of Latin America for information and opinion to supplement written sources. But they have not engaged in fieldwork with the passionate intensity of the anthropologist, and they have not conducted interviews with the sociologist's eye to quantification.

Finally, traditionalism has been characterized by the relative isolation of Latin American studies from the field of comparative politics. While there may be some difficulty for an area specialist in remaining intellectually alert to experimental departures in his discipline, the ties between traditional Latin Americanists and the discipline of political science, especially the field of comparative politics, seem unusually tenuous. Symptomatically, virtually no general treatises in comparative politics incorporate Latin American data,[7] whereas data on the Soviet area regularly are introduced, and the inclusion of materials on Asia in textbooks devoted to comparative politics no longer signifies radical innovation.

On the negative side, therefore, we conclude that traditional research has failed to provide adequate data—regardless of the methodological criterion invoked—on important countries in Latin America, has been analytically careless, and has suffered from incomplete assimilation into the discipline of political science.

Symptoms of Transition

Traditional political research on Latin America, it perhaps should be stressed, has not disappeared. Traditionalism continues

[7] Brief chapters on Mexico and Brazil were included in the textbook edited by Marx (1949); and a brief chapter on Argentina appeared in Ogg and Zink (1949). Token representation of Latin American countries in these textbooks does not require qualification of the generalization made in the body of the paper.

to survive in the current environment of rapid change within the discipline of political science. Under prevailing circumstances, the same individual may concurrently carry on both traditional and nontraditional research. Despite the persistence of traditional features, however, contemporary political science may be regarded as predominantly transitional in its nature. In concepts, emphases, and methods, it tends to challenge traditionalism. It is less concerned with formal procedures, written prescriptions, interesting anecdotes, governmental structure, recommendations for public policy, and normative judgments. It is somewhat more concerned with power, interests, parties, groups, elections, processes of decision-making, operational rules of the game, conceptual self-consciousness, analytical devices, methodological rigor, and the potentialities of quantification.[8] In the Latin American field, it is represented in some of the work of Alexander (an economist), Blanksten, Brandenburg, Fitzgibbon, Gil, Johnson (a historian), Kantor, Kling, Lieuwen (a historian), Lipset (a sociologist who is not a Latin American specialist), Padgett, Scott, Silvert, Stokes, and Taylor and in some of the reports of the American Universities field staff. These men, of course, are not united by a common disciplinary ideology; some, indeed, view modernizing trends in research with anything but enthusiasm, some appear indifferent to the divisions within the discipline of political science, and some who profess to embrace nontraditional objectives probably would not escape a blackball if they applied for active membership in the club of behavioral political scientists. Their research, nevertheless, seems motivated by a desire to shift the traditional focus of political studies of Latin America.

[8] No term enjoys universal acceptance to designate modernizing tendencies within political science, but "behaviorism," with all its ambiguities, is probably the most widely employed label for the movement that has gained momentum since the Second World War. While recognizing that there is "no single way of characterizing" the intellectual components of this movement, Easton (1962: 7–8) has compiled a list of items that "probably includes all the major tenets of the behavioral credo":

"(1) Regularities: There are discoverable uniformities in political behavior. These can be expressed in generalizations or theories with explanatory and predictive value. (2) Verification: The validity of such generalizations must be testable, in principle, by reference to relevant behavior. (3) Techniques: Means for acquiring and interpreting data cannot be taken for granted. They are problematic and need to be examined self-consciously, refined, and validated so that rigorous means can be found for observing, recording, and analyzing behavior. (4) Quantification: Precision in the recording of data and the statement of findings require measurement and quantification, not for their own sake, but only where possible, relevant, and meaningful in the

The outstanding contributions of the transitional phase of political science to Latin American studies, in the opinion of this writer, are Scott's *Mexican Government in Transition* (1959) and Silvert's *A Study in Government: Guatemala* (1954). The attempt to apply an explicit scheme of political analysis and to integrate that scheme into a general model of political change sets off Scott's achievement from the bulk of research on Latin American politics. Not content with "simple empirical data-gathering," he deliberately aims for generalization and justifiably claims that "The principal difference between this and other studies of Mexican government, at least with regard to substantive materials, is that the data is presented within a particular frame of reference, based upon what is hoped to be an internally consistent and logical method." He conscientiously and successfully executes a research design which draws inspiration from interest group analysis (as developed by Bentley and Truman) and the model of differences between non-Western and Western systems of politics elaborated by Kahin, Pauker, and Pye in their report on comparative politics in non-western countries (1955). Within his conceptual boundaries, Scott organizes and presents a significant body of Mexican political data, with special attention to the party system and the presidency. The book, appropriately for a work illustrating research in a culture in transition, does not sever links with the past: value judgments are not absent, democracy is retained as a relevant criterion for assessing change, and

---

light of other objectives. (5) Values: Ethical evaluation and empirical explanation involve two different kinds of propositions that, for the sake of clarity, should be kept analytically distinct. However, a student of political behavior is not prohibited from asserting propositions of either kind separately or in combination as long as he does not mistake one for the other. (6) Systematization: Research ought to be systematic; that is to say, theory and research are to be seen as closely intertwined parts of a coherent and orderly body of knowledge. Research untutored by theory may prove trivial, and theory unsupported by data, futile. (7) Pure science: The application of knowledge is as much a part of the scientific enterprise as theoretical understanding. But the understanding and explanation of political behavior logically precede and provide the basis for efforts to utilize political knowledge in the solution of urgent practical problems of society. (8) Integration: Because the social sciences deal with the whole human situation, political research can ignore the findings of other disciplines only at the peril of weakening the validity and undermining the generality of its own results. Recognition of this interrelationship will help to bring political science back to its status of earlier centuries and return it to the main fold of the social sciences." (See also Eulau 1963; Dahl 1961, 1963.)

the research procedures are sufficiently conventional to reassure defenders of the traditional culture.

Although Silvert (1954) does not subscribe to as specific a research strategy as Scott, his work on Guatemala is distinguished by its conceptual sensitivity, its seizure of opportunities to generalize (especially with regard to the phenomenon of nationalism), its appreciation of the links between cultural norms and political practices, and its wealth of detail.

Aside from Scott's study of Mexican government and politics and Silvert's study of Guatemala, which manifest numerous features of political science in transition, research associated with the current transitional phase can be grouped under the following headings: studies of parties, interest groups, and elections; analyses of (political) system's traits; improvements in the quality of political reporting and data collection; experiments in quantification; and evidence of assimilation into the field of comparative politics.

STUDIES OF PARTIES, INTEREST GROUPS, AND ELECTIONS

The largest volume of transitional research in Latin American politics falls into this category, and the yield in this sector of Latin American studies has been a relatively rich one. Political scientists, perhaps relying upon a somewhat plastic interpretation of interest groups, have not been deterred by the pessimistic implications of Silvert's conclusion (1959: 77) that "Interest or pressure groups are few in Latin America. Where caudillistic one-party rule holds sway, there is insufficient complication to give much room to variegated pressure groups."

Published studies concerned with the role of groups, parties, and elections in Latin American political systems include: Blanksten (1959), which classifies a variety of groups that compete for power and influence, distinguishes among the kinds of party systems operating in Latin America, and persuasively argues for the comparative analysis of groups in order to facilitate theory construction; Fitzgibbon's (1957) review of "The Party Potpourri in Latin America"; Abbott (1951) on the contemporary political parties of Chile; Lieuwen (1961), a substantial analysis of the diverse effects of military organizations upon Latin American politics; Johnson (1958), a strikingly successful effort to establish and support a consistent thesis about the relationship between the rise of a social group and the contemporary patterns of politics in Uruguay, Chile, Argentina, Mexico, and Brazil; Johnson (1962), in a chapter contributed to a book on *The Role of the Military in Underdeveloped Countries;* Kantor (1953), a study of the Peruvian Aprista movement; Kantor (1958), on the Costa Rican election of 1953; Gil (1962), on the political parties of Chile; Schneider (1958), on Communism in Guatemala; Taylor (1963), on Uruguay; and Alexander's (1949, 1957, 1958) prolific and policy-oriented work.

Political scientists stimulated by the group approach have showered more attention upon Mexico than upon any other Latin American country. In addition to Scott's book, there are Brandenburg (1958), a useful compilation of business organizations in Mexico, originally prepared as a report for the Committee on Comparative Politics of the Social Science Research Council; Kling (1961), a study confined to a single business association; Padgett (1960); and Taylor (1960b).

ANALYSES OF POLITICAL SYSTEMS

Contemporary methodological ferment in political science has been marked by, among other things, a quest for comprehensive frameworks of analysis, and a by-product of this quest has been the passage of the phrase "political system" into the stream of discourse of the discipline. While only a limited amount of empirical research reflects the application of the "systems model," the terminology has rapidly established its status in the vocabulary of political science.

Perhaps the most influential version of this approach has been formulated by Almond, in a paper ultimately republished as the introductory chapter to *The Politics of Developing Areas* (1960).[9] To this volume, Blanksten (1960) has contributed a substantial section which seeks to adapt Almond's concepts to Latin American phenomena and to recast a considerable quantity of the available data on Latin America within Almond's categories. Conforming to the present stage of development of political science, Blanksten, rather than offering a novel explanation of behavior derived from the exploitation of newly discovered raw materials, introduces a fresh synthesis of Latin American social, economic, and political data.

[9] Easton (1957: 383–400) has also developed a scheme designed for the investigation of political systems.

Several writers, without self-consciously utilizing an overarching scheme of political analysis or a uniform vocabulary, have attempted to identify and explain aspects of political behavior which appear widely distributed in Latin America. To a degree they have engaged in the analysis of traits of an ideal type—the usage is Weber's and carries no utopian connotations—of political system in Latin America, although they have not explicitly and deliberately organized their findings and interpretations within a framework of systems analysis. Their unit of analysis consequently may not achieve the levels of generality required for comparative political analysis pointed in cosmopolitan directions. But their studies of the nature and functions of violence, instability, and nationalism in Latin America may be regarded as exercises in analysis of a system's traits. Illustrations of such research and interpretation focusing on widely diffused political traits in Latin America include Stokes (1952), a study which emphasizes the pervasiveness and integral quality of violence in Latin American political systems and provides a taxonomy of violence in this area; Kling (1956), which argues a particular thesis to account for the chronic replacement of leading personnel by methods not authorized by written constitutional documents; and Silvert (1961b), which discusses implications of nationalism for the area and recognizes the diverse perspectives inherent in the concept of nationalism.

IMPROVEMENTS IN THE QUALITY OF POLITICAL
REPORTING AND DATA COLLECTING

Specialists in Latin American affairs are accustomed to deplore the treatment of Latin American news in the mass media. They are disposed to describe news coverage of the area as shallow, inadequate, distorted, and spasmodic. Latin American events, they complain, are not accorded equal space with other geographical areas in the columns of newspapers. In their view, journalistic accounts often cater to the popular stereotype of Latin American politics as an entertainment composed of recurring acts of inexplicable violence. Specialists inevitably have expressed regret at the absence of reliable sources which might provide a steady flow of relevant information.

The problem of creating an abundant supply of accurate information for analysis has not been solved, and newspaper headlines continue to be monopolized by accounts of recent and impending outbreaks of violence in Latin America. But some publications, perhaps inspired by the vision of a less traditional climate for Latin American studies, have contributed a dimension of depth to the reporting of selected Latin American conditions and have made a serious effort to improve and stabilize the gathering and presentation of certain kinds of data. Thus, the *Reports* of the American Universities field staff devoted to Latin America incorporate analyses by scholars with prolonged field experience. The *Reports* do not embrace the entire Latin American area and they are not a substitute for a comprehensive file on the sequence of events in Latin America. These *Reports*, nevertheless, comprise brief, readable, and authoritative interpretations of politically relevant developments which have engaged the attention of their authors. Among the subjects of the *Reports* have been "The Peruvian Elections of 1962 and Their Annulment" (Patch 1962a); "Personalities and Politics in Bolivia" (Patch 1962b); "Political Universes in Latin America" (Silvert 1961d); and "The Annual Political Cycle of Argentina" (Silvert 1961c). Such essays not only draw upon firsthand experiences but also reflect a level of training, depth of knowledge, and sophistication of orientation that ordinarily cannot be assimilated into the mass media. While not constituting exhaustive or orthodox scholarship, they usually manage to avoid emphasizing the transient and ephemeral. They may not qualify for space in scholarly journals, but they are more durable than the daily newspaper or the weekly periodical.

Two other publications, with more regular publication schedules than the *Reports* of the American Universities field staff, now systematically attempt to collect and organize Latin American data of interest to political scientists: the *Hispanic American Report*, established in 1948 and published monthly by the Hispanic American Society of Stanford University, and the *Statistical Abstract of Latin America*, compiled annually since 1955 by the Center of Latin American Studies, University of California, Los Angeles. The editors of the *Hispanic American Report*, believing that the political sector dominates Latin American society today, concentrate on printing summaries of political events in Latin America, particularly as reported in U.S. and Latin American newspapers; the periodical consequently performs some of the services of a press-clipping agency for Latin

American scholars. The *Statistical Abstract*, which progressively has expanded the range of topics on which it collects and tabulates data, is an extremely valuable and readily accessible source of quantified information. The *Abstract* not only prints statistics on population, education, and economic developments which are relevant as background and explanation (in the form of independent variables) for political analysis, but has begun to print election statistics and other data of a directly political nature.

Thanks to the vagaries of status considerations, probably few political scientists wish to compete with journalists. To describe a product of their research as a contribution to the elevation of the standards of journalism, therefore, is not to invite an expression of effusive gratitude. Yet, as has been pointed out, much of traditional political science, in its implicit definition of task as well as techniques of research, has not been sharply differentiated from journalism. And the transitional period has witnessed the appearance of at least one volume by a political scientist that raises a standard to which journalists of good will, talent, and high aspiration might repair. Blanksten's *Peron's Argentina* (1953b), written with considerable literary skill, brings together a mass of factual material on the Peron regime which was hard to come by. As his Preface suggests, he encountered and overcame the kinds of obstacles and restraints which political groups hostile to the public dissemination of uncensored information are likely to impose. Blanksten's study is without the apparatus of hypotheses, concepts, and generalizations attributed to modern social science, but in this writer's opinion it represents a notable contribution to elevating the quality of political reporting on Latin America. (See also Alexander 1951.)

EXPERIMENTS IN QUANTIFICATION

There is a good deal of evidence to suggest that the thrust towards science as an appurtenance of modernization carries with it a commitment to the goal of quantification. If political science follows in the methodological footsteps of the natural sciences and of such social sciences as economics, sociology, and psychology, with a corresponding slackening of its bonds with history and public law, then we can anticipate the substitution of quantitative measurements wherever feasible for impressionistic, qualitative appraisals.

In general, during the present transitional phase the few modest attempts at quantification in Latin American political studies deserve commendation for their good intentions rather than for their accomplishments. While they demonstrate sensitivity to the cues emanating from the culture of modern social science, their methods and procedures with few exceptions are extremely vulnerable to adverse criticism.

Fitzgibbon has made a heroic effort to subject an important concern of traditional political science (the state of democracy in Latin America) to statistical analysis. In a series of studies, he has sought to determine rankings according to the scoring of items included in a scale of democracy among the countries of Latin America and fluctuations at intervals in relative rankings (Fitzgibbon 1951, 1956a, 1956b; Fitzgibbon and Johnson 1961). Utilizing a panel composed of specialists on Latin America in both academic life and journalism, Fitzgibbon requested members of the panel to rank (with the letters A, B, C, D, and E) the individual countries of Latin America with respect to fifteen criteria, for example, educational level, standard of living, freedom of press and speech, freedom of elections, and civilian supremacy over the military. The letter grades were then translated into numerical scores, and the resulting computations were subjected to a variety of statistical analyses. The tables prepared on the basis of accumulated scores indicated the relative rank of each country in accumulated total scores (and hence rank in the "democratic" scale). The surveys were conducted in 1945, 1950, 1955, and 1960 and consequently register changes in assessments made by members of the panel during these intervals.[10]

Fitzgibbon reports his findings with considerable caution, but the obvious limitations of the surveys should be appreciated. In the first place, each participant in the polls responds on the basis of individual, subjective judgments; the application of uniform standards by the judges cannot be assumed. Secondly, the criteria of democracy evaluated by each participant contain unavoidably large components of ambiguity. While the ultimate findings are reported with mathematical precision, the figures originate in subjective responses to a relatively ambiguous field

[10] For a more traditional attack on a closely related problem, see the symposium, in which Fitzgibbon (1950) also participated, on "Pathology of Democracy in Latin America."

of questions. Finally, as Lipset has observed, "The judges were asked not only to rank countries as democratic on the basis of purely political criteria, but also to consider the 'standard of living' and 'educational level.' These latter factors may be conditions for democracy, but they are not an aspect of democracy as such" (1959: 74).

Notwithstanding these substantial reservations, Fitzgibbon's surveys remain one of the most elaborate efforts at quantification of Latin American phenomena by a political scientist. While a few other political scientists have introduced quantified data and have appropriated some of the language of mathematics, the scope of their studies ordinarily has been modest and their statistical methods have been much less complex and sophisticated than Fitzgibbon's. Thus, Kling (1959) has attempted to test the hypothesis that a shift from *caudillismo* to interest-group politics is accompanied by a decline in the proportion of governmental revenues derived from the "external" sector; but his analysis rests on an impressionistic appraisal of conformity to *caudillismo* in the political behavior of Latin American countries, and the data gathered on the sources of revenue in Latin America are not complete. Silvert (1961a) has conducted a limited survey of two Guatemalan communities in an attempt to determine varied intensities of nationalistic sentiment. Regrettably, a planned survey including the capital city, which might have provided a basis for broader generalization, was not completed.[11]

Perhaps Lipset, a sociologist, has made the most successful marriage between quantified technique and categories of continuing relevance to political scientists. In a study not confined to Latin America (1959: 69–105), Lipset has attempted to ascertain possible relationships between selected social and economic conditions and the stability of democratic political systems, and he establishes a correlation between indices of wealth, industrialization, education, and urbanization, on the one hand, and the countries which, on the other hand, he groups together under the heading of "democracies and unstable dictatorships" in Latin America. Collectively, the countries classified by Lipset as "democracies and unstable dictatorships" (Argentina, Brazil, Chile, Colombia, Costa Rica, Mexico, and Uruguay) rank higher on

[11] A recently published volume by Almond and Verba (1963) incorporates survey material on Mexico.

his social and economic indices than countries classified as "stable dictatorships" (the remaining thirteen states of Latin America). Whereas the social and economic indices rest on an impressive foundation of statistical data, the political taxonomy, unfortunately from the point of view of the development of greater precision in political science, largely depends upon qualitative judgments. Hence, Lipset, in classifying a Latin American country as democratic, employs the criterion "whether a given country has had a history of more or less free elections for most of the post-World War I period"; and even this standard is stretched in order to accommodate Mexico, on the ground that the Mexican system "does introduce a considerable element of popular influence." In conceding that "the judgments of experts and impressionistic assessments based on fairly well-known facts of political history will suffice for Latin America," he provides additional disturbing evidence to support the conclusion that we have not solved the problem of evolving quantified indices for important political variables.

Thus far, Silvert and Bonilla have mounted the most direct attack on the problem of quantifying politically relevant variables in Latin America, and they have also conducted the most elaborate experiment in the application of quantitative and survey techniques to an intra-area comparative study. In *Education and the Social Meaning of Development: A Preliminary Statement* (1961) they seek to determine the relationship of class position, social mobility, and national identification to processes of social modernization. By administering questionnaires to groups in Brazil, Chile, Argentina, and Mexico, they sought to ascertain class position, extent of political participation, degree of religiosity, and attitudes toward nation-oriented values and development values among their respondents. The results, not yet published in final form, have been reported with elaborate statistical tables constructed on the basis of the replies to the questionnaires. More than any published work, comparative or monographic in nature, devoted to the analysis of Latin American politics, this intra-area comparative study consistently relies upon quantitative and survey methods.

It is both ironic and admirable that Latin American scholars, despite the historic bias in favor of philosophical, speculative, and polemical literary enterprises in their academic environments, have assumed leadership in the quantitative study of voting behavior in Latin America. Although some would argue that the most impressive achievements of modern political science lie in the field of voting behavior studies, U.S. scholars apparently have been dubious of the value of conducting such studies in Latin America. (Or have political scientists interested in Latin America lacked adequate statistical training?) But some Latin American social scientists have responded promptly to the challenge of adapting the techniques of voting behavior studies to the Latin American milieu. Thus, modeling his work on ecological studies of voting patterns in France and relying upon aggregate statistics, Germani (1955, 1960) has attempted to establish correlations between membership in occupational groups and vote secured by various political parties in the Argentine federal capital during several elections. The journal *Revista Brasileira de Estudos Políticos* has devoted a special issue to analyses by Carvalho (1960) and cooperating scholars which also stress the geographical distribution of the vote among political parties in the election of 1958 in Brazil. And Soares (1961, 1962) is engaged in testing, by means of a comparative study employing advanced statistical techniques, a highly original and stimulating hypothesis regarding possible relationships between economic development and political radicalism as manifested in voting behavior.

EVIDENCE OF ASSIMILATION INTO THE FIELD OF
COMPARATIVE POLITICS

The relationship between Latin American studies and political science in general, and comparative politics in particular, remains awkward. No political scientist concentrating on the Latin American area seems to be so centrally situated professionally as, for example, Lucian Pye (an Asian specialist) or David Apter (an African specialist). Political research on Latin America, rather than flowing into the somewhat turbulent mainstream of modern political science, often appears to drift in an isolated channel of its own, with its sponsors perched along the banks of the more swiftly moving waters of the discipline. Authors of textbooks and treatises in the field of comparative politics therefore ignore Latin American data without evident pangs of remorse or expectations of censure for failure to recognize conspicuously pertinent research.

During the transitional phase, nevertheless, there has been some seepage of Latin American materials into two types of books in comparative politics: anthologies (or readers) and symposia on underdeveloped countries. Thus, *Comparative Politics: Notes and Readings,* edited by Macridis and Brown (1961), and *Foreign Policy in World Politics* (1958), edited by Macridis, include selections dealing with Latin American countries. Likewise, Kautsky (1962) reprints articles on Latin America and Johnson, ed. (1962) , incorporates chapters on militarism in Latin America contributed by himself, Edwin Lieuwen, and Victor Alba. In addition, Blanksten (1960), as has been noted, is the author of the Latin American section in the influential volume on *The Politics of Developing Areas,* edited by Almond and Coleman (1960).

Scattered and fragmentary evidence also encourages the conclusion that closer integration between Latin American studies and the field of comparative politics may take place in the not-too-distant future. Lipset's analysis of the concomitants of democracy, embracing Latin America as well as other areas of the world, is included in his systematic treatise on comparative politics (Lipset 1960), which, incidentally, may be the most rigorously executed major work in the field. Almond and Verba (1963) include survey materials on Mexico; and Scott is scheduled to contribute a volume on Mexico to the comparative politics series of books to be edited by Almond, which will attempt to adhere to a common conceptual framework.

Toward Modernization

There is some disenchantment among social scientists with the preparation of elaborate agenda for research. The unstructured character of much of academic life, the traditional value attached to the scholar's prerogative of determining his own research priorities and pursuing his own idiosyncratic interests, militate against the fulfillment of collectively promulgated research plans. The frequent gap between announced, grandiose intention and modest result also breeds a wariness, if not an outright distrust, of enterprises with the professed aim of shaping the directions of scholarly research. Hence, Lane probably reflects the prevailing mood when, in reviewing *Essays on the Behavioral Study of Politics* (Ranney, ed., 1962), he praises the book because its "programs for future research—until recently so large a portion of the literature—are economical and useful" (Lane, 1963: 163). In the light of Lane's comment, we should strive at least for economy, even though usefulness may be beyond our grasp.

Although we cannot rely upon a unique intellectual or financial panacea to produce rapid modernization in political studies of Latin America, we can seek to obtain benefits from our exercise in self-conscious appraisal. Subject to the constraints of the properly hallowed principle of scholarly self-determination, moreover, we can attempt to identify elements in a program of research that might accelerate the trend in the direction of modernization. At the sacrifice of nuance and qualification, I should submit the following recommendations, in summary form, designed to improve the state of research in Latin American political affairs. That these suggestions are offered in the imperative tense is a testimonial to their author's quest for economy and not to his confidence in their merit.

INCREASE PRODUCTIVITY

Measured by virtually any relevant standard, the *quantity* of serious research on Latin American politics is inadequate. Modernization, among other things, simply requires an increase in the volume of research conducted on Latin American affairs. Doubtless many will be gratified if an expanded program of research yields products of uniformly high quality, reflecting the application of modern methods and theory. But the requirements for personnel capable of adding to our store of knowledge of Latin American politics along almost any dimension are so great that we cannot be overly fastidious in setting boundaries of methodology. When we can turn to no post-World War II monographic studies of many Latin American countries (ranging from El Salvador to Chile in political importance) by political scientists, when existing monographic studies (of Honduras and Ecuador, for example) are not updated and analytically refined by successive generations of scholars, we can only echo the alleged demand of Samuel Gompers for labor: "More!" Any developed subject matter incorporates an underbrush of research of indifferent quality, but one symptom of development is the availability of abundant supplies of goods—in this case, research goods—for consumption or possible reprocessing. The experience of Russian area studies in the United States, moreover, indicates that an expansion in quantity need not inhibit improvements in quality. (And Russian area studies, we might note parenthetically, have confronted and surmounted a more formidable language barrier than Latin American studies.) There is, then, a compelling need to recruit a much larger number of able scholars to the Latin American field and to allocate appreciable resources for the support of their research. Academic norms still dictate that scholars be allowed to exercise maximum choice in the selection of fields of specialization, but there seems to be some correlation between the distribution of funds by governments and foundations in the post-World War II era and the fields of specialization elected by graduate students.

An exhaustive list of concrete research proposals cannot and probably should not be compiled, but members of the Seminar on Latin American Studies (of which this volume is a result) identified the following problems, by way of illustration, as deserving the attention of political scientists:

1. Contemporary analyses of Latin American constitutions as sources of relevant political symbols and values, the function of constitutions in setting limits to expressions of political opposition.

2. Political leadership—the recruitment and socialization of elites, rigidity and flexibility among elites, a taxonomy of political leadership.

3. The changing nature and role of the Church in Latin America.

4. Sources of cohesion, consensus, and national integration in Latin America.

5. Modifications in the nature and role of interest groups in the light of rural-urban migration, efforts at national unification, and movements toward international integration (common markets, for example) among Latin American states.

6. The content and influence of communication, including mass media, in Latin America.

7. The social correlates of political radicalism and democratization in Latin America, bases for initiation of drastic social and political change in Mexico.

8. The construction of theoretically oriented typologies of political actors and regimes in Latin America; a classification of

regimes on the basis of their response to general problems, including economic development.

9. Studies of the process of political socialization. How are political values and attitudes acquired in Latin America? How may they be modified? How may techniques of governmental engineering be employed to promote effective democratic procedures?

10. The changing political role of women in Latin America.

11. The scope and functions of voluntary associations in Latin America, including an analysis of factors encouraging their prevalence or absence.

12. The content, functions, and domestic and international effects of ideology and political thought in Latin America.

13. The influence of new election procedures upon political participation.

14. The role of the army in the process of development.

15. The politics of diplomatic appointments, the composition of foreign office personnel, and perceptions of role by foreign policy officials.

16. The relationship between resource allocation, especially investment in education, and the development of political participation and democratization.

17. The prevailing rules of the political game in Latin America.

18. Intra-area comparative studies of political parties.

19. Relationships between the type of violence employed and the nature of a political system; the possible influence of guerrilla warfare, for example, in shaping the character of the Castro regime in Cuba.

20. The significance of area-wide movements, such as Christian Democracy, for Latin American political behavior.

21. Personality and party politics in Latin America.

22. The relationships between economic stagnation and political change.

23. The impact of United States policies, international politics, and international institutions upon decision-making in Latin America.

24. Private enterprise and governmental policies in Latin America.

25. The foreign policies of the major powers in Latin America.

26. Studies of the termination of regimes, particularly the con-

ditions accompanying the demise of leaders who have exercised power for prolonged periods.

27. Problems of diplomatic and military intervention.

28. The effect of the emergence of new social and political groups upon foreign policy decisions in Latin America.

29. The political consequences of the norm of diplomatic asylum. Does the observance of this principle inhibit the evolution of techniques of political compromise?

30. Problems in the development of national character and national identity in Latin America.

31. The relationship between styles of decision-making and social and economic development.

32. The political worlds of Latin American intellectuals.

33. Comprehensive, insightful treatises on subjects of large significance, as distinct from intensive explorations of relatively minor topics.

34. The translation into English of basic documents and books prepared by Latin Americans.

35. Monographic treatments of individual countries in Latin America which have been neglected by contemporary political scientists, including Brazil, Paraguay, and the Central American republics.

36. A study of transnational politics. In the words of Samuel P. Huntington:

Latin America is a political community, and . . . events in one country frequently have effects on other countries. Lieuwen . . . brought this out clearly in his book on the Latin American military; a radical (or conservative) coup in one country will often trigger off similar coups in other countries. A broad analysis of how transnational revolutionary, reform, and conservative movements operate on a continental basis would be most illuminating. The model for such a study exists in R. R. Palmer's *The Age of the Democratic Revolution* [1959]. Palmer conclusively shows how similar political currents ebbed and flowed and interacted with each other throughout the western world from Williamsburg to St. Petersburg in the late 18th century. Someone should do a similar job for Latin America in the mid-twentieth century.

UTILIZE THE CONCEPTS OF POLITICAL DEVELOPMENT AND
POLITICAL MODERNIZATION AS A FRAMEWORK FOR
ORDERING LATIN AMERICAN DATA

Although many participants in the Seminar endorsed this approach, Samuel P. Huntington, in a memorandum which is

quoted below, presented the most comprehensive and systematic
statement on the research implications of the approach:

Political development—from traditionalism to modernization—seems
to offer the best framework for analyzing Latin American politics.
Political development, however, is a complex process. At a minimum, it
takes place through four channels:

1. *Mass mobilization,* including increased communications, national
identifications, integration, socialization, participation—all dealing with
the attitudes and behavior of people-in-the-mass. To what extent are
traditional attitudes and behavior patterns breaking down and being
replaced by modern ones? To what extent are the masses of the people
being brought within the political arena, broadly conceived?

2. *Interest articulation,* including both the forms and methods of interest-group organization (are these modern or traditional?) and the
substance of the interests articulated (are these modern or traditional?).
To what extent is politics pre-empted by institutional interests (Church,
army) and to what extent do associational interests play a role?

3. *Elite broadening,* including, particularly, the expansion of the
number and type of political activists and the assimilation of new types
of individuals into leadership roles. Who performs political leadership
functions? Where do they come from? How are their sources and skills
changing in the modernization process?

4. *Institutional development,* including the generation and growth of
political organizations and ideologies: parties, executives, legislatures,
judicial bodies, the rules of the game among political leaders. To what
extent is there emerging an autonomous political culture with its own
organizations, attitudes, and practices distinct from those of other
groups in society?

In any society, some political development undoubtedly takes place
in all four channels. Of crucial importance, however, is the balance in
development among the four channels. In many instances, development
in one channel may conflict with or retard development in other channels. Rapid mobilization of previously apolitical masses may lead in
the direction of a "mass society" (see Kornhauser) hostile to the emergence of a complex structure of "intermediate" interest groups or of
autonomous political institutions (channels 2 and 4). The anarchy and
instability occasioned by mass mobilization without compensating interest articulation, elite assimilation, and institutional strengthening
may, in turn, prepare the way for an unassimilated, revolutionary
counter-elite to impose a totalitarian "solution" to the modernization
imbalance. Conversely, rapid assimilation of rising elite groups into
political leadership positions may slow down mass mobilization (the
classic British pattern). Or . . . a high rate of interest articulation and
organization may lead to the activation of traditional interests opposed
to other aspects of political development in channels 1 and 3. Specialized studies of political development in each individual channel are
necessary—and particularly in channels 3 and 4, which have tended to

be neglected. Even more important, however, are studies which will analyze the interaction among events in the four developmental channels. Do rapid or revolutionary changes in one channel necessarily lead to rapid or revolutionary changes in other channels? In policy terms, should the United States aim for a "balanced" political development across the board in all four channels? If so, perhaps a most scholarly and yet directly policy-relevant use of resources would be to analyze each Latin American society in terms of its developmental progress in each of the four channels. Where gross imbalances are discovered, American efforts should be devoted to pushing development in the channels where it has lagged the most. Obviously, this approach cannot become too formal or overly systematic. But it does perhaps offer a framework and some criteria for giving the term "political development" somewhat more meaning than it usually has.

PLUG THE WIDEST GAPS

Certain omissions in the literature dealing with Latin American political life verge on the scandalous. There are no book-length studies by political scientists of Brazil since Vargas or of Argentina since Peron. There is no book-length study of Chilean politics since World War II. Despite the dramatic emergence of a professedly Marxist-Leninist government in Cuba, there is no book-length study by a political scientist of contemporary Cuban politics; in fact, the best book on the Castro regime is by a journalist: Theodore Draper, *Castro's Revolution: Myths and Realities* (1962).[12] The research opportunities offered by these important segments of Latin America would appear unusually inviting. Systematically organized data, interpretations, and analyses are so scarce that a political explorer of these territories is under no obligation to equip himself with methodologically impeccable instruments of investigation; the work of a Tocqueville on Brazil or Argentina will be warmly welcomed! [13]

SPECIFY THE DEPENDENT VARIABLES

The dependent variable, for a political scientist, is an aspect of politics which he seeks to explain. Thus, for some students of North American politics, voting behavior may serve as the de-

[12] Political scientists have contributed briefer commentaries on Castro's Cuba; among them are Blanksten (1961), Fitzgibbon (1961), Kling (1962).

[13] A future Toqueville, writing on Brazil, may wish to consult Lipson (1956); various social and political studies sponsored by the University of Minas Gerais, including the works of Machado Horta *et al.* (1958); and Lambert (1953).

pendent variable. What are political scientists working in the Latin American field trying to account for? Among the multitude of "factors," "forces," and "conditions" in Latin America, which aspects of Latin America life do political scientists describe with a view toward explanation? Presumably political scientists utilize political variables as their point of departure; but the encyclopedic approach, inherent in many studies, incorporates a miscellany of social, economic, and political facts and often fails to identify clearly the political phenomenon under analysis. Are we trying to explain—that is, correlate with other relevant variables—instability? Or *caudillismo?* Or the emergence of a one-party system? Or centralized decision-making? Or the prevalent means for the selection and recruitment of politically active personnel? Or democracy? Or the legitimation of procedures for solving problems of succession? Whichever it is, let us be specific. We then can enlist social, economic, psychological, and possibly other political data to function as independent variables for purposes of explanation. Adherence to the research convention of specifying the dependent political variables is a relatively simple device for improving the symmetry of research, but heretofore it has not been absorbed into the main currents of political research on Latin America. Yet the regular application of this convention would facilitate comparison between one study and another, circumvent the limitations of a purely descriptive report, possibly introduce a much-desired element of cumulativeness into Latin American studies, and perhaps add to the durability of each separate research effort.

EXPLOIT THE AREA APPROACH IN ORDER TO
CONTROL FOR SELECTED VARIABLES

Political scientists concentrating in Latin American studies have not taken sufficient advantage of the potentialities of an area focus to contribute directly to the conversion of the study of foreign governments into a field eligible for the label "comparative politics." By assisting in this transformation, incidentally, Latin American specialists also can create a more favorable intellectual environment for the growth of empirical political theory. As Eulau (1962: 397) has pointed out,

Comparative analysis, truly to deserve its name, might have fared better, and done so earlier, if all students of government—the domestic brand as well as the foreign—had been concerned with a method which comes closer to the laboratory experiment than any other we have in controlling a few variables. For . . . "control" is the *sine qua non* of all scientific procedure.

While Eulau, drawing upon his experiences in a comparative study of state legislative systems, argues the merits of utilizing the controls inherent in a single, albeit heterogeneous, culture, such as that of the United States, the area approach makes it possible to impose controls over a larger terrain. If we seek to ferret out the combinations of variables that warrant generalizations about political behavior, an area orientation enables us quite readily to isolate and identify those attributes which are widely distributed among the units we wish to compare. By the same token, the area approach quickly may lead us to discard, for explanatory purposes, other variables that do not discriminate between one system and another. Thus, if political activists in a number of countries share a common language and racial background, but in some of these countries a high degree of instability in the selection of key governmental personnel prevails while in other countries a mode of peaceful accession to office has evolved, we are justified in concluding that language and race cannot function as exclusive explanatory variables of instability. Likewise, the popular hypothesis that susceptibility to the appeals of Communism or political radicalism correlates with such variables as low income and low levels of literacy can be subjected to fairly rigorous testing in the Latin American milieu. (The case of Cuba, while not providing conclusive evidence, indicates that a relatively high per capita income and a relatively high literacy rate do not by themselves immunize a population against Communism.)

In so far as a number of Latin American societies share common linguistic, racial, religious, economic, and institutional traits, some variables can be held "constant" in a comparative study of politics within the Latin American area. By deliberately exploiting the possibilities of "controlling" for these selected variables in area-centered research, Latin American specialists can demonstrate a constructive role for area studies in the development of theoretical propositions derived from comparative analysis. As Silvert noted almost a decade ago, in the Preface to his monograph (1954: ix) on Guatemala, "A general awakening of awareness among area specialists of the importance of relating their geographical interests to broader trends is of special significance to the political scientist."

SYNTHESIZE THE FINDINGS ON MEXICO WITH A VIEW TOWARD
FORMULATING MORE INCLUSIVE GENERALIZATIONS

Political scientists have made more progress in collecting and analyzing data on Mexico than on any other Latin American country. There are reasonably comprehensive treatises on Mexican government and politics, the Mexican party system has been examined intensively by several scholars, some reports on Mexican interest groups have been published, and Mexico has been the subject of important and substantial studies by historians, economists, and anthropologists. Indeed, we now have available some insightful essays on the psychology and family structure of Mexicans. Certainly, gaps in our knowledge of Mexico remain and will remain, but the problem of data-collection obviously is less acute with regard to Mexico than with regard to Brazil.

Political scientists now seem to be in a position to outline the configuration of the modern Mexican political system: stability in the tenure of presidential office, peaceful accession to governmental posts, the predominance of a single party in electoral contests, the integration of organized interests into the formal structure of a dominant party, the presidency as a focal institutional objective of the competition for access and influence among the various interests, and the relatively low visibility of public decision-making. The time, therefore, appears ripe for social scientists to go beyond data-collection and case analysis and to engage, with whatever cautions seem appropriate to them, in the creation and testing of hypotheses, the formulation of generalizations and theories, and the construction of tentative models of political change grounded in Mexican events of the last half-century.

Assuming the feasibility of building on the present base of Mexican studies, political scientists might proceed to design research projects for the erection of a superstructure of empirical theory. Perhaps a tri-level structure may be contemplated:

1. At the first level of research we might try to establish, systematically and rigorously, the social, economic, and psychologi-

cal concomitants of the contemporary Mexican political system. What are the nonpolitical variables associated with the Mexican political system?

2. At the second level, we might attempt to correlate the rates of change among the nonpolitical variables with the rates of change of the political variables since the Mexican revolution. Did changes in certain political variables—shifts in power among competing groups, the emergence of a single dominant party— precede changes in social and economic institutions? Were certain social and economic changes—shifts in land tenure—introduced prior to the achievement of political stability? What has been the sequence of change, the rate of change, and the relationship between political and nonpolitical variables in the process of change? Did economic, social, and political changes, evidently of crucial significance, take place concurrently?

3. Finally, we might venture to construct a comprehensive model of political change in Mexico and attempt to extrapolate hypotheses from such a model which can be tested comparatively in the Latin American area. Thus, political behavior in Mexico since the beginnings of the Mexican revolution may be viewed as changing from discernible instability and *continuismo* to apparent stability and rotation in presidential office, from *caudillismo* to institutionalized leadership, from amorphous personalist parties to a structured political party aggregating social and economic interests; and some may perceive change in Mexico as manifesting movement from less democratic to more democratic norms or from a parochial to a participant political culture. An effort to integrate these diverse aspects of change may yield a model of political change. We also may try to assimilate into this model the social and economic concomitants of the components of political change.

Certain hypotheses—phrased here as questions—suggested by the process of change in Mexico then may be tested by means of comparative analysis elsewhere in Latin America: Is a single-party system regularly a concomitant of a certain stage of modernization in Latin America? Given the other variables of the Latin American environment, do stability, a single-party system, a more participant political culture, and certain kinds of social and economic change indeed cluster? Does charismatic leadership emerge and subside with some regularity—that is, in association with other identifiable variables—in the Latin American setting? At what point in political development—to employ Lasswell's phrase—does "restriction by partial incorporation" come into play, with the result that persons and groups hostile to a regime are content to express their opposition in nonviolent forms? Clearly, comparative studies inspired by analysis of the Mexican experience could help us to generalize with a good deal more empirical certainty about the significance of variables in the Mexican system which recur elsewhere in Latin America and those which are unique or discrete to Mexico. A less parochial treatment of our Mexican findings consequently may enable us effectively to move in the direction of comparative political analysis.

To put it another way, case studies ordinarily are advertised as preliminary explorations (pilot projects) to blaze the trail for more ambitious research expeditions, and Mexico is ready for the research expedition with visions—and hopefully not delusions—of grandeur.

ESTABLISH EMPIRICAL REFERENTS FOR DISTINCTIVE
CONCEPTS EMPLOYED IN LATIN AMERICAN STUDIES

Political scientists have inherited a language comprising numerous concepts which lack precise empirical referents. Such terms as "democracy" and "dictatorship," for example, do not convey identical meanings to diverse audiences.

Specialists on Latin America obviously cannot assume responsibility for the elimination of all semantic ambiguity from the vocabulary of political science, but they may appropriately undertake the task of clarifying such concepts as "instability," "violence," and *caudillismo,* which are regularly applied to the analysis of Latin American political data. Thus, "instability" is not a unidimensional phenomenon in Latin America, and the goal of "operationalizing" its meaning involves both taxonomic and analytical problems. Instability assumes a variety of complex forms in Latin America, with differential consequences for Latin American political systems. Some kinds of instability merely rotate governmental personnel; other kinds of instability are accompanied by shifts of power among competing social and economic groups. If we propose to speak of some countries as "more unstable" than other countries, we require a more elaborate tax-

onomy of instability than we now possess, and we could profitably develop measurements for differentiated types of instability.

Although Stokes (1952) has developed a useful classification of
forms of violence in Latin America, political scientists have been
slow to locate violence in Latin America within a broader framework of studies of violence. In recent years, research on "internal
wars," "unconventional warfare," and "revolutions" has prolif-
erated. There would appear to be value in attempting to integrate research on violence in Latin America with such studies
and to consider the multiple functions performed by violence in
Latin American political systems.

The concept of *caudillismo* especially is susceptible to greater
refinement. In an effort to develop more precise connotations for
the term, political scientists might raise questions posed in
studies of leadership in the United States: How are individuals
socialized and recruited into roles of political leadership in Latin
America? What elements are common in the backgrounds of
Latin American political leaders? What changes, if any, have
taken place in the nature (including personality characteristics
and styles) of Latin American political leaders, and what are the
accompanying characteristics of such changes? Under what circumstances do persons assume or lose power in Latin America?
What are the rewards of the exercise of leadership? Such studies,
by systematically collecting data on a large sample of Latin American political leaders and going beyond such biographical works
as Alexander (1962b), could present results in a quantified form
that might serve to provide an empirical referent for *caudillismo*.

PROBE IN NEW DIRECTIONS FOR THE NATURE AND ORIGINS
OF POLITICALLY RELEVANT VALUES,
ATTITUDES, AND ALLEGIANCES

Traditionally, documents, constitutions, proclamations, and
speeches have been consulted as statements of Latin American
political values. But alternative techniques, applying somewhat
different concepts, have been developed in the study of political
attitudes and loyalties in the United States. Hence, the concept
"political socialization" seems to have emerged as a powerful tool
for the analysis of North American political behavior; it is a
concept which apparently can account for the attitudes of children toward authority (Greenstein 1960; Easton and Hess 1962)

and the voting behavior of most adults (Campbell *et al.* 1960: 147). An observation of Bryce regarding Uruguay suggests that the concept also may shed light on party affiliations in Latin America: "The parties have become largely hereditary; a child is born a little Blanco or a little Colorado, and rarely deserts his colour" (Bryce 1926: 359). It would seem particularly relevant to investigate how processes of political socialization work to produce both continuity and change in a Latin American political system, since internalization of the norm of violence would appear capable of either perpetuating or modifying the pattern of decision-making in a Latin American country.

The adaptation of interview techniques to the Latin American environment should provide an especially rich yield of fresh generalizations and insights. Almond (1954) has demonstrated that a comparative study, unfortunately not including Latin American respondents, can be conducted to determine the social and psychological characteristics of those who respond to and ultimately reject Communist appeals and that the results can be presented in statistical form. Lane (1962), assisted by a tape recorder, has conducted prolonged, intensive, depth interviews with a small number of respondents in an effort to discover "Why the American Common Man believes what he does." Lewis, in *The Children of Sánchez* (1961), reports in massive detail the results of taped interviews with a family in Mexico, but Lewis' research reflects his orientation as an anthropologist. Similar potentially exciting and original work utilizing such techniques remains to be carried out by political scientists.

Nor have library materials been exhausted as sources for clues to the motivation and values of political man in Latin America. Political scientists thus far have not examined political novels, such as those of Mariano Azuela, Carlos Fuentes, and Luis Spota, with a view toward securing insights, illustrations, confirmatory evidence, or "emotional closure" for their propositions about political behavior.

In any event, since there is general agreement that the written constitutions and laws do not, in Carl J. Friedrich's phrase, constitute "effective regularized restraints" in Latin America, we advantageously can employ new weapons in order to attack the problem of "legitimacy" and "the rules of the game" in Latin America. If the constitution does not prescribe the effective rules of the game, what are the operating rules governing political conflict in Latin America? Needler (1962) recently has argued the thesis that a "legitimacy vacuum" accounts for the instability and violence of Latin American politics. But may not violence itself become an accepted, and therefore "legitimate," value within a culture? Procedures for reaching decisions, including decisions on the selection of government personnel, do become institutionalized in Latin America, but they may not be the procedures formulated in a written document. To discover the effective rather than the formal rules of the political game in Latin America represents a continuing challenge to political scientists.

EXPLORE THE FEASIBILITY OF STUDIES OF
PUBLIC POLICY FORMATION

Although some social scientists have popularized the model of decision-making by a "power elite" in the United States, intensive studies of specific governmentally determined decisions at the national and local level tend to indicate that public policies in the United States reflect the interplay of complex interests and a pluralistic model of power. In the case of Latin America, political scientists continue to ascribe "power" to abstract, evidently monolithic, entities—the landowners, the army, the president. Yet, we have not made a series of empirical studies to determine the process by which specific decisions have been reached. What groups and individuals, exercising what degrees of power, have participated in decisions to initiate programs of land reform or modifications in tax legislation? By what process has a decision been reached to nationalize a public utility? Is there anything distinctive about Latin American policy-making processes? A comprehensive analysis of existing case studies is needed to see if any common patterns exist in the policy-making process. In general, who takes the initiative in pushing policy measures and in generating support (consensus building)? What are the veto groups on different types of policy? Are the patterns of negotiation and bargaining different from those in the United States? How have they changed in Latin America over the years? It is true that public decision-making in Latin America seems characterized by lower visibility than in the United States; but studies of the formation of specific public policies, if feasible, might make it possible to associate the concept of "power" more meaningfully with particular groups and institutions in Latin America.

An economist rather than a political scientist is responsible for the only substantial comparative study of public policy formation in the Latin American area, namely, Hirschman (1963). Drawing upon detailed studies of land reform in Colombia, attempts to introduce change in Brazil's Northeast, and the problem of inflation in Chile, Hirschman generalizes about the processes of development. Although he is an economist with a pronounced policy orientation, Hirschman continuously is concerned with the behavior of public decision-makers. With notable sophistication and subtlety, he analyzes the semantics of public problem-solving and coins the term "reform-mongering" to describe the process by which economic development takes place. The centrality of the concepts of power, conflict, political style, and decision-making in his work, the sustained concern with evolving models and theories which can facilitate prediction and at least partially control solutions, and the integration of concepts from multiple disciplines (including history and social psychology) make *Journeys toward Progress* an outstanding and highly stimulating contribution to the study of the formation of public policies.

EXAMINE INSTITUTIONS AND BEHAVIOR IN THE LIGHT
OF THE CONCEPT OF FUNCTIONALISM

Clearly, parties, legislatures, and constitutions do not perform similar functions in different political cultures. In the United States and Great Britain, political parties may be significant vehicles for carrying on electoral contests. In the Soviet Union, the Communist Party functions as the center of decision-making and the principal arena of conflict. But what functions are discharged by one-party and multiple-party systems in Latin America? What functions are performed by legislatures in Latin America, and if the functions differ between one country and another, what are the correlates of such differences?

Edelman's concept of "symbolic reassurance" (1960), I believe, will prove a useful adaptation of the functional approach for political scientists concerned with Latin American behavior. Whereas Lenin advocated that revolutionary theory (symbols) should serve as a guide to revolutionary action, Edelman points out that in certain contexts symbols produce political quiescence. The symbols, in other words, may gratify certain personality needs and maintain some groups in a state of inactivity or quiescence, while the tangible resources, nominally the stakes of political competition, are awarded to other groups. Although numerous facets of political behavior in Latin America may be subjected to clarifying analysis through the application of Edelman's concept, I shall confine myself to one illustration—the functional role of opposition parties in Mexico. On the basis of Edelman's thesis, for example, we may hypothesize that support for opposition parties in Mexico, at least on the part of some Mexicans, is not intended to challenge the authority of the regime or to register dissatisfaction with the distribution of tangible rewards but to reassure some individuals that they have not violated values acquired early in life, even though those values no longer correspond to their "tangible interests." Certainly, we also are warranted in hypothesizing that the "leftist" and "revolutionary" declarations by Latin American political leaders likewise often function as symbolic reassurance and are designed to induce political quiescence.

ADAPT THE CONCEPTS OF COMMUNITY POWER STUDIES
TO STUDIES OF LOCAL POLITICS IN LATIN AMERICA

Silvert has emphasized the importance of the village and the hacienda in Latin American political life. Huntington, in his memorandum quoted above, suggested comprehensive studies of local decision-making:

The study of political systems in villages and cities has leapt forward in the United States in the past decade. The trigger book here was Floyd Hunter's 1953 study of Atlanta's *Community Power Structure*. Hunter's research seemed to show a fairly monolithic and concentrated local power structure. His findings have been challenged as to their methodology and general applicability, most notably in the writings of Robert Dahl and his disciples. Other studies have compared the power structures existing in American and English cities. Others have analyzed the changes in the distribution of power in a single city over time. These studies have shown the effects of modernization in the breakdown of narrow oligarchical rule and the rise of a more pluralistic elite structure. The techniques, methods, categories, and theories developed in this rich and extensive literature might easily be applied to the study of medium-sized Latin American cities. Two studies have been made of cities just south of the border: namely, those by Form and D'Antonio (1959) and by Klapp and Padgett (1960).

Studies of local decision-making, moreover, could provide a focus for collaboration between anthropologists and political scientists.

MOVE TOWARD RESOLUTION OF THE PROBLEM OF RESEARCH
PRIORITIES BY CLARIFYING THE CHOICE OF REFERENCE
GROUPS FOR POLITICAL SCIENTISTS SPECIALIZING
IN LATIN AMERICAN STUDIES

The problem of research priorities is a problem in the choice of reference groups. To the members of which groups do we wish to look for standards to guide our research? To those who encourage political scientists to utter banal pleas for good will in the Western Hemisphere? To those who seek to maintain a clientele for Latin American studies by stressing the quaint, the deviant, and the exotic? To those who demand a prompt identification of friend and foe in Latin America? To those who pressure political scientists to provide simple capsule solutions to complex, enigmatic problems? (On behalf of pursuing alternative values, political scientists, in fact, might consider the declaration of a moratorium on premature prescriptions of public policy.) To those who merely wish political scientists to contribute a large fund of facts to an interdisciplinary area program? To those who believe that the development of empirical theory about Latin American political behavior, within the framework of comparative political analysis, holds out the greatest promise for contemporary political science? Although this paper has not repudiated eclecticism, it has tried to imply that political scientists who would study modernization in Latin America must not resist the modernization of themselves.

BIBLIOGRAPHY

Abbott, Roger S.
   1951   The role of contemporary political parties in Chile. American Political Science Review 45 (No. 2): 450–63.
Alexander, Robert J.
   1949   The Latin American *Aprista* parties. Political Quarterly 20 (No. 3): 236–47.

Alexander, Robert J.
  1951 The Peron era. New York.
  1957 Communism in Latin America. New Brunswick, N.J.
  1958 The Bolivian national revolution. New Brunswick, N.J.
  1962a Today's Latin America. New York.
  1962b Prophets of the revolution: profiles of Latin American leaders. New York.
Almond, Gabriel
  1954 The appeals of communism. Princeton, N.J.
Almond, Gabriel, and Sidney Verba
  1963 The civic culture. Princeton, N.J.
Almond, Gabriel, and James S. Coleman (eds.)
  1960 The politics of developing areas. Princeton, N.J.
Amadeo, Santos P.
  1943 Argentine constitutional law. New York.
American Academy of Political and Social Science
  1940 Annals 208 (March): 1–186.
Blanksten, George I.
  1953a Ecuador: constitutions and caudillos. Berkeley and Los Angeles.
  1953b Peron's Argentina. Chicago.
  1959 Political groups in Latin America. American Political Science Review 53 (No. 1): 106–27.
  1960 Latin America. In The politics of developing areas, Gabriel A. Almond and James S. Coleman, eds. Princeton, N.J.
  1961 Fidel Castro and Latin America. A paper prepared for the 1961 annual meeting of the American Political Science Association.
Brandenburg, Frank R.
  1958 Organized business in Mexico. Inter-American Economic Affairs 12 (No. 3): 26–50.
Bryce, James
  1926 South America: observations and impressions. New York. (New edition corrected and revised.)
Campbell, Angus, et al.
  1960 The American voter, [by] Angus Campbell, Philip E. Converse, Warren E. Miller, and Donald E. Stokes. New York.
Carvalho, Orlando M., et al.
  1960 [Analysis of election of 1958.] Revista Brasileira de Estudos Políticos, No. 8 (April).
Christensen, Asher N.
  1951 The evolution of Latin American government. New York.
Clagett, Helen L.
  1952 The administration of justice in Latin America. New York.
Cleven, Andrew N.
  1940 The political organization of Bolivia. Washington, D.C., The Carnegie Institution of Washington.
Dahl, Robert A.
  1961 The behavioral approach in political science: epitaph for a monument to a successful protest. American Political Science Review 55 (No. 4): 763–72.
  1963 Modern political analysis. Englewood Cliffs, N.J.
Davis, Harold Eugene (ed.)
  1958 Government and politics in Latin America. New York.

Draper, Theodore
1962   Castro's revolution: myths and realities. New York.
Easton, David
1957   An approach to the analysis of political systems. World Politics 9 (No. 3): 383–400.
1962   Introduction: The current meaning of "behavioralism" in political science. *In* The limits of behavioralism in political science. Philadelphia, American Academy of Political and Social Science (October), pp. 7–8.
Easton, David, and Robert D. Hess
1962   The child's political world. Midwest Journal of Political Science 6 (No. 3): 229–46.
Echaiz, René León
1939   Evolución histórica de los partidos políticos chilenos. Santiago, Chile.
Edelman, Murray
1960   Symbols and political quiescence. American Political Science Review 54 (No. 3): 695–704.
Eulau, Heinz
1962   Comparative political analysis: a methodological note. Midwest Journal of Political Science 6 (No. 4): 397.
1963   The behavioral persuasion in politics. New York.
Eulau, Heinz, Samuel J. Eldersveld, and Morris Janowitz
1956.   Political behavior. New York.
Fabregat, Julio T.
1949   Los partidos políticos en la legislación uruguaya. Montevideo.
Fitzgibbon, Russell H.
1948   The constitutions of the Americas. Chicago.
1950   Pathology of democracy in Latin America. American Political Science Review 44 (No. 1): 100–49.
1951   Measurement of Latin American political phenomena: a statistical experiment. American Political Science Review 65 (No. 2): 517–23.
1954   Uruguay: portrait of a democracy. New Brunswick, N.J.
1956a How democratic is Latin America? Inter-American Economic Affairs 9 (No. 4): 65–77.
1956b A statistical evaluation of Latin-American democracy. Western Political Quarterly 9 (No. 3): 607–19.
1957   The party potpourri in Latin America. Western Political Quarterly 10 (No. 1): 3–22.
1961   The revolution next door: Cuba. Annals of the American Academy of Political and Social Science 334 (March): 113–22.
Fitzgibbon, Russell H., and Kenneth F. Johnson
1961   Measurement of Latin American political change. American Political Science Review 55 (No. 3): 515–26.
Form, William H., and William V. D'Antonio
1959   Integration and cleavage among community influentials in two border cities. American Sociological Review 24 (December): 804–14.
Germani, Gino
1955   Estructura social de la Argentina: análisis estadístico. Buenos Aires. Chap. 16.
1960   Política e massa. Belo Horizonte, Minas Gerais, Brasil, Faculdade de Direito, Universidade de Minas Gerais.
Gibson, William Marion
1948   The constitutions of Colombia. Durham, N.C.

Gil, Federico G.
  1962 Genesis and modernization of political parties in Chile. Latin American Monographs No. 18. Gainesville, Fla.
Gomez, R. A.
  1960 Government and politics in Latin America. New York.
Gonzales Calderon, Juan A.
  1930–31 Derecho constitucional Argentino. Buenos Aires.
Greenstein, Fred I.
  1960 The benevolent leader: children's images of political authority. American Political Science Review 54 (No. 4): 934–43.
Hirschman, Albert O.
  1963 Journeys toward progress: studies of economic policy-making in Latin America. New York, The Twentieth Century Fund.
Holt, Pat M.
  1963 United States political science and Latin America, p. 3 (mimeo, dated April 5).
James, Herman G.
  1923 The constitutional system of Brazil. Washington, D.C., The Carnegie Institution of Washington.
Johnson, John J.
  1958 Political change in Latin America: the emergence of the middle sectors. Stanford, Calif.
  1962 The Latin America military as a politically competing group in a transitional society. In The role of the military in underdeveloped countries, John J. Johnson, ed. Princeton, N.J.
Johnson, John J. (ed.)
  1962 The role of the military in underdeveloped countries. Princeton, N.J.
Jorrin, Miguel
  1953 Governments of Latin America. New York.
Kahin, George McT., Guy J. Pauker, and Lucian W. Pye
  1955 Comparative politics in non-western countries. American Political Science Review 69 (No. 4): 1022–41.
Kantor, Harry
  1953 The ideology and program of the Peruvian Aprista movement. Berkeley, University of California Press. (A Spanish version also has been published: Ideología y programa del movimiento Aprista. Mexico City, 1955.)
  1958 The Costa Rican election of 1953: a case study. Latin American Monographs No. 5. Gainesville, Fla.
Kantor, Harry, and Eugenio Chang-Rodríguez
  1961 La América Latina de hoy. New York.
Kautsky, John H.
  1962 Political change in under-developed countries: nationalism and communism. New York.
Klapp, Orrin E., and L. Vincent Padgett
  1960 Power structure and decision-making in a Mexican border city. American Journal of Sociology 65 (No. 4): 400–06.
Kling, Merle
  1956 Towards a theory of power and political instability in Latin America. Western Political Quarterly 9 (No. 1): 21–35.
  1959 Taxes on the "external sector": an index of political behavior in

Latin America? Midwest Journal of Political Science 3 (No. 2): 127–50.

1961 A Mexican interest group in action. Englewood Cliffs, N.J.

1962 Cuba: a case study of a successful attempt to seize political power by the application of unconventional warfare. Annals of the American Academy of Political and Social Science 341 (May): 42–52.

Lambert, Jacques

1953 Le Brésil, structure sociale et institutions politiques. Paris.

Lane, Robert E.

1962 Political ideology: why the American common man believes what he does. New York.

1963 *Review of* Essays on the behavioral study of politics, edited by Austin Ranney. American Political Science Review 57 (No. 1): 163.

Lanz Duret, Miguel

1947 Derecho constitucional mexicano. Mexico City.

Lascano y Mazón, Andrés Maria

1942 Constituciones politicas de América. Havana.

Lewis, Oscar

1961 The children of Sánchez. New York.

Lieuwen, Edwin

1961 Arms and politics in Latin America. New York. Revised edition.

Liñares Quintana, Segundo V.

1945 Los partidos politicos: instrumentos de gobierno. Buenos Aires.

1946 Gobierno y administración de la república argentina. Buenos Aires.

Lipset, Seymour Martin

1959 Some social requisites of democracy: economic development and political legitimacy. American Political Science Review 53 (No. 1): 69–105.

1960 Political man: the social bases of politics. New York.

Lipson, Leslie

1956 Government in contemporary Brazil. Canadian Journal of Economics and Political Science 22 (No. 2): 183–98.

Loewenstein, Karl

1942 Brazil under Vargas. New York.

Lopez Rosado, Felipe

1955 El regimen constitucional mexicano. Mexico City.

MacDonald, Austin F.

1949 Latin American politics and government. New York. (Revised edition, 1954.)

Machado Horta, Raul, *et al.*

1958 Perspectivas do federalismo brasileiro, [by] Raul Machado Horta, Gerson de Britto Mello Boson, Orlando M. Carvalho, Onofre Mendes, Jr., and Washington Peluso Albim de Souza. Belo Horizonte, Minas Gerais, Brazil, Universidade de Minas Gerais.

Macridis, Roy C.

1958 Foreign policy in world politics. Englewood Cliffs, N.J.

1961 Comparative politics: notes and readings. Homewood, Ill.

Marx, Fritz Morstein (ed.)

1949 Foreign governments. New York.

Mecham, J. Lloyd

1934 Church and state in Latin America: a history of politico-ecclesiastical relations. Chapel Hill, N.C.

Mendieta y Nuñez, Lucio
1942 La administración pública en México. Mexico City.
1947 Los partidos políticos. Mexico City, Biblioteca de Ensayos Sociológicos, Instituto de Investigaciones Sociales, Universidad Nacional.
Miranda, José
1957 Reforma y tendencias constitucionales recientes de la América Latina (1945–1956). México City, Instituto de Derecho Comparado, Universidad Nacional Autonoma de México.
Needler, Martin
1962 Putting Latin American politics in perspective. Inter-American Economic Affairs 16 (No. 2): 41–50.
Ogg, Frederic, and Harold Zink
1949 Modern foreign governments. New York.
Padgett, L. Vincent
1957 Mexico's one-party system: a re-evaluation. American Political Science Review 51 (No. 4): 995–1002.
Palmer, Robert Roswell
1959 The age of the democratic revolution: a political history of Europe and America, 1760–1800. Princeton, N.J.
Patch, Richard W.
1962a The Peruvian elections of 1962 and their annulment. Reports, West Coast South America Series, Vol. 9: No. 6 (September).
1962b Personalities and politics in Bolivia. Reports, West Coast South America Series, Vol. 9: No. 5 (May).
Peaslee, Amos J.
1950 Constitutions of nations. Concord, N.H. (2nd ed., The Hague, 1956.)
Pierson, William W., and Federico G. Gil
1957 Governments of Latin America. New York.
Ranney, Austin (ed.)
1962 Essays on the behavioral study of politics. Urbana, Ill.
Rowe, L. S.
1921 The federal system of the Argentine republic. Washington, D.C., The Carnegie Institution of Washington.
Schneider, Ronald M.
1958 Communism in Guatemala, 1944–1954. New York.
Scott, Robert E.
1951 Argentina's new constitution: social democracy or social authoritarianism? Western Political Quarterly 4 (No. 4): 567–76.
1959 Mexican government in transition. Urbana, Ill.
Silvert, Kalman H.
1954 A study in government: Guatemala. New Orleans, Middle American Research Institute, Tulane University.
1959 Political change in Latin America. In The United States and Latin America. New York, The American Assembly, Columbia University (December): 77
1961a The silent voices: the nation and the village. In Reaction and revolution in Latin America: the conflict society. New Orleans, pp. 35–46.
1961b Nationalism in Latin America. In Latin America's nationalistic revolutions. Annals of the American Academy of Political and Social Science 334 (March): 1–9.
1961c The annual political cycle of Argentina. Reports, East Coast South America Series, Vol. 8: No. 6 (December 12).

1961d Political universes in Latin America. Reports, East Coast South America Series, Vol. 8: No. 7 (December 17).

Silvert, Kalman H., and Frank Bonilla

1961 Education and the social meaning of development: a preliminary statement. New York: American Universities Field Staff, Inc. (mimeographed).

Soares, Glaucio Ary Dillon

1961 Economic development and political radicalism. Boletim do Centro Latino-Americano de Pesquisas em Ciências Sociais. Rio de Janeiro, UNESCO. Vol. 4 (No. 2): 117–57.

1962 Desenvolvimento econômico e radicalismo político: o teste de uma hipótese (Chile). America Latina 5 (No. 3): 65–83.

Stevenson, John Reese

1942 The Chilean popular front. Philadelphia.

Stokes, William S.

1950 Honduras: an area study in government. Madison, Wis.

1952 Violence as a power factor in Latin-American politics. Western Political Quarterly 5 (No. 3): 445–68.

1959 Latin American politics. New York.

Stuart, Graham

1925 The governmental system of Peru. Washington, D.C., The Carnegie Institution of Washington.

Tannenbaum, Frank

1943 A note on Latin American politics. Political Science Quarterly 58 (No. 3): 415.

Taylor, Philip B., Jr.

1960a Government and politics of Uruguay. New Orleans.

1960b The Mexican elections of 1958: affirmation of authoritarianism? Western Political Quarterly 13 (No. 3): 722–44.

1963 Interests and institutional dysfunction in Uruguay. American Political Science Review 57 (No. 1): 62–74.

Tucker, William P.

1957 The Mexican government today. Minneapolis.

Vanorden Shaw, Paul

1930 The early constitutions of Chile 1810–1833. New York.

Wallace, Elizabeth

1894 The constitution of the Argentine republic and the constitution of the United States of Brazil. Chicago.

Whitaker, Arthur P.

1956 The Argentine upheaval. New York.

6. Economic Research in Latin America

CARLOS MASSAD

The term "revolution of expectations" has become common in Latin American literature as an elegant euphemism to dramatize the generalized dissatisfaction with the economic and social conditions in the area. Such discontent and the corresponding yearning for change are not alien to economists or to other social scientists. In the face of a situation that calls for change, the economist finds it very difficult to disown responsibility either for criticizing policy measures or for suggesting them. He is strongly tempted to start work with a value judgment as to how the world should be and then proceed to enumerate, to a greater or lesser degree, those changes which would seem to help in the attainment of the ideal situation.

The initial value judgment is not necessarily shared by everyone; and, since it is the starting point, discussion is likely to center upon it. As a result, the defense of a particular value judgment may become the focus of the professional activities of many economists. Economic analysis then is used consciously or unconsciously in the promotion of a particular view of the world. Economists tend to become classified according to the value judgments they defend, and their work is suspect. Even the tools of analysis are not exempt. When an economist becomes suspect of serving a particular political system, his work is attacked and discarded by one group and simultaneously is stoutly defended and overemphasized by another. In this type of debate, of course, empirical evidence is hardly relevant except as far as it upholds a specific position. In this environment, sets of affirmations illustrated by casual references to data tend to become generally accepted by each group, almost acquiring the status of a doctrine whose chief elements appear over and over again in documents, addresses, and international agreements. One cannot blame Latin American economists alone for an approach that may be deemed unscientific. The pressure for development combined with the rather unsatisfactory provision of tools of economic analysis necessary to tackle problems of growth compels economists in Latin America, and presumably elsewhere, to assume attitudes based mostly on personal preference and intuition rather than on objective findings.[1]

Economic tools lend themselves to the study of ways of attaining an optimum, starting from given institutional structures, but they are often inadequate for the analysis of the far-reaching and long-range implications of changing given institutional structures. If the institutional structures were changed in a certain way, would the community, after fulfilling all the marginal conditions, reach a higher welfare maximum? This question is being pressed on both economists and politicians in Latin America. While the economists contend that this is a matter for the politicians to answer, the politicians in turn deem it to be a "technical" affair and pass the question back to their economic advisory committees. Phrases containing the word "reform," such as "tax reform," "land reform," and "educational reform," actually imply a comparison of alternative "structures" on the basis of their effect on welfare.

In the face of strong pressures to answer questions they are not prepared to answer, Latin American economists scan other social sciences in the hope that there they will find satisfaction for their demands. It has come to be a matter of general agreement that economists cannot do a good job in such areas of the world as Latin America unless they also have a firm knowledge of sociology, social psychology, anthropology, and other related subjects. In the Latin American field it is often expected that economists will furnish the insights about society that other social scientists provide in places where development of the social sciences is more balanced.

Obviously, the problems of adjustment to a different institutional structure are not merely economic, and perhaps not

[1] This is in some measure unavoidable. This writer's intuition, however, tells him that an attempt to answer through research at least the questions set forth in the following pages will push forward the boundary of knowledge and push back the realm of intuition.

mainly economic. The basic dissatisfaction with existing social and economic conditions and the urge to change the institutional structure makes the need for an interdisciplinary approach to research in the social sciences more pressing for Latin America than for the United States or Europe. Attempts to meet the situation, however, have usually failed.[2]

In what follows, a brief summary is presented of what has been done in economic research in Latin America, and some preliminary steps to further research in the area are indicated; three research subjects are discussed in some detail. Neither bibliographical references nor references to individuals claim to be exhaustive, and they are strongly influenced by the fact that this writer is more familiar with literature on Chile than on other Latin American countries.

Surveying the Field: A Bird's-Eye View

Research in economics in Latin America is of rather recent date. Most of the efforts before World War II were essentially of a historical or a sociological character. They attempted to arrive at broad explanations of social and economic processes and to provide national ideologies and national approaches to development.[3] Economic studies in Latin America received momentum with the establishment of several international agencies. Most of these, such as the International Bank for Reconstruction and Development (IBRD), the International Monetary Fund (IMF), the Food and Agriculture Organization (FAO), and the

[2] As a result of the particular type of training obtained, there is no common language that social scientists can speak. It appears that the most profitable approach to this matter at its present state is through a cluster of groups, each with one main approach, economic, sociological, political, or some other, using the specialist in the other field primarily to advise on the general questions within his realm.

[3] On this point see Hirschman (1960). Among the work done by foreign scholars in this period in relation to Chile are Fetter (1931) and Ellsworth (1945). Fetter (1931) emphasizes as inflationary factors the poor banking practices at the time and the permanent attempt of the highly influential agricultural landlords to reduce the real burden of their heavy mortgages. His approach is somewhat similar to that of the present-day structuralists. Ellsworth (1945) examines the impact of depression on Chile's trade, the protective system of tariffs and exchange controls imposed as a consequence of the depression, and the government's effort to stimulate economic development. Ellsworth's analysis of inflation places him closer to present-day monetarists.

Organization of American States (OAS), rather than doing economic research proper, prepared economic studies of a somewhat general and descriptive nature on Latin American countries and on specific economic sectors. The UN Economic Commission for Latin America (ECLA), for example, not only conducted this kind of study but, in addition, provided descriptions of current economic events. It attempted to point out the main areas to which economic policy should be directed in order to accelerate development. A basic study of this type is Prebisch's (1950; or UN DEA 1950b) *The Economic Development of Latin America and Its Principal Problems.* (See also UN DEA 1950a; Singer 1950; UN ECLA 1963.)[4]

Foreign trade became a focal point of interest and the chief element in the interpretation of the long-run development of Latin American countries. Prebisch states that the benefits of technological progress do not reach the underdeveloped countries (countries of the "periphery") in a measure comparable to that achieved by the developed countries (those of the "center"). The secular deterioration of the terms of trade of the countries producing primary products is a sign that the policy of growth based on the traditional theory of comparative advantage would only mean that the "center" will permanently grow at a faster rate than the "periphery," thus widening the gap between developed and underdeveloped areas. The only course of action open to the peripheral countries, therefore, is industrialization under protective tariffs (Hirschman 1960). The "Prebisch thesis," as it has come to be called, started a lively debate, mostly outside Latin America. Viner (1952, 1958) and Haberler (1960), without considering themselves centrally interested in Latin America, strongly contested Prebisch on this matter on both empirical and theoretical grounds.

Later work by ECLA and by other economists (Pinto 1962) has contributed to the discussion by synthesizing the economic

---

[4] A recent UN ECLA publication (1963), also by Prebisch, presents a restatement of his position, drawing on the experience of ECLA since the early 1950s. This publication presents further elaboration on the same points touched upon in 1950, particularly in connection with the limitations imposed by foreign trade on the development process, the terms-of-trade agreements, and the international distribution of income. The document places much more emphasis than previous publications on policy measures that could be used to achieve a higher rate of development.

history of the area connected with the period of political independence into two stages: the first, beginning about the middle
of the nineteenth century and closing with the great depression
of the early 1930s, was a stage of *crecimiento hacia afuera* (out-
ward-directed growth). Latin America was exporting mainly food
and raw materials and importing practically all the manufactured products consumed locally. Dependence on foreign trade
was extreme, and the fluctuations in domestic activity induced by
the world market were outstanding topics of concern. The second
stage, beginning shortly after the great depression and reaching
its peak during and shortly after World War II, is one of *crecimiento hacia adentro* (inner-directed growth). Import difficulties
caused by the war, tariff barriers, and exchange controls acted
as incentives to the domestic import-substituting industries.

During this second stage the need for general planning became
clear. Government intervention was usually piecemeal and contradictory (UCIE 1956, 1960), and ECLA took the lead in preparing programming techniques to be applied in Latin America.
The technique offered by ECLA starts out by determining, on
the basis of historical information, a capital-output ratio. It
then goes on to establish the volume of investment needed to
achieve alternative growth rates. Thence it proceeds with estimates of future consumption that may be deemed reasonable
and contrast domestic savings with the required investment for
each alternative growth rate. On this basis a tentative rate of
growth, such that the difference between investment and domestic savings may reasonably be covered by foreign capital, is
selected as a goal. The projected import needs are compared
with the projected capacity to import; the difference between
them is the amount of imports that must be substituted for by
domestic production. More detailed analysis of different sectors
of production is then undertaken, and finally the global projections are revised accordingly (UN ECLA 1955).

This technique has been criticized on several grounds: it relies
heavily on the use of capital-output ratios, which are very difficult to interpret economically and to measure empirically (Grunwald 1960), it does not provide for flexibility within the plan
itself, and it does not take into consideration the policy measures
to be adopted in order to induce economic units outside the gov-

ernment to operate in a way consistent with the plan. Demand
and supply of products and factors of production are deemed to
be price-inelastic. The technique emphasizes consistency in economic decisions without due regard for economic efficiency. Some
of these problems are recognized in ECLA's publications, but no
systematic effort has been made by ECLA to overcome them.
Even though studies using this particular ECLA programming
technique were made in several countries, such as Argentina,
Bolivia, and Colombia, the main result obtained was not in
terms of planning but rather in terms of making the idea of
planning more widely accepted in Latin America.*

The emphasis placed on import substitution as compared with
export promotion has changed over time. Initially, the promotion of exports was viewed only as a secondary element essentially
determined by exogenous variables, but the development of
exports was later emphasized in the context of economic integration. Originally, import substitution was encouraged within
the frontiers of each country, whereas more recently the drive
has been for import substitution on an international scale within
Latin America. Latin American countries showed a relatively
high rate of growth until the early 1950s, but the process slowed
down after the Korean war. ECLA economists argued that the
area of relatively easy substitution of domestic production for
imported goods was shrinking, and that the emphasis had to be
placed once more on inner-directed growth. This time, however,
they stressed that the process should operate under different
structural conditions. Import substitution could not proceed unless the area of the market was considerably expanded. Since the
terms-of-trade problem was still present, a way had to be found
to expand the market while maintaining import restrictions
needed to secure incentives for domestic industries. The answer
was to be found in the economic integration of Latin America.
Integration thus appeared as a natural third stage in the development of the area. Recently ECLA research has been centered on
the integration issue. It should be noted that the development

* The new Latin American Institute for Economic and Social Planning,
financed by the Special Fund of the UN and the Inter-American Development
Bank, has undertaken the task of improving planning techniques, advising
governments on development policy questions, and training personnel for the
application of planning techniques. These functions were previously performed, in a more limited way, by ECLA.

of this research still follows the general lines set forth by Prebisch in his *Economic Development of Latin America and Its Principal Problems* (1950). The idea of import substitution and the drive for economic integration were already implied in the statement Prebisch made in 1950.

Even though ECLA's position [5] has had a strong influence on the thinking of economists in this hemisphere, its work has usually been of a rather general nature without probing in depth into specific aspects. For example, ECLA has done little in the field of economic behavior and policy measures designed to stimulate economic units outside the government to operate in a way consistent with the goals set in economic programming. In the main, studies in depth have been left to other institutions; very few of them, however, have met high professional standards.

The Instituto de Economía de la Universidad de Chile (UCIE) took the lead as a nongovernmental national institution doing economic research in Latin America. Up to 1954 UCIE devoted its resources to preparing the first current estimates of national income and product accounts done in Chile and to analyzing the current economic events in the light of these estimates (UCIE 1954, 1955). Later, after preparing a general survey of the economic development of the country (UCIE 1956), the Institute published a number of studies on specific economic problems, most of them referring to the economy of Chile.[6] At present UCIE is also responsible for a graduate program of Latin American economic studies, and its research program includes not only applied economics but theoretical studies as well. In addition, several textbooks are being prepared with emphasis on subjects particularly relevant to the Latin American scene.

[5] Among Latin American economists who at one time or another have been, or still are, connected with ECLA, are Celso Furtado of Brazil; Juan Noyola of Mexico; Jorge Ahumada, Julio Melnik, Aníbal Pinto, Osvaldo Sunkel and Pedro Vuskovic of Chile, Norberto González and Manuel Balboa of Argentina, and Jorge Alcázar of Bolivia. Non-Latin Americans include Alexander Ganz and Dudley Seers, who were connected with ECLA for an extended period, while Thomas Balogh, Hollis Chenery, Nicholas Kaldor, Jan Tinbergen, and John Chipman, among others, have been short-term consultants of ECLA. Many of these have contributed to the elaboration of the ECLA position.

[6] Regional quarterly surveys on employment and unemployment, a series of monographs on the economics of transportation in Chile, and another on agricultural economics, covering such aspects as allocation of credit, economic analysis of taxation, and subdivision of agricultural land.

Another important institution devoted to economic research is the Centro de Investigaciones Económicas of the Instituto Torcuato di Tella, Argentina (ITT), which has published several studies on aspects of the Argentine economy (1962a, 1962b). The Instituto Brasileiro de Economia of the Fundação Getúlio Vargas, Brazil, has devoted most of its efforts until very recently to compiling and publishing national income and other data.

Other centers engaged in economic research are, to name a few, the Centro de Estudios sobre Desarrollo Económico de la Universidad de los Andes, Colombia; the Centro de Estudios de Desarrollo Económico (CENDES), Venezuela; the Centro de Investigaciones Económicas de la Pontificia Universidad Católica, Chile; and the Faculty of Economics of the Universidad de Concepción, also in Chile. All these centers have devoted themselves to research on well-defined specific problems, with varying degrees of success. The results obtained are necessary building blocks for an understanding of the general development process.

Communication between ECLA and the various Latin American research institutions has been hampered occasionally by their methodological approaches. ECLA's analysis and subsequent policy conclusions are frequently based on a priori reasoning. Starting from a global position that has become almost an "ideology" (Hirschman 1960), ECLA selects problems for study and approaches them within the context of this position. The independent research institutes, on the other hand, have concentrated on detailed empirical studies of specific aspects of the economy. These studies are conducted without any particular a priori (explicit) ideological viewpoint. In fact, it is believed that sectoral studies and micro-studies are valuable independently of one's ideological view and, furthermore, that an accurate global analysis can be based only on the prior existence of such studies.

Both approaches have their merits, particularly when there is formal intellectual intercourse. Aside from Prebisch's work already cited, however, it is difficult to find formal presentations of the basic framework of analysis underlying ECLA's work. It has been presented in seminars and in oral debates but more as a strong criticism of "orthodox" economics than as a coherent body of theory. Even though the attack on "orthodox" economics has been quite strong, however, and is usually centered on the assumptions on which existing theories are based, a new body of consistent theory that will dispose of or change the assumptions under criticism has not been articulated (Seers 1962, 1963).

In this context, what have come to be known as structural defects of the economic and social systems have been brought up for discussion. Land ownership and land tenure arrangements, income distribution, tax systems and patterns of government expenditure, educational levels and systems, monoproduction and problems of duality in Latin American economies together with such aspects as the structure of political power and voting rights, pressure groups and their relative strength, are usually included among the structural components of the basic framework of development. The necessity for reforms designed to overcome structural problems is now widely accepted.

The subject of structural maladjustment is closely connected with the discussion of inflation in Latin America and its relation to growth. This is the second main subject to which professional attention has been devoted in Latin America. The debate on inflation reached a point a few years ago where contestants tended to be classified into one of two groups: the structuralists and the monetarists. The structuralists state that inflation is an expression of deep-seated defects in the economic structure and that the anti-inflationary policy attempting to apply a brake on monetary expansion will only paralyze growth and cause unemployment. Monetarists argue that inflation impairs development and that in order to stimulate the latter, inflation must be stopped by monetary restriction (Grunwald 1961). Felix (1960), Kaldor (1957), Noyola (1956), Pinto (1960), Prebisch (1961), Seers (1962), and Sunkel (1958) line up on the structuralist side. It is difficult to find exponents of the monetarist side; the position has been represented chiefly in International Monetary Fund reports, which are not easily available. A major Latin American economist who is not on the structuralist side of the debate is Campos (1961a, 1961b). A conference on inflation and growth held in Rio de Janeiro in January, 1963, gave an opportunity for most of the actors in this debate to present papers for discussion. The conference showed that the two schools of thought are coming closer together, even though much remains to be done to formalize the alternative hypotheses and to subject them to empirical testing.[7]

[7] A challenging hypothesis is certainly an excellent intellectual stimulus, particularly when it is taken as such without becoming an "ideology."

The Lack of Information, an Important Drawback

Very little of the research done up to now has been empirical. Most Latin American economists prefer to set up hypotheses and present them in a polemical way rather than test them against data. This attitude is partly due to the fact that the fields of econometrics and statistics are as yet insufficiently developed in the area and partly to the fact that data are not easily available. Some countries in Latin America have not had a population census in recent years, and reasonably good series of wages are not available in any Latin American country. National income and product information does exist in practically all countries, but it is generally unsatisfactory, and in many cases one might do better with an educated guess. Regular unemployment data are available only for some areas in two or three countries, and indices of physical output, when they exist, have a very limited scope. The lack of information is certainly no stimulus to empirical research, nor does it enhance objectivity.

This general picture does not imply that efforts are not being made to fill the gap. As a matter of fact, more and more is being done in Latin America to improve the training of economists, to keep research on an objective basis, and to foster the availability of information. Some of these efforts have been extremely successful, but they are still far from being sufficient. Chile has perhaps passed the "take-off" stage in this matter and is ahead of the rest of the countries in the area.

Two gaps need to be closed in order to tap research possibilities. First, there is the need to publish, in as many Latin American countries as possible, reports that contain the available statistical information, including complete explanations of the methodology used for both collecting and processing the data presented.[8] If at all feasible, this should include some of the statistical information obtained by governmental or private institutions which has been neither processed nor published. Clear definitions of concepts and methods used in obtaining the data

---

[8] Obviously the data have no value per se but only in regard to their use for analysis. Some theoretical framework is needed to select what is important and what is irrelevant, but as a first step it might be better to concentrate on an evaluation of what is available. On statistics relevant for analysis, see, for example, UN Statistics Dept. (1959), Messy and Pedersen (1963).

should be made available, so that economists will not be tempted to carry their analyses farther than the data warrant.

This work might prove burdensome, but it would be exceedingly valuable. Aside from facilitating research, both because the data would be readily available and because its value could be more easily assessed, publications of this kind would disclose the gaps in statistical information in terms of quality and coverage. In addition, the publication of such bodies of information would allow social scientists and statisticians to suggest ways and means of improving the data.[9] On the other hand, research production on problems relevant to Latin America would be enhanced within the area as well as in other countries, thus fostering collaboration among Latin American social scientists and between them and scholars with similar interests elsewhere.

A second gap which, in my opinion, badly needs to be filled involves solid descriptions of particular aspects of the economic and social environment in Latin American nations. By description is meant not merely the orderly presentation of particular institutions or general aspects of social organization. A descriptive study of the kind suggested here should also point out at least the direction of the economic and social effects obtained.[10] This kind of study may be useful for research in other disciplines in so far as it provides information on institutions whose effects are not merely economic. There are many fields where studies of this type would be warranted: taxation generally, social security, wage legislation and policy, the operation of the labor market, income distribution, financial institutions and policies, land tenure, and other topics of economic discussion about which very little if anything is known. While students of money and banking in Latin America have easy access to material on the purposes

[9] Sample surveys offer the possibility of filling important gaps and improving on available information at relatively low cost. People trained in sampling techniques are, however, very scarce in Latin America today.

[10] A study that fits snugly into this frame, and that is mentioned here by way of illustration, is *La tributación agrícola en Chile, 1940–1958*, published by UCIE (1960a). This study presents the tax legislation applicable to agriculture in Chile during the period involved and compares the effects envisaged by the legislator with those actually obtained. It also points out the main aspects of the problem on which further study is needed. The monograph also includes a rough estimate of the effects on agriculture of the foreign trade policy pursued by the government, of indirect and direct subsidies, and of domestic price controls. The UCIE has also published a series of studies of this type on the subject of maritime and truck transportation in Chile (see also Ross and Christensen 1959).

and functions of the Federal Reserve System of the United States (U.S. Federal Reserve System 1959), they do not have comparable material relative to their own central banks.[11] Studies of some characteristics of the labor force are available for a few countries in Latin America such as Argentina (ITT 1961) and Chile (UCIE 1959; UC INSORA 1962). Very little is available, however, on social security and the other aspects of the national economies mentioned above.

Work on the availability of statistical information and methodology and on the description of some aspects of the economy will pave the way for research on a vast number of well-defined specific problems. If this preliminary and basic research were done, the selection of a research project could then be made with a better perspective on the relative importance of alternatives in order to increase the understanding of the economy of a particular country of Latin America or of the region as a whole.

A Research-Minded Approach to "Reforms"

Even though the selection of research topics should usually be left to the researcher, three leading subjects are discussed in the following pages: land reform, fiscal reform, and economic integration. These are not necessarily presented because they are high-priority subjects in my own opinion but because they serve as illustrations of very important problems involving structural changes and, furthermore, because they constitute the kind of topics that are to be of central interest in Latin America in the next decade. Whatever his preference with respect to research in Latin America, the economist cannot ignore the fact that sooner or later some conditions which are usually included in his very comfortable *ceteris paribus* will change. He will find it difficult to avoid the pressure, both from his own intellect and from the community, to devote his energies to finding out the alternative paths these changes might follow and the implications of treading a given path.

LAND REFORM

Land reform and agrarian reform are terms that, although accepted and used by everybody in Latin America today, mean dif-

---

[11] The Centro de Estudios Monetarios Latinoamericanos (CEMLA) has only recently started to fill in this gap.

ferent things to many people. These terms have different meanings as they relate to two main aspects of the problem, the goals and the methods of land and agrarian reform.

With respect to the goals of land and agrarian reform, there appears to be a conflict at some point between the economic consequences and other social consequences. This conflict is usually taken as a matter of course; it is assumed that in order to achieve maximum economic efficiency, one has to sacrifice social efficiency to some degree, and vice versa. Yet it is in reality not known whether such conflict actually exists. Is social "efficiency" a meaningful analytical category and, if so, how could it be evaluated? This very broad problem, as applied to land and agrarian reform or to any other type of institutional change, is a field where the joint work of several branches of the social sciences is called for. For some scholars and policy-makers, the goal of economic efficiency overrides all social implications; the positions of others range through the entire spectrum, to the point where social considerations swamp those from the economic field.

To my knowledge, no research has gone very far to date in the attempt to point out the most likely changes resulting from alternative policies with regard to agriculture, in terms of output per unit of input and of total output and its composition, either in the short or in the long run.[12] Little has been done by economists in Latin America to describe the existing situation with respect to land tenure,[13] agricultural policy, the possibility of introducing new techniques of cultivation, new products, existing marketing systems and their weak points, the degree of integration of the agricultural population with the market for manufactured products, income elasticities of demand of the agricultural population for manufactured products, or possibilities of profiting from economies of scale in industry through a redistribution of income in agriculture.

There is at least as much diversity with regard to methods as with regard to goals,[14] ranging from complete socialization of

[12] One of the few works in Chile that comes close to this subject is Bray (1960). Bray's conclusions are in conflict with those of ECLA (UN ECLA 1953).

[13] The Inter-American Committee for Agricultural Development (ICAD) of the OAS has recently undertaken a study of land tenure in several countries of Latin America.

[14] It is not always easy to distinguish between goals and methods. For example, family farms are a goal for some people, while for others they are

land ownership to limited-tax, credit, and price incentives to produce the changes envisioned.

A set of general questions will be helpful in pointing out the research projects which economics might cover in relation to land and agrarian reform in Latin America:

1. What is the present situation in the country or area under consideration, and what are the main weaknesses in economic and social terms?

2. What are the goals sought by political parties and other institutions, what policies and methods are advocated, and what are the alternatives that have a high probability of being followed?

3. How have other countries tried to achieve some or all of the goals? What can be learned from their experience?

4. What are the criteria for evaluating alternative proposals for land and agrarian reforms?

5. How can these criteria be used to determine minimum and maximum size and other characteristics of the agricultural units that would best fit the goals?

6. What are the alternative policy measures that could be followed to arrive at the desired situation, and what are the alternatives with respect to institutional organization?

7. How can the changes envisaged be integrated into the general development effort at the regional and national levels?

8. What are the resources needed to put the necessary changes into effect, and how can they be obtained within the context of the general development policy envisioned?

Each of the foregoing questions involves a number of more specific queries leading to research projects. An attempt will be made below to point out at least some of the specifics.

The answer to the first question would fall under my general category of descriptive studies mentioned in preceding paragraphs. Land tenure systems in Latin America are said to be dominated by three main types: the plantation, the hacienda, and the *minifundio*. The first two have been analyzed for some countries in a general way. For Chile there are some studies on the hacienda system, although they do not adequately cover the economic aspects (McBride 1936; Borde and Góngora 1956). With

---

just one way of achieving some other goal. The distinction is bound to be in some measure arbitrary.

regard to the *minifundio,* some work has also been done, but it has been piecemeal (UCIE 1960a; UCIG 1961).

Several incidental questions are pertinent: (a) What are the prevalent land tenure systems? (b) What is their relative importance in terms of income, output, employment, and use of capital? (c) What is the distribution of production and other rights and obligations among the parties involved? (d) What is the impact of such distribution upon incentives to work, to save, and to invest? (e) Is there any relationship between any special form of land tenure and size of tract, use of capital, employment, type of agriculture, management, market orientation, or introduction of new techniques? (f) What is the existing legislation with respect to these factors? (g) What is the impact of existing land tenure systems on social mobility? (This is just one of the questions that would certainly appeal to sociologists.) (h) Is one particular tenure system more suited to some specific product?

The second main question is whether the major job should be undertaken by political scientists and sociologists, leaving to the economists only those aspects relative to the feasibility of carrying through any or all of the various land reform programs proposed by different groups.

The third main question points to an evaluation of the experience in different countries or areas. Research devised to answer this question would be particularly useful if it focused on a cost-and-benefit type of analysis. Of course, the social and political implications should certainly be included. Some of the more important questions to be asked are the following: (a) What was the prevalent tenure system before the change? (b) What were the goals expected to be achieved by the reform? (c) What were the specific policy measures applied to achieve these goals? Expropriation? Taxation? Credit policy? Other policies? (d) Were these policies effective in achieving the goals? If so, in what measure? If not, why not? (e) What was the cost, in terms of resources, of achieving those results? (f) What was the impact of the change in other sectors of the economy?

The answer to the fourth main question is probably the most crucial to a clarification of the subject of land and agrarian reform. Even rough answers to it would help diminish the emotional factor that emerges whenever the subject is discussed or analyzed. In any discussion there is a natural tendency to blend economic, agrarian-technical, sociological, and political criteria. When no attempt is made to isolate one criterion from the others, substantial emotional content is thrown into the debate. Another element which is bound to muddle the discussion is the relative importance assigned to each of these different criteria. In fact, the four main criteria of evaluation mentioned above— the economic criterion, the social criterion, the agrarian-technical criterion, and the political criterion—undoubtedly call for research not only by economists but also by sociologists, agronomists, political scientists, and other social scientists. In studying these four main criteria, researchers are very likely to find many points of common concern, and areas will certainly be found that call for interdisciplinary work.

I am not qualified to discuss the social, agrarian-technical, or political criteria. With respect to the economic criterion, however, the relevant research should cover at least two aspects: What are the specific criteria that should be considered under this heading, and do these criteria lend themselves to measurement? If so, how? If not, how can alternative proposals be compared on these grounds? Under the economic criterion, some of the pertinent questions should refer to the effects of the change envisaged on income distribution, composition of expenditures between consumption and savings, changes in demand which stimulate or discourage other sectors of the economy, investment incentives within agriculture, demand for resources and employment, absorption of new techniques, more advantageous use of natural resources, changes in the pattern of agricultural production, and changes in foreign trade.

The answer to main question (5) involves simultaneous consideration of the economic, social, agrarian-technical, and political criteria. It also involves a pointing out of the relationships among them in a way that would facilitate choices among alternatives and provide better knowledge of the implications of particular choices. The answers to these questions would be closely related to the results of studies carried out to answer main questions (6) and (8). What question (5) purports to set forth is, above all, a technique or a model geared to clarify the analytical categories into which the specific criteria would fall and relationships would be singled out. This kind of model or technique should be, at least in a very rough way, a byproduct of the work done by social scientists from different disciplines in their attempt to answer the previous main questions and in discussing jointly the results obtained.

Main question (6) involves an exploration of possible alternatives of policy and would draw heavily upon experience. There will certainly be a relationship among the policy measures, the time and resources needed to arrive at the ideal situations envisaged, and the economic and social strains produced in the process. Some of the problems to be tackled under this heading are (a) the use of expropriation and incentive policy to induce the changes desired (emphasis should be placed on determining the type of incentives that can be expected to work effectively in the particular area or country); (b) the institutional organization needed to carry out the policy; and (c) the strategy of the reform, that is, would it be applied area by area or measure by measure throughout the country?

Main question (7) emphasizes the fact that land reform is being conceived in Latin America as part of a wider effort to change the economy and the society. The changes brought about in the agricultural sector of any country will definitely affect other sectors of the economy, while changes in policy with respect to other sectors will certainly affect agriculture. Under this heading some important questions are the following: (a) How would the market for industrial products operate as a consequence of the changes in agriculture, and what are the industrial and other activities that might be expected to expand or to contract? (b) Are the changes in demand for different factors of production consistent with those in the rest of the economy? This question is particularly relevant in the case of factors with low elasticity of supply, in the shorter and medium runs. (c) How would the changes envisaged affect the balance of payments, the pattern of trade, or the exchange rate? (d) Will the internal terms of trade be affected and in what way? (e) Would the new pattern achieved in agriculture be a stable one? If not, what can be done to make it so, or in what way can it be expected to alter, and how would these changes affect the rest of the economy? (f) Are the policy measures envisioned for other sectors of the economy compatible with those in agriculture? (g) What would be the result for the country as a whole in terms of efficiency, of stability, and of growth possibilities?

Main question (8) is geared to a determination of where and how the resources needed to carry out changes in agriculture would be obtained: (a) What amount of domestic resources could be devoted to this particular effort, and how might they be secured? (b) What amount of foreign resources could be obtained, and how? (c) How would these needs be distributed over time? (d) What is the opportunity cost of the resources involved? (e) According to the benefits that are likely to accrue, would this use be the most profitable one from the point of view of growth? (f) Could domestic resources be obtained without endangering the achievement of other goals? (g) Should the main effort with respect to credit, development of new and better seeds, extension, and other innovations in agriculture, come from the government, or should there be important participation from the private sector?

While the foregoing questions imply an enormous amount of research, not only by economists but also by other social scientists, it would be naive to think that nothing should be done in the way of land and agrarian reform in Latin America until this huge research effort is completed. Some changes will take place regardless of research, but one would hope that social scientists will be able to contribute as much as possible to clarifying the problem, pointing out some of the main consequences of alternative paths of action, and developing techniques of analysis and research procedures suited to approach a problem of such complexity.

FISCAL REFORM

The problem of changes in fiscal policy has aroused far less discussion among the general public than land and agrarian reform. This, however, does not mean that there is no pressure to undertake some changes in this area. There is agreement on the crucial role of government in Latin America both in reducing the rate of inflation and in facilitating or promoting a higher rate of increase in per capita output. There is no agreement, however, on the ways and means of achieving this end. Neither is there always agreement with respect to facts, and here much could be learned through intelligent description of the existing situation.

Fiscal policy in Latin America, both with regard to taxes and to expenditures, has developed on an *ad hoc* basis, attempting to solve specific problems one at a time as they arise. As a consequence, examples of inconsistencies in policy and of contradictory measures are common. Likewise, it is extremely difficult to know in advance what taxes, tax exemptions, subsidies, and sundry regulations apply to a particular activity in a specific region or country. At the same time, the effort to comply with existing legislation is a costly one.

Descriptive studies in the field of fiscal policy should aim, in the view of this writer, at answering questions like the following: (a) What are the characteristics of the present tax system in terms of types of taxes and tax exemptions? (b) Who pays the taxes? (c) What are the incentives, or lack of incentives, built into the system? Have they been rationally aimed at a target, or are they just an unexpected result? (d) Have taxes affected the allocation of resources and, if so, how? (e) Have tax exemptions or subsidies been effective in promoting enterprises benefiting from them? (f) Are tax receipts elastic with respect to money income or to real income? (g) Are there particular incentives to use specific factors of production? Have these incentives been effective and in what measures? (h) How good a job is being done with respect to tax collection? (i) How have tax collection procedures affected the economic impact of the tax system?

In regard to expenditures, some of the relevant questions would be the following: (a) How does the proportion of government expenditure for consumption compare with that for investment? (b) How much is devoted to education, public works, housing, and other investment projects? (c) How much is used to cover deficits of public enterprises? (d) What other transfer payments are being made? (e) How are decisions made to distribute expenditures among alternatives? (f) How are expenditures greater than regular tax income financed? (g) What has been the impact of government expenditures and government deficit on the allocation of resources, on the general price level, and on the balance of payments?

These are just a few of the many questions that could be asked in describing the present system. Further work in the field of public finance would be particularly welcome in Latin America if it centered around the kind of problems most often encountered. Some of the more pressing general questions are the following:

1. How could fiscal policy contribute to the acceleration and orientation of economic growth?

2. What are the relationships between fiscal policy and inflation?

3. What can be done to improve fiscal decision processes and institutions?

4. What can be done to improve tax collection? Should the collection of the present taxes be improved?

5. How can social scientists improve the understanding of nationalization? When and how might it usefully be undertaken?

6. How can fiscal studies both contribute to the understanding of economic integration and make it proceed faster in Latin America?

Research in regard to main question (1) may cover several specific aspects: (a) What can fiscal policy do to increase savings? (b) What types of fiscal measures create effective saving incentives? (c) Are government-savings investment mere substitutes for private-savings investment? (d) Is it ever possible to cut current government spending? If so, how? (e) Are there rational ways to decide on the extent of public investment? (f) How should projects be evaluated? (g) How would this evaluation change for different clusters of projects? (h) How should one go about deciding the cut-off point each year for carrying out projects? (i) How could the debt-incurring capacity of the government be estimated? Is this a relevant concept? (j) When should internal indebtedness be preferred as opposed to external debt? (k) What kinds of incentives could be offered to promote particular activities?

With respect to main question (2), the importance of the role of government deficit in inflation was one of the few opinions shared by the participants in the recent Rio de Janeiro conference on inflation and growth. One of the facts singled out was that tax receipts in most Latin American countries do not tend to increase at the same rate as money income. Thus, either the tax rates have to be adjusted periodically (leading to rather awkward changes in the tax structure), or the deficit increases, since expenditures are quite inelastic in actual terms. (a) What can be done, then, to make tax receipts more elastic with respect to changes in money income? (b) What specific taxes are best fitted to achieve this objective? (c) Are there any changes in tax administration and collection systems that would help in this regard? (d) What other types of built-in stabilizers are practicable?

On the other hand, in countries where inflation has been a fact of life for some time, escalator clauses are incorporated into many types of contracts, including labor contracts. (a) What is the role of such clauses in public and private finance? (b) What are the problems connected with and the advantages derived from the domestic sale of dollar bonds and other constant-purchasing-power obligations? (c) Is it advisable to allow the private sector to use any type of readjustment clauses in private contracts, or is some regulation of such contracts called for? (d) Does the type of government expenditures, as distinct from their level, make any difference in terms of inflationary impact?

In many Latin American countries government income depends rather heavily on taxes levied on a few export products, making revenues highly dependent upon foreign trade conditions. While in times of booming exports expenditures are increased, expenditures cannot be reduced easily when the export market deteriorates, and a deficit or an increase in the deficit is generated. (a) What can be done to diminish the impact of fluctuations of foreign trade on government finance? (b) What fiscal measures are indicated, if deficit spending is not, to maintain domestic demand in the face of falling export markets? How can monetary and fiscal analyses and policy be coordinated in Latin America?

In regard to main question (3), every once in a while discussion starts in Chile, for example, as to whether the executive or the legislative branches of government should have the exclusive right to take the initiative in legislation relative to government expenditures, wage policy, social security, and so on. (a) How can the decision processes in this matter be improved? (b) What kind of restraints, if any, are to be imposed on the powers of the legislative and the executive branches? (c) Should some fiscal decisions be decentralized and given over to local government, or at least to branches of the central government in different areas of the country? (d) What decisions could be decentralized, and how? (e) How can local and central governments be coordinated, and in what areas? Questions of this type should be appealing to political scientists as well as economists.

The problem of tax collection is not merely administrative. There might be instances where the economist would recommend non-enforcement of a given set of taxes rather than have enforcement carried to its ultimate consequences. By tightening or loosening collection procedures, it might be possible to minimize the undesirable effects of a poor tax system which for political or other reasons is difficult to change. On the other hand, the possibility of enforcing some tax laws or regulations is very closely related to the attitudes of both taxpayers and tax collectors. (a) How can these be changed? (b) What types of penalties and rewards are most effective? (c) How can some new techniques such as aerial photography be used for taxation purposes?

In countries that have suffered inflation for some time, the yield of real estate taxes, usually levied on some estimated value base which remains fixed for long periods of time, tends to decrease in real terms. (a) Are there any methods to reassess tax values easily? (b) What kind of self-policing schemes [15] would it be worth while to try? (c) Under what conditions? (d) Could the system of tax retention at the source be applied more widely? (e) What kinds of taxes make for easier collection? (f) Given the magnitude of existing deficits, should simplicity of collection be made a central criterion for selection of a tax structure in Latin America?

Main question (5) is as conducive to emotional outbursts as land reform, and an objective analysis of it is as badly needed. (a) What are the economic and social criteria to be used in reaching decisions about nationalization? (b) According to such criteria, what would be an appropriate target? (c) What is the available evidence in this area? (d) Should former owners be compensated? If so, how? (e) Under what conditions could state-owned enterprises be expected to be successful, or more successful than privately owned ones? (f) How would the Chilean Empresa Nacional de Petróleos, for example, compare with private forms of this type operating in other countries? (g) Does the Banco del Estado de Chile, to use another example from Chile, operate dif-

---

[15] Such as that proposed by A. C. Harberger to the Conference on Taxation (sponsored jointly by OAS, IDB, and ECLA) held at Santiago, Chile, December, 1962.

ferently from private commercial banks? Should it? (h) Very much has been said in Chile about the private commercial banks favoring some individual or group of individuals and thus facilitating the concentration of economic power. Would nationalization be a solution to this problem? What are the alternatives?

There are many questions relative to the effect of fiscal policy on economic integration that warrant the attention of social scientists. If the Latin American Free Trade Zone is to move toward a more advanced form of integration, the problem would certainly come up as to whether tax and fiscal policy—and other economic policies—should be uniform for all the countries involved or whether some differences should be maintained. If a common external tariff is put into effect, how should customs revenue be allocated among different countries? Could fiscal policy help to redistribute, if needed, the benefits from integration? How? What types of taxes will least affect the possibility of competition among the various countries involved? How could the possible losses in revenue due to decrease in tariff barriers, if any, be offset? Should income taxes be coordinated among those countries in order to avoid sharp differences among them? What subsidies are to be accepted? How could government, monetary fiscal, and planning decisions be coordinated? Is there a need to reach some agreement in regard to the treatment of private investment, both foreign and domestic?

ECONOMIC INTEGRATION

The other main field of research opportunities mentioned above is that of economic integration. Several questions that might appeal to the researcher have been raised by Dell (1959), by Urquidi (1960), and by Massad and Strasma (1961). Rather than extend this presentation, it seems appropriate to refer the interested reader to these works. Some subjects, however, have not been given adequate consideration. With this idea in mind, I should like to suggest further research on points such as the following:

1. Economies of scale are very often mentioned as one of the main justifications for integration. However, in many countries we find that in a wide variety of industries large firms coexist with small ones. Are economies of scale really important for some industries? If so, for what industries and under what conditions?

2. As integration proceeds, some criteria will have to be used in order to decide upon the location of the new industries or investment projects to be fostered. Can the "comparative advantage" criterion be applied in practice? How should it be revised to avoid full ranking of all products? In what industries are "factor endowments" likely to be a decisive element? How would "comparative advantage" change with investment in education, with land and agrarian reforms, with sharply different patterns of industrial development? Or should one forget about "comparative advantage" because of unpredictable technical developments?

3. Closely connected with the preceding questions is that of external economies. The lack of reasonable estimates of their importance is often used to justify practically any project. What industries are more likely to produce external economies and of what type? How can they be evaluated? How would their importance change under different investment complexes? What part of them would accrue to a particular country or area or to what part of the whole group of countries? How can the benefits be distributed among the countries involved? What about "external diseconomies"?

The three subjects developed in the preceding pages share several elements in common. They are "reforms" that are usually approached with more emotion than analysis. Research about them should include descriptive studies that will break ground for comparative analyses leading to the discovery of factors peculiar to the Latin American scene and of the elements that may be considered of value for underdeveloped areas in general. They all require the study of both alternative policy measures and institutional organizations, as well as their integration into a more general policy or planning framework.

Research on these subjects, then, will most probably yield as a byproduct a set of meaningful conclusions as to the value of economic theory in its present state and indicate the main lines along which theoretical work should proceed. On the one hand, problem-centered and comparative economic studies are likely to contribute more to knowledge than all-inclusive national studies, which are necessarily superficial. On the other hand, the far-reaching implications of these "reform" problems would preclude an excessively narrow approach to economic research in

Latin America and would provide points of contact among social scientists of various disciplines studying this region of the world. Last but not least, the types of projects presented to the researcher facing these "reform" problems will direct our work toward providing statistical, econometric, and other tools of analysis and make available a testing ground for theoretical constructions. Clearly, many types of research projects can provide these byproducts. The "reform" problems presented here, however, because of their wide scope, can give a focus to research and a coherence to the efforts of economists and other social scientists to improve understanding of the workings of Latin American economic and social systems.

Of course, the problems of land and agrarian reforms, fiscal policy, and economic integration do not by any means exhaust the reservoir of research for the social scientist in Latin America. Other topics, such as the role of education or of foreign trade in economic development; the relationships between stability and growth, including the testing of alternative hypotheses about inflation; transportation; labor and capital markets; industrial organization and the economic effects of monopolies; the rapid urbanization under way in Latin America and its economic impact; the problems presented by differences in the degree of development within the countries and among them; methods of economic and social planning, and the organization of planning; and economic history, are of great importance to the understanding of Latin American economics and lend themselves to additional work.[16]

From the choice of research topics presented in this paper, it should be obvious that this writer leans toward policy-oriented research. His preference is shared by most economists working in Latin America. This is so in part because Latin American economists cannot avoid formal or informal responsibility in policy-making. But, perhaps more important, the kind of social and economic changes Latin America is asked to undertake, as recognized in the Act of Bogotá and by the Alliance for Progress, are

[16] For other interesting research areas see the report prepared by Wood (1962) on the Inter-American Conference on Research and Training in Economics held at Santiago, Chile, in August, 1962, under the auspices of the Joint Committee on Latin American Studies of the Social Science Research Council and the American Council of Learned Societies. There is also a Spanish version of the report published by UCIE (1962).

bound to attract the interest and imagination of the social scientist. In order that this interest may become effective, it is necessary to bear in mind at least three facts.

First, the collection and evaluation of information is much more difficult in Latin America than in the United States or in Europe. This fact makes research a more costly undertaking and points to the need for research groups that are able to obtain information from primary sources.

Second, there is no tradition in Latin America that regards knowledge as a cumulative process, mainly owing to the situation described in general terms in the first pages of this paper. Continuity of work is not assured, as elsewhere, through publications; and, in my opinion, it will not be easy to correct this situation. In the meantime, teamwork is probably one of the few alternatives left to insure that there will be some degree of continuity. In other words, a group that becomes interested in a problem will provide both the necessary stimulus through discussion and the possibility of continued research on a particular set of problems, even though some of the members of the group move out to other jobs.

Third, in order to have more and higher quality research done on economics in Latin America, more and better researchers are needed. Efforts are being made in the Latin American nations in this direction, but foreign scholars will be needed for several years, not only for intellectual cross-breeding, which would be a permanent need but also to help carry out the work to be done. At present there are not enough well-trained Latin American social scientists to perform the tasks which in other areas of the world are done by local social scientists. To help effectively, however, and especially to help his Latin American colleagues develop or adapt tools of analysis appropriate for the kind of problems to be faced, the foreign scholar should normally plan for an extended stay. One-month visitors are welcome; one-year colleagues are needed!

BIBLIOGRAPHY

Borde, Jean, and Mario Góngora
  1956 Evolución de la propiedad rural en el Valle de Puangue. Instituto de Sociología, Universidad de Chile. Santiago. 2 vols.

240   Carlos Massad

Bray, James
1960 La intensidad del uso de la tierra en relación con el temaño de los predios en el valle central de Chile. Santiago, Pontificia Universidad Católica de Chile.
Campos, Roberto
1961a Two views on inflation in Latin America. *In* Latin American issues: essays and comments, A. O. Hirschman, ed. New York, The Twentieth Century Fund.
1961b Inflation and balanced growth. *In* Economic development for Latin America, H. S. Ellis, ed. New York.
Dell, S.
1959 Problemas de un mercado común en América Latina. Mexico City, CEMLA.
Ellsworth, P. T.
1945 Chile: an economy in transition. New York.
Felix, David
1960 Structural imbalances, social conflict and inflation. Economic Development and Cultural Change 8: No. 2 (January), 113. Chicago.
Fetter, Frank W.
1931 Monetary inflation in Chile. Princeton. (Also in Spanish; Universidad de Chile, 1937.)
Grunwald, Joseph
1960 Inversión, relación capital-producto y crecimiento económico. Trimestre Económico 27 (April–June): 274.
1961 The "structuralist" school on price stability and economic development—the Chilean case. *In* Latin American issues: essays and comments, A. O. Hirschman, ed. New York, The Twentieth Century Fund.
Haberler, Gottfried
1960 Comercio internacional y desarrollo económico. De Economía 13: No. 68 (October–December), 1089. Madrid.
Hirschman, Albert O.
1960 Ideologies of economic development in Latin America. *In* Latin American issues: essays and comments, A. O. Hirschman, ed. New York, The Twentieth Century Fund.
Instituto Torcuato di Tella. Centro de Investigaciones Económicas.
1962a Oferta de la mano de obra especializada (universitaria y técnica) en la República Argentina. Buenos Aires.
1962b Relevamiento de la estructura regional de la economía Argentina. Buenos Aires. 4 vols.
Kaldor, Nicholas
1957 La inflación chilena y la estructura de la produción. Panorama Económico 11: No. 180 (November 22), 738. Santiago.
McBride, G. M.
1936 Chile: land and society. New York, American Geographic Society Research Series No. 19.
Massad, Carlos, and John D. Strasma
1961 La zona de libre comercio en América Latina—algunos problemas por resolver. Universidad de Chile, Instituto de Economía. Santiago.
Messy, Roger, and Hans T. Pedersen
1963 Statistics for economic development with special reference to national accounts, and related tables. Paper presented to the Conference on Inflation and Growth in Latin America, Rio de Janeiro, January.

Noyola, Juan
1956 El desarrollo económico y la inflación en Méjico y otros países latinoamericanos. Mexico City, Escuela Nacional de Economía, UNAM. Investigación Económica 16: No. 4, 603.
Pinto, Aníbal
1960 Ni estabilidad ni desarrollo—la política del fondo monetario. Santiago.
1962 Chile: un caso de desarrollo frustrado. Santiago. 2nd edition.
Prebisch, Raul
1950 The economic development of Latin America and its principal problems. United Nations, Department of Economic Affairs.
1959 Commercial policy in the underdeveloped countries. American Economic Review 49 (May): 251–73.
1961 El falso dilema entre desarrollo económico y estabilidad monetaria. Boletin Económico de America Latina (CEPAL) 6: No. 1.
Ross, Stanford G., and John B. Christensen
1959 Tax incentives for industry in Mexico—a report. Cambridge, Mass. Law School.
Seers, Dudley
1962 A theory of inflation and growth in underdeveloped economies based on the experience of Latin America. Oxford Economic Papers 14: No. 2 (June), 173.
1963 The limitations of the special case. Bulletin of Oxford University Institute of Statistics 25: No. 2 (May).
Singer, H. W.
1950 The distributions of gains between investing and borrowing countries. American Economic Review 40 (May): 473.
Sunkel, Oswaldo
1958 La inflación chilena: un enfoque heterodoxo. Trimestre Económico 25 (October–December): 570.
United Nations, Department of Economic Affairs
1950a Economic survey of Latin America in 1949.
1950b The economic development of Latin America and its principal problems, [by] Raul Prebisch. (Original text in Spanish.)
United Nations, Economic Commission for Latin America
1953 Análisis de algunos factores que obstaculizan el incremento de la producción agropecuaria. Santiago, April.
1955 Análisis y proyecciones del desarrollo económico: introducción a la técnnica de programación. Mexico City.
1963 Décimo periodo de sesiones. Mar del Plata, Argentina, May.
United Nations, Statistics Department
1959 Series estadísticas para uso de los países menos desarrollados en relación con sus programas de desarrollo económico y social. Informes Estadísticos, Series M, No. 31. (Also in English and French.)
U.S. Federal Reserve System
1954 The federal reserve system: purposes and functions. Washington, D.C. (Spanish translation. Fondo de Cultura Económica. Mexico City.)
Universidad de Chile, Instituto de Economía
1954 Cuentas nacionales 1953. Santiago.
1955 Informe económico 1954. Estudios de las cuentas nacionales. Panorama Económico 7 (January 6): 8.
1956 Desarrollo económico de Chile, 1940–1956. Santiago.

Universidad de Chile, Instituto de Economía
1959   La población del Gran Santiago, 1952–1959. Santiago. (Ocupación y
        desocupación, a series of monographs on employment and unemploy-
        ment, based on periodical surveys.)
1960a La tributación agricola en Chile, 1940–1958. Santiago.
1960b Subdivisión de la propriedad agrícola en una región de la zona cen-
        tral de Chile. Santiago.
Universidad de Chile, Instituto de Geografía
1961   Valle de Putaendo. Estudio de la estructura agraria. Santiago.
Universidad de Chile, Instituto de Organización y Administración
1962   Estudio de recursos humanos de nivel universitario en Chile. Santiago.
Urquidi, V.
1960   Trayectoria del mercado común latinoamericano. Mexico City, Cen-
        tro de Estudios Monetarios Latinoamericanos.
Viner, Jacob
1952   International trade and economic development. New York.
1958   Stability and progress; the poorer countries' problem. *In* Stability
        and progress in the world economy, D. Hague, ed. London.
Wood, Bryce
1962   Report on Inter-American conference on research and training in
        economics. Santiago, August, 1962. (Spanish version published by
        Universidad de Chile, Instituto de Economía.)

7. Research on Latin America
in Sociology

REX HOPPER

There was a time when Abraham Flexner's famous essay on "The Usefulness of Useless Knowledge" made sense. Within limits it still does. Nevertheless, it is also true that the leisurely pace of the conventional conception of the nature of research is anachronistic in a world which, as Moore has remarked, "is full of revolutions" in the sense of "rapid, extensive, and fundamental social change . . . " (Hoselitz and Moore 1963: 360). Such a world needs, even if it does not want, the kind of knowledge sociological research is designed to provide. Moreover, it is increasingly demanded that we provide it. The kind of "pure science" which was once tolerated as a luxury because there seemed to be all the time in the world is rapidly becoming an urgent necessity as time appears to be running out. In this context we would do well to ponder Norbert Wiener's dictum that "the hour is very late and the choice of good and evil knocks at our door" (Hilton 1963: 368). The world has a right to expect that sociology contribute to the rational basis of the choices confronting mankind. Planners and politicians, technicians and citizens are likely to be impatient with and disrespectful of the practitioners of a science who try to waive this responsibility for contribution to knowledge of the consequences of feasible alternatives and equally inclined to respect those who will assume it.

The foregoing remarks are particularly applicable to Latin America. The region has become the "land of mañana" in a strikingly new sense. Specifics of what tomorrow holds are difficult to foresee; clearly, however, Latin America is being caught up and swept along in a process of development that is world-wide in its nature and in its implications. Certainly the area presents a tremendous research challenge to sociologists.

At this point may I brashly suggest that a research program resting on the deliberate choice of one view of the scientific enterprise be developed? This choice does not necessarily imply the rejection of the antonymous view; rather it represents an emphasis deemed to be desirable at this juncture in sociological research in Latin America. I suggest that research be planned against the backdrop of the acceptance of the conception of science as a social invention designed to do better what men have always wanted to do anyway: call the shots and make things jump through hoops—or more seriously, predict and control events.

I would not, of course, decry, much less attempt to impede or proscribe, the work of those who choose to adopt the more idealistic view of science as a sort of interesting game played by an intellectual elite who should be supported in their pursuit of "pure science" as they choose to define it. I would only insist that such a conception is inadequate to present research needs and is almost certain to be regarded as useless by the policy- and decision-makers in Latin America. As Costa Pinto (1963) has remarked,

> In these societies everything is on the table for debate and all debate is a political debate. Development in Latin America today is not only a transition from plantation system to factory system. In fact, what is under debate is the whole heritage of the archaic society—the economic, political, and intellectual heritage—as well as the archaic society itself—its structure, its values, its prospects. Living in a transition of this scope, any decision is a political decision—*in the highest meaning of the word.* So social situations soon become social actions and social actions become political decisions. [Italics supplied.]

Surely it is the social responsibility of sociologists to contribute to a body of scientific knowledge which *will* illuminate social situations, *could* inform social actions, and *might* even influence political decisions.

It could easily be argued that Latin America provides one of the world's best proving grounds for work on a problem with which sociologists have always wrestled: the relationship of sociology to social problems. Or, more accurately, the problem of the process by which a *social* problem is translated into or restated as a *sociological* problem. Adams (1963: 5) has also recently discussed this matter in a brief paper. I would like him to speak for both of us:

> It is clearly evident from the direction that the work that the Latins themselves do that the attention to real contemporary problems is the important thing. This is, somehow, separated from the improved techniques that have developed in the U.S. and Europe. *The logical thing, it would seem, would be to encourage the development of methodology and theory on problems of importance.* If it is possible to make detail analyses of personal pronouns and firewood, why cannot such attention be given to economic choices and political bents?
> In summary the history of anthropological development in Latin American studies indicates that both theoretical and applied work should be encouraged, but *that also* some special attempt should be made to focus the interest of competent theory and methods on problems of greater importance. [Italics supplied.]

With these caveats I now turn to the matter at hand. In what follows I propose (1) to deal briefly with trends in the development of sociology in Latin America, (2) to discuss the chief areas under research cultivation, and (3) to outline what seem to be the indicated next steps.

Previous Surveys of Development

To my knowledge, one of the earliest—if not the earliest—attempts to survey the state of sociology in Latin America was undertaken by Bernard in 1933 for the *Encyclopedia of the Social Sciences* (Bernard 1937). Subsequently, and over a period of some twenty years, several books, various chapters in books, and numerous articles have dealt with the subject. I myself did such a summary in 1945 (Hopper 1945). There is no present need to characterize these contributions; they reflect the situation as it was ten to twenty years ago. The same must be said for most of the chapters on Latin America appearing in the various symposia on world sociology. In any case each succeeding contribution draws on its predecessors to such an extent that to read one is to have read them all.

More recently, the Centro Latinoamericano de Pesquizas em Ciências Sociais has issued a series of reports on the social sciences in various Latin American countries. The project was launched in 1958 and was to have covered eight countries. To date, reports on Chile (Donoso and Zarbas 1959), Colombia (Arboleda 1959), Costa Rica (Campos Jimenez 1959), Venezuela (Silva Michelena 1960), and Uruguay (Solari 1959) have been published, and reports on Argentina, Brazil, and Mexico are forthcoming.[1] Each of these reports was organized in terms of commonly agreed-upon topics: historical background, teaching, research, publications, employment opportunities and professionalization, and problems confronting the social sciences. The net result is a valuable set of sources on the state of sociology in Latin America today. The present survey makes use of these reports, and it also leans heavily on Germani's attempt at a region-wide statement on the development and the state of Latin American sociology (Germani 1959a, 1959b).

Stages in the Development of Sociology

For quite evident reasons it is difficult to generalize about the twenty countries of Latin America. Any attempt to generalize about the development of sociology in the region is subject to the same difficulty. Nevertheless, Germani feels, and I concur, that throughout the region the past fifteen years have witnessed rapid changes which are likely to result in increasing regional similarities in the relatively near future. This course of events, when taken in conjunction with factors which have been directly implicated in the development of sociology in Latin America, gives ground for the belief that, despite regional differences, it is possible to formulate some generalizations about the state of sociology throughout the region.

Among the factors that have made for similarities in the development of sociology in Latin America is the fact that the Latin American countries do share a common cultural heritage and do possess a series of characteristic cultural traits which mark them off as a socio-cultural area vis-à-vis other regions of the world. Latin Americans experience an undeniable sense of "belonging," of "community,"—and even of a "common destiny." More specifically, there is a certain parallelism in the types of social problems with which the various countries have been con-

[1] An earlier survey on Brazil was published by Costa Pinto and Carneiro in 1955.

fronted. In addition, the currents of foreign intellectual influences which played a role in the development of the Latin American nations—influences whose impact was not only national but international and even continentwide in scope—are similar. Then there is the relative hegemony of a few centers of influence which served to filter, channel, and diffuse both the indigenous and foreign intellectual currents affecting the development of Latin American thought. The concentration in two or three centers (Spain, Argentina, Mexico) of most editing and publishing activity and the great similarity in the traditions and organization of the universities of the Latin American region are two examples. This last factor operated not only during the colonial period but also after Independence, when the universities modeled themselves after the institutions of continental Europe, notably France. In this context, Germani also calls attention to the negative importance for the development of sociology of such features of university organization as the methods for recruiting faculty, the form of compensation, the significance and status attached to university teaching in Latin America, and the whole set of attitudes which resulted from these practices.

All in all, Germani concludes that the existence of a traditional conviction of the reality of a "Latin American sociology" is neither accidental nor arbitrary. The sense of this conviction is that of a scholarly tradition which is manifest in the majority of sociological studies produced by Latin American authors and is evident in the similarity of attitudes, orientation, and fields of interest found among sociologists. He adds that most foreign observers, looking at the matter from the outside, have taken this for granted. But, Latin American sociologists themselves take the same position. In Germani's words (1959a: 435),

There is no doubt at all that Latin American sociologists are aware that they are indeed a regional group. The existence of a regional association—a type of organization not to be found in other continents—constitutes the institutionalization of this sentiment of community.[2]

Against this background, it is suggested that the course of development in Latin American sociology since Independence can

---

[2] The regional organization referred to is ALAS (Asociación Latino Americano de Sociología), which was founded in 1950 and which, beginning in 1951, has held biennial continentwide congresses.

be traced or surveyed through three stages or periods.[3] These stages not only coincide with important historico-social changes in the region; they also tend to parallel the general process of the development of sociology as an autonomous discipline anywhere.

THE PRE-SOCIOLOGICAL PERIOD

Germani labels the first period the phase of "pre-sociological thought." It stretches from the anarchic years following the revolutionary struggle for independence to the beginning of this century. Only the briefest characterization seems to be called for here.

First, a word about the socio-psychological roots of the initial epoch. The influence of European and Anglo-American events and ideas on Latin American thought during this period was strong. Under the impact of these events and ideas, the Latin American elites who launched the revolution proposed "to transform the colonies into modern states." As Germani wryly puts it, "the reality was otherwise and years of anarchy and dictatorships followed hard on the revolutionary period." The depth of the resultant disillusionment was eloquently expressed by Bolivar in his famous observation that "Those of us who have served the Revolution have plowed in the sea." For some participants and observants and observers, however, their very disenchantment with the Revolution led to the development of the belief that its failure was the consequence of the disparity between "the ingenuously rationalistic dreams of the revolutionary fathers and a social reality which they did not understand." The remedy was clear to the succeeding generation: an understanding of the actual, present social reality was a prerequisite to its transformation.

Hence "social realism" became one of the dominant characteristics of pre-sociological thought. It represented, quite simply, the clear conviction that society is a datum and that a science of the social is a fundamental and necessary foundation on which to base any program of societal reconstruction. It is interesting to

[3] For present purposes the colonial period can be omitted from consideration, although, as Germani remarks, there was much writing that represented *"reflexiones sobre lo social."* Indeed there was, and I have found some of it most useful in my own work on the struggle for independence in Latin America.

note that this point of view was formulated in the New World prior to the introduction of Positivism, and, for that very reason, prepared the way for the rapid spread of Comtean Positivism when it was introduced during the second half of the nineteenth century. Thus the soil was prepared for the cultivation of a science of the social, and a positivistic sociology became one of its chief manifestations. In Germani's words, Positivism, both the domestic and imported varieties, spread throughout Latin America, even though its particular development in any one country was modified by varying intellectual, political, and social factors in each case. As Zea (1949: 47) puts it, "It is possible to speak of an Hispanic-American positivism: but by the same token one can speak of a Mexican, Argentine, Uruguayan, Chilean, Peruvian, Bolivian, or Cuban positivism."

Positivism was incorporated in the sociology of the period in two ways. On the one hand, the positivistic orientation predominated in speculative and theoretical writings—usually the work of those engaged in university teaching. On the other hand, there emerged a considerable body of literature written in the tradition of the social realist school. In these works, Positivism provided the conceptual apparatus in terms of which writers approached the task of describing and analyzing the concrete social phenomena that they were examining.

A second characteristic of the pre-sociological stage is found in the fact that it was the period of the *pensadores*—the thinkers.[4] The literary output of such men cannot easily be classified under any of the usual categories, such as historical, political, philosophical, or scientific. For the *pensamiento* of the *pensadores* has a very special meaning in the history of ideas in Latin America; it is most nearly approximated by the work of the French *philosophes* of the eighteenth century. In an attempt to clarify the meaning and significance of this characteristic, Germani cites José Gaos to the effect that *pensamiento* is something which forms a vital part of daily existence and which is, therefore, concerned with problems tied to the circumstances of a given time and place, and, in consequence, requiring urgent attention. However, there is one striking peculiarity in *pensamiento:* in spite of the nature of the objects of its concern, the manner in which it

---

[4] Many Latin American scholars still prefer to be known as *pensadores* rather than to be identified with a specific discipline.

deals with its subject matter is in accord with the methods and
style of philosophy and science (Germani 1959a: 437). The tradition of the *pensadores,* whatever it is, has been an important influence in Latin American scholarly work.

A third characteristic of the period under examination has to
do with the aesthetic interests of the *pensadores.* In general they
were literati who paid much heed to beauty of style and to capacity for originality in the expression of ideas. Naturally, this
emphasis had great influence on the nature of the social analyses
which they undertook.

The warrant for this brief characterization of the work of the
pre-sociological period is its continuing powerful influence on
the later stages of the development of sociology. In defining the
task of the sociologist as perceived both by the public and by
sociologists themselves, we must take these factors into account.

THE INSTITUTIONALIZATION OF SOCIOLOGY

We may now turn to the second phase in the development of
sociology in Latin America, which might be designated as the
period of the institutionalization of the discipline.

The last half of the nineteenth century was the period of the
organization of former colonies into Latin American nation-
states. As we have seen, the period was also marked by the dominance of Positivism as a theoretical concept in terms of which the
task of structuring the national life was approached. One salient
sector of this total effort was the reorganization of the already
established universities and the development of new ones. It was
in this context that, toward the end of the nineteenth century,
sociology as a discipline was first introduced into Latin American
universities. As early as 1877 there was an Institute of Social Science in Caracas which was affiliated with the University. Chairs
of sociology were also established in Bogotá in 1822, Buenos
Aires in 1896, Asunción del Paraguay in 1900, and Ecuador in
1906. The process continued, and by the close of the first quarter
of the century "the teaching of sociology was established in virtually all countries" (Germani 1959a: 440). Brazil was an exception. Costa Pinto (1955) states that the teaching of the social
sciences on the university level did not get under way until 1930
in Brazil. Thereafter, however, developments were very rapid:
many chairs were established, and the inauguration of the Free

School of Sociology and Politics in São Paulo in 1933 antedated similar institutions in other countries by twenty years.

It scarcely seems necessary to outline the factors operating in promoting this relatively rapid development. Obviously the continuing conviction that the study of social reality demanded a social science was a powerful influence. But what is most significant at this point is the way in which and the circumstances under which sociology found its place in the university structure and curriculum. For the most part the newly established chairs of sociology were located in the faculties of law and philosophy. It is evident that these affiliations could not fail to be significant in determining the nature of the development of the discipline. Indeed, Germani (1959a: 440) argues that "Much of the content and the orientation of Latin American sociology, even up to the present, derives directly from these academic connections." This influence was not limited to matters of theoretical and methodological orientation but also was present on the more practical levels of recruitment of personnel and pedagogical practices. Out of a welter of such influences, these should be underlined as features which resulted from the affiliation of sociology in Latin America with the faculties of law and philosophy:

1. The holder of a chair in sociology (*el catedrático*) was rarely a full-time professor. Usually, what is more, he was not a professor who might also engage in other activities; rather he was an individual primarily engaged in another profession, who might also teach sociology.

2. An appointment as a university professor was much sought after because it conferred social prestige and enhanced standing in the primary occupation.

3. In the nature of the case professorships were rarely held by people who had been formally trained in sociology—even when the incumbents had been trained in the field of law. Not infrequently, appointees were politicians or prominent public figures.

4. There were no criteria for the determination of professional specialization or competency. This was especially true of the disciplines deemed to be "nontechnical," of which sociology was one. In consequence, a professor might well be teaching all over the map, so to speak. Simultaneously or successively he might be lecturing on, for example, the philosophy of law, introduction to law, constitutional law, criminal law, and sociology. And it

was almost certain to be the case that the incumbent's formal professional training had not been in sociology.

5. Even in those rare instances where a professor gave full time to his university work, it was still virtually certain that he would be teaching in several and distinct subject-matter areas— a type of "moonlighting" made necessary by the low level of compensation.

6. The faculty was inevitably drawn almost exclusively from the upper class, given the nature of the social structure. The same composition held true for the student body, though to a somewhat lesser degree.[5]

7. Finally, teaching was not linked up with research. Very little research was undertaken in the context of the university sociology programs. There was writing, of course, but there was little writing that resulted from research in any technical sense.

In view of the conditions just outlined what did the publications of the gentlemen scholars of this period look like? Many of the professors published texts based on the courses they offered. They also published books and articles on various special themes. The nature of their published work led Poviña (1941) to describe the period as a time when attention was directed to "systematic sociology" and "*sociological* specialization." And, indeed this is accurate if the comparison is with the work of the earlier period of pre-sociological thought. With few exceptions, scholarly production was not original; it was largely devoted to the effort of an organized and systematic transmission of the sociological knowledge of the epoch—particularly that emanating from the great centers of Europe and North America. In the early years, as we have seen, the positivistic orientation was dominant and the works of Comte, Spencer, and their followers were cited widely. Later, neopositivistic and nonpositivistic points of view were introduced. During this "borrowing phase" the work of the principal European sociologists and even of the outstanding North Americans became known and was used. As there was no specialization in their preparation, so was there no specialization in the writings of the academics. The same author was likely to

[5] Germani (1959a: 442–43) adds the comment that, though changes are occurring in the university structure, this picture of university organization remains accurate still "for a considerable number of Latin American universities."

write on a great variety of subjects and from a number of disciplinary viewpoints. Yet, it must be added, Latin American sociology was not greatly different from sociology in Europe and North America during the nineteenth and early twentieth centuries.

But the winds of change were already blowing. One especially significant shift was the development of a very strong antipositivistic school. As early as 1904 an antipositivist movement was in full swing in Mexico. Interestingly enough, the leader's mantle was worn by Antonio Caso, an outstanding philosopher and sociologist of the day. Once launched, the movement swept throughout Latin America; it was especially influential in philosophical circles. Its effects on sociological thought varied, however, from country to country. Although a sociologist headed the campaign in Mexico, philosophical antipositivism in Brazil seemed to have little effect on the development of sociology (Germani 1959a: 445).[6] Germani suggests Argentina as the more typical case. The waxing of Argentine antipositivism marked the waning of Argentine sociology as a scientific discipline. In short, the antipositivistic movement created a climate of opinion that was decidedly unfavorable to the development and growth of the scientific spirit generally and for the sciences of man particularly. Psychology and sociology were hardest hit by the attack.

The strongest impact of antipositivism was felt in the field of methodology. Under German influence there developed a conceptual distinction between the "sciences of nature" and the "sciences of the spirit and culture." In consequence, sociology came to be viewed by many as chiefly a speculative and philosophical discipline. The methodological repercussions were, of course, serious. It came to be held that sociology could and should utilize intuition as a means of arriving at truth. The usual techniques and procedures of scientific investigation were to be discarded.

An important body of literature grew up in defense of this "intuitive" orientation. In Germani's view, the predominance of Spain, Mexico, and Argentina in intellectual matters again func-

[6] There is an interesting problem here. Why is it that in the two Latin American countries where Positivism seemed to have taken deepest root—Brazil and Mexico—the reactions to the challenge to Positivism should have been so different?

tioned to facilitate and intensify the new development. It is his affirmation that virtually everything published in these three countries from roughly the 1930s to the beginning of the present decade can be classified as representative of this antipositivistic and antiscientific trend. In Germani's own words (1959a: 447),

All of Dilthey was published, works of Rickert, and Windleband, much of Scheler, Vierkandt, Spann, Freyer, Springer, and naturally, the greater part of Husserl and other phenomenologists. More recently Sartre, Heidegger, Merleau-Ponty and others have found wide acceptance in sociology. To all these are to be added, of course, the works of many Latin Americans and Spaniards. The writers, notably Ortega y Gasset, were especially influential in mediating the acceptance of German influence in Latin American philosophy and sociology.

Viewed against the background of our characterization of the first period in the development of Latin American sociology, the appeal of the *verstehen* movement as a solid foundation for the kinds of research to which most Latin Americans were already predisposed becomes rather evident. Indeed our colleagues to the south came to aver that the methods of "antipositivism" were the only really scientific means of arriving at knowledge of the social world.

Meantime, there were significant new developments in Europe and the United States. As an extraordinarily competent Latin American sociologist sees these novelties, they look somewhat like this:

1. On the one hand, world sociology—i.e. sociology which seeks to transcend national or regional limitation—was breaking new trails. The era of the dominance of Durkheim, Pareto, Weber, Simmel, and others seemed to be drawing to a close. What now seemed called for was advances beyond the level of their admitted achievements. What was needed was greater methodological rigor coupled with cumulative advances in theory—this to be accomplished through a more fruitful intersection between hypotheses, investigations, new conceptual schemes, and new researches.

2. Additionally, the growing inter-relationships between European and North American sociologists pointed in the direction of profound modifications on both sides of the Atlantic. Indeed, it gave promise of being the foundation for the development of a truly "world sociology."

3. All this was not, of course, a purely "intellectual" development. The volume and intensity of the social changes characteristic of the contemporary world had again given new significance to the sciences of man as the one rational instrument with which these changes might be confronted.

4. Meantime, in Europe there was a great upsurge of interest in

"empirical studies," in the development of more technically adequate methods, in the institutionalization of sociology as worthy of university status, and in the necessary reorganization of universities and the creation of institutes especially devoted to training in sociology. Somewhat oddly, this was paralleled in the United States by an increased interest in theory which seemed to suggest both a sloughing off of provincialism and more importantly, an eschewing of "planless empiricism." [7]

It is against the background of the antipositivistic movement in Latin America and the foregoing sketch of recent development in world sociology that the next stage of development of sociology in Latin America comes into focus.

THE BEGINNINGS OF SCIENTIFIC SOCIOLOGY

In the midst of his description of the prevalent type of university organization in Latin America, Germani cautiously remarks that there have been recent tendencies toward university reforms which may portend the beginnings of scientific sociology in Latin America.[8] The suggestion of such a possibility need not involve any casuistric discussion of the term "scientific." All that is intended for present purposes is to raise this question: is there a likelihood that the traditional type of "university sociology" which we have been considering may be superseded to some degree at least by the kind of sociological orientation which has come to characterize the great international training centers during the past fifteen or so years? As of now, however, "university sociology" is still dominant throughout the region. Teaching is speculative, content eclectic, subject matter poorly defined, teachers are largely untrained and unspecialized, little research is undertaken, and what there is continues the tradition of the *pensadores,* for very few investigators have been trained in modern methods of research. The very organization of the universities is inadequate as an environment in which to teach and do research in the modern sense—especially in so sensitive an area as sociology.

[7] In this context it is interesting to speculate whether these remarks—together with all that has been said about the Latin American concern with social problems—throw some light on the present extraordinary vogue in Latin America of such U.S. sociologists as Parsons, Merton, Moore, and the late C. Wright Mills.

[8] Germani (1959a: 443) knows whereof he speaks, for he has certainly been a key leader in this development. Given the circumstances under which he had to work, his reorganization of the sociology program in the University of Buenos Aires and the establishment of a department of sociology stand as a most remarkable achievement.

Nevertheless, there is rapidly emerging a new generation of sociologists who have been the leaders in the reorganization of old establishments and in the organization of new institutes and schools in which training in scientific sociology is being introduced. Two international institutions have been formed to train social scientists and to promote social research. The Centro Latinoamericano de Pesquisas em Ciências Sociais in Rio de Janeiro is primarily a research agency. La Facultad Latino Americana de Ciencias Sociales (FLACSO) in Santiago de Chile is a teaching and training institution. Both were established in 1957 under the joint sponsorship of UNESCO and the respective governments and function under the supervision of the same Board of Directors. Certainly they may well become focal points of the new sociology.

Similar developments are occurring throughout the region. Everywhere there are to be found representatives of the new breed of sociologists, whose image of themselves and of their discipline differs drastically from the views of their intuitively grounded predecessors and contemporaries. The emerging image is mirrored in the kind of research its proponents are undertaking. We have dealt with this theme elsewhere and will return to it shortly (Hopper and Hopper 1962). Yet everywhere in Latin America, we find the two types of sociology coexisting. As Germani observes, the problem posed by this coexistence is very complex indeed, for, it is not merely a matter of "modernizing" certain sectors of Latin American sociology; in a sense this has already been done. Rather, it is basically a problem of changing attitudes, of reorientation with reference to the values to be served, of the adoption of a different and more adequate scientific position, accompanied, of course, by substantial changes in organizational structure and in the teaching and research staffs (Germani 1959a: 449–50).

Research in Sociology

THE CHANGING SELF-IMAGE OF LATIN AMERICAN SOCIOLOGISTS

It was suggested above that the new generation of Latin American sociologists includes a significant number who see themselves and sociology in a new light. This group has little in common with their predecessors or with the older scholars of the present period. To elaborate on this observation will help explain the current situation and will introduce the discussion of research activity and needs.

Three facets of the new self-image of the Latin American sociologists stand out. First, there is a clearly discernible shift in the sources to which the new men of sociology turn for their own professional growth and development. In oversimplified form, this change may be said to represent a shift from European to American models of the nature and function of sociological research. As one of the most eminent Latin American sociologists remarks: "The reference group to which Latin American social scientists often turn is that ideally constituted by their colleagues in the United States, England, and, to a lesser extent, France (Germani 1960a).

A second facet of this changing image may be phrased as the shift from an emphasis on sociology as a "cultural" and/or "national" discipline to a conception of sociology as a "natural" or "universalistic" science. Though this shift is under way, it is far from complete. Every university in which sociology is taught, every center of sociological research, and every sociological association in Latin America is a battleground of the struggle between the "culturalists" and the "naturalists"—between the coterie of "gentlemen scholars" representative of the past and the recently emerged group of trained professionals who look to the future.

This discussion of the "new" Latin American sociology will of course have a familiar ring for those acquainted with the history of sociology elsewhere. What is happening in Latin America is obviously a variation on a theme. However, it is something more as well; it also illuminates the thesis that *such developments are not mere recapitulations*. Rather, the three aspects of the Latin American experience constitute evidence in support of the thesis that such shifts depend upon prior and (or) correlative changes in the self-image of practicing sociologists. For example, there *has* been a significant change in the Latin American image of the role of the professor. From conversations, personal observations, and teaching experience in several Latin American countries, I can report that for the professor to consider himself a "gentleman scholar" in the traditional manner is no longer deemed adequate. Nor is it enough for him to use the classroom as a platform for expounding little more than his personal opinions. Rather, he must learn the importance of the toilsome business of research among real people and on real problems.

Secondly, there has been a shift in attitude toward teaching and students. In the new image, teaching is no longer a matter of the "master" casting pearls before the swine. Nor is it an activity that can be relegated to subordinate assistants while the master goes about his main business of extracurricular activities. In short, in the earlier image the *cátedra* was regarded as a sinecure or status symbol for men whose chief professional interests were nonacademic; the newer conception of a university professorship turns upon challenge and responsibility.

In similar fashion the image of the student role is changing. Students are no longer pictured as nuisances who clutter up the academic scene and induce guilt feelings in an occasional *catedrático* because he accepts little or no responsibility for their work. Rather, students are coming to be seen as charges working in a joint educational endeavor. The new conception is affecting the status of the "perennial" student and of the "political" leader who enrolls as a student in order to infiltrate the student body; both find themselves being downgraded in academic esteem.

Of course, these attitudes are not universal. They are felt to a greater or lesser degree in different faculties. The need for full-time professors and full-time students is increasingly recognized. Regular attendance in classes and regular work assignments throughout the academic year are displacing the traditional views of classes as having no real functions and of education as cramming for final examinations. In such matters, Latin America still has a long way to go despite the substantial changes in both image and practice already recorded.

Changes are also occurring in the field of administration. Sociology is slowly emerging from its traditional position as an appendage to the curricula of faculties of law or philosophy; sociologists are establishing the discipline and organizing its programs in terms of models clearly derived from the "reference groups" mentioned earlier. In consequence, the working relationships developing among faculty members and between faculty and students in such centers as Bogotá, Buenos Aires, Caracas, Rio de Janeiro, São Paulo, and Santiago are both exciting and encouraging.

And, we might add, because the task of our Latin American coworkers must be carried out in a milieu of rapid transition and dramatic social upheaval we have much to learn from them—if we will trouble to inform ourselves—as they wrestle with the problem of establishing a fruitful relationship between social theory and social structure.

RESEARCH ORIENTATION OF THE NEW GENERATION

We now turn to the implications of these changes in orientation for the *kind* of research Latin American sociologists want to do and are increasingly undertaking. The earlier image of sociology as a cultural discipline meant that sociologists delved into and rationalized the details of the uniqueness of the national ethos. The work of these sociologists was impressionistic, literary, unsystematic, descriptive, speculative, and moralistic (Germani 1960a: 6). In contrast, the image of the role of the sociologist in the contemporary situation held by the emerging group of well-trained and self-conscious professionals has been formulated by one of their number (Fals Borda 1961: 21) in these forceful words:

We have the grave responsibility of studying the sweeping changes which envelop us. This we must do in order to provide the scientific data necessary to the alleviation of the conflicts inherent in the transition period and to the reduction of institutional dysfunctioning. Nothing less will justify our science and our profession. Anything less will reduce our professional "caucuses" and congresses to irrelevant academic disquisitions held in ivory towers. And, we'd do well not to forget that the social processes operative in the real world are not only undermining the traditional social structure; they are also destroying the foundations of the ivory towers.

An analysis of the research production of the "new professionals" in Latin America sustains this view of the nature of the shift under examination. A basic and general concern with social change breaks down into specific and intense interest in the investigation of urbanization, industrialization, social stratification and mobility, the family, and demographic studies—especially immigration and internal migrations. There is a growing interest in the difficult area of political sociology, in the sociology of development, of occupations, and of education. In these directions, we are observing work far more significant than the mere imitation of sociological fashions dominant in other countries.

Granted, Latin American scholars have always been interested, in one way or another, in problems of change, development, mobility, social structure. What is new is the context within which researchers are working. Three statements characterize the modern frame of reference:

1. There is recognition of the utility—not to mention the urgent necessity—of such studies in the face of the continent-wide social, economic, and political situation.

2. There is an equally important insistence on the need to project such research against the background of an accumulating body of theory and principle and with a view to making substantial contributions to that body of theory.

3. There is increasing methodological sophistication, manifested not only in an awareness of the need for such sophistication but also in the acquisition of the requisite technical skills.

Throughout Latin America research increasingly approximates this mold. The direction and rate of change in research orientation is most manifest and most advanced in the centers in Buenos Aires, Bogotá, Rio de Janeiro, São Paulo, and Santiago.

In what follows, then, the focus of attention is the reflection in sociological research of these changes in the image of sociology. The problem here is not one of finding evidence but one of an embarrassment of riches—that is to say, the problem of organization. Perhaps the matter can best be handled through the use of selected materials illustrating the fact of changing images as a recurrent finding in various areas of research that did not, naturally, have this problem as a central concern.

RESEARCH ON SOCIAL CHANGE

It is no exaggeration to say that the basic research interest of the present generation of Latin American sociologists is the study of processes and problems of social change. Nor is it too much to say that their reporting of their work is replete with references to and evidence of changes in the attitudes, values, conceptions, and aspirations of members of the various sectors of the social structure. The research reports of Fals Borda illustrate this point; they are crammed with evidence of the "changing mentality" at the core of the rapidly changing scene in Latin America. The comment is particularly apt for his monograph on *Peasant Society in the Colombian Andes: A Sociological Study of Saucio* (1955; Spanish version, 1961), and his essay on "The

Transformation of Latin America and Its Social and Economic Implications" (1961). He opens his discussion of the rural population of Colombia with these words (Fals Borda 1955: xviii):

The whirlwind of the social revolution which promises to be the distinctive characteristic of this century is beginning to pull the rural population into its vortex. One would have thought that four centuries of monotonous labor would have completely numbed any awareness of the possibility of progress and would have left the country people resigned and docile. However, they are slowly coming to see that they have been exploited and despised . . . [they] manifest an unprecedented dissatisfaction and are becoming aware of themselves as a class.

Similarly, Fals Borda's essay on "The Transformation of Latin America" affirms the causal role of the "human factor" in social transformation, documents changing images—especially those held by the middle class, the urban proletariat, and the rural proletariat—and describes consequent changes in the stratification system, in the power structure, and in the institutional constellation. All these changes Fals Borda (1961: 1–2) sees as potentially productive of increased tension, violence, and revolutionary upheaval unless a more adequate democratic leadership emerges.

For a second illustration we turn to the work of the Argentine sociologist, Germani. Virtually everything he undertakes takes the form of an empirical study designed to make theoretically useful contributions to the investigation of Latin America in the process of transition from a traditional to an industrial and urban society. Especially noteworthy are his "Problems and Strategy of Research in Less Developed Countries: Latin America" (1960a) and his recent book on *Política y sociedad en una época de transición* (1962). In all of Germani's work there is much evidence of the correlation between the process of transition under analysis and the changing conceptions of the role of the new elite, the middle class, and the urban and rural proletariats. Like Fals Borda, Germani recognizes the insistent social forces generated and released by these changing images. For example, he attributes the failure of the Peronist regime to the fact that it offered only an ersatz political participation to the masses. Moreover, while recognizing that the fall of Peron was brought about by a conjunction of diverse factors, he holds that the principal factor was the inability of the Peronist movement to become the vehicle for the genuine expression of the interests and the aspirations of the "popular classes." Finally, he argues that the need to provide institutions adequate to the demands of the images held by the masses continues to be the central problem of Latin America in transition.

DEMOGRAPHIC AND URBANIZATION STUDIES

For the sake of convenience, demographic research and studies in urbanization will be considered together. What can such work tell us about changing images? It may be well to preface an answer with a brief reminder of the facts of population growth in Latin America:

The stark fact is that total population increased by about four-fifths between 1920 and 1950, a rate of growth well above the world average; and that the population of Latin America, growing at a rate of about 2.5 per cent per year, may double within the next thirty years

for a total of close to 600 millions. Significant for our purposes is

the fact that the growth of urban population in Latin America was even greater than that of the total population—reaching levels as high as 7 per cent per year [in Venezuela]. In seven of the fifteen countries for which data are available urban population at observed rates of growth would double in less than 18 years; and in one—Venezuela—in about ten years (Hauser, ed., 1961: 76).

Such is the general picture. In this context we must content ourselves with three illustrations of a wealth of material embedded in the work being done in these areas. First is a statement taken from a large-scale and magnificently designed project of which we have had a preview:

The difficulties normally attending the modernization of agrarian societies are exacerbated in Latin America by the accelerating population growth. . . . [The decades since 1920] have witnessed drastic social changes associated with urbanization, improved communications, and increased political participation. *As a consequence, Latin Americans today have aspirations that resemble those of their neighbors in Canada and the United States.* [Italics added.] [9]

It is these new aspirations that give content to the changing images. Obviously, the details cannot be provided here, but they

[9] The research program mentioned is a five-year project planned by the International Population and Urban Research Center of the University of California at Berkeley and the International Center for Comparative Social Research of the University of Buenos Aires.

are easily accessible to researchers. With unanimity scholars report and document such changes in aspirations—changing aspirations in food habits, changing patterns of dress, changing beliefs about relations between the sexes, changing conceptions of political participation, and changing hopes with reference to the possibility of upward mobility.

A second illustration comes from the work of Fals Borda (1961: 17–32). In a discusssion of the contention that the industrial revolution did not get under way in Latin America until the third decade of the twentieth century, he writes

Such a transformation was not possible earlier because Latin America had not undergone *the necessary modification in beliefs, attitudes and motivations—that is, the pre-requisite changes in the ethos of the people had not occurred.* It took over a hundred years to lay the foundation for these changes.

Following a brief and plausible consideration of the various factors which may have contributed to awakening the people to a critical outlook toward the existing order, Fals Borda points to the development of an awareness of social injustice and a set of new aspirations, needs, and ambitions. These changed images, he insists, provide the fuel for the forces of the revolution now sweeping over Colombia. He concludes that "this is the new milieu in which the Latin America of today is being formed, and these are the forces which alone will explain the transformation which is taking place" (Fals Borda 1961: 18).

A third illustration comes from the report of a recent seminar on *Urbanization in Latin America.* Relevant to our interest is the section of the "Conclusions of the Seminar" which summarizes the findings relevant to the "Demographic Aspects of Urbanization":

The discussion disclosed the similarity between the character of urbanization in Latin America and in Asia, [though it was also found that] the degree of urbanization in Latin America was intermediate between that of the economically more advanced nations in Oceania, North America and Europe, and the least economically advanced nations of Asia and Africa.

With this qualification, then

In Latin America as in Asia it is apparent that:
1. There is a larger urban population than is justified by existent levels of agricultural and nonagricultural productivity.

2. Rapid urban growth is more the result of economic "push" factors from the rural countryside than "pull" factors in the cities. *The "pull" from the cities tends to be social rather than economic.*

3. Urbanization in large measure has been independent of industrialization.

4. Urban population is concentrated in the large cities, especially in the capital cities, which continue to grow more rapidly than other urban places (Hauser, ed., 1961: 76).[10]

Four observations are in order with reference to these findings and the problem of changing images: First, if for whatever reasons people are deserting the country for the city, even though they are still needed on the farm, it can be concluded that they migrate because they *want* to and not because they are forced to. We suggest that they are lured by the city because their aspirations are changing. Second, a more sociological interpretation of the "push" and "pull" factors supports this hypothesis. Certainly economic conditions in the countryside have not worsened appreciably since the upsurge of urbanward migration. Rural people *could* have remained where they were *had they been content to do so.* Changing images and aspirations have rendered rural life in poverty less satisfactory than urban life in poverty. Both the "push" and "pull" factors turn out to be social when viewed from this vantage point. Third, since it has been found that urbanization "in large measure has been independent of industrialization and represents the transfer of poverty from the countryside to the city," this too suggests that the migration is a function of changing images—even if the images are erroneous in so far as job opportunities are concerned. Fourth, and finally, the fact that the flow of migration is mainly to the large cities suggests that the motives for movement have to do with images of a way of life rather than a panicky desire to escape the grinding poverty of the country. Indeed, one of the interesting facets of the rapid redistribution of population over the last three decades has to do with the changing character of urban living itself. Urbanization in Latin America has not been a function of industrialization. Indeed, urban concentration in the distributive

10 The report is published as the outcome of the seminar jointly sponsored by the Bureau of Social Affairs of the United Nations, the Economic Commission for Latin America, and UNESCO in cooperation with the International Labor Organization and the Organization of American States. The seminar was itself an index of a new day in Latin American research.

sense has been characteristic of the continent for a very long time. Both the physical environment (geography, topography, and climate) and the social environment (Spanish and Portuguese institutions) contributed to the concentration of population in urban port areas. In short, urban concentration was a function of a system of land occupancy and resulted in "urbanization" in an ecological sense rather than the development of an urban "style of life" in the modern sense.

All this is changing. The recent intensification in rural-urban migration is accompanied by significant changes in the socio-psychological climate of the cities. People who have for centuries been concentrated in "cities" in the numerical sense are now rapidly evolving the attitudes and values—the "life style"—usually associated with the concept of urbanization. And the newcomers from the countryside are sharing in these changing conceptions of a way of life—as are the relatives who are left down on the farm. A wealth of evidence supports these affirmations and they are subjects for sociological research. Furthermore, we can suggest the need to study the role of the mass media in this context. The urban proletariat, the rapidly growing "middle group"— hardest hit by inflation—*and* the rural proletariat are being bombarded by and are responding to the images of an increasingly industrialized, commercialized and urbanized way of life. (See Hopper and Hopper 1961: 15–31; Bogart 1959.) In short the process of modernization is in full swing. C. P. Snow's warning of the explosive potential in lower-class awareness of the disparity between rich and poor (Snow 1959: 43–44), if unheeded by the decision-making elite, may foreshadow the institutionalization of a totalitarianism of the right or left rather than an institutionalization of the processes of change and industrialization within a progressively more democratic framework.

RURAL SOCIOLOGY

Rural sociology is a third research area which merits mention. Indeed, rural sociologists were the "pioneers" among U.S. scholars to interest themselves in research in Latin America. In 1960, in a special issue devoted to "Education and Social Change in Latin America," the editors of *Rural Sociology* reported that not only was Latin America "the first major [foreign] area into which American rural sociologists ventured," it is also the area in which "more rural sociologists have worked . . . than in any other portion of the globe."

The names of Carl Taylor, T. Lynn Smith, Olen Leonard, Lowry Nelson, and Nathan Whetten come immediately to mind. These five men were invited to spend a year attached to an American Embassy for the purpose of studying rural life in five countries. They did not attempt to develop a common research design but did agree to organize their investigations around the following topics: population, type-farming regions, man-land relations, basic social institutions, and local communities or locality groups. They also agreed to use *ad hoc* sampling techniques. As might be anticipated, the reports resulting from this comprehensive project vary in the degree to which they approximate the ideal set forth in the agreement on research objectives. Nevertheless, the published volumes became and remain classics in the field (cf. Smith 1964; Whetten 1948; Taylor 1946; Nelson 1952; Leonard 1952). Taylor has described this pioneering effort in an article entitled "Early Sociological Research in Latin America" (1960). In addition, the work of Ford (1955) on Peru and of Whetten (1961) on Guatemala, although no part of this series, fits into the same pattern of research.

The research of these North American rural sociologists was paralleled—indeed, to some extent preceded—by active interest among Latin American scholars. The uneven quality of their studies was to be expected, given the course of the development of sociology in Latin America. What follows is but a sample of the more interesting and valuable Latin American contributions to the literature of rural sociology.

Discussion must begin with Freyre's classic two-volume study of plantation life in Brazil, *Casa grande e senzala: Formação da familia brasileira sob o regime de economia patriarcal.* First published in 1935, it is now in its ninth edition. Menezes' *O outro nordeste: Formação social do nordeste* (1937) is a less well-known contribution. Still another indication of the interests of the period is Carneiro Leão's *A sociedade rural* (1941). Despite the biasing influence of Oliveira Vianna's racist prejudice, mention must be made of his *O campeador rio-grandense* (1952) and other works. Similar but less imposing studies of other regions include Thales de Azevedo's *Gauchos* (1943) and Milliet's *Roteiro do café e outros ensaios* (1939).

The Brazilian Serviço de Informação Agrícola also has published a series of analyses of regional social structure and development. These include Diegues' *O engenho de açucar no nordeste* (1952); Batista Filho's *A fazenda de café* (1952); and Laytano's *A estância gaucha* (1952). Diegues also has published a study of *População e açucar no nordeste do Brasil* (1954).

In Argentina, the case is quite different. Bagu and his collaborators, in writing *Estratificación y movilidad social en Argentina* (1959), remark that, in the field of rural sociology, "The only work published continues to be Carl C. Taylor's *Rural Life in Argentina*." In his view this work is indispensable for anyone interested in the socio-economic structure of Argentine agriculture. This apparently astounding gap in Argentine scholarship becomes less surprising when it is recalled that the period between the time of Taylor's work in Argentina and Bagu's comment virtually coincides with the "dark age" of the Peron regime (1946–55).

For Uruguay two items may be noted, namely, Solari (1953), *Sociología rural nacional,* and Vidart's *La vida rural uruguaya* (1955). The following studies are suggestive of work being done in Venezuelan rural sociology: Hill (1959), Martinez and Verburg (1960), and Merchan (1961). The work of Fals Borda in Colombia has already been mentioned in an earlier context. It is enough to add here a reference to his study, *El hombre y la tierra en Boyacá* (1957).

In Mexico Mendieta y Nuñes has long been interested in *El problema agrario* (published in 1937 and in its seventh edition by 1954) and has written various treatises on agrarian questions. Examples of other work on rural sociology in Mexico are Mendieta y Nuñes (1960, 1961), Fernández y Fernández (1957), and Herzog (1959).

The foregoing sketch of work in rural sociology provides the backdrop for a brief account of subsequent developments. As elsewhere, the separation between rural and urban sociology is tending to break down in Latin America. In consequence, a shift in focus has occurred which has resulted in the transformation of the traditional concern with rural and urban communities into an interest in the analysis of the processes of internal migration, urbanization, modernization, and social stratification. In short, it is increasingly recognized that, to be basically significant, research in rural sociology must now be conducted within the framework of the analysis of the dynamics of social change. Freyre's *Sobrados e mucambos* (2nd ed., 1951) and *Nordeste* (1st ed., 1937), in which he continued to trace the changes in the patriarchial family in Brazil, serves nicely, in subject matter, to symbolize this trend. As Bastide put it, the "sobrados e mucambos are the ancient *casas grandes* and *senzalas* transported from the country to the city and taking a new and unaccustomed aspect because of the street that joins the houses" (Bastide 1945). In this new setting the plantation mansion becomes a luxurious townhouse and the slave quarters are debased into the even more miserable slums of the city. Needless to say, the slaves of the *senzalas* become the impoverished "free men" of the shanties.

Also representative of the changing orientation are studies which, though lesser in scale, are more meritorious as scientific contributions. Among these are: Moreira's "Rural Education and Socio-Economic Development, Industrialization and the Growth of Urban Population in Brazil"; Pearse's "Some Characteristics of Urbanization in the City of Rio de Janeiro"; Brandão Lopes' "Aspects of the Adjustment of Rural Migrants to Urban-Industrial Conditions in São Paulo, Brazil"; Germani's "Inquiry into the Social Effects of Urbanization in a Working-Class Sector of Greater Buenos Aires"; and Matos Mar's study of "The Barriadas of Lima: An Example of Integration into Urban Life," all chapters in *Urbanization in Latin America* (see Hauser 1961), and Medeiros' *O processo de urbanisação no Rio Grande do Sul* (1958). Mention should be made, too, of the work of Gonçalves de Sousa, for example, his "Aspects of Land Tenure Problems in Latin America" (1960).

The following listing of recent works will suggest something of the scope of current research in rural sociology by both North American and Latin American scholars: Alvers-Montalvo's study of supervised agricultural credit in an Andean community (1960), Fujii and Smith's work in Brazil (1959), Harris' (1956) and Hutchinson's (1957) community studies in Brazil, Sariola's article on colonization in Bolivia (1960), Smith's article on the rural community (1958), Senior's study of the Laguna region in Mexico (1958), Diegues' study of social change in rural Latin America (1963), Moraes Filho's analysis of social aspirations in Brazil (1962), Costa Pinto's paper on social change in Latin America

(1962), and Diegues' study of the social conditions for industrialization in Brazil (1962). Wagley's recently published general study of Brazil (1964) contains excellent materials on the urbanward drift so characteristic not only of Brazil but of all Latin America. Wagley's analyses of the tensions resulting from urbanization in Brazil is equally valid for the continent when he writes that most of the social values of Brazilian culture "were shaped for an agrarian society of a semi-feudal Brazil and are out of keeping with the dynamic metropolitan centers of modern Brazil." These are but a few of the results of recent research on rural Latin America.

RESEARCH ON SOCIAL STRATIFICATION AND MOBILITY

By necessity, this discussion will be cursory. No attempt will be made to review the literature. Rather, we shall limit ourselves to an effort to distill the major and recurrent emphases to be found in a somewhat bewildering variety of studies.[11]

The evidence of drastic changes in the social structure of Latin American countries and of changing images of man is clear and plentiful in reports of research on social stratification and mobility. Even when there is sharp divergence of opinion in evaluation of the desirability of the changes, there is complete consensus with reference to the sheer fact of social upheaval and regrouping. On this score, then, one illustration will suffice, a statement by one of Latin America's best-informed sociologists (Germani 1960a: 13):

Social stratification in Latin America is changing at a fast rate from the traditional pattern to new forms. There are [of course] considerable differences between various countries. . . . But everywhere the contrast between the old and the new, co-existing within the same area, is the most conspicuous truth characterizing the Latin American situation.

For this reason social scientists in Latin America have concentrated attention on stratification and mobility during the last fifteen years. To the series on the middle classes published ten years ago by the Pan American Union, a quantity of material has been added. Noteworthy among the recent contributions is the

[11] Representative of sources of bibliography on the subject are: Estratificación y movilidad social: fuentes bibliográficas, Centro Latino-Americano de Investigaciones Sociales (1960); American Assembly (1959); Adams *et al.* (1960); Hirschman, ed. (1961); UN ECLA (1950).

important survey on urban stratification in Chile, Argentina, and Brazil (Centro Latino-Americano 1961).

Most of the present research is carried out within the framework of the familiar and widely used traditional-industrial society continuum and is designed to aid in the analysis of the process of modernization in Latin America. There is no need to tarry here on a detailed characterization of the traditional society in Latin America. Suffice it to say that the traditional society is described as one in which the prevailing type of action is fixed or prescribed more or less rigidly for every situation; it is resistant to change and enamored of the past and is limited in institutional specialization. With reference to class structure the traditional society is a hierarchial two-caste system characterized by virtually no upward mobility (Hauser, ed., 1961: 48).

All this is changing—and with mushroomlike rapidity. In the words of Fals Borda (1961: 5),

There is general agreement that the most important feature of the changes now occurring is the appearance of new social groupings which in one way or another are sharply modifying the traditional flattened pyramid which, until recently, was used to give graphic representation to the system of social stratification.

These new groups are seen as forces acting to propel Latin America in the direction of a new "ethos."

There also is consensus among competent observers on the major features of the new alignments of the class structures. The process of modernization is resulting in the formation of a new upper class, a changed and enlarged middle group, and an urban and rural proletariat (Fals Borda 1961):

With few exceptions, the sanctum of the traditional aristocracy now shelters not only the people of distinguished ancestry but also a new aristocracy of money—of industrialists and business men. As yet these new rich have not been able to ascend to the heights of the social pyramid represented by full acceptance in the ranks of traditional aristocracy. But bank notes are beginning to supply the results once achieved in high society only by means of a certificate of ancestry.

The new middle class, as has been repeatedly observed, is a middle *group* rather than a class in view of its heterogenous origins. However, it is becoming increasingly "self-identifying" (Germani and Silvert, MS.) and is rapidly growing. For example, it has been estimated that 50 percent of the population of Argentina and Uruguay and 40 percent of the population of Chile belong to this "middle stratum." The group is predominantly urban and composed of:

1. A relatively small group of functionaries, traders, and artisans who for centuries have filled the gap between the power elite and the masses of people; this group continues much as it was.

2. The descendants of proud families of the traditional society who have entered the professions because they have lost their wealth and fallen in the social scale by virtue of the changing image of social prestige.

3. Former members of the lower classes and immigrants and their descendants who have taken advantage of the new opportunities for upward mobility offered by industry, technology, education, and, especially, life in the cities.

However, a middle group is also developing in the rural areas. It is composed of former absentee landowners who have mechanized their agricultural operations and now live on their holdings, personally engaging in agricultural pursuits. In the new context, such activity no longer carries the stigma of "hand labor." Also to be counted among the ranks of the rural middle group are those few peasants whose standard of living has risen sharply.

Though it is sometimes so argued, the evidence does not warrant the conclusion that this middle group can be looked to as the bulwark of democracy. To date, at least, they seem more inclined to imitate the traditional upper class; they are generally conservative, somewhat intolerant, stubbornly defensive of their own interests, and woefully blind to the mounting claims of the rural and urban proletariat. The middle group is at best an exponent of "limited democracy" and has been quite unable to come to terms with the need to incorporate the masses into the process of social, economic, and political modernization.

The urban proletariat is incorporating into its ranks displaced elements from the rural areas who are accommodating themselves to an urban environment without complete abandonment of their "country customs." Such rural elements have responded to the demand for industrial labor, have been caught up in the process of technological innovation, and have been stimulated to new aspirations by improved means of transporation and communication. They also have been the object of a great deal of political persecution. All this has left them a dissatisfied and frustrated group capable of the violent uprisings and bloody "revolutions" that now and again erupt in Latin America. One of the important consequences of the "population explosion" in Latin America is the exceptionally rapid growth of this volatile and angry urban proletariat, which is, as yet, imperfectly socialized to the "life style" of an industrial culture. Research reports also show that a rural proletariat is forming as a result of the beginnings of mechanized agriculture. The rural proletariat is made up chiefly of young men who do not care to go back to the hoe and the ax and prefer to hire themselves out for daily wages. They, like their urban counterparts, form the disgruntled elements in rural Latin America.

All this is a far cry from the two-class system of the traditional Latin American society. These new group alignments have had repercussions in other sectors of the social structure: in the power structure, where the power monopoly of the traditional upper class is being challenged by the emerging middle class and the new upper class; in the family; in the position of women in public life; in religious, educational, and economic institutions; and in striking changes in the impact of the mass media. And always lurking in the background are the masses of the urban and rural proletariat who represent the shock troops of the "revolution of rising expectations." All these phenomena call for further sociological research.

FLACSO AND RESEARCH ACTIVITY

One way of "sampling" the ranges of research activity in Latin America is to take a look at the programs developed by the Centro in Rio de Janeiro and FLACSO in Santiago, both of which have been mentioned above. Now I want to limit myself to the utilization of an interesting paper by Heintz (1962) on "research models" prepared for the Second International Seminar on Sociology. The idea for these "research models" orginated some years ago (1959) in the Department of Sociology of FLACSO with two purposes in view:

1. To provide relatively simple research projects to be used by Latin American sociology professors as a means for giving their students some intensive training in the field of theory-oriented empirical research.

2. To test a series of hypotheses taken from current literature on sociological theory.

In the intervening years the original objectives have been retained. But experience has suggested a significant shift in emphasis and the addition of an important third aim. I shall have occasion to return to this paper later in the context of the discussion of research strategy, at which point these modifications will be considered. At the moment my interest is in what the paper tells us about the central concerns of research activity in Latin America.

Heintz makes it quite clear that he is "exclusively concerned with making some specific proposals concerning possible research models." He also points out that, given the uses for which they are intended, pretesting becomes necessary before the models are offered for use. At the time the paper was written, some of the models had already been pretested and others were being studied as part of the training program of FLACSO.

Against this background twelve examples of research models were presented, classified under four general categories. In each instance the description of the model was so organized as to show the sociological theory which it is designed to utilize and illuminate, the relevance of the hypotheses formulated to problems that are important to Latin America, and the problems involved in transforming the selected problems into theoretically relevant and testable hypotheses. In this presentation I shall do no more than summarize the statement of the theoretical problem deemed to be especially relevant to a selected range of crucial social problems.

The first category, in line with what was said earlier, has to do with *General Theory of Social Change.* The first model suggests a theoretical framework for the study of "value orientations." The research problem is an investigation into the "relationships between the distribution of dominant and variant value orientations and the distribution of power." The value orientations to be studied are "those proposed by Florence Kluckhohn and Fred Strodtbeck. It is assumed that modern rational authority systems tend to be homogeneous whereas traditional power systems tend to be heterogeneous."

The second model in the same category is designed to explore the "rising expectations of the masses" through the study of the "relationships between level and degree of structuring of expectations in the field of consumption, expectations concerning the use of patterns of social mobility, participation in groups which pursue social change, and expectations concerning social change without participation (through external agents over which there is no control)."

The third model in this category has to do with "family socialization" with special reference to semi-integrated lower-class families. The intent is to study the "consequences of the nonconvergence of power and moral authority between the socializing agents for the socialization of the child."

The second major category of models is designed to open up the investigation of the *General Dynamics of Economic Development*. The process of economic and social development becomes the general criterion for the selection of relevant problems. Three models are presented.

The first is labeled "industrialization"; the problem claiming attention is the "interrelationship between participation in ideological groups and industrial work commitment." The second is a design for the investigation of "urban socialization through local groups"; like the model of "rising expectations of the masses," it was pretested in 1961. The problem is outlined as the study of the "socialization of rural immigrants through participation in formal groups created on an ecological basis and working towards better personal and social conditions of the inhabitants of the local urban area." The third model in this group has to do with rural organization—the "agricultural work organization in transition"—and is directed to an attempt to assess "functionality and dysfunctionality of elements of modern technology and rational organization with regard to traditional work organization in agriculture."

The third major category focuses on an aspect or sector of the general problem of the dynamics of economic development under the heading *Political Aspects of Economic and Social Development*. A project for the study of "insecurity and authoritarianism in the working class," a research model for study of "working-class nationalism in different phases of economic development," and a plan of study on "middle-class authoritarianism and the channelizing of aggression towards lower class" round out this category.

The fourth and final major category carries the general design of the research program one step further. It is devoted to *Some Critical Problems of Economic Development*. Here the first model is intriguing indeed. The label is "national organization" but the subtitle is "particularistic deviations within bureaucracy." The statement of the problem focuses attention on "the impingement of particularistic values and the system of interchange of favors upon bureaucratic roles." The second model, again one which was pretested in 1961, brings "technological innovation" under examination in the context of a rural society "dominated by traditional big landowners." The third and final model directs attention to "emergent roles, collective goals, and organizational means" to economic development in an underdeveloped society.

Research Strategy and Problems

Two general observations come to mind. First, I shall not be talking about "filling in research gaps." The notion of theoretical and methodological gaps may be quite appropriate for more developed disciplines concerned with Latin America. I do not find it so in the case of sociology. Researchers become aware of "gaps" only when research has been so undertaken as to be cumulative. However valuable in many respects the scholarly work in Latin American sociology has been to date, it certainly has not been cumulative. This noncumulative character of scholarly activity is, of course, a direct result of the coexistence of two schools of Latin American sociology. The emergence of the "new school" has been so recent and the number of "new sociologists" is so relatively few that the volume of their research has been small. Therefore, it is in no sense deprecatory of their achievements to suggest that, in terms of research activity, the situation is almost all "gap." It is precisely this fact which accounts for most of what follows in this presentation.

The second observation is derivative of the first. I shall be discussing the need for a research strategy that will be based on the firm decision to identify the key people and institutions of this emerging "new group," to support and build on what they are already doing, and to assist them in their efforts to extend their influence among other people and into other centers of teaching and research.

THE CONTEXT OF RESEARCH

Research strategy for Latin American sociology seems to call for a willingness to build a research program focused around the analysis of social change or, if preference dictates, the sociology of development. What has been said earlier needs no repetition here. As far as Latin America is concerned, this is the greatest need and enlists the greatest interest. Certainly research focused on social change is what our Latin American colleagues are asking for. Yet, in the paper mentioned earlier by Heintz outlining a research program for FLACSO, he wrote "there is no generally accepted theory of economic and social development—indeed there is hardly any such theory at all." Yet this is no time to hone and polish erudite theories. A massive attack on these problems is needed.

Next I suggest that a research program focused on the sociology of development be directed toward large-scale research on centrally crucial social problems. These problems should be identified by our Latin American sociologists rather than by "outsiders." There will be thus greater stimulus for research—more than enough to do if we begin in this way (see Fernandes 1963). I am not proposing so-called action research—much less an action program. I am proposing that research strategy in Latin America could well be pointed toward providing aid in the techniques of translating social problems into researchable sociological problems. In short, I am advocating that what FLACSO is doing on the training level be systematically extended to research planning.

A third suggestion on research strategy has to do with a matter which I believe to be the core of any social research strategy for Latin America. At this juncture in the development of sociology nothing is of more importance than the need to give sustained attention to the problem of developing a better organizational structure in which competent and highly trained men and their successors can work. The contribution already made by both the Centro and FLACSO point the way. FLACSO is demonstrating the desirability of a close linkage between teaching and research.

The Centro in Rio has performed surveys, and research of regional, not only national, significance.

Research agencies of national governments are obliged to function under certain handicaps and disadvantages. A more adequate research strategy calls for the creation of "supplementary" institutions. Such supplementary institutions would be able to implement the sort of research programs that Latin America now seems to require better than the present national agencies, and they would be able to extend their influence. The proposed agencies, being private or voluntary rather than public, would be able to provide for the stability, continuity, and security which research requires. Their "demonstration effect" would be important. There would be nationalistic opposition, but surely the combined organizational ingenuity of sociological policy-makers in both Americas should be able to find ways to circumvent these criticisms. I suggest that research strategy calls for identifying the men and agencies—and in some instances creating the agencies—that show most promise and arranging to assist the men in doing the work they want to do.

RESEARCH PROJECTS AND PROBLEMS

The foregoing discussion provides the background for the following outline statement of suggestions regarding research projects and problems. It has been prepared with two purposes in mind: to direct attention to research areas, to the work that is being done in these areas, and to the men who are doing the work; and to suggest a few items for an agenda of "future problems" that are already called for. Since I assume that the study of social change is central in any area of substantive research, there is no separate category for this topic.[12]

At the outset three items might well claim attention which do not so much represent research projects as suggestions about

[12] In this connection the recommendations of the International Social Science Council Round Table on the Uses of Survey Data in Comparative Research (Chateau de la Napolue, June 29–July 3, 1962) are important, two items especially so. First it was recommended that the theme for the "Development of a Substantive Programme of Comparative Research" be "Comparative research on processes of social, cultural, and political change as they relate to economic growth." Second, that top priority be given to research in Latin America (Rokkan 1962: 35–36). Attention should be called here to Germani's valuable discussion (1963b: 373–92) of "Problems of Establishing Valid Social Research in the Underdeveloped Areas."

types of research that need to be undertaken in Latin America. First, and obviously, there is the need to intensify and step up the pace of the kinds of research discussed in earlier sections of this paper. Second, there is the need for innumerable sociographic studies. If the "social world" of the United States remains poorly mapped, think of the extent of the unexplored and unmapped social territories in Latin America. Mere descriptions are not being called for though even they might have value. What is lacking at present are descriptive and analytical studies feeding into an over-all plan designed to provide grounds for comparison and generalization. Strickon, in his paper on anthropological research in Latin America,[13] refers to Steward's *The People of Puerto Rico* as a model, though one which must be expanded upon, of the sort of work that still remains to be done in Latin America. Strickon also remarked that the Steward report, "as is often the case with the work of anthropologists, is weak in its study of urban groups." The fact that these observations refer to anthropological research is totally irrelevant. The point is that there is much to be studied on all levels—from small villages, to the towns and the middle-size cities, to the great metropolitan centers. Sociologists should do their part in the effort. Germani and his associates in Buenos Aires have made a good beginning, and the atmosphere at the Institute of Sociology of the University of Buenos Aires is somewhat like that at the University of Chicago when their Department of Sociology was beginning its studies of its own metropolitan area. Third, we need replications of studies already carried out and published. Unfortunately, this tradition is not firmly established in sociology. The literature abounds in studies that have never been seriously checked though they may have been severely criticized. It would be good to have a sociological re-run of Hirschman's studies of the decision-making process in the job of dealing with inflation in Chile, land reform in Colombia, and the work of SUDENE in the drought-ridden northeast of Brazil (Hirschman, 1963). I have heard it repeatedly suggested that someone should take a second look at the Cornell–Peru Vicos Project as reported by Holmberg and others (see Adams *et al.* 1960: 63–107). The classic study by Pierson (1942) on race relations in Salvador, Bahia, could be easily continued, not so much to verify his conclusions but to see the effect of almost a generation on this social process.

13 See Chapter 4 of this book.

A Miscellany of Suggestions for Sociological Research

There is no thought of total coverage in what is offered below. Rather, it is a sort of annotated listing of things I should like to see done. The items represent research "themes" or topics; they are not formulations of research problems or of specific projects. Finally, there is a rough sort of priority rating in the order in which the categories are arranged.

THE SOCIOLOGY OF REVOLUTIONARY SOCIAL CHANGE

The study of social change, especially, of revolutionary social change, should be given high priority not only because the problems are socially crucial but also because they are theoretically central to Latin America sociology. In a world of revolutionary changes, Latin America is of special strategic importance for research. The research opportunities are unusually great because the events to be studied are "laid out" in an exceptionally usable fashion and because the competencies and skills for such investigations are also increasingly available in the region. In short, as Rokkan has remarked in a slightly different though related context, "Through its Western heritage and the resulting degree of similarity in culture and institutions, Latin America lends itself particularly well to the application of the social science knowledge and methods developed in the highly advanced countries" (1963: 31–38). Sociologists would be remiss indeed if they ignore this research challenge. Here, then, are some specific suggestions in this important area, any one of which, of course, would need to be broken up into an array of interrelated research problems: (1) the dynamics of social revolution; (2) the ideological component in revolutionary social change; (3) the independence movement in colonial Brazil; (4) the second Mexican revolution; (5) the Aprista movement in Peru; (6) the Bolivian revolution; (7) the Cuban revolution; (8) the revolutionary process in Haiti; (9) the Trujillo regime; and (10) the Peronista movement in Argentina.

THE SOCIOLOGY OF DEVELOPMENT

These salient topics occur to me: (1) structural marginality in Latin America (cf. Costa Pinto 1963); (2) socio-economic development and political structure (Almond and Coleman 1960; Blanksten 1960; Scott 1959, etc.); (3) socio-economic development and the institutionalization of political behavior in Argentina and Mexico: a comparative study; (4) changing patterns of agricultural landholding in Latin America: an inquiry into land reform programs (cf. Higbee 1963, etc.); (5) studies of imbalances in development.

URBANIZATION AND INDUSTRIALIZATION

This is an area in which much is already being done. In addition to suggestions made in earlier contexts, I limit myself to two:

1. Studies of the urban shantytowns of Latin American cities. Little has been done on this subject, although such "slums" are perhaps the major problem of Latin American cities. There are the *favelas* of Rio de Janeiro and São Paulo, the *villas miserables* of Buenos Aires, and others with their special names. Only Lewis in his outstanding books (1959, 1962) on Mexico has really described this urban poverty.

2. Comparative studies of social change in selected Latin American cities to be done by a team or teams of carefully selected and technically competent Latin American and North American specialists. The following pairs of cities might well be selected: Buenos Aires and Córdoba, Mexico City and Monterrey, São Paulo and Porto Alegre, Bogotá and Cali, Caracas and Maracaibo. Five are, of course, metropolitan centers; the others are rapidly developing middle-size cities. These five pairs are suggested because they may reasonably be expected to yield especially valuable comparative data.

INSTITUTIONAL STUDIES

I have in mind here the usual sociology of institutions. Systematic research on *religious institutions* would certainly seem to be indicated. Some work of this nature is constantly in progress, of course. In Brazil, for example, Willems has been studying religious activities in small communities for some time (Willems 1945). However, few materials are available in English, and little has been done in the description and analysis of the "religious factors" in contemporary change and resistance to change. What is needed is something akin to Lieuwen's (1960) analysis of the role of the military in Latin America.

Another important field is the *sociology of education*. Some of the Brazilian work in this area especially merits mention. The Centro Brasileiro de Pesquisas Educacionais of the Instituto Nacional de Estudos Pedagógicos, Ministry of Education and Culture in Rio de Janeiro, has published several studies of uneven value, among them Lambert's *Os dois Brasis* (1959). Fernandes also is working in this field (see Fernandes 1962: 97–121, 1960a: 7–13, 1960b: 67–119). Fernando de Azevedo, Cardoso, and Wilson Cantoni have likewise been involved, scientifically and by conviction in these studies. The central values underlying the approach of these students are those of democracy, planned social change, and mass education. These are surely research needs in Latin America. I venture to suggest that such research is becoming urgent in the light of the possible impact of automation on the countries of Latin America. Witness, for example, the Brazilian government's present consideration of automation as a solution to its development problem in the still rural traditional society of the northeast. If automation becomes relatively general, what are the likely consequences vis-à-vis an ideological commitment to mass education? For what will the masses need to be prepared and how will different means influence possible outcomes? Many significant research questions cluster about this aspect of technological change.

Sociology of the family is another area calling for intensified research. Not too long ago Germani began a paper with the observation that "in Argentina there are no investigations dedicated to the study of the impact of technological changes on the structure and functioning of the family" (Germani 1962). This holds for the rest of the region.

The *sociology of industry* is an especially important research task. There are innumerable opportunities for sociological research in Latin America industry. Studies of IKA (Industria Kaiser de Argentina) and FIAT of Argentina would be an important contribution. Study of the role of organized labor would give valuable sociological insights.

Political sociology is central in any research program on Latin America. Studies on what it is now conventional to call "anomic movements" are needed. Coleman has pointed out that such movements represent a "political phenomenon found throughout the countries of Africa-Asia, and to a lesser extent in Latin America" (Almond and Coleman, eds., 1960: 556).

There are a host of sociological research problems and projects which could be fruitfully carried out in Latin America. We are fortunate now to have a "new group" of Latin American sociologists such as Germani, Costa Pinto, Fernandes, Nogueira, Fals Borda, and others too numerous to mention by name who are leading sociological research into empirical and theoretical fields never before cultivated. There are few sociologists in the United States interested in Latin America. If we are to keep up with them and be of some help to our South American colleagues— we must go to work.

BIBLIOGRAPHY

Adams, Richard
  1963 Some supplementary notes on the work of anthropology in Latin America. Unpublished paper presented to the Seminar on Latin American Studies of the American Council of Learned Societies and the Social Science Research Council. Center for the Advanced Study in the Behavioral Sciences, Stanford, California. July.
Adams, Richard, *et al.*
  1960 Social change in Latin America today. New York.
Alers-Montalvo, Manuel
  1960 Social system analysis of supervised agricultural credit in an Andean community. Rural Sociology 25 (No. 1): 51–64.
  1961 Sociologia: introducción a sua uso en programas agrícolas rurales. Turrialba, Instituto Interamericano de Ciencias Agricolas de OEA.
Almond, G. A., and J. S. Coleman (eds.)
  1960 Politics of the developing areas. Princeton, N.J.
American Assembly
  1959 The United States and Latin America. New York, Columbia University.
Arboleda, Jose Rafael, S.J.
  1959 Las ciencias sociales en Colombia. Rio de Janeiro, Centro Latino-Americano de Pesquisas em Ciências Sociais, No. 7.
Azevedo, Fernando J. de
  1942 A cultura brasileira. Rio de Janeiro, Serviço Gráfico do Instituto Brasileiro de Geograria e Estatística.
  1950 Brazilian culture. Translated by William Rex Crawford. New York.
  1960 La ciudad y el campo en la civilización industrial. Política, No. 11, July.
Azevedo, Thales de
  1943 Gauchos. Bahia, Notas de Antropologia Social.
Bagú, Sergio
  1959 Estratificación y movilidad social en Argentina. Rio de Janeiro, Centro Latino-Americano de Pesquisas em Ciências Sociais, Publicação No. 6.
Bastide, Roger
  1945 Latin American sociology. *In* Twentieth Century Sociology, Georges Gurvitch and Wilbert E. Moore, eds. New York.

Bastide, Roger, and Florestan Fernandes
1959   Brancos e negros em São Paulo. São Paulo. 2nd ed.
Batista Filho, Olavo
1952   A fazenda de café. Rio de Janeiro, Serviço de Informação Agrícola.
        Documentário da Vida Rural, No. 2.
Bazzanella, Waldemiro
1960   Problemas de urbanização na América Latina: fontes bibliográficas.
        Rio de Janeiro, Centro Latino-Americano de Pesquisas em Ciências
        Sociais, No. 2.
Beegle, J. Alan, Harold F. Goldsmith, and Charles P. Loomis
1960   Demographic characteristics of the United States–Mexican border.
        Rural Sociology 25 (No. 1): 107–62.
Bernard, L. L.
1937   The social sciences as disciplines: Latin America. In Encyclopedia of
        the social sciences I: 301–20.
Blanksten, George I.
1960   The politics of Latin America. In The politics of the developing
        areas, Gabriel A. Almond and James S. Coleman, eds. Princeton,
        N.J., pp. 455–531.
Bogart, Leo
1959   Changing markets and media in Latin America. Public Opinion
        Quarterly, Summer, pp. 159–67.
Borges, Thomas Pompeu Accioly
1960   Relationship between development, industrialization and the growth
        of urban population in Brazil. In Urbanization in Latin America,
        Philip M. Hauser, ed. UNESCO. Chap. V, pp. 149–69.
Brandão Lopes, Juarez
1960   Aspects of the adjustment of rural migrants to urban-industrial con-
        ditions in São Paulo, Brazil. In Urbanization in Latin America,
        Philip M. Hauser, ed. UNESCO. Chap. IX, pp. 234–48.
Bryson, Lyman (ed.)
1960   Social change in Latin America today. New York, Council on Foreign
        Relations. (Also Vintage Book No. V 196, 1961.)
Campos Jimenez, Carlos Maria
1959   Las ciencias sociales en Costa Rica. Rio de Janeiro, Centro de
        Pesquisas em Ciências Sociais, No. 8.
Cardoso, Fernando Henrique
1962   Capitalismo e escravidão no Brasil meridional—o Negro na sociedade
        escravocrata do Rio Grande do Sul. São Paulo, Difusão Européia do
        Livro "Corpo e Alma do Brasil" séries, Vol. VIII.
Carneiro Leão, Antonio
1941   Sociedade rural. Rio de Janeiro.
Carroll, Thomas F.
1961   The land reform issue in Latin America. In Latin American issues:
        essays and comments, Albert O. Hirschman, ed. New York, pp. 161–
        201.
Centro Latinoamericano de Investigações Sociais, UNESCO. Rio de Janeiro
1959a   Estratificación y movilidad social: fuentes bibliográficas.
1960   Problemas de urbanização na América Latina.
1961   Estratificação e mobilidade social (Nota). Boletim 4: No. 4 (Novem-
        ber). [Devoted to papers presented at the Seminar on Stratification
        and Social Mobility, held in Buenos Aires, September 26, 1961. See
        pp. 271–72 for brief summary in English, Spanish, and Portuguese.]

Coale, Ausley J.
1963 Population and economic development. *In* The population dilemma, Philip M. Hauser, ed. New York, American Assembly, Columbia University, pp. 46–69.
Costa Eduardo, Octavio
1948 The Negro in Northern Brazil: a study in acculturation. New York, Monographs of the American Ethnological Society, No. 15.
Costa Pinto, Luiz Aguiar
1953 O Negro no Rio de Janeiro, relações de raça numa sociedade em mudança. São Paulo.
1963 The process of social change in Latin America. Unpublished paper presented to the seminar on Latin American studies, sponsored by the Joint Committee on Latin American Studies of the American Council of Learned Societies and the Social Science Research Council. Center for Advanced Study in the Behavioral Sciences. Stanford, Calif., July.
Costa Pinto, Luiz Aguiar, and Edison Carneiro
1955 As ciências sociais no Brasil. Rio de Janeiro, Campanha Nacional de Aperfeiçoamento de Pessoal de Nivel Superior. Séries Estudos e Ensaios, No. 6.
Diégues, Manuel, Jr.
1952 O engenho de açucar no nordeste. Rio de Janeiro, Serviço de Informação Agrícola. Documentário de Vida Rural, No. 1.
1954 População e açucar no nordeste do Brasil. Rio de Janeiro.
1963 Mudanças sociais no meio rural latino-americano.
Donoso, Luiz V., and Alejandro Zorbas D.
1959 Estado actual de las ciencias sociales en Chile. Rio de Janeiro, Centro Latino-Americano de Pesquisas em Ciências Sociais, No. 9, Fuentes Bibliográficas.
Duverger, Maurice, *et al.*
1959 As classes sociais e os partidos políticos. Rio de Janeiro, Centro Latino-Americano de Pesquisas Sociais, No. 3 (mimeographed). Round table.
Fals Borda, Orlando
1955 The peasant society in the Colombian Andes. Gainesville, Fla. (Spanish edition: Campesinos de Los Andes, 1961.)
1957 El hombre y la tierra en Boyacá. Bogotá.
1961 La transformación de la América Latina y sus implicaciones sociales y económicos. Revista la Nueva Economía 1: No. 2.
Fernandes, Florestan
1958 O padrão de trabalho científico dos sociólogos brasileiros. Revista brasileira de estudos políticos.
1960a Dados sobre a situação do ensino. Brasiliense, No. 30: 67–119.
1960b A educação como problema social. Commentarios 1 (No. 4): 7–13.
1962 Sociologiques et grand public au Brésil. *In* Transactions of the Fifth World Congress of Sociology. International Sociological Association 1: 97–121.
1963 A sociologia numa era de revolução social. São Paulo, Editora Nacional. Biblioteca universitária, series 2, Ciências sociais, Vol. 12. [Includes papers previously published in French, Portuguese, and English.]
Fernández y Fernández, Rámón
1957 La reforma agraria mexicana. Trimestre Económico 24: No. 94.

Ford, Thomas R.
1955 Man and land in Peru. Gainesville, Fla.

Freyre, Gilberto
1937 Nordeste; aspectos da influência da câna sobre a vida e a paisagem do nordeste do Brasil. Rio de Janeiro. 1st edition.
1951 Sobrados e mocambos—decadência do patriarcado rural e desenvolvimento do urbano. Rio de Janeiro. 2nd ed. 3 vols. (English translation, The mansions and the shanties: the making of modern Brazil, New York, 1963.)
1952 Casa-grande e senzala—formação da família brasileira sob o regime de economia patriarcal. Rio de Janeiro. 7th ed. 2 vols. (English translation by Samuel Putnam, The masters and the slaves, New York, 1946.)
1959 Ordem e progresso—processo de desintegração das sociedades patriarcal e semipatriarcal no Brasil sob o regime de trabalho livre: aspectos de um quase meio século de transição do trabalho escravo para o trabalho livre; e da monarquia para a república. Rio de Janeiro. 2 vols.

Fujii, Yukio, and T. Lynn Smith
1959 The acculturation of the Japanese immigrants in Brazil. Gainesville, Fla. Latin American Monograph Series, No. 8.

Ganón, Isaac
1959 Estratificación y movilidad social en el Uruguay. Rio de Janeiro, Centro Latino-Americano de Pesquisas em Ciências Sociais, No. 5. Fuentes Bibliográficas.
1961 Estratificación social de Montevideo. Boletim do Centro Latino-Americano de Pesquisas em Ciências Sociais 4 (No. 4): 303–30.

Garmendia, Dionisio Jorge
1961 Algunas consideraciones metodológicas sobre una investigación de estratificación y movilidad sociales. Boletim do Centro Latino-Americano de Pesquisas em Ciências Sociais 4 (No. 4): 331–48.

Germani, Gino
1959a Desarrollo y estado actual de la sociología Latino-americana. Boletim del Instituto de Sociología, Cuaderno 17. Buenos Aires, Universidad de Buenos Aires.
1959b Development and present stage of sociology in Latin America. In Transactions of the Fourth World Congress of Sociology 1: 117–37.
1960a Problems and strategy in less developed countries: Latin America. Paper to the North American conference on the social implications on industrialization sponsored by UNESCO and held at University of Chicago, September.
1960b Inquiry into the social effects of urbanization in a working class sector of Greater Buenos Aires. In Urbanization in Latin America, Philip H. Hauser, ed. UNESCO, pp. 206–33.
1963a Política y sociedad en una epoca de transición de la sociedad tradicional a la sociedad de masas. Buenos Aires, Editorial Paidos, Biblioteca de Psicología social e sociología. (Collected essays, many previously published, with some revision.)
1963b Problems of establishing valid social research in the underdeveloped areas. In Industrialization and society, Bert F. Hoselitz and Wilbert E. Moore, eds. UNESCO, pp. 373–92.
1963c Uses of social research in developing countries. In Industrialization and society, Bert F. Hoselitz and Wilbert E. Moore, eds. UNESCO.

286 Rex Hopper

Germani, Gino, and Kalman H. Silvert
  Politics, social structure, and military intervention in Latin America.
  MS.
Gillin, John P.
  1951 The culture of security in San Carlos: a study of a Guatemalan community of indians and ladinos. New Orleans, Middle American Research Institute, Tulane University.
Gonçalves de Souza, João
  1960 Aspects of land tenure problems in Latin America. Rural Sociology 25 (No. 1): 26–37.
Graciarena, Jorge, and Maria A. R. Sautu
  1961 La investigación de estratificación y movilidad social en el Gran Buenos Aires. Boletim do Centro Latino-Americano de Pesquisas em Ciências Sociais 4 (No. 4): 277–302.
Gross, Jacquelyn
  1963 Gold coasts and shantytowns in Latin America. The New York Times Magazine, June 23.
Hagen, Everett
  1962 On the theory of social change. Homewood, Ill.
Harris, Marvin
  1956 Town and country in Brazil. New York.
Hauser, Philip (ed.)
  1961 Urbanization in Latin America. UNESCO.
  1963 The population dilemma. American Assembly, Columbia University.
Heintz, Peter
  1962 Research models for Latin America. Unpublished paper prepared for presentation at the Second Interamerican Seminar in Sociology, Princeton University, September 10–12, 1962.
Higbee, Edward
  1963 Farms and farmers in an urban age. New York.
Hill, George
  1959 El campesino venezolano. Caracas.
Hilton, Alice Mary
  1963 Logic, computing machines, and automation. Washington, D.C.
Hirschman, Albert O.
  1963 Journeys toward progress. New York.
Hirschman, Albert O. (ed.)
  1961 Latin American issues: essays and comments. New York.
Hopper, Rex D.
  1945 The status of sociology in Latin America. In Intellectual trends in Latin America: Latin American Studies I. Austin, Texas.
Hopper, Rex D., and Janice H. Hopper
  1961 Mass culture in Latin America. Política, No. 18 (October–November).
  1962 Latin American man: a changing image. Unpublished MS. presented at the annual meeting of the American Sociological Association, Washington, D.C., August–September.
Hoselitz, Bert F., and Wilbert E. Moore (eds.)
  1963 Industrialization and society. In Proceedings of the Chicago Conference on Social Implications of Industrialization and Technical Change, September 15–22, 1960. Publication of the International Social Science Council with the assistance of the École Pratique des Hautes Études (VIE Section). Paris, and The Hague, UNESCO.

Hutchinson, Harry W.
1957 Village and plantation life in northeastern Brazil. Seattle, American Ethnological Society.
Ianni, Octavio
1961 A constitutioçáo do proletariado agrícola no Brasil. Revista Brasileira de Estudos Políticos, No. 12 (October): 27–46.
Labbens, Jean, and Aldo E. Solari
1961 Movilidad social en Montevideo. Boletim do Centro Latino-Americano de Pesquisas em Ciências Sociais 4 (No. 4): 349–376.
Lambert, Jacques
1959 Os dois Brasís. Rio de Janeiro
Laytano, Dante de
1952 A estância gaucha. Rio de Janeiro, Serviço de Informação Agricola. Documentário da Vida Rural, No. 4.
Leonard, Olen
1952 Bolivia: land, people and institutions. Washington, D.C.
Lewis, Oscar
1959 Five families: Mexican case studies in the culture of poverty. New York.
1962 The children of Sanchez. New York.
Lieuwen, Edwin
1960 Arms and politics in Latin America. New York.
Martinez, G., and J. Verburg
1960 Estado Yaracuy: trabajo de sociología rural. Caracas.
Matos Mar, J.
1961 The barriadas of Lima: an example of integration into urban life. In Urbanization in Latin America, Philip M. Hauser, ed. UNESCO.
Matthews, Herbert L. (ed.)
1959 The United States and Latin America. American Assembly, Columbia University.
Medeiros, Laudelino
1958 O processo de urbanização no Rio Grande do Sul. Porto Alegre, Faculdade de Sociologia, Universidade do Rio Grande do Sul, Estudos Sociais.
Mendieta y Nuñes, Lucio
1937 El problema agrario. Mexico City.
1961 Efectos sociales de los cambios en la organización agraria. Revista Mexicana de Sociología, May–August, pp. 359–83.
Mendieta p Nuñes, Lucio, et al.
1960 Efectos de la reforma agraria en tres comunidades de la república mexicana. Mexico City.
Menezes, Djacir
1957 O outro nordeste: formação social do nordeste. Rio de Janeiro.
Merchan, Antonio
1961 Algunos aspectos sociales de la realidad agraria venezolana. Proceedings of the Sixth Latin American Congress of Sociology. Caracas. Vol. II: 181–222.
Millet, Sergio
1939 Roteiro do café e outros ensaios. São Paulo. Coleção Departamento de Cultura, Vol. 25.
Moore, Wilbert E.
1955 Labor attitudes toward industrialization in underdeveloped countries. American Economic Review, Supplement 65: 156–65.

Moore, Wilbert E.
1961 The social framework of economic development. *In* Tradition, values, and socio-economic development, Ralph Braibanti and Joseph J. Spengler *et al.*, eds. Durham, N.C., Duke University Commonwealth Studies Center. (Also London, 1961.)

Morais Filho, Evaristo de
1962 Aspirações atuais do Brasil: análise sociológica.

Moreira, J. Roberto
1960a Rural education and socioeconomic development in Brazil. Rural Sociology 25 (No. 1): 38–50.
1960b Educação e desenvolvimento no Brasil. Rio de Janeiro, Centro Latino-Americano de Pesquisas em Ciências Sociais, No. 12.

Nelson, Lowry
1952 Rural Cuba. Minneapolis.

Pearse, Andrew
1961 Some characteristics of urbanization in the city of Rio de Janeiro. *In* Urbanization in Latin America, Philip M. Hauser, ed. UNESCO.

Pereira, Luiz
1960 A escola numa área metropolitana. São Paulo, Universidade de São Paulo, Faculdade de Filosofia, Ciências e Letras. Boletim No. 253, Sociologia No. 8.

Pierson, Donald
1942 Negroes in Brazil: a study of race contact in Bahia. Chicago.
1945 Brancos e pretos na Bahia, estudo de contacto racial. São Paulo.

Pierson, Donald, and Mario Wagner Vieira da Cunha
1947 Research and research possibilities in Brazil with particular reference to culture and cultural change. Acta Americana 5: 18–83.

Pierson, Donald, *et al.*
1951 Cruz das Almas: a Brazilian village. Washington, D.C.

Poviña, Alfredo
1941 Historia de la sociologia en Latino-América. Mexico City, Fondo de Cultura Económica.

Oliveira Vianna, F. J.
1952 O campeador Rio-Grandense. Rio de Janeiro.

Rios, José Arthur
1961 Estratificación y movilidad en Rio de Janeiro. Boletim do Centro Latino-Americano de Pesquisas em Ciências Sociais 4 (No. 4): 377–79.

Rokkan, Stein
1963 The development of cross-national comparative research: a review of current problems and possibilities. *In* Social Science Information 1: No. 3, N.S. Paris and Le Havre, International Social Science Council, pp. 21–38.

Sariola, Sakari
1960 A colonization experiment in Bolivia. Rural Sociology 25: No. 1.

Senior, Clarence
1958 Land reform and democracy. Gainesville, Fla.

Silva Herzog, Jesús
1959 El agrarismo mexicano y la reforma agraria. Mexico City, El Fondo de Cultura Económica.

Silva Michelena, J. A.
1960 El estado actual de ciencias sociales en Venezuela. Rio de Janeiro, Centro Latino-Americano de Pesquisas em Ciências Sociais, No. 11. Fuentes Bibliográficas.

Smith, T. Lynn
 1957 Current social trends and problems in Latin America. Gainesville, Fla., Latin American Monograph Series No. 1.
 1958 The rural community with special reference to Latin America. Rural Sociology 23 (No. 1): 52–67.
 1964 Brazil: people and institutions. Baton Rouge, La., 3rd revised edition.
Smith, T. Lynn, and Alexander Marchant (eds.)
 1951 Brazil: portrait of a half a continent. New York.
Snow, C. P.
 1959 The two cultures and the scientific revolution. London.
Solari, Aldo
 1955 Sociología rural nacional. Montevideo, Facultad de Derecho y Ciencias Sociales.
 1959 Las ciencias sociales en el Uruguay. Rio de Janeiro, Centro Latino-Americano de Pesquisas em Ciências Sociais, No. 4.
Steward, Julian H., et al.
 1956 The people of Puerto Rico: a study in social anthropology. Urbana, Ill.
Taeuber, Irene B.
 1963 Population growth in underdeveloped areas. In The population dilemma, Philip M. Hauser, ed. American Assembly, Columbia University, pp. 29–45.
Taylor, Carl C.
 1946 Argentina rural life. Baton Rouge, La.
 1960 Early rural sociological research in Latin America. Rural Sociology 25 (No. 1): 1–8.
Tumin, Melvin, and Arnold Feldman
 1961 Social class and social change in Puerto Rico. Princeton, N.J.
United Nations Economic Commission for Latin America
 1950 Economic survey of Latin America.
Vidart, Daniel D.
 1955 La vida rural uruguaya. Montevideo. Departamento de Sociología Rural, Ministerio de Ganadería y Agricultura.
Wagley, Charles
 1961 The Brazilian revolution: social change since 1930. In Social change in Latin America today: its implications for United States policy. New York, Council on Foreign Relations, pp. 177–230.
 1964 An introduction to Brazil. New York.
Whetten, Nathan
 1948 Rural Mexico. Chicago.
 1961 Guatemala: the land and the people. New Haven.
Williems, Emilio
 1947 Cunha: tradição e transição em una cultura rural do Brasil.
Zea, Leopoldo
 1949 Dos etapas del pensamiento en Hispano-América. México City, El Colegio de México.

8. The Study of Latin American Law and Legal Institutions

KENNETH L. KARST

The current surge of law-school interest in Latin America is part of our general national response to the region's social revolution. It is also curiously parallel to a similar sudden increase in interest in Spanish law around the turn of the century, just after the United States had acquired new responsibilities in the Caribbean and the Philippines. That interest faded in all but a handful of schools, not to be revived until very recently. With the advantage of hindsight, it is possible to understand why Latin American legal studies remained an academic backwater even during the past generation of ferment in the comparative study of law. First, much of the law of Latin America is of a derivative nature; it derives from the private law of Europe, France and Spain in particular, and from the public law of Europe and the United States. For classic comparative purposes, one might as well study European law as that of Latin America. The European literature is more plentiful, it is also better, and it is authoritative in Latin America as well. Second, and more important, the scholars who gave the greatest push to comparative law studies in the United States were largely Europeans, many of them refugees from Germany. They naturally focused their work on the comparative study of European and Anglo-American law.

For the last half-century, the trend of legal study and research in the United States has been toward an operational policy-oriented analysis and criticism of rules and principles in their social context. Legal scholarship in this country is not typically technical and conceptual, concerned only with the statement of rules. It is also concerned with the justification of rules and with the institutions through which they are formulated, communicated, and applied. Necessarily, scholarship of this kind must attempt to make use of the data and perspectives of the other social sciences.

Such trends were not realized in the civil-law countries, such as those of Latin America, until recently. Instead, much of the substance of legal analysis by the very best civil-law scholars of these countries has been deductive. From the time of the Renaissance their tradition has been one of annotation of the masters. Furthermore, their basic modern code, the Code Napoléon, was a product of the French Revolution, which also aroused a healthy distrust of judges as instruments of the aristocracy. The position of the judiciary was deliberately lowered. The law was written in language thought to be clear enough to avoid the need for judicial interpretation. Judges were to be functionaries charged with the application of policies made up by others, and their main analytical problem was deductive. In contrast, the common-law system has required its judges to make policy; legal analysis has been forced into legislative considerations, that is, considerations of the common good.

Although the civil-law system has steadily moved away from the tradition of the sterile judge and although civilian scholarship is moving closer to the functional analysis favored in this country, early comparative-law studies in the United States have concentrated on the driest kind of deductive technical analysis and comparisons of rules, more or less in a social vacuum. Abstract scholasticism of this kind has only hampered the comparative study of law. The new interest in Latin American law thus coincides with the recognition of the need to de-emphasize the more formal comparative techniques of the past generation. For the comparative study of law in its social context, Latin America offers special attractions which Western Europe does not have:

1. The role played by law in the community is different in Latin America from its role in the United States; in this sense, the Western European countries are probably more similar to us than the civil law countries of Latin America.

2. It is possible to understand, for example, how the French legal system works by reading books. This, regrettably, is less true of Latin America. The differences between the law as writ-

ten and the law as it operates in society may in themselves be instructive as to what is essential about a system of law and perhaps even be productive of generalizations which bear extensions to other systems.

3. The social structure of some Latin American countries is so markedly different from our own, perhaps more so than that of any Western European country, that there are exceptional opportunities for legal studies of the "contrastive" type.

4. The rapidity of social change in most of Latin America puts a strain on legal institutions. Under such circumstances it may be possible to gain insights into the workings of a legal system which would be harder to achieve in a more smoothly functioning system.

When civil-law scholars began to come to the United States from Europe, only a few American law schools made places for them on their regular law faculties. A course in comparative law was regarded by many as an expensive frill. Now, a generation later, nearly every major law school in the country offers at least one comparative law course.[1] The purposes of comparative study are many, but the one purpose which seems to have had the greatest influence in gaining acceptance for such courses is that of giving the student "perspective," helping him to understand the fundamentals of his own system better by studying how another system deals with analogous basic problems. To most of our students, it does not seem profitable to study foreign law for its own sake; comparative law is something else.

There have been a number of experiments with comparative-law teaching materials, but out of this experience have emerged only two widely used books (Schlesinger 1959; Von Mehren 1957). They present an interesting contrast in method. The book by Schlesinger seems aimed at giving the student a kind of panorama of the civil-law system and therefore dips briefly into a large number of subjects. The other, by Von Mehren, seems deliberately limited in scope and treats only a few subjects. The treatment, however, is thorough enough in each case so that the student is required to do his thinking in terms of the other system by the time he finishes studying each section.

Opinions differ as to the relative effectiveness of the two attacks on the subject; but if the main goal is to give the student

[1] The 1964 Directory of Law Teachers lists 75 men who are currently teaching courses in comparative law.

an understanding of what is fundamental in a legal system, the more selective but more thorough treatment seems better suited to the purpose. The implication is that one must, after all, teach foreign law in order to permit comparative study. There are obvious difficulties in using such a method in a course of thirty class hours. On the other hand, the panorama technique never leads the student deeply enough into a foreign system to give him any real understanding of the way lawyers within the system must think. Neither of these two popular casebooks deals with Latin America except in passing; both concentrate on Western Europe.

The study of Latin American comparative law requires an even greater adjustment on the student's part. Not only must he adjust to another juridical structure and frame of mind; he must also adjust to a social context further removed from his own than that of Europe. The teaching of Latin American comparative law is even more clearly required to transcend disciplinary boundaries for the purposes of imparting legal understanding and perspective. Any legal analysis takes place against a background of assumptions about a society, whether the system analyzed be foreign or domestic. Take away the familiar assumptions, and it is impossible to construct a legal system without replacing them with new assumptions.

For the purpose of giving our students new comparative perspectives, Latin American law is best taught in institutional terms. For example, the North American system of constitutional guarantees, which so many Latin American countries have formally copied, rests on an institution which does not exist in most of Latin America, namely, an independent judiciary. To understand how and to what extent individual liberties are protected in Latin America, one must study the institutional framework within which claims against the government are processed. For the same reasons, research in Latin American law seems best oriented toward institutions and not toward a comparison of rules or principles. Thus, interdisciplinary cooperation is necessary for such studies, even though they may deal with ordinary problems in the law of contracts or torts. In comparative study as well as in the analysis of our own domestic law, it is getting to be true that there is no such thing as purely legal study or research.

Several law schools have established special teaching programs on Latin America. In practice, these programs have amounted largely to special teaching programs for Latin Americans. There are hundreds of lawyers in Latin America who have spent a year or two in one of these schools (Eder 1950) and have emerged with certificates or special degrees, for example, Master of Comparative Law. Undoubtedly there are exceptions. To an outsider, however, the instruction given to these visitors seems none too rigorous. Perhaps there is no easy way to make it more demanding, in view of the students' level of preparation, but an effort to do so ought to be made. In addition, a few law schools have regularly accepted some Latin Americans among their graduate students. There is probably no graduate program which does not make some concessions to its foreign students (i.e., give them easier treatment than that given to its domestic students), but it would seem that fewer concessions have been made by the schools which do not have special Latin American programs.

The number of courses in law devoted to Latin America is increasing.[2] Some such courses are straight Latin American law, for example, Latin American civil law, taught largely by the "magisterial" (lecture) method common in civil-law countries. Other courses emphasize the comparison of Latin American and North American solutions to related legal problems, while at least one law-school seminar has been devoted to Latin American institutions in general, such as the army or the Church. Finally, some courses emphasize Latin American public international law: the principle of nonintervention, the right of asylum, the OAS, and other similar topics.

North American literature on Latin American private law has been weighted toward the problems of North Americans who do business in Latin America: how to qualify, taxes to be expected, labor regulations, etc.[3] With respect to public law, the political

[2] Some of the books used in these courses are de Vries (1961), Thomas and Thomas (1963), and Karst (1964). There are now about 35 law-school faculty members involved in some phase of Latin American studies, with more than one-third of them in the schools which have set up special Latin American programs. See the reports of the Director of International Legal Studies, Harvard Law School (1954–61, 1961–63), particularly the latter (pp. 5–15) for a description of recent and current Latin American studies at the School.

[3] See Association of the Bar of the City of New York (1961). The Pan American Union staff periodically issues summary statements of the laws of the various Latin American countries relating to business, and a number of private associations publish similar materials in pamphlet form. The Depart-

scientists have done better than the lawyers, but their output of literature has been limited, and even that has been focused on constitutional law (Grant 1954, 1948; Blanksten 1951; Amadeo 1943). Writings on public international law are more plentiful, but are perhaps of less immediate interest to the scholar who seeks to relate Latin American law to Latin American society (Szladits 1955; Bayitch 1961).[4]

Much of the Latin American literature is equally barren. It naturally is representative of the current style of legal analysis. There is article after article on the true nature of one concept or another, including polemics carried on for years without any of the participants going beyond logical deductions from the codes or from the writings of the great jurists. Changes are on the way,[5] but they may be slow in coming. The articles by students which usually win prizes in competitions are generally of the classical type. They show the most "scholarship," i.e., familiarity with the classics. Originality is sometimes rewarded, but it is a stylized and conceptual kind of originality, the ability to make new deductions from old sources. The deficiencies of the secondary literature would be more tolerable if the primary sources, particularly court decisions, were more readily available; but most judicial opinions are never published at all and are thus lost for all practical research purposes, even though one may find them in the files of the various courts. One who had the money to publish opinions might still find it hard to create enthusiasm for the project among Latin American judges; civilian training pays little attention to the decisions of courts.

There are two libraries in the United States which may be said to have rather complete collections of Latin American legal materials: the Harvard Law School Library and the Library of Con-

---

ment of Commerce publishes a series of booklets containing information for businessmen, some of which relates to the laws of the countries described. The PAU has also published studies on the following subjects: copyright protection, double taxation, international judicial cooperation with respect to service of process and taking testimony abroad, and problems relating to international waterways.

4 The indispensable bibliography is Szladits' (1955–63). See also various bibliographies published by the Library of Congress.

5 The work of two Argentine law professors, both trained in the United States, indicates the high quality of analysis which is possible within the civil-law framework (Cueto-Rúa 1957, 1961; Carrió 1959a, 1959b, 1961a, 1961b).

gress. Apart from these, fewer than ten can be called adequate, in the sense that they have collections sufficient to enable a scholar to do most of the basic library work on his subject. In Latin America the number of barely adequate law libraries surely does not reach ten, and no collection approaches the completeness of the two best North American ones.

Research Opportunities

While it may be proper to suggest that certain subjects for research are basic, or perhaps deserving of a degree of priority, the fact is that virtually no research in Latin American law or legal institutions will run the risk of duplicating existing work. The following suggestions are examples of two kinds of research problems, some of which are basic, relating generally to the functioning of law in Latin American society, and others that are concerned more particularly with the ways in which some of the distinctive characteristics of the society are reflected in its law. Many of these subjects overlap. The subjects are not, in general, recommended for study in all countries of Latin America. Most of them seem suitable for separate study in each country. A further narrowing may also be justified, either because of varying social backgrounds or for the purpose of taking samples representative of national characteristics. Still, the law and the legal institutions of Latin American countries tend to be quite centralized in fact, even though some of the larger countries are formally federal in governmental structure.

In addition to the following list of research topics and problems, an outline of research subjects on the general topic of land reform is presented. Land reform is obviously not entirely, perhaps not even principally, a "legal" subject. It does, however, offer an illustration of the kind of research which is necessary if legal scholars are to analyze the operation and the effect of various alternative legal rules and institutions.

THE JUDICIARY

Despite the relatively low position of the judge in the civil-law scheme, he remains central to any study by North Americans of Latin American legal institutions. The assumption on which so much of our own law is based, namely, the existence of a strong independent judiciary, generally cannot be made in Latin America. Since our domestic legal analysis is carried out against so different an institutional background, it is necessary to understand where the judiciary stands in Latin America in order to understand other differences which may be uncovered by study.

1. *Appointment, removal, discipline, status* (Clagett 1952; Scheman 1962a, 1962b, 1963). How are judges selected? To what extent is there a judicial career ladder? What connections do judges have with political parties? For what reasons may they be removed? What has been the experience of the country with respect to stability of judicial tenure? (Let us consider the recent Argentine case, for example. When Perón fell in 1955, his appointees, who had themselves replaced the pre-Perón judiciary almost entirely, were swept out of office; the provisional government appointed new judges, but the Constitution requires that all judges be approved by the Senate, and there was no Congress. Thus, in 1958 President Frondizi was permitted to select a new judiciary when he took office. When Frondizi was removed in 1962, the entering President Guido dissolved the Congress, so that his appointments were also temporary. His successor will undoubtedly also have the chance to make new appointments, which must be approved by the new Senate.) How and to what extent has the opportunity to make new appointments to replace uncooperative judges been used? What pressures are there outside constitutional or other legal requirements in favor of longer judicial tenure? How are judges disciplined, short of removal, for showing too much independence? How well are judges paid? What are the motives for accepting a judgeship? (One Venezuelan professor stated that lawyers are induced to become judges casually, while they wait for something better to come along.) What is the judge's status in the community?

2. *Law-making, creativity* (Carrió 1961b; Barrancos y Vedia 1961). It never has been strictly true that a civil-law judge is prevented from contributing to the growth of the law. From the early nineteenth century there has been, on the continent of Europe, a fairly steady evolution in the direction of a greater creative role for judges, even in private-law matters. (In French administrative law, judges have come to occupy a position some-

what equivalent to that of the common-law judge.) Similar trends are identifiable in Latin America, but they would seem not to have progressed so far. One explanation for the difference may be that European judges have acquired a degree of independence thus far denied to most of their Latin American counterparts. To what extent are the judges conscious of their own freedom or lack of it? Would they prefer a more creative role, or does their training preclude such a preference?

3. *Creating a new constitutionalism* (Blanksten 1951; Amadeo 1943; Clagett 1945; Eder 1961, 1960; Trueba Urbina and Trueba Barrera 1963). Granting that judges cannot by themselves set effective constitutional limits on the governments of Latin America, would it still be possible for them to contribute to that end? The King's justices in England did not begin their task of regularizing the use of governmental power by attempting to limit the King; rather, they began with sheriffs and tax collectors. Is there something of the same nature in, for example, the Mexican writ of *amparo*, or the Brazilian writ of security, both of which give judges limited powers to correct illegal acts of government officials? Judicial correction of the President of Mexico is unthinkable, but cannot the judges contribute to the growth of constitutional limitations that would eventually reach the highest officers in the government? The historical parallel can be overdone, but research on the judges' part in the constitutionalization of Latin America would surely be justified. Part of the research would be difficult, since it would require a survey of a good sample of the judges in question, as well as interviews with other interested persons. But much of the job could be done in a good law library.

Similarly, research is needed into the role played by the judiciary during states of siege and *de facto* governments. This research would not simply be a law-library job.[6] Rather, what is needed is historical research, emphasizing individual interviews with men who were judges during such times and with knowledgeable lawyers and military men.

---

[6] There already exists a thorough review of the Argentine and Brazilian cases on *de facto* governments (see Irizarry y Puente 1955). The Pan American Union legal staff has recently completed its study of states of siege, made on behalf of the Inter-American Juridical Committee.

4. *Principled decision-making.* Two basic reasons for requiring judicial decisions to be based on principle are to assure equal treatment by the law of the various persons who come before it and to assure a measure of stability so that individuals can order their activities with some confidence. Where judges are not independent, it is difficult for them to rest their decisions on principle; those who exercise influence over the decisions are interested less in equality or stability than in the outcome of given cases as they affect particular persons. To what extent are judicial decisions in the various Latin American countries principled? The answer may be that it is always possible to dredge up a presentable principle if one tries, whatever the legal system may be. In fact, there are nearly always competing principles, so that choices must be made. Even so, the question may be asked: Is equality before the law a reality, or not? It is hard to avoid the impression that criminal justice is dispensed on a class basis in many Latin American countries.

This kind of research is emphatically not suitable for library work; by the time an opinion is written, the factual background of the case has been carefully filtered, and an "unprincipled" decision is not likely to be evident in an opinion. Yet the subject is important enough to justify a study, for example, of the criminal complaints which come to the police of a given city, along with the disposition of the complaints, including those cases which are immediately dismissed by the police and those which are subjected to the various possible judicial dispositions. Criminal law is one branch of the law which can be counted on to affect both the rich and the poor and thus may offer more possibilities for the kind of class comparison here suggested than would the disposition of, say, actions for breach of contract. Official cooperation for such a study probably would not be easy to get.

THE ORDERING FUNCTIONS OF LAW

In our own society we are accustomed to the law as a potential force, in the background of all our activities, lending order even where it is not directly applied by any arm of the government. The same should be even more true of civil-law countries, for civilian training emphasizes law as a guide to conduct rather than as a settler of disputes. To what extent does law perform this guiding function in Latin American societies? This is in part a question of social psychology: Who are the persons governed by law, in the sense that the existence of legal institutions makes a difference in what they do? Which branches of the law are involved? Who is conscious of the law as a threat or a protection? If one were to stop ten strangers on the street in Mexico or Buenos Aires, asking each where he would look for protection in a case of public or private injustice, how many would mention the law? It might be guessed that the number would be smaller than the corresponding number in London or Chicago. What are the substitutes for the law's protection? One's union, a trade association, a relative in a Ministry? There must be private or semi-official substitutes for ordering men's affairs, or there would be a major social breakdown. But the consequence is that equality of treatment becomes a casualty, as those without private protection are aware.

In this connection, further analysis of the role of the executive dispensation is needed. In a system where it is always possible to hope that the President of the Republic might be brought to smile on one's cause, there are strong pressures working against a resolution of disputes through the ordinary channels. Decision-making on a principled basis becomes difficult, and the principle of equality before the law suffers. The Latin American "tradition" of bypassing the regular authorities in favor of an appeal to the highest level dates back at least to the days of the Viceroys.

There is also room for consideration of the concept of law prevailing among the lawyers themselves. To what exent does their training, with its emphasis on the law's symmetry and structure, create the impression of law as a static institution, unsuited for creative uses? The use of legal institutions as vehicles for social change will surely be impeded by such a conception of the nature of law.[7]

Research should be done on the extension of law to the poor. What part does law play in the life of the great urban slums of Latin America? For example, how are real property "rights" protected where everyone is a squatter? How do the informal shadow governments of such areas administer justice? What is the cost of official justice? What portion of the population never seeks

[7] For a study of the principal influences on Latin American conceptions of law, see Kunz (1950).

official justice because it never has enough at stake to make such an appeal worth while?

LEGISLATION

Who effectively makes the laws? Where does the initiative for legislation reside? How are laws drafted? What is the mechanism for clearing legislation with interested groups? How is lobbying, or its equivalent, carried on when the executive governs by decree? How does the law-making function differ between countries in which there is a strong legislative body, such as Venezuela or Brazil, and countries in which there is no effective independent congress, as in Mexico or in the Argentina of 1962–63?

These politically oriented questions are related to the earlier theme of judicial creativity. If the political branches of the government are partly immobilized, must not judges take a more active legislative role, even in a codified system? How are the basic codes modified to meet changed conditions: by amendment, by supplemental statute, by judicial reinterpretation? Why have so many projected code revisions failed, even when the projects were commissioned by congresses? If there is no congress in session, codes and statutes cannot be modified; may not judges legitimately change their interpretations of the old codes to adapt them to present needs? For example, has the recent experience of Argentina contributed to such an attitude on the part of Argentine judges?

Under what circumstances does a Latin American government seek to influence the behavior of individuals or private institutions by promising benefits, and when does the government rely on threats? (Consider, for example, the various alternatives for slowing the flight of capital from a given country.) What are the factors in the economy, or more generally in the society, which suggest one or another legislative technique?

PUBLIC ADMINISTRATION

1. Regularizing administrative action is an important step toward constitutional government. The Spanish tradition of authoritarian government has died hard in Latin America. Judges who sit in judgment on administrative acts are apt to think of themselves not as protectors of individuals against government, but rather as government functionaries charged with

the protection of all the people against the private depredations of selfish individuals. How and to what extent does the judiciary exercise control over the administration? What other controls are there, either within the executive branch or outside of it? (The institution of the *controlador* in Chile, a kind of comptroller general and *ombudsman* rolled into one, is worth a separate study in itself.)

2. Government enterprises are sufficiently common in Latin America to warrant a study of the enforcement of their obligations and also of the degree of their subjection to obligations borne by their predecessors or their private counterparts, such as labor regulations and contractual obligations. Such questions are traditionally a concern of administrative law in the Latin American scheme.

3. To the one good study of public utility regulation in Latin America (Cavers and Nelson 1960) should be added studies of other industries and studies of utility regulation in particular countries.

4. The relations between the public administration and its employees merit study: civil-service laws, relations with government-employee unions, the responsibility of the individual government official for wrongful official conduct which harms someone.

PATERNALISM IN THE LAW

Every society has its public wards, that is, persons who are especially protected by the law against their own folly. If a child agrees to a contract for seven years of dancing lessons, any country's law is likely to let him out of it. In Latin America, the class of persons with a claim to such protection is large. The indigenous peoples and the masses of illiterates, both found in varying percentages in any nation's population are numerous in Latin America taken as a whole. In addition, the beneficiaries of various government programs, from ordinary welfare to land reform, are disabled from making their own choices in a number of important respects. The lawmakers of Latin America appear to doubt the capacity of large numbers of persons to take care of themselves in the complexities of the modern world, to doubt the honesty of those who deal with such people, or both. There is an amazing proliferation of requirements for written permissions, official registration, and the like, in all legal relationships, and not merely in those which involve persons of supposedly reduced capacity. What are the origins of such rules? To what extent are they compatible with the strong individualism of the civil codes? Why are they so common? Are there justifications for such disabilities beyond the political desirability of keeping control centralized?

SOCIAL SECURITY AND WELFARE FUNDS

1. In Mexico, for example, where a large number of new rights have been created by social security legislation, the very nature of property can be said to be changing, just as it has been changing in the United States under the influence of insurance systems, pension plans, widespread ownership of corporate shares, etc. Who participates in such social security programs? Lewis (1960) feels that much of the rural-indigenous population of Mexico does not. How are the new rights enforced? To what extent are lawyers and traditional legal institutions involved?

2. Pension and welfare funds have accumulated sufficient capital to be of great potential importance in development programs. Some such funds are government-controlled, while others are in the control of private groups such as labor unions. Research is needed on the administration of these funds and on means of enforcing the trustees' responsibilities; to what extent is there a danger of creating a new form of "social welfare *caudillo*"? How can such funds be protected from inflation? How can they be channeled into investments which are sound, considering the funds' needs, or investments which contribute to the country's development?

LOCAL GOVERNMENT

A high degree of centralization characterizes all Latin American governments, despite the formal federalism of some of them. It would be rewarding to study existing local governments—their structure, their functions, and their financing—at least in part in order to see whether there is any possibility of using local government as a means of educating citizens in responsible participation in public affairs. This subject is related to the preceding ones, for central governments have never entrusted local governments with any substantial powers, for fear of the potential development of competing political power centers.[8]

LAW AND DEVELOPMENT

The inclusion of lawyers in the early planning stages of projects aimed at development is something which U.S. planners tend to take for granted. In Latin America, the tendency is otherwise: after decisions are made, lawyers are invited to put them in "legal" form, with the result that decisions are often made without adequate attention to the institutional problems which they may raise. The following topics are just a few examples which point out the importance of the institutional framework for development; the list is intended to be suggestive, not exhaustive.

1. *National planning agencies.* In many of the Latin American countries, new agencies have been created to draft national economic plans and in some cases to oversee their execution. What will be the relation of these agencies to the legislature and the other executive departments? How will the new agencies' decisions be executed? To what extent will the new agencies be given enforcement powers? What protection can be given to individuals or groups affected by the new agencies' decisions? Can institutions be devised to give such agencies some continuity through changes in political administrations?

2. *Inflation.* It may not be possible to prevent inflation in Latin America; in some instances it may not even be desirable. How can legal institutions be adjusted to mitigate the undesirable effects of inflation? The Chilean concept of the "living wage" should be studied. Much legislation is cast in terms of multiples of a "living wage," an amount set periodically by administrative action on the basis of the purchasing power of money. A similar device is used in Brazil for setting progressive income tax rates; research might be usefully directed toward the community of interest which such an arrangement creates between upper-bracket taxpayers and unions pushing for increases in the minimum wage.

[8] For a description of urban problems in Latin America, see Haar (1963). A vitalized city government might accomplish more toward the solution of such problems than a strong national government.

3. *Nationalization.* Can varying standards of compensation be devised according to the activity or property nationalized (i.e., public utilities, manufacturing, or land)? To what extent can international standards be made effective? In what way? [9]

4. *Regulation of financial institutions.* Does the orderly development of credit facilities demand a general tightening of commercial banking practices, as well as the creation of new government credit or guarantee programs?

5. *Commercial law, contracts.* How has the law of agency and of contracts adjusted to a commercial society in which mutual distrust is the rule? What changes in the assignment of business risks have been made in adjustment to the availability of insurance? To what extent are the terms of private business dictated by the government (by statutory limits, by entry of the government into the market as a competitive bidder, etc.)?

What has been the impact of the theory of social security on private contracting? Our North American economy developed earlier, during a period when the security of the individual was sacrificed to the security of transactions. Social legislation came later in the United States. The countries of Latin America, committed as they are to a system of social security, must find a way to develop in spite of the limitations on economic freedoms implicit in such a system. Can institutions be devised that will meet this need and at the same time maintain the essentials of a free-market economy?

Research is needed on the forms of association for economic activity, ranging from private enterprise to government monopolies: How are the responsibilities of managers enforced? What are the implications of the various forms of association for economic growth? How are consumers protected against arbitrary pricing policies? How are the rights of shareholders, cooperative members, partners, etc., defined and enforced? What sectors of a national population are potential participants in the various forms of association?

An important area to be studied in Latin America is the pub-

[9] See the section on p. 309, "Legal Research Opportunities in Land Reform," for further research possibilities on expropriation as they relate to land reform. The problem of nationalization is part of a broader subject for research: the limitations imposed on development activities by constitutions and constitutional traditions.

lic issuance of corporate securities.[10] Public participation in business ownership is rare in Latin America. Why? Can new laws (regulating issuance of securities, authorizing the creation of new kinds of ownership interests) encourage an increased sale of shares to the public? Do present securities regulations adequately protect the investor? Can an international securities market be created for countries which are too small to have markets of their own? Might guarantees be devised to encourage United States investors to participate in publicly-held securities in Latin America?

Likewise, the problems of secured transactions calls for research.[11] The use of trust receipts, inventory financing, negotiable bills of lading, etc., has been made difficult in Latin America because of rather strict interpretation of requirements for the transfer of possession in transfers of ownership. Greater flexibility in commercial transactions demands the creation of new legal institutions and rules, which in turn demand research.

The commercial codes have generally been left in their original forms, some of them dating back 100 years. Changes in the legal framework for commerce have been made in other legislation, which often remains badly indexed. Meaningful reform must rest on research.

6. *Labor law.* Many Latin American countries have adopted labor legislation which "on paper" ranks with the most enlightened in the world. Non-enforcement is a recurrent problem. How can labor laws be adjusted so that they can be enforced, and still retain a maximum of enlightenment? To what extent does current legislation on wages, work rules, and the like, affect economic development (effects on inflation, featherbedding, etc.)?

7. *Economic integration.* The contrasting experience of the Latin American Free Trade Area and the integration of Central America's economy should be instructive for lawyers. What kinds of trade barriers have proved easiest (and hardest) to re-

[10] The Pan American Union's legal staff is considering a study of these questions.

[11] A research project on these questions is also under current consideration by the Pan American Union. For a number of years, Hessel Yntema of the University of Michigan Law School has been directing Latin American students in a research project on comparative negotiable instruments law; this study is nearing completion.

move? What kinds of sanctions and inducements have been effective (and ineffective) in securing the removal of trade barriers? To what extent are the constitutional and regulatory institutions of the United States and the European Common Market adaptable to Latin America?

TAXATION

The International Program in Taxation being carried out at Harvard Law School is at present the only large-scale university program of research and study on taxation in Latin America. The program's accomplishments are impressive,[12] yet many research opportunities remain:

1. What are the tax traditions of a nation? What kinds of taxes have historically been accepted, and what kinds have been resisted as too burdensome? Resisted by whom? Must taxes be hidden to be accepted by the public?

2. Who pays taxes? The impact of various types of taxation on the several social or economic groups in a country should be studied. Such a study would involve difficult survey work, since tax avoidance is itself a long-standing tradition.

3. What are the alternative revenue sources? To what extent are the Latin American governments capable of raising revenue through nontax means, such as government-owned businesses? (Many public utilities normally run a deficit operation.)

4. What is the differential between taxation and borrowing for development purposes? It may be cheaper for a developing country to borrow at low interest from an international lending agency than it is to levy more taxes, especially if the tax might have the effect of withdrawing capital from the pool available

[12] Members of the program have participated in the following works: volumes on Mexico and Brazil in the World Tax Series (Harvard University 1957a, 1957b), Ross and Christensen (1959), Shoup et al. (1959), Oldman and Surrey (1960). Oldman is now engaged in a similar study of taxation for the government of El Salvador. In addition, in 1954 the program held a conference on agricultural taxation and economic development. The Law School published the papers of this conference, and one of its key participants has since published a book on the subject (Wald 1959; cf. Sakolski 1957). Harvard personnel have taken a leading role in organizing the Joint Tax Program, sponsored by the OAS, BID, ECLA, and the Harvard Law School. In 1961, in Buenos Aires, the Joint Tax Program held a conference on tax administration the proceedings of which will soon be published by the OAS. In 1962, a similar conference was held in Santiago, Chile, on the subject of tax policy.

for investment. Detailed studies of the effects of various forms of taxation on investment are needed.

5. Can tax reforms redistribute income? To what extent does a tax reform redistribute income in a country where a large share of the population has never paid direct taxes? How can direct taxes on high-income groups be made to replace hidden taxes, such as processing or manufacturing taxes, which are levied on all consumers as part of the retail prices they pay?

6. The Alliance for Progress program demands tax "reform" and not simply the enactment of laws. Can it make this demand stick, in view of the political resistance to real reform? Who are the opponents of particular tax reforms? How are they organized? Have the proponents of real reform any political strength outside the pressures of the *Alianza?*

7. How can taxes be used to complement or accelerate desired changes in land-tenure structures? After a land distribution, to what extent can taxation on agriculture be used to divert funds from agriculture to other sectors in need of capital? During a land reform program, to what extent can taxation be used to obtain the funds needed to finance the land distribution?

8. The Harvard study of tax-incentive legislation in Mexico should be duplicated for other countries (Pan American Union 1963; American Bar Association 1963; Surrey and Hill 1961). There should be emphasis in any such study on the manner in which such laws have worked in practice. Studies of this kind suffer from an inherent difficulty in isolating the particular motives for business decisions. To what extent are tax incentives crucial, in that they are sufficient to tip the balance of such decisions?

9. If nonpayment of taxes is usual, then a major share of the blame must go to the systems used to assess and collect taxes. New administrative techniques must be developed to meet the peculiar needs of the Latin American countries. In any case, some substitute must be devised for the present practice of delayed enforcement of tax obligations, followed by "all is forgiven" periods which in effect give a discount or bonus to the taxpayer who does not pay when his tax is due. What alternatives are there for a government which desperately needs money and cannot wait for the fruits of a long-range taxpayer-honesty campaign?

FAMILY LAW

In all but a few countries of Latin America, the consensual or free-union type of marriage predominates in large sections of the population. To what extent have marriage and divorce laws contributed to this practice or reacted to it? How has this kind of relationship affected rules for the establishment of paternity, obligations of support, and inheritance? How do such rules work in practice? Are there legislative incentives to family life: tax or other inducements, invalidation of restraints on marriage, husband-wife privileges, or difficult requirements for divorce?

LAW AND THE CHURCH

Does the Church act as a lobby or as patron of a political party? Does the Church control property? Are there any limitations in law or in fact on Church holdings? Such problems as the Mexican dispute over free, compulsory, government-supplied textbooks in Church-operated schools need to be explored.

LEGAL LIMITATIONS ON THE PRESS (Castaño 1962)

Probably all Latin American constitutions include a guarantee of freedom of the press, but there are always means of keeping the press in line. In Mexico, for example, criticism of the president in a large daily newspaper must be kept veiled. The government has a monopoly on newsprint, and there are other more subtle controls. The law of defamation and *desacato* (a crime based on public disrespect for certain classes of government officials) may also be an effective limitation. What kinds of remedies, judicial or nonjudicial, are available to an editor who feels suppressed?

Legal Research Opportunities in Land Reform

As stated earlier, land reform, a central problem for most Latin American nations, offers an excellent broad topic for legal research and study. Such research necessarily calls for cooperation with many other disciplines. The various topics suggested below extend into many fields other than law. They are concerned with many different levels of agricultural development and with various types of cultivation. Yet all of them indicate the necessary preoccupation of legal studies with the whole of Latin American society and with what might be called a "high priority" problem such as land reform.

THE SETTING [13]

1. Is there an inventory of rights to the land? Who owns the land? How are the rights of ownership distributed? How did the tenure pattern reach its present stage? [14]

2. How do the land tenure arrangements relate to agricultural production: Its organization? Its volume? The kinds of crops? The extent and quality of extension services? Which is cause and which effect: Is the land-holding system an important cause of the production pattern, or is the system itself largely the result of the demands of economic efficiency, as determined by soils, slopes, climates, markets, etc.? [15]

3. Under what circumstances and to what extent does subsistence farming imply a lack of connection to and understanding of the money economy?

4. What is the relationship between land tenure and socio-economic conditions? Solon Barraclough (mimeo, 1962) of the FAO conducted a study of the relationship between the land-tenure structure of an area and the education of the people living there. Such studies seem likely to lead to the expected conclusion, that peonage and poor education go together, but they should not be avoided just because "everyone knows" the answer. Similar studies might be addressed to the relation between the pattern of land tenure and such matters as health, housing, habits of dress, consumption of food, and political attitudes.

5. What is the situation of the indigenous population (see

---

[13] The outstanding bibliography, necessary for any serious research in this area, is Carroll's (1962). Valuable background material may be found in general works by McBride (1936), Taylor (1948), Ford (1955). See also Parsons *et al.*, eds. (1956), ILO (1957), Carroll (1961).

[14] The latter question is treated in a study of a valley in Central Chile (Borde and Góngora 1956).

[15] The OAS, the Inter-American Development Bank, and other agencies have formed the Inter-American Committee for Agricultural Development (CIDA) for the purpose of studying questions such as those suggested here. Their report should be published soon (see also Jacoby 1953; FAO 1961; and U.S. Department of Agriculture 1962). The latter collection of papers deals with "research perspectives and problems."

ILO 1953)? The definition of who is "indigenous" causes problems, but there is general agreement that the Indians of such countries as Peru and Ecuador stand at the bottom of the economic and social ladders and have virtually no political influence. Even in Bolivia and Mexico, where the revolutions had a strong base in the indigenous groups, these groups—in so far as they remain separate—have not generally attained a condition of equality with the rest of the population. In general, such people live in rural areas. What are their occupations? What migratory currents are discernible? Are population shifts traceable to a scarcity of rural land? To poor rural labor conditions which may be connected with the land-tenure structure? To what extent are these groups capable of assuming the economic responsibilities which should be implicit in a distribution of land? Could any incapacities be compensated for by the use of traditional indigenous communal-ownership forms? What rural education resources can be brought to bear on existing incapacities?

6. What are the current concepts of property rights? Latin American legal scholarship has provided a good base for investigation of the prevailing conceptions among lawyers of the nature and function of private rights of property (see Vivanco 1954, 1962). (The same may be said concerning the historical sources of such legal conceptions.) There is less to work on when it comes to an investigation into the popular understanding of rights of ownership, yet in a setting of potential revolutionary change perhaps the "popular" idea of property is the more important one.

7. Who leads a village, and how do village leaders come to their positions? The work of some Colombian sociologists shows great promise, both for its own sake and as a model for future investigations (Fals Borda 1955; Guzmán et al. 1962). Obviously, any land-reform program must rely on available and potential local leadership resources. Who is now interested in the training of future village leaders? In Chile and in Venezuela, Church-sponsored training programs are actively pursuing this goal (see Domínguez 1961). Their methods and their degree of success deserve study.

8. To what extent does Latin American caciquismo rest on a land base? What changes have resulted from development away from the traditional social structures and toward a more industrialized—or at least more "modern"—society?

9. What is the real situation of *campesino* communities? Who supports projects such as the construction of a rural school house or the digging of a flood-control channel? How can the *campesinos'* interest be aroused and held? Each of the Colombian government's community-action groups has typically included one sociologist who has acted as adviser and reporter; the National University of Colombia (Bogotá) has published some case studies of this kind (Fals Borda 1955; see also Holmberg 1960, for an analogous problem in Peru).

10. The rural-education programs of the Church in Chile and Venezuela are indicative of a broader social consciousness among the Catholic clergy of those two countries than is to be found, say, in Argentina or Colombia. In Chile, the growing Christian Democratic Party has close ties with the Church and at the same time advocates what amounts to a peaceful revolution, with rapid and drastic land and tax reforms, and a whole range of programs normally identified with socialistic movements (see Mensaje 1962; Domínguez 1961; Ducoin 1958). How have these attitudes come to prevail among the clergy? What are the ages and the social and economic backgrounds of the churchmen who most actively propagate the doctrine of social reform? What are the techniques thought by the clergy to be legitimate in promoting this viewpoint?

11. What is the role of the armed forces in land reform? One reason why land reform is now a dead issue in Argentina is that the highest leaders of the military almost surely would not tolerate a reform of substantial proportions. What are the origins of this attitude? It is sometimes said that the officer corps is drawn from the landholding class, but that is too simple an explanation; there are too many officers and too few landholding families. What are the origins of *Nasserismo?* (The *Nasseristas* are young officers who want to create a social revolution with a strongly nationalistic flavor.)

12. Does the structure of the land-tenure system affect the government's policy toward the construction of roads, irrigation dams, rural electric facilities, etc.? Historically, rural investments in such social overhead capital items have increased after a land reform, but it is not self-evident that similar investments would not have been made in, say, Mexico, in the absence of reform. This is an especially slippery research subject, because of the lack

of any "control" country or region which is similar enough in all its varied political-economic conditions to justify comparison.

13. To the extent that foreign capital is invested in land, what kind of land tenure arrangements prevail? Are the foreign owners guilty of the same repressive practices which have characterized domestic *latifundios?* Have foreign owners tried to improve the labor conditions on their land or to offer health services, housing, or education to their workers? To what extent have such efforts succeeded in alleviating political pressure for more radical solutions?

14. Who takes the risks of the market for agricultural products? Does the market price directly affect what the *campesino* gets if he owns his own farm? Or is there a middleman who takes the risks of the market and reaps the benefit of its rises? To what extent does the land-tenure structure affect the response of agriculture to demand? Is the producer associated with one or another form of tenure more flexible or more rigid in adjusting to the market?

THE ORIGINS OF LAND REFORM

1. What is the political situation in regard to land reform (Hirschman 1963; Lleras Restrepo 1961; Carroll 1964)? Who supports land reform legislation? What are the histories of the agrarian movement's leaders—their education and training, their political associations? What do they expect from a reform? Who are the opponents of land reform? What are their fears, the motives for their opposition? What are the tactics of proponents and opponents? Can the differences in tactics from one locality to another be explained by reference to differing local political situations?

2. Is there political-economic awareness of the necessity for land reform? Since conditions of poverty or near-slavery do not in themselves produce a popular demand for reform, it is necessary to add a degree of awareness of the possibilities of change. Silvert (1961) has written of the varying degrees of "national" society in Latin America, defining a national society as one in which, among other things, there is rapid political communication among all parts of the country and a widespread sense of popular involvement (if not participation) of the public in public affairs. One might expect basic reforms to come soonest in

such societies, but Argentina and Uruguay are two examples of national societies as Silvert has defined them, and neither has seen a land reform of a fundamental nature. Then whose awareness is critical and of what must they be aware?

3. What are the political and socio-psychological effects of the Alliance for Progress? How has the North American pressure for reform operated? In what ways does the "interventionist" character of the *Alianza* contribute to its chances of failure? To what extent is it possible to bypass reluctant governments and speak directly to those portions of society which may be more favorable to reform? Among the people of Latin America, which ones are aware of the *Alianza,* and what do they think of it? Has the *Alianza* changed internal balances of political power? What legislation or other institutional changes may be said to have flowed directly from the *Alianza?* To what extent have these new institutions been designed simply to please the U. S. government, without any changes of substance being made? To what extent has money from the *Alianza* gone to reform projects, and to what extent has it been used to bail out unrealistic government budgets or to solve current monetary crises?

4. What are the necessary economic preconditions for land reform (Furtado 1962, 1963)? Reforms do not take place in times of widely shared prosperity. With that exception, it is dangerous (in the absence of study) to generalize about the economic conditions which precede various types of land reform. Is it possible to draw any conclusions of this nature?

5. What is the relationship between land reform and industrialization? Land reforms have, with the exception of Venezuela (which is so frequently a special case, because of its petroleum), taken place in countries which have not been highly industrialized. Does the presence of a growing and important industry accelerate or retard the drive for land reform? Do manufacturers want reforms in the hope of creating a larger class of rural consumers for their products? Do industrial unions want reforms for political and ideological reasons or for bread-and-butter reasons? Will the intensification of agriculture (often said to demand a land reform) be accelerated by what Hirschman calls "backward linkage," that is, the creation of an increased demand for agricultural products through the establishment of industries that use or process such products (Hirschman 1958;

see also Flores 1961; Urquidi 1962; Furtado 1959)? What kinds of industries are most likely to produce the demand for agricultural products that would require, in turn, the agricultural intensification said to be needed to induce reform?

6. Does intensification of agriculture imply a reform of the land-tenure structure? The classical *latifundios* are extensively, rather than intensively, cultivated. Will a distribution of land ownership be sufficient in itself to bring about more intensive cultivation? Or will intensification require a so-called "integral" reform, with expanded agricultural credit and extension services to go with the distribution? Upon what factors will the varying answers to this question rest: climate, soils, the educational level of the *campesinos*, the types of production existing before the reform, the "credit" system of the hacienda?

TENANCY REGULATION AND WAGE-HOUR LEGISLATION

1. Prominent among the features of tenancy legislation are provisions guaranteeing security of tenure, regulating rents, and regulating or prohibiting certain kinds of contracts (for example, for marketing) which have the effect of binding the tenant closely to the owner (Abensour *et al.* 1957). These laws should be analyzed to determine the scope of the new rights and duties they create. How often have they been invoked? With what success on the part of the tenant? How does their usage relate to *campesino* pressure for land in a given area? Which procedures have been effective, and which obstructionistic? (See Barry 1961.)

2. An Argentina law gave rural tenants an option to purchase the land which they occupied, but this law had little effective use because the government never had the money to give credit to tenants who wanted to buy. A thorough exploration of this abortive scheme would surely be worth the effort because it would require investigation into so many of the political and economic factors which have recently governed the exploitation and tenure of land in Argentina.

3. To what extent is agricultural labor included in minimum-wage and similar legislation? Some of the objectives of a land reform can be attained without changes of ownership, provided that far-reaching labor legislation is enacted and enforced. What are the conditions which have made enforcement of such legislation possible in Uruguay, for example? What are the types of

sanctions which are most effective? What administrative mechanisms are effective?

4. In 1960, the State of São Paulo, Brazil, enacted a rural minimum-wage law—or, perhaps more accurately, a minimum-living-conditions law—in the form of a progressive tax on rural land. The law taxes rural land at rates which increase according to the size of the owner's holdings, but permit him to evade the tax if he complies with a rather detailed set of requirements relating to the way he treats his labor force. Wages, housing, sanitation facilities, even electrification are all considered in determining whether the owner is making a "rational" use of his land. If he is, the progressive feature of the tax rates does not apply to him. The law is still on the books, but the national Congress transferred the functions of assessment and collection of property taxes from the states to the municipalities, where landowners are more influential. Research into the operation of the law, and particularly into any instances of its application, would be useful. Research into the political maneuvering which resulted in Congressional action is also called for.

COLONIZATION OF STATE-OWNED OR VACANT LAND

1. There now has been extensive experience with colonization in at least a dozen major Latin American countries, and it should be relatively easy to determine the cost of colonization.[16]

2. Colonization, by definition, requires the movement of people from one place to another. What persons volunteer to go? Why do they want to leave? Who chooses among competing applicants? On what basis are the actual selections made?

3. How do the colonists respond to their transplantation? The early experience in Bolivia suggested that the people of the *altiplano* resisted the colonizing movement into the hot and humid Oriente; now, Bolivian officials insist that the reverse is true, that they have a surplus of applicants. What made the difference? The officials say that the more recent efforts at colonization have been better planned and more adequately financed. Now the colonist is given more to work with when he gets to his new home: roads, electricity, housing, and the like. But even such

[16] Some officials of the Inter-American Development Bank unofficially estimate the cost of colonization projects undertaken with the support of the Bank at from 20,000 to 50,000 dollars per family settled.

investments cannot always insure the success of a colony. There have been several attempts to move people from the depressed Laguna region of Mexico to such places as Yucatán and Campeche. Some of these colonies suffered from inadequate preparation, but others were based on a heavy advance investment. More than half of the colonists, even in some of the better-prepared colonies, have returned to the Laguna. Why do they go back? A thorough survey of the people who went home and the people who stayed would probably reveal causes that were not entirely economic.

ACQUISITION OF PRIVATE LAND WITHOUT EXPROPRIATION

Rights of first refusal may enable the state to substitute itself for a potenital buyer of land, or the owner himself may wish to sell to the state for such a purpose. In such cases, the principal problem is the valuation of the land. To what extent are such practices authorized by law? What has been the experience under such laws?

EXPROPRIATION: AFFECTABILITY OF LAND

1. Recent land reform legislation tends to emphasize concepts like "the social function of ownership," declaring affectable (i.e., subject to expropriation) all land the ownership of which fails to fulfill its social function. This is said to be the case when the land is worked indirectly or when it is idle or when it is worked by employees who are inadequately paid. What have these standards meant in practice? Who has escaped affectability on the ground that his ownership is fulfilling its social function? To what extent have extra-legal considerations played a part in determining whose land is to be taken and whose land exempted?

2. What are the procedures for determining affectability? Who makes the actual selection of the land which is to be taken? What avenues of appeal are there? How long must a petitioning group wait before action is taken on its request for lands? What determines the length of the delay?

3. Nearly all reform legislation includes an exemption for property under a certain size. Under what circumstances have these exemptions been respected? Survey work is needed to furnish even the basic data on this subject.

4. In the early days of the land reform in Mexico, land was

often invaded by *campesinos* who were not willing to wait for the formalities of land adjudication. But since this took place during a revolution, it has been accepted as just another natural element of violence. In Venezuela, after the Betancourt government took office, *campesino* invasions became frequent. Venezuela was not suffering an armed revolution at the time; in fact, many of the invasions were directed by the very *campesino* leagues which had been the key to President Betancourt's electoral success. This wave of invasions lasted for about a year and a half during 1959–60, and then stopped. The reason they stopped is not clear; perhaps it was a reduction in *campesino* pressure or perhaps a hardening in the government's attitude. The Ministry of Agriculture appointed a special group to study the invasions. The group made its investigation, but its report has not been made public. Some Venezuelans say that the fact that the invasions stopped is proof of the political success of the land reform. An independent study of this crucial period in the history of the Venezuelan land reform would be invaluable. A survey of the recent attempted invasions in the Peruvian *sierra* and in northern Mexico would also be of interest in connection with studies of the techniques of agrarian agitation.

EXPROPRIATION: PAYMENT PROBLEMS

1. When land is expropriated without payment, a frequent excuse is the necessity to obtain capital to carry forward the goals of a social revolution and the lack of money to pay for the land. On the other hand, confiscation may discourage the investment of foreign capital in other parts of the agricultural sector or in other sectors of the economy (cf. Bronfenbrenner 1955). What has been the net effect of the confiscatory land reforms in Bolivia and Cuba on investment in agriculture, both governmental and private? (No doubt it is impossible to separate the psychological effects of the land reforms from those of the revolution in general.) In particular, how does the timing of expropriation affect private investment? It would seem that a prolonged delay between the first mention of expropriation and the expropriation itself would simply magnify the problem of capital flight, particularly in agriculture.

2. Can international standards for expropriation, and remedies for their breach, be formulated? The Draft Convention on

the International Responsibility of States for Injuries to Aliens, a model multination treaty prepared by two Harvard Law School professors at the invitation of the International Law Commission (Sohn and Baxter 1961), states as a general principle that an expropriation is wrongful if prompt and full compensation is not paid. But the Draft Convention makes an exception in the case of an expropriation for purposes of general economic and social reform, provided a reasonable part of the compensation is paid promptly and the rest paid with reasonable interest over a reasonable period. What purposes do such international standards serve? Has any social-revolutionary government ever respected a pre-existing foreign treaty when its obligations became heavily burdensome? Is it possible to devise an international agreement that provides built-in sanctions against a government not yet in being which are not dependent on the frailties of post-expropriation diplomacy?

3. Where bonds have been issued to the owners of land expropriated in a reform program, what has their value been? Has there been a market in which such bonds could be traded? In the Mexican case, there has been such a market; the Mexican government has occasionally taken advantage of the depressed market price to buy up its debts at a very great discount, so that its borrowing capacity would not be embarrassed by agrarian bonds that were outstanding. What is left of the market for these bonds? What is the attitude of the Mexican government toward the bonds? In Venezuela, three classes of bonds have been established, with varying maturity dates, interest rates, and transferability. To what extent are the transferable bonds actually transferred? What relation does their market value bear to par? Is there any real trading of "nontransferable" bonds, comparable to the purchase of similarly nontransferable future inheritances? To what extent is it feasible to permit holders of agrarian bonds to use them to pay certain kinds of taxes or other obligations to the government or to accelerate the deferred payment of the bonds on condition that their proceeds be invested in favored sectors of the local economy?

4. Who makes the real decisions in evaluating expropriated property? To what extent do courts participate in the valuation? To what extent are such courts independent of the political branches of the government in their review of the administrative

decision? In a country like Venezuela, where the state is really the only important buyer of rural land, how can "market" values be determined? In the event of a dispute over value, does the state take immediate possession?

5. Should a bank which holds the equivalent of a mortgage on expropriated land be permitted to collect its debt at maturity, even if the payment to the owner is deferred for, say, twenty years? Or should the lender's recovery also be deferred? What will be the effect on future lending and agricultural investment of a policy of expropriating lenders' security interests in this manner?

DISTRIBUTION OF LAND: PROBLEMS OF STRUCTURE

There is little in the Latin American literature on cooperatives which attempts to evaluate the relative performance of various forms of agricultural organization. The Rockefeller Foundation's researchers in Mexico have been investigating such questions in the state of Sonora, and their report should be available soon. Similar studies would be useful over a wide range of areas and crops. Rural cooperatives seem likely to increase in number and importance, bringing with them all the problems of management and control which plague any corporate economic unit. Some sophistication is required to be a member of a cooperative; members must understand the nature of their obligations. The unhappy history of joint borrowing (a cousin of the credit cooperatives) in Mexico suggests that a major educational effort will be needed if the cooperative movement is to succeed. The study of the problems of various forms of agricultural cooperatives (production, credit, marketing, etc.) is a research opportunity of the first magnitude. Does the decision to grant land in individual parcels or to some kind of organization depend on the type of production expected?

2. What should be the size of the parcels of land distributed? Many economists are now skeptical of the validity of the doctrine that there are optimum sizes for agriculture. The optimum size varies too much according to price levels, the cost of seed, fertilizer, labor, and machinery, and other factors (Barraclough and del Canto 1960). Perhaps it is more universally agreed that there are *minimum* sizes—at least within the limits of a given technology. In a given area, and assuming a given type of cultivation,

what is the minimum size of a parcel of land which must support a family of average size either on a subsistence-farming basis or through the cultivation of a cash crop? What is the maximum size plot, assuming the employment of machinery likely to be available, which can be cultivated by one family?

3. During a violent social revolution, there may be no opportunity to give an adequate screening to candidates for settlement on land taken by the state. But all land-reform legislation in Latin America establishes qualifications which must be met by applicants for land, and most of the laws also provide preference lists against the possibility that the number of applicants and their needs will be greater than the available land. Who gets the land in fact? Who decides this? To what extent are the beneficiaries who are chosen qualified, in terms of education or experience, to run their own farms? Are they required to prove themselves during a test period, as under our Homestead Act? Do such test periods work?

4. Most land-reform beneficiaries in Latin America have not been required to pay for their land. The exceptions have generally been beneficiaries of colonization schemes. Obviously, peons who have nothing cannot be required to pay cash for land. But it is not fanciful to suggest that they pay something, sometime. Some anthropologists say that the *campesinos* "want" to pay at least a token amount, so that they will feel that they have bought their land. The reasons are apparently not simply related to possible feelings of guilt; such *campesinos* think that their rights over the land are insecure if they merely receive it as a gift. Another motive for requiring some kind of payment would be to syphon off some of the profits of agriculture, just as a tax would do, for the benefit of other sectors of a developing economy. Is it true that political considerations often make it impossible to demand any payment from *campesinos* who were settled in the course of a fundamental land reform?

5. Title is only a concept which helps us to think about certain rights in relation to things; it may have different meanings, depending on how those rights are restricted. Nevertheless, the assumption is still made, and probably accurately, that title means a great deal to the *campesino*. In particular, one might study the *campesino*'s attitude toward investment and toward community-action projects, his interest in producing more, and

his political orientation, all in relation to his title, or lack of title, to his land. May title also be withheld for political reasons, such as the desire to control the votes of beneficiaries? Where lending institutions insist on a showing of title before they will give credit to farmers, as was apparently the case in the first years of the Bolivian reform, it is of the highest economic importance to the *campesino* to have his title clearly defined. What steps are being taken to make titles definite and to register them? What survey work still needs to be done? What new institutions can be developed to make the definition and registry of ownership faster and more convenient? What contributions can aerial photography make to an improvement in the definition and registration of land titles? What substitutes for title may be used in granting credit?

6. What restrictions are imposed on the transferability of the beneficiary's interest (Palomo Valencia 1959)? Some people believe that if a beneficiary is allowed to transfer his parcel, he will soon sell it in order to get cash to pay for a medical emergency, for a wedding, or even for debts incurred in the operation of his farm. It is feared that just as the hacienda traditionally encroached on the lands of the Indian village, so will a new landholding class buy up all of the good land. Thus, the Mexican, Bolivian, Venezuelan, and Cuban laws all require written government approval before a beneficiary can sell his interest. The other side of the coin is that such a rule binds the beneficiaries to the land, whether or not they want to be farmers and whether or not they have any talent for farming. Since the parcel, in Mexico at least, is often too small to support the family that owns it, the owner is tempted to make an illegal contract with someone else to whom he rents the parcel, and then work for a third owner as a peon. Although the Mexican law explicitly forbids the rental or sale of land received in the land reform, everyone who was asked about the practice said that it is to be found in all regions of the country. Even in Venezuela, where the parcels tend to be larger and credit is more freely available, such illegal rentals are known. How extensive are such arrangements in countries which have undertaken land reform? What are the devices used? Do the limitations on transfers have any current usefulness? Are they maintained for political reasons, to keep the control in the hands of the *campesino* bureaucracy

which has developed in the wake of every land reform? Is there an economic reason for permitting land to become the object of purchases and sales, namely, to establish a market value for it and to permit an accurate estimate of the economic role of the land itself, as distinguished from management, seed, fertilizer, machinery, etc.? Would the freeing of land on the market release still more *campesinos* to fill the ranks of the urban unemployed? Is there thus a national political reason for keeping these people in the rural areas?

7. What persons become leaders after the land is distributed? What are their backgrounds and training, their attitudes, their political affiliations? What are their leadership functions? To what extent do they manage the farming operations of others? By what means?

RURAL EDUCATION AND EXTENSION SERVICES

1. What are the educational needs of the *campesinos?* These needs must be identified with some precision, and priorities should be established. Literacy, for example, may be less of an immediate need than an understanding of basic cultivation techniques. Other items of apparently high priority would seem to be teaching the value of saving and investment, teaching community cooperation in such activities as building public facilities, teaching about the farm credit system, and especially teaching the borrowers to be responsible in their dealings with credit, and, finally, teaching the *campesino* the need to educate his children.

2. An inventory of rural educational resources is much needed. How many farmers can one extension agent serve effectively? How many extension agents are now available, and how many more must be trained? Are the training facilities adequate? What needs to be done to make them so? Can the extension agents' work be supplemented by the work of such personnel as the credit supervisors of the banks that loan to the *campesinos* and the local officers of the campesino leagues?

3. How can the conscientious farmer be rewarded for improving his cultivation techniques, sending his children to school, or taking part in community-action projects? Such rewards need not be, probably should not be, primarily economic. Sanctions for inadequate performance are harder to devise. A man's credit cannot be cut off without jeopardizing his next crop entirely.

Money fines are effective only where there is money to pay the fines. Taking away the offender's parcel of land is appropriate only for very serious offenses. Public reprimands are likely to be counterproductive.

AGRICULTURAL CREDIT

1. Assuming that there is not enough money to make adequate loans to everyone who needs them, how is the allocation to be made? Is everyone's credit reduced a little, or is adequate credit given to some and none to others? If the latter policy is followed, what are the official and real standards for establishing priorities?

2. To what extent have borrowers failed to repay their loans? In Venezuela, one responsible estimate is that 40 percent of the money loaned is not repaid. In Mexico some estimates run even higher. Why do borrowers default? A number of reasons are regularly suggested: (a) The loans are not large enough in the first place. Such loans are often barely sufficient to cover current farm expenses, forcing the *campesino* to skimp on seed or machinery rental, with the result that his crop is poor. (b) The farmer may have been told by politicians that he really need not repay. (c) The parcels are too small to produce enough to feed a family and repay loans also. (d) The farmer does not know how to use the money efficiently; he needs help from an extension service. It is probable that all of these factors are responsible for some failures, but the basic survey work on such problems has not been done. Do the *campesinos* really hide their crops (the only security the lending banks have)? What are the techniques used for cheating?

3. Most governments in Latin America have, as part of their land-reform programs, established special banks to make loans to beneficiaries who have received land. These organizations deserve study: How do they carry a banking operation to a part of the population that has no experience with banks? Have they been able to decentralize their operations to an extent which permits local supervision of the uses to which the money loaned is put? How can corruption be kept to a minimum by administrative checks without hampering the day-to-day functioning of the banks? What are the standards used for ruling on applications for credit? Who has the effective power of decision?

4. What are the requisites for making group borrowing effec-

tive, so that the group really is responsible for its debts, even though there be only one member in default?

5. With the aid of large grants from the Alliance for Progress, various supervised credit programs are just now getting under way. Supervised credit requires the lending banks to go into the agricultural extension business on a large scale. Soon there should be a sufficient body of experience under these new programs to justify an evaluative study.

6. What is the role of private lenders in agricultural credit? The Alliance for Progress and the Mexican government have recently made available a large sum of money to a guarantee fund of the Bank of Mexico. This fund will guarantee agricultural loans made by private banks and will also be used for loans to private banks at low interest rates for the purpose of making further loans to farmers. (The private banks which make the loans have no political reason for being soft about collecting.) Is this just another scheme to aid the rich farmers, as its critics on the political left have argued? Or does it afford commercial-bank supervision of loans which come in effect from the government?

7. Since the lands are usually nontransferable, the only security normally available to the banks which lend to beneficiaries of a land-reform program is the crop which is produced with the aid of the loaned money. This fact has put the lending banks into the food-marketing business. In Venezuela the government has recently attempted to allow the Agricultura Bank to evade this nonbanking function by establishing a new marketing corporation (called ADAGRO), which takes the crops from the farmers and distributes them. Before long, there will be enough data to justify a comparative analysis of the old and new systems. Similar studies may be made in Mexico, where the Banco Ejidal has had similar marketing responsibilities.

AGRICULTURAL MARKETING

1. When the bank takes a farmer's crop and markets it, the farmer has little participation in the marketing process. If one of the goals of a land reform is the development of responsibility among the *campesinos*, would it not be better to give them a role in marketing? In view of the admitted lack of marketing experience of the majority of *campesinos,* one answer may be

the establishment of marketing cooperatives. But such an arrangement also involves the danger that the individual farmer will have his affairs run by a new class of rural bureaucrats and that the desired training in responsibility will be lost. What has been the Latin American experience with marketing cooperatives? What conditions are needed before such a cooperative can succeed? What kind of training program is implicit in a decision to organize marketing cooperatives?

2. The structure of the distribution system in Latin American countries needs to be studied. The recent introduction, in all major Latin American countries, of supermarket chains of the North American type seems to be changing the old pattern of numerous middlemen. What difference does the new system make in the prices received by the individual farmer? Does this new distribution system modify the prices paid by consumers and thus the demand for agricultural products? Do new marketing institutions aid the process of changing some of the numerous subsistence farmers into farmers who produce for the market? Would it be feasible to get the food-distributing chains or food processors into the business of financing producers, as some food-processing companies do in the United States?

MINIFUNDIO: THE UNECONOMICALLY SMALL PARCEL

1. Under what circumstances does a tiny parcel imply a devotion to subsistence farming?

2. Is the owner of a small parcel condemned to primitive methods of cultivation? What opportunities might there be for cooperative use of machinery, or even cooperative labor in the North American pioneer tradition? What are the costs of machinery rental to *minifundio* owners (per hectare, per unit of the product, etc.)?

3. What provision is made for the consolidation of small parcels? (See Moral López and Jacoby 1962.) In 1945, Mexico adopted a law providing a method of partly voluntary, partly compulsory consolidation of very small plots. In nineteen years the law has never been applied. Why was it adopted? What were the political forces behind the law, and why did they lose strength when it came to implementation? There have been some model consolidation projects in Chile. What did they cost? Where did displaced individuals go? What have been the eco-

nomic results of the consolidation? To what extent can these model projects be reproduced elsewhere? Are the changes implicit in such a consolidation generally acceptable to the people who must make them?

LAND REFORM AND WATER RIGHTS

In many regions of Latin America, water rights are even more important to the farmer than his formal land rights. Some land-reform legislation deals expressly with water problems, making provisions for the distribution of water rights along with the land. Elsewhere (Colombia's Cauca Valley Corporation, for example) public control over water rights has been exercised in such a way as to exact compliance by individual farmers with directives concerning conservation, production techniques, etc. Although the FAO has described water legislation in Latin America, what is needed now is an effort to study water law in its geographic-economic context, preferably on a narrow regional basis.

BROAD-SCALE EFFECTS OF PAST AND CURRENT REFORMS

Studies of this breadth are dangerous, for they invite excessive generalizations.

1. A study of the economic effects of Mexican land reform would be valuable.[17] It has been suggested that the intensification of Latin American agriculture demands a land reform. Can it be said that the Mexican reform resulted in such an intensification? What have been the measurable economic effects of the reform? How has capital been diverted to industrialization? Have production patterns (kinds of crops, type of cultivation, etc.) changed as a result of the reform? Has the reform made any difference in the productivity of land devoted to agriculture?

2. What were the political effects of the Mexican land reform? It has been called a political success, in that it stopped the violence of the Revolution and consolidated the position of the official party in the rural areas. To whom does the *campesino* feel loyal? How is his political reliability maintained? What

---

[17] Evaluative articles on the Mexican reform may be found in the now defunct Boletín de Estudios Especiales del Banco Nacional de Crédito Ejidal. See also Simpson (1937), Whetten (1948), Senior (1958), Tannenbaum (1929) for evaluations of the Mexican land reform program. A preliminary evaluation of the Cuban land reform may be found in Conchol (1963).

are the origins of the current rural unrest; and what political solutions are foreseen?

3. Did the Mexican land reform bring about socio-economic mobility? Is the *campesino* now better able to change jobs, or change his residence, than he was before the reform?

4. What became of the *hacendados* after expropriation? Where do they live? What are their occupations? Their investments? There ought to be data available in all the countries which have experienced reforms.

5. A before-and-after study of beneficiaries would be valuable. How have the various reforms been felt in the lives of communities where they have taken place? Patterns of dressing, eating, education, hours of work, leisure activities, etc., may have been changed. (See Barraclough 1962.)

6. What kinds of local institutions, governmental or private, have replaced the hacienda's services: health and welfare, police protection, recreation, etc.?

BIBLIOGRAPHY [18]

Abensour, Emmanuel S., Pedro Moral López, and Erich J. Jacoby
1957   Los arrendamientos rústicos: principios de legislación. United Nations, Food and Agricultural Organization.
Amadeo, Santos Primo
1943   Argentine constitutional law: the judicial function in the maintenance of the federal system and the preservation of individual rights. New York.
American Bar Association (Committee on International Trade and Investments, Section of International and Comparative Law)
1963   The protection of private property invested abroad. Chicago.
American Bar Foundation
1962   First work plan for Latin America. Chicago.
Association of the Bar of the City of New York
1961   Selective English language materials on doing business in Latin America. Record 16: 286–303.
Banco Ejidal
1953–61 Boletin de Estudios Especiales. Mexico City.
Barraclough, Solon
1962   Agrarian structure and education in Latin America. UNESCO (mimeographed).
Barraclough, Solon, and Juan del Canto
1960   La unidad económica en la agricultura. Santiago, Universidad de Chile.

[18] Those marked with an asterisk (*) are especially recommended for those who wish to begin the study of legal institutions in Latin America.

Barrancos y Vedia, Fernando N.
1961   Sobre los jueces y la jurisprudencia. Revista Jurídica de Buenos Aires, 1963–III, pp. 137–47.

Barry, Alfredo M.
1961   Fuero rural: sus problemas actuales. Revista Jurídica de Buenos Aires, 1961–III, pp. 169–217.

Bayitch, Stojan A.
1961   Latin America: a bibliographical guide to economy, history, law, politics, and society. Coral Gables, Fla.

Blanksten, George I.
1951   Ecuador: constitutions and caudillos. University of California Publications in Political Sciences 3: No. 1.

Borde, Jean, and Mario Góngora
1956   Evolución de la propriedad rural en el valle de Puangue. Instituto de Sociología, Universidad de Chile. Santiago. 2 vols.

Bronfenbrenner, M.
1955   The appeal of confiscation in economic development. Economic Development and Cultural Change 3: 201.

Carrió, Genaro R.
1959a Recurso de amparo y técnica judicial. Buenos Aires.
1959b Algunos aspectos del recurso de amparo. Buenos Aires.
1961a Nota sobre el caso de los números vivos. Revista del Colegio de Abogados de la Plata.
1961b Los jueces crean derecho. Revista Jurídica de Buenos Aires, 1961–IV, pp. 225–33.

Carroll, Thomas F.
1961   The land reform issue in Latin America. In Latin American issues: essays and comments, A. O. Hirschman, ed. New York, The Twentieth Century Fund, pp. 161–201.
1962   Land tenure and land reform in Latin America: a selected, annotated bibliography. Washington, D.C., Inter-American Development Bank (mimeographed). (Preliminary version.)
1964   Land reform as an explosive force in Latin America. In Explosive forces in Latin America, J. J. TePaske and S. N. Fisher, eds. Columbus, Ohio, pp. 81–125.

Castaño, Luís
1962   Régimen legal de la prensa en México. Mexico City.

Cavers, David Farquhar, and James R. Nelson
1960   Electric power regulation in Latin America. Baltimore.

Chonchol, Jacques
1963   Análisis crítico de la reforma agraria cubana. Trimestre Económico 30 (1): 69–143 (No. 117).

Clagett, Helen
1945   The Mexican suit of "amparo." Georgetown Law Journal 33: 418–37.
1952   Administration of justice in Latin America. New York.

*Couture, Eduardo J.
1958   Fundamentos de derecho procesal civil. Buenos Aires. 3rd edition.

Cueto-Rúa, Julio
1957   El common law: su estructura normativa, su enseñanza. Buenos Aires.
1961   Fuentes del derecho. Buenos Aires.

DeVries, Henry P.
1961   Inter American legal studies. New York, Parker School of Foreign and Comparative Law, Columbia University. 2 vols. (mimeographed).

330   Kenneth L. Karst

*Diez, Manuel M.
  1961   El acto administrativo. Buenos Aires.
Directory of Law Teachers
  1964   St. Paul, Minn.
Domínguez Correa, Oscar
  1961a   El campesino chileno y la acción católica rural. Estudios socio-religiosos latino-americanos. Oficina Internacional de Investigaciones Sociales de FERES, Fribourg, Centro de Investigaciones y Acción Social, Santiago. No. 15.
  1961b   La tierra es la esperanza. Santiago, Instituto de Educación Rural, Centro de Estudios e Investigaciones Sociales.
Ducoin, Georges
  1958   Economía y bien común según la doctrina social de la iglesia. Santiago.
Eder, Phanor James
  1950   A comparative survey of Anglo-American and Latin-American law. New York.
  1961a   Habeas corpus disembodied: the Latin American experience. In Twentieth century comparative and conflicts law, edited by Kurt H. Nadelmann, Arthur T. von Mehren, and John N. Hazard on behalf of the Board of Editors of the American Journal of Comparative Law. Leyden, pp. 463–67.
  1961b   Judicial review in Latin America. Ohio State Law Journal 21: 570–615.
Fals Borda, Orlando
  1955   Peasant society in the Colombian Andes: a sociological study of Saucio. Gainesville, Fla.
Flores, Edmundo
  1961   Tratado de economía agrícola. Mexico City.
Food and Agriculture Organization of the United Nations
  1961   Report of the FAO regional land reform team for Latin America. Rome. Publication No. 1388 (mimeographed).
Ford, Thomas R.
  1955   Man and land in Peru. Gainesville, Fla.
*Fraga, Gabino
  1962   Derecho administrativo. Mexico City. 9th edition.
Furtado, Celso
  1959   Formação econômica do Brasil. Rio de Janeiro. (Translated as The economic growth of Brazil. Berkeley and Los Angeles, 1963.)
  1962   Reflexiones sobre la pre-revolución brasileña. Trimestre Económico 29 (3): 381 (No. 115).
  1963   Brazil: What kind of revolution? Foreign Affairs, April, pp. 526–35.
Goldschmidt, Roberto
  1962   Nuevos estudios de derecho comparado: problemas generales del derecho privado, derecho civil, y derecho judicial civil, derecho mercantil, derecho de autor, derecho de tránsito terrestre. Caracas. Publicaciones de la Faculdad de Derecho, Universidad Central, Vol. 27.
*Gorla, Gino
  1959   El contrato. Barcelona. 2 vols. (Translated from the Italian Il contratto by Ferrandis Villela.)
Grant, J. A. C.
  1948   Judicial review by executive reference prior to promulgation: the Colombian experience. Southern California Law Review 21: 154–71.

1954 Judicial control of legislation. American Journal of Comparative Law 3: 186–98.
1962–63 El control jurisdiccional de la constitucionalidad de las leyes. Revista de derecho. Faculdad de Derecho, Universidad Nacional Autónoma de México.

Guzmán, Germán, et al.
1962 La violencia en Colombia: Estudio de un proceso social. Bogotá. Vol. I: 92–99. (Monografías Sociológicas, No. 12.)

Haar, Charles M.
1963 Latin America's troubled cities. Foreign Affairs 41: 536–48.

Handbook of Latin American Studies
1935–62 Gainesville, Fla. 24 volumes to date.

Harvard University, International Program in Taxation
1957a Taxation in Brazil. Boston. World Tax Series.
1957b Taxation in Mexico. Prepared by Harvard Law School, International Program in Taxation in consultation with the United Nations Secretariat. Boston.

Harvard University Law School, International Legal Studies
1954–61 Report of the director. Cambridge, Mass.
1961–63

Hirschman, Albert O.
1958 The strategy of economic development. New Haven.
1963 Journeys toward progress. New York.

Holmberg, Allan
1960 Changing community attitudes and values in Peru: a case study in guided change. In Social change in Latin America today, [by] Richard Adams et al. New York, pp. 63–107.

International Labor Organization of the United Nations
1953 Indigenous people: living and working conditions of aboriginal peoples in independent countries. Geneva, Report No. 35.
1957 The landless farmer in Latin America.

Irizarry y Puente, Julius
1955 The nature and powers of a "de facto" government in Latin America. Tulane Law Review 30: 15–72.

Jacoby, Erich H.
1953 Inter-relationship between agrarian reform and agricultural development. Rome, Food and Agriculture Organization of the United Nations.

Karst, Kenneth L.
1964 Latin American legal institutions: problems for comparative study. 3rd edition (mimeographed).

Kunz, Joseph Laurenz
1950 Latin American philosophy of law in the twentieth century. New York.

*Linares Quintana, Segundo V.
1953–63 Tratado de la ciencia del derecho constitucional argentino y comparado. Buenos Aires. Vols. 1–9.

Lleras Restrepo, C., et al.
1961 Tierra: Diez ensayos sobre la reforma agraria en Colombia. Bogotá.

McBride, George M.
1936 Chile: land and society. New York, American Geographic Society Research Series.

Mensaje
1962 [Editorial] Revolución en América Latina: visión cristiana. Mensaje, No. 115. Santiago.

Moral-López, Pedro, and Erich H. Jacoby
1962 Principles of land consolidation legislation. United Nations, Food and Agriculture Organization.

Oldman, Oliver, and Stanley S. Surrey
1960 Preliminary survey of the tax system in Argentina (mimeographed).

*Orgaz, Alfredo
1954 Nuevos estudios de derecho civil. Buenos Aires.

Palomo Valencia, Florencio
1959 Historia del ejido actual. Mexico City.

Pan-American Union
1963 Sistemas de protección jurídica a las inversiones privadas extranjeras en Latinoamérica. Provisional text (mimeographed).

Parsons, Kenneth H., Raymond J. Penn, and Philip M. Raup, (eds.)
1956 Land tenure. Proceedings of the International Conference on Land Tenure and Related Problems in World Agriculture (Madison, Wisc., 1951). Madison.

*Puig Brutau
1951 Estudios de derecho comparado; la doctrina de los actos proprios. Barcelona.
1952 La jurisprudencia como fuente del derecho; interpretación creadora y arbitrio judicial. Barcelona.
1953–59 Fundamentos de derecho civil. Barcelona. (Incomplete.)

Ross, Stanford G., and John B. Christensen
1959 Tax incentives for industry in Mexico. Cambridge, Mass.

Sakolski, Aaron Morton
1957 Land tenure and land taxation in America. New York, R. Schalkenbach Foundation.

*Salvat, Raymondo Miguel
1958– Tratado de derecho civil argentino: parte general. Buenos Aires. 10th edition. 10 vols.

*Satanowsky, Marcos
1957 Tratado de derecho comercial. Buenos Aires. 3 vols.

*Sayagués Laso, Enrique
1959 Tratado de derecho administrativo. Montevideo. 2 vols.

Schlesinger, Rudolf B.
1959 Comparative law: cases, text, materials. New York. 2nd edition.

Scheman, L. Ronald
1962a Brazil's career judiciary. Journal of American Judicature Society 46: 134–40.
1962b The social and economic origin of the Brazilian judges. Inter-American Law Review 4: 45–72.
1963 The Brazilian law student: background, habits, attitudes. Journal of Inter-American Studies 5: 333–56.

Senior, Clarence
1958 Land reform and democracy. Gainesville, Fla.

*Sentís Melendo, Santiago
1957 El juez y el derecho. Buenos Aires.

Shoup, Carl Summer, Walter Sterling Surrey, and Oliver Oldman
1959 The fiscal system of Venezuela: a report. Baltimore.

Silvert, Kalman H.
1961 The conflict society: reaction and revolution in Latin America. New Orleans.

Simpson, E. N.
1937 The ejido: Mexico's way out. Chapel Hill, N.C.

Sohn, Louis Bruno, and R. R. Baxter
1961 Responsibility of states for injuries to the economic interest of aliens. American Journal of International Law 55: 545–84.

*Soler, Sebastián
1951 Derecho penal argentino. Buenos Aires. 2nd edition. 5 vols.

Surrey, Walter S., and Dumond Peck Hill
1961 Investment transactions between private individuals across national frontiers. Ohio State Law Journal 22: 520–45.

Szladits, Charles
1955–63 A bibliography on foreign comparative law: books and articles in English. New York, Parker School of Foreign and Comparative Law, Columbia University. 3 vols. (Kept up to date by supplementary list in American Journal of Comparative Law.)

Tannenbaum, Frank
1929 The Mexican agrarian revolution. New York.

Taylor, C. C.
1948 Rural life in Argentina. Baton Rouge, La.

*Tena Ramírez, Felipe
1963 Derecho constitucional Mexicano. Mexico City. 6th edition.

Thomas, Ann Van Wynen, and A. J. Thomas, Jr.
1963 The Organization of American States. Dallas.

Trueba Urbina, Alberto, and Jorge Trueba Barrera
1963 Legislación de amparo. Mexico City.

United States Department of Agriculture
1962 Agrarian reform and economic growth in developing countries. Washington, D.C.

Urquidi, Victor L.
1962 Viabilidad económica de América Latina. Mexico City.

Vivanco, Antonino C.
1954 Introducción al estudio del derecho agrario. Buenos Aires.
1962 Derecho agrario y reforma agraria en América Latina. Journal of Inter-American Studies 4 (No. 2): 233–45 (April). Gainesville, Fla.

Von Mehren, Arthur Taylor
1957 The civil law system: cases and materials for the comparative study of law. Englewood Cliffs, N.J.

Wald, Haskell P.
1959 Taxation of agricultural land in underdeveloped countries. Cambridge, Mass.

Whetten, Nathan L.
1948 Rural Mexico. Chicago.

Participants in the Seminar
on Latin American Studies

Continuing Members of the Seminar

Robert N. Burr, University of California, Los Angeles
Raymond Carr, St. Antony's College, Oxford
Joseph Grunwald, The Brookings Institution, Washington, D.C.
H. Field Haviland, Jr., The Brookings Institution, Washington, D.C.
Robert Heussler, The Ford Foundation, New York
Frederick A. Olafson, Johns Hopkins University
Robert E. Scott, University of Illinois
Carl B. Spaeth, Stanford University
Ralph W. Tyler, Center for Advanced Study in the Behavioral Sciences, Stanford, California (Chairman)
Charles Wagley, Columbia University
Richard J. Walter, Stanford University (Secretary)
Bryce Wood, Social Science Research Council, New York

Participants in Special Sessions

POLITICAL SCIENCE, JULY 11–13

James S. Cunningham, U.S. Foreign Service
E. McC. Dannemiller, Lieutenant Colonel, U.S. Army Special Warfare School, Fort Bragg, N.C.
Robert H. Dix, Yale University
John C. Dreier, Johns Hopkins University
Clarence N. Faust, The Ford Foundation, New York
Samuel P. Huntington, Harvard University
Merle Kling, Washington University
John N. Plank, Department of State, Washington, D.C.
Ronald M. Schneider, Columbia University
Kalman H. Silvert, Dartmouth College
W. Howard Wriggins, Department of State, Washington, D.C.

ECONOMICS, JULY 18–20

William S. Barnes, School of Law, Harvard University
Abram Bergson, Harvard University
Hollis B. Chenery, Agency for International Development, Washington, D.C.
Emile Despres, Stanford University
Evsey Domar, Massachusetts Institute of Technology
Arnold C. Harberger, University of Chicago
Carlos Massad, Instituto de Economía, Universidad de Chile

ANTHROPOLOGY, JULY 22–24

Richard N. Adams, University of Texas
Munro S. Edmonson, Tulane University
William Madsen, Purdue University
Sidney W. Mintz, Yale University
Benjamin D. Paul, Stanford University
A. Kimball Romney, Stanford University
Arnold Strickon, Brandeis University

LAND TENURE AND LEGAL INSTITUTIONS, JULY 31–AUGUST 2

Richard N. Adams, University of Texas
James O. Bray, Stanford University
Thomas F. Carroll, Inter-American Development Bank, Washington, D.C.
James S. Cunningham, U.S. Foreign Service
Evsey Domar, Massachusetts Institute of Technology
Edmundo Flores, Princeton University
Ira Michael Heyman, University of California, Berkeley
Kenneth L. Karst, Ohio State University
John H. Merryman, Stanford University
James J. Parsons, University of California, Berkeley
Hugh Popenoe, University of Florida
L. Ronald Scheman, Pan American Union, Washington, D.C.

SOCIOLOGY, AUGUST 5–7

Wendell Bell, Yale University
Kingsley Davis, University of California, Berkeley
Wayne H. Holtzman, University of Texas
Rex Hopper, Brooklyn College
Wilbert E. Moore, Princeton University
J. M. Stycos, Cornell University

HISTORY AND LITERATURE, AUGUST 14–16

Howard F. Cline, Hispanic Foundation, Library of Congress
Fred P. Ellison, University of Texas
Melvin J. Fox, The Ford Foundation, New York
John J. Johnson, Stanford University
Ernest R. May, Harvard University
Luis Monguió, University of California, Berkeley
Robert A. Potash, University of Massachusetts
Stanley J. Stein, Princeton University
Schuyler C. Wallace, Foreign Area Fellowship Program, New York

About the Authors

CHARLES WAGLEY is Professor of Anthropology and Director of the Institute of Latin American Studies at Columbia University. He has been identified with Latin American studies for over twenty years. His most recent book is *An Introduction to Brazil*.

JAMES J. PARSONS is Professor of Geography and Chairman of the Department of Geography at the University of California at Berkeley. He is the author of *Antiqueno Colonization in Western Colombia*, *San Andrés and Providencia: English-Speaking Islands in the Western Caribbean* and *The Green Turtle and Man*, as well as numerous articles on the historical and economic geography of Latin America.

STANLEY J. STEIN is Professor of History at Princeton University. He has done field research in Brazil and in Mexico and has held a Research Fellowship in Entrepreneurial History at Harvard and a Guggenheim Fellowship. His publications include *Vassouras: A Brazilian Coffee County, 1850–1900*, *The Brazilian Cotton Textile Manufacture, 1850–1950*, and articles on Brazil and Mexico.

ARNOLD STRICKON is an Assistant Professor of Anthropology and Chairman of the undergraduate Latin American Studies Program at Brandeis University. He has done field research in Argentina and the British Caribbean and is presently preparing for publication a study of an Argentine ranching community. He has published several articles on Argentine social structure and the ecology of cattle ranching in the New World.

MERLE KLING is Professor of Political Science at Washington University, St. Louis, and is currently (1946–65) a Research Associate of the Center of International Studies, Princeton University, where he is engaged in a study of Latin American revolutions. He has taught in Mexico and is the author of *A Mexican Interest Group in Action* and articles on Latin American politics.

CARLOS MASSAD is Director of the Instituto de Economía, at the University of Chile, Santiago. He is the author (with John D. Strasma) of *La zona de libre comercio en América Latina: problemas por resolver,* published by the Instituto de Economía.

REX HOPPER is Professor of Sociology at Brooklyn College of the University of the City of New York and is the author of several papers on the sociology of Latin America, some of which were written with the collaboration of Janice H. Hopper.

KENNETH L. KARST is Professor of Law at Ohio State University in the fields of constitutional law and comparative law. He has held a Ford Foundation law faculty fellowship, and his publications include *Latin American Legal Institutions: Problems for Comparative Study* and numerous articles on constitutional law and on public law issues relating to private charities.